CT Anatomy for Radiotherapy

Other Health & Social Care Books from M&K include:

Research Issues in Health and Social Care
ISBN: 978-1-905539-20-8

Self-assessment in Limb X-ray Interpretation
ISBN: 978-1-905539-13-0

Self-assessment in Paediatric Musculoskeletal Trauma X-rays
ISBN: 978-1-905539-34-5

Self-assessment in Axial Skeleton Musculoskeletal Trauma X-rays
ISBN: 978-1-905539-47-5

Self-assessment in Musculoskeletal Pathology X-rays
ISBN: 978-1-905539-14-7

Spiritual Assessment in Healthcare Practice
ISBN: 978-1-905539-27-7

Perspectives on Death & Dying
ISBN: 978-1-905539-21-5

CT Anatomy for Radiotherapy

Pete Bridge
David J. Tipper

CT Anatomy for Radiotherapy
Pete Bridge
David J. Tipper

ISBN: 978-1-905539-54-3

First published 2011

British Library Cataloguing in Publication Data
A catalogue record for this book is available from the British Library

Notice
Clinical practice and medical knowledge constantly evolve. Standard safety precautions must be followed, but, as knowledge is broadened by research, changes in practice, treatment and drug therapy may become necessary or appropriate. Readers must check the most current product information provided by the manufacturer of each drug to be administered and verify the dosages and correct administration, as well as contraindications. It is the responsibility of the practitioner, utilising the experience and knowledge of the patient, to determine dosages and the best treatment for each individual patient. Any brands mentioned in this book are as examples only and are not endorsed by the publisher. Neither the publisher nor the authors assume any liability for any injury and/or damage to persons or property arising from this publication.

To contact M&K Publishing write to:
M&K Update Ltd · The Old Bakery · St. John's Street
Keswick · Cumbria CA12 5AS
Tel: 01768 773030 · Fax: 01768 781099
publishing@mkupdate.co.uk
www.mkupdate.co.uk

Designed and typeset in 11pt Helvetica Neue by Mary Blood
Printed in England by H&H Reeds Printers, Penrith

To my ever-supportive parents, my inspirational Jacqui and my wonderful kids, Connor and Rhiannon. *(PB)*

'We ought to write a book', we said; it seemed like a great idea at the time, but the practicalities were a little more complicated than first anticipated, combining a busy work schedule and family life. My heartfelt thanks go to all who have supported me over the last 12 months. Judith, Alex, Amy and Izzy, we can take that holiday in Disneyland now – you've earned it! Thank you. *(DJT)*

Contents

About the authors

Pete Bridge BSc MSc

Pete is a senior lecturer in Radiotherapy and Oncology at Sheffield Hallam University, where he teaches radiotherapy planning, radiation physics, and CT anatomy. He is the course leader for the MSc Radiotherapy Planning course as well as the facilitator for CPD short courses on CT Anatomy and structure outlining (prostate, brain and breast). Pete has worked clinically as a therapy radiographer in Manchester, Auckland, Dundee and Derby. He is particularly interested in structure outlining for radiotherapy planning.

David J. Tipper DCR(R) PgCert (MRI) PgCert (CT)

David is the Cross-Sectional Imaging Manager for Sheffield Teaching Hospitals NHS Trust, Northern General Hospital, Sheffield, UK. He has worked clinically as a diagnostic radiographer for 18 years and now has what he describes as his dream job. He chose to specialise in cross-sectional imaging early on in his career, and has worked clinically in CT and MRI for nearly 15 years in Derby and now in Sheffield. David has an almost obsessive interest in cross-sectional anatomy and also lectures regularly on the subject.

Acknowledgements

The grateful thanks of the authors are extended to:
David Bottomley, Consultant Clinical Oncologist, for the foreword; Chris Bragg, Medical Physicist for tracking down elusive tumour images; Hazel McCallum, Medical Physicist, for MVCT images; Sue Warren at TomoTherapy Inc for tomotherapy images; David Scott at Varian Medical Systems Inc for kVCT images; Angela Duxbury for support and advice.

All CT images in the book were acquired using a 64 slice GE™ VCT Lightspeed scanner. The MR images were acquired on a Siemens Avanto 1.5T MRI scanner. Structure outlining and 3-dimensional reconstruction were performed using Varian Medical Systems' ECLIPSE™ planning system contouring tools.

Foreword

The CT scanner is an indispensable component in the armoury of the modern radiotherapy consultant. It permeates most aspects of the patient journey: diagnosis and staging, tumour localisation, radiotherapy planning and increasingly on-treatment verification. Although CT interpretation has long been the preserve of medical and selected radiotherapy planning staff, recent developments in image-guided radiotherapy (IGRT) have made these skills essential for a much wider range of staff. This book addresses this new training need at both pre- and post-registration levels. From the clinical oncologist's perspective, this book offers the potential for radiotherapy staff to unlock these skills and extend their roles to structure outlining and routine CT verification.

The use of radiotherapy-dedicated positioning and slice orientation for image interpretation makes this book much more user-friendly than existing texts. Structures identified are all relevant to radiotherapy practice as potential tumour sites, critical organs or useful indicators of lymph node positions. The reader is guided through the principles of CT in a detailed but accessible manner. I am sure that readers will particularly appreciate the inclusion of dedicated lymph node sections and details of the 'Deep Spaces' of the head and neck. The importance of these in the understanding of tumour progression cannot be overemphasised. The intracranial chapter also features some highly relevant CT-MR fused images as well as some useful tips on interpretation of this potentially daunting modality. Combining the authors' knowledge of both radiotherapy requirements and CT image interpretation has produced a text that provides the detail required, but in a highly focused manner. Thus it remains relevant to radiotherapy while providing a high enough level of detail to satisfy the most inquisitive of students.

This book should become one of the essential texts for those training or working in radiotherapy at any level. I have no hesitation in commending it to you.

Dr David Bottomley MB BS MRCP FRCR
Consultant in Clinical Oncology, St. James's Institute of Oncology, Leeds, UK
2010

Preface

This book is essentially a celebration of the wedding of two revolutionary (no pun intended) technologies. The first linear accelerators were used clinically in the 1950s. Combined with localisation from plain radiographs, the art of accurate tumour treatment was relatively crude, and knowledge of bony and surface anatomy was an essential skill for a therapy radiographer. Twenty years later the first CT scanners were peering into patients to reveal the position of soft tissue structures. It did not take long for the obvious application to tumour localisation to enrich radiotherapy planning. Since then, the two technologies have steadily evolved and converged until modern times where they have combined to form the Image-Guided radiotherapy machines that are increasingly essential for verification of accurate conformal radiotherapy. This convergence perhaps finds its ultimate expression in the 'hybrid' tomotherapy machines where the two devices are inseparable. Now it is rare indeed to find a patient on a linear accelerator who has not arrived there via a CT bore.

A similar story concerns the two radiography professions. Despite their shared history and professional body, the scope of practice of the diagnostic radiographer and therapy radiographer have never been so close as today. Radiotherapy education has also evolved so that today's radiotherapy student has to complement their knowledge of surface anatomy and 2-dimensional radiograph interpretation with cross-sectional anatomy and CT image interpretation. This book was born out of the growing demand for a radiographic anatomy text suitable for interpretation of radiotherapy CT images. Existing texts are primarily prepared for the diagnostic radiographer and often present the radiotherapy practitioner with significant problems. Radiotherapy scans are designed to be reproducible rather than comfortable and often require a different plane of images from those of our diagnostic colleagues. This frequently requires the student to thumb between three images from the textbook in order to identify structures at the anterior, middle and posterior of a single axial radiotherapy scan. This book aims to teach CT image interpretation with a strong focus on structures relevant to radiotherapy, utilising radiotherapy positioning, immobilisation methods and imaging techniques.

The text is aimed not only at the pre-registration radiotherapy student, but also at staff working with Image-Guided Radiotherapy equipment, CT-simulators or CT scanners. It will also be of value to radiotherapy planning staff wishing to update their knowledge of CT anatomy and advanced practitioners wishing to specialise in advanced planning or structure outlining.

This book is a product of collaboration between the diagnostic radiography and radiotherapy disciplines and it aims to provide enough detail of essential diagnostic CT interpretation skills while remaining relevant and focused on radiotherapy. I hope you find it to be a useful and enjoyable read that will nurture a growing interest in the endlessly fascinating world of cross-sectional anatomy.

Pete Bridge, 2010

Anatomy of the human form is a fascinating subject. The word anatomy is derived from the Greek word *anatome* (*ana* – up or through, and *tome* – to cut), and describes the study of form, historically by cutting up or dissecting the subject to reveal the various systems and structural complexities within. Most anatomical terminology is based on Greek or Latin descriptions, and is quite straightforward, often linked to adjacent anatomy in some form or other. Medical imaging now enables us to collate our knowledge of cadaveral anatomy with the living patient, and we now cut or dissect our patients using CT and MRI scanners providing detailed 2- or 3-dimensional images. Radiology provides increasingly detailed morphological information on every aspect of the human form, and, linked with detailed anatomical and pathological evaluations, endeavours to provide clinical teams with the best possible information to facilitate optimal patient care and treatment. However, understanding of human anatomy is vitally important in Radiology, and without a grasp of basic old-fashioned anatomical knowledge, even the most exquisitely detailed 3-dimensional image can be meaningless. Our aim is to help you to understand each CT section, not only its CT appearance, but to bring the CT anatomy to life, in more than just the 2-dimensional plane. Remember CT sections are just that; they are plural, so rather than using just one CT image, use all of the CT data and tools at your disposal. We hope to provide you with a level of understanding that enables you to recognise different anatomical regions, structures and systems, following which, you should be able to demarcate normal and abnormal structure boundaries for your Radiotherapy practice. I hope I may even inspire you to delve deeper into the fascinating subject of human anatomy as I have done throughout my career, and urge you to always remember, anatomy is everything in Radiology.

David J. Tipper, 2010

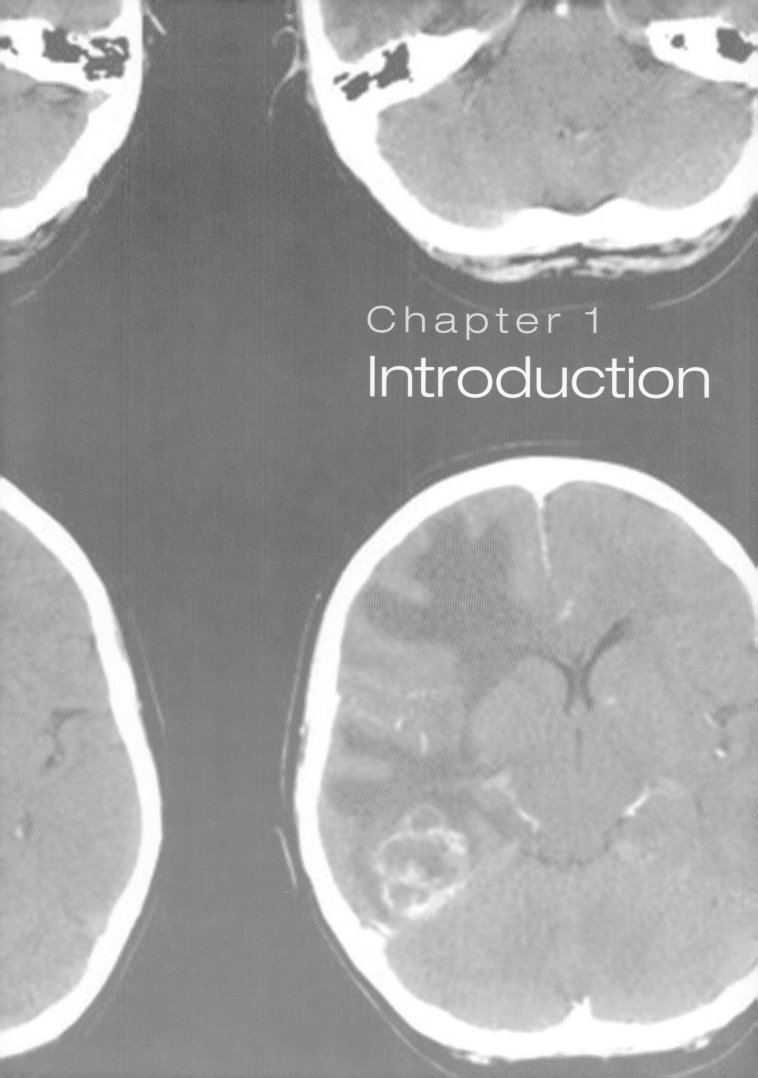

Chapter 1
Introduction

1.1 Purpose of the book

This book is intended to prepare the radiotherapy professional for CT interpretation of radiotherapy planning or image-guided radiotherapy scans. This introductory chapter provides some background details related to CT equipment and principles as well as potential problems and hints to aid image interpretation. All essential structures relevant to radiotherapy are described and depicted on labelled CT images covering the whole body. Each region of the body has its own chapter and within that chapter, various anatomical systems are described along with an overview of their CT anatomy on transverse sections. Three-dimensional images have been reconstructed from CT outlines and are presented to aid understanding of the relationships between structures. Labels and outlines are provided on real CT images alongside notes relating to image interpretation and tips for identifying structures. Within a region of the body each structure has its own identifying number, enabling them to be traced throughout the CT series with ease. The structure index contains a full list of these labels. After the different systems have been discussed, the full CT anatomy of the region is presented on labelled images alongside corresponding blank CT scans. Intracranial CT images are complemented with MR and fused images where this represents common clinical practice. To aid the reader with this, there is a short introduction to some common MR imaging sequences and hints on image interpretation.

The CT images in the book were all obtained using standard radiotherapy planning protocols and use immobilisation and positioning techniques familiar to those found in radiotherapy. This distinguishes the book from other CT texts which utilise diagnostic views and patient positions. It must be borne in mind, however, that individual departments vary in positioning requirements almost as much as individual patients vary in anatomy. The reader is urged to use the images in this text to engender an understanding of how different structures relate to each other so that this knowledge can be applied to their own clinical practice.

Each chapter concludes with a short self-test to consolidate and check learning. Answers to these can be found at the back of the book. The final chapter provides an overview of alternative CT imaging systems, including megavoltage CT, with some image interpretation. The emphasis of the book, however, remains on providing interpretation skills using standard kilovoltage CT images with a view to undertaking radiotherapy planning or IGRT delivery.

1.2 CT Principles and Equipment

1.2.1 CT Development

Medical imaging has utilised the mechanical movement of an x-ray source and imaging media to demonstrate layers or 'slices' in the human body since the early 1920s in the form of 'stratigraphy' (*stratum* – layer), later recognised as 'tomography' (*tomos* – Greek meaning section or slice). Further exploration of this concept, linked with reconstruction algorithms that can be traced back to theories by mathematician J.H. Radon in 1917 and evolution of the computer processing power necessary to process and reconstruct large amounts of data, led to development of CT as we know it.

Computerised Axial Tomography (CAT or CT) has revolutionised radiological diagnosis since its introduction into the clinical setting in 1972. CT was developed by several individuals, including Allan Cormack, Dr James Ambrose and Dr Robert Ledley. The most notable, however was sir Godfrey Hounsfield, a UK-born electrical and mechanical engineer. His name was immortalised in the name of the quantitative measurement scale used to evaluate CT images: the 'Hounsfield Scale'.

In 1971, Hounsfield and Ambrose conducted studies of the first clinical prototype on human and bovine brain specimens. Images from these studies demonstrated clear demarcation between tumour tissue and surrounding normal grey and white matter. Following this success, the first clinical examination of a real patient successfully demonstrated a dark cystic lesion in the brain and highlighted the clinical potential of CT. Following Dr Robert Ledley's work in 1974, developing the first whole body scanner, a new era of medical imaging investigations began. CT's ability to record very small differences in tissue contrast demonstrated the potential to demarcate disease process in relation to adjacent tissues. Given the potential for CT to image previously difficult areas such as intracranial tissues, it rapidly became the accepted imaging modality of choice for many clinical queries. As diagnostic confidence and imaging capabilities grew, it also became clear that radiotherapy accuracy could be greatly improved by utilising CT images in the tumour staging, treatment planning and more recently treatment verification processes. CT technology has evolved rapidly ever since, resulting in the current 'third generation' scanner, on which today's CT equipment is based.

1.2.2 Basic CT Principles

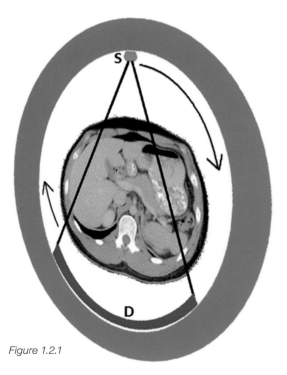

Figure 1.2.1

Figure 1.2.1 illustrates the arrangement of the x-ray tube source (S) and detector array (D) in a typical modern scanner. A number of detector elements are arranged in an arc and rotate around the isocentre of the gantry simultaneously with the x-ray tube. Numbers of detector elements and rows vary between manufacturers; however the principle remains the same.

The source emits a heterogeneous 'fan' beam of x-radiation that is collimated and filtered to specific body areas and types and aimed towards the patient in the centre of the gantry aperture. This beam is attenuated to differing extents depending on the tissue density, atomic number and electrons per gram of the tissue in its path. The detector array records the emergent attenuated beam, collecting data from multiple measurements as it rotates around the patient.

The detectors contain scintillation crystals that emit visible light when irradiated. The intensity of this light is proportional to the attenuation of the original beam. The light is then converted into an electrical signal. The detector array is able to measure many thousands of signals with each rotation of the x-ray tube and these are then subjected to sampling and reconstruction.

During image reconstruction, absorption values are assigned to each picture element (pixel) within each slice. A 2-dimensional image representation of the body area of that particular slice location is formed and typically shown on a 512 x[multi] 512 image matrix. This image resolution is sufficient for resolving sub mm changes in tissue contrast. The resolution of the whole CT system is dependent upon the size of each single detector, with some systems capable of resolving 0.5 x[multi] 0.5mm with similar sized detector elements.

1.2.3 Spiral CT

Spiral or 'helical' imaging can be achieved by simultaneously moving the table and patient though the scanner during image acquisition. The resulting spiral or helix of cross-sectional data is then produced with tiny gaps in it which are later interpolated by the reconstruction algorithm software. This is best imagined as resembling a spring viewed from the side. Figure 1.2.2 demonstrates the path of this spiral acquisition captured incidentally as the result of a patient coughing during a scan. The faster the table moves, the more the helix of the spring is pulled apart and the wider the gaps become, as shown in Figure 1.2.3. This impacts negatively on image detail, although patient dose and scan times are reduced.

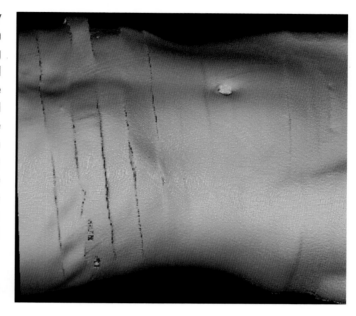

Figure 1.2.2

Slower and reduced table movement – **Slower scan time** – Smaller gaps in helix – increased image detail – **Increased CT dose**

Faster and increased table movement – **Faster scan time** – Bigger gaps in helix – reduced image detail – **Reduced CT dose**

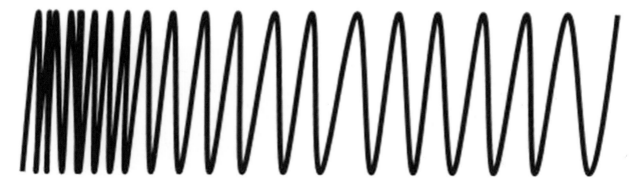

Figure 1.2.3

The ratio between the amount of table movement and tube rotation of the beam is called 'pitch' and can have a sizeable effect on both image quality and patient dose. If the table moves through the gantry slowly then the pitch will be lower, giving greater image detail but at the expense of increased patient x-ray dose.

1.2.4 Multi-slice CT

Multi-slice CT has been available since the early 1990s. Multi-slice scanners use an array of detector rows to acquire up to 64 'slices' of data per tube rotation. This can be described as volumetric acquisition and has the benefit of greater tissue coverage together with considerably reduced scan times. At the time of publication, diagnostic systems with 128, 256 and even 320 multi-slice detector scanners are available and ever more complex cone beam reconstruction algorithms are being developed.

1.3 CT Interpretation

1.3.1 Viewing axial images

Although it is possible to reconstruct images in the sagittal and coronal planes, most of the CT images in radiotherapy are traditionally displayed and viewed in the 'axial' or 'transverse' plane. Figure 1.3.1 illustrates a series of axial scans through the thorax. When displayed, each image is viewed caudally, i.e. from the patient's feet upwards. When viewing each image, this must be taken into account. Thus the left side of the patient in Figure 1.3.2, which can be identified by the location of the heart, is on the right side of the image.

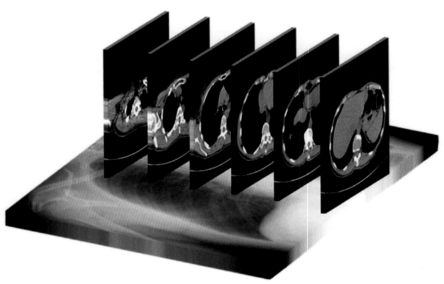

Figure 1.3.2 also indicates that each slice is not merely a 2-dimensional image, but also has a measurement of depth. This depth is the slice thickness and is commonly manipulated at acquisition. Each image is also divided into a matrix of typically 512 x[multi] 512 pixels in the X and Y axes, although greatly simplified in the figure. Because each pixel also has depth, it has a volume in all three axes, and is called a volume element, or 'voxel'. Ideally, to enable maximum image resolution and minimal distortion during post processing, each voxel should be cuboidal (or 'isotropic'), for example, 0.5mm x 0.5mm x 0.5mm[multis]. During image reconstruction, each voxel is allocated a grey shade associated with specific tissue types within the cross-section; this is dependent upon the attenuation coefficient of the tissues.

Figure 1.3.1

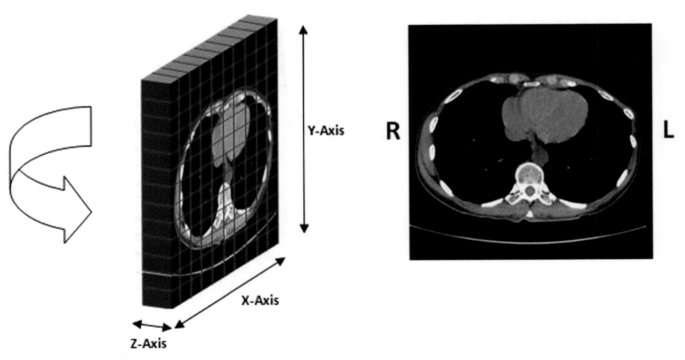

Figure 1.3.2

1.3.2 Slice thickness and 'partial volume' effect

Ideally, for maximum image resolution, scanners should use the smallest slice thickness possible. This can present difficulties since imaging a whole chest or pelvis using 0.5mm slices would provide 400 to 500 images for analysis and planning. There are also patient dose and image noise implications to consider here; generally a thin slice requires a higher dose to reduce image noise to acceptable levels. Most radiotherapy planning scans therefore tend to utilise 3mm–5mm slice thickness as a compromise between image noise, patient dose and number of images produced.

The detrimental effect of slice thickness on image resolution and hence upon the demarcation of structure boundaries is known as the partial volume effect. Figure 1.3.3 shows two slices of differing thickness; the image on the left is over 10mm, and the image on the right is 5mm thick.

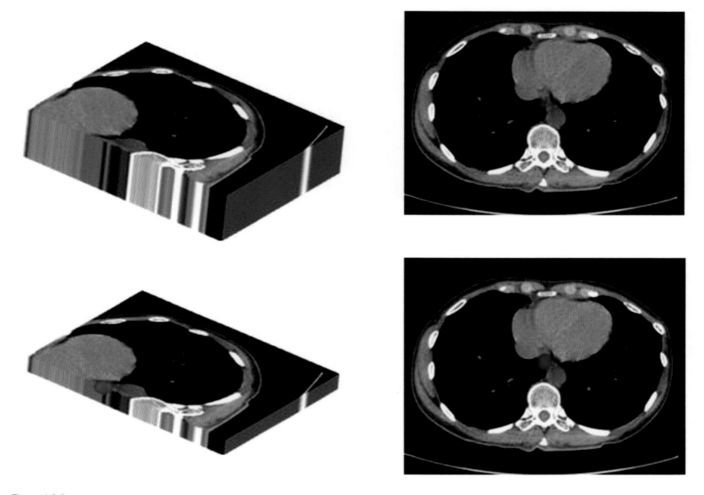

Figure 1.3.3

Attempting to identify a 5mm lymph node (marked in red) on the thick slice is fraught with difficulty, with the boundaries appearing less resolute and the overall attenuation value difficult to appreciate. This is because the slice thickness contains normal tissues above and below the node. By using thinner slices, the affected node will occupy the whole slice thickness and its borders and attenuation value will be more resolute and accurate. Any measurements or demarcation of borders will be more accurate on the thinner slice. The same applies for tortuous or rounded structures that may pass through part of the slice, where only part of the structure occupies the slice or other structures are superimposed.

1.3.3 Viewing the whole series of images

The value of using a range of images to aid interpretation cannot be emphasised enough. Figure 1.3.4 illustrates the thoracic aorta in red on all slices in the series. All such tubular structures running superiorly or inferiorly will be present on more than one image and can be traced above and below the slice being examined. This can help to distinguish between tubular and spherical structures such as lymph nodes. A similar technique can be adopted to assist with locating borders or determining centres of structures. It is important to view the images in this text not as isolated slices, but rather as part of a series and to interpret them in conjunction with adjacent slices.

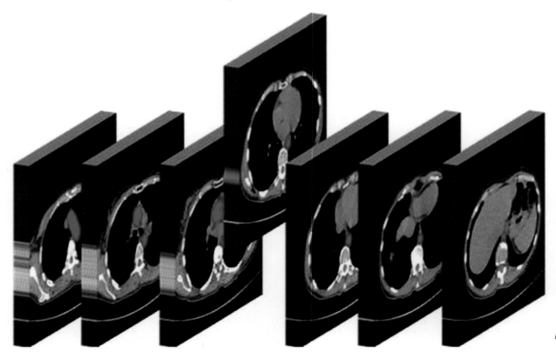

Figure 1.3.4

1.3.4 Using Hounsfield Units

CT images are displayed using the convention of standard x-rays with the more dense 'radio-opaque' structures such as bone appearing white, and less dense 'radiolucent' structures appearing darker on the images. Sir Godfrey Hounsfield realised that he could plot specific attenuation units or values for each specific body tissue type falling within each pixel of the image. It would then be possible to calculate and plot any range of tissue densities found in a cross-section of human anatomy within each pixel of the image displayed. Thus an image of multiple tissue densities can be produced that is linked to reproducible measurable units of attenuation. These units are aptly named 'Hounsfield Units' (HU), and follow a scale centred on water, where water measures 0 HU. Tissues of greater density or attenuation value have positive values, and densities of lower attenuation are given negative values. CT systems are capable of measuring an approximate range from +3000HU to -1000, although in practice the scale maximum is set at +1000HU. Figure 1.3.5 demonstrates the Hounsfield Scale with further detailed breakdown of HU between +100HU and -5HU illustrating the range of units for soft tissues and fluid.

This diagram indicates one of the inherent problems experienced when differentiating between soft tissue types with similar HU values. In order to view all the attenuation values, at least 2000 shades of grey (from black to white) would be required. Today's monitors are capable of displaying over 250 grey tones, but the human eye can only distinguish between a maximum of 50–100 dependent upon ambient conditions. It is clear here then that small changes in tissue density would be missed if over 250 shades of grey were used. This failure to detect subtle changes in represented tissue density would lead to poor diagnosis and demarcation of structures, particularly between tissues possessing similar densities.

By selecting the proportion of relevant HUs we wish to display, we can greatly improve the possibility of distinguishing between differing tissues. This method of image manipulation is called grey level mapping, or 'windowing'. Windowing reflects the method used in CT to maximise image contrast by choosing a median HU value called the 'Level' and a range of HU either side of this called the 'Width'. A wide window displays a large range of HU, and is useful for visualisation of detail across a wide range of tissue densities, such as in bones. By looking at the HU in Figure 1.3.5, it is evident that bone HU values range from approximately 200HU to 1000HU; for optimal image detail all these HU must be displayed. At the other extreme, when identifying tissue types where the HU variation is much narrower, the width must be reduced. For intracranial imaging, normal

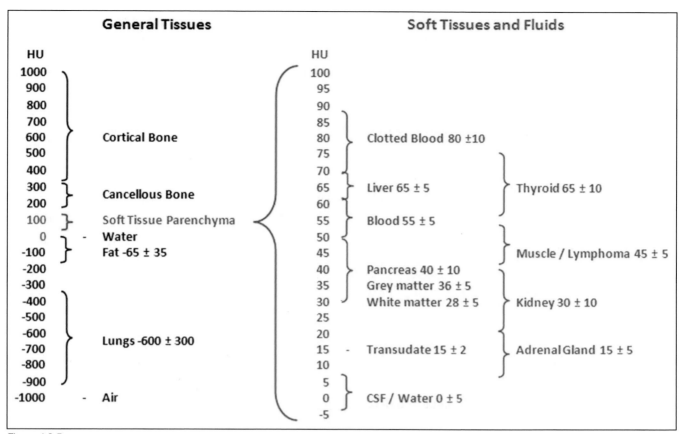

General Tissues

HU	
1000	
900	
800	
700	Cortical Bone
600	
500	
400	
300	Cancellous Bone
200	
100	Soft Tissue Parenchyma
0	– Water
-100	Fat -65 ± 35
-200	
-300	
-400	
-500	
-600	Lungs -600 ± 300
-700	
-800	
-900	
-1000	– Air

Soft Tissues and Fluids

HU		
100		
95		
90		
85		
80	Clotted Blood 80 ±10	
75		
70		Thyroid 65 ± 10
65	Liver 65 ± 5	
60		
55	Blood 55 ± 5	
50		
45		Muscle / Lymphoma 45 ± 5
40	Pancreas 40 ± 10	
35	Grey matter 36 ± 5	
30	White matter 28 ± 5	Kidney 30 ± 10
25		
20		
15	– Transudate 15 ± 2	Adrenal Gland 15 ± 5
10		
5		
0	CSF / Water 0 ± 5	
-5		

Figure 1.3.5

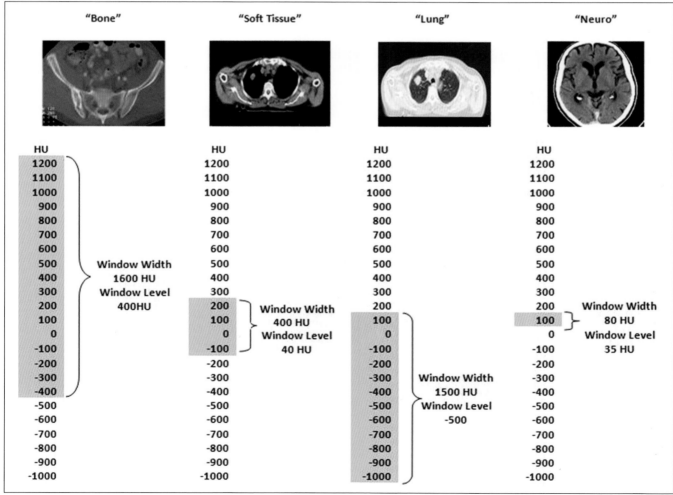

"Bone"	"Soft Tissue"	"Lung"	"Neuro"

HU	HU	HU	HU
1200	1200	1200	1200
1100	1100	1100	1100
1000	1000	1000	1000
900	900	900	900
800	800	800	800
700	700	700	700
600	600	600	600
500	Window Width	500	500	500
400	1600 HU	400	400	400
300	Window Level	300	300	300
200	400HU	200	Window Width	200	200	Window Width
100		100	400 HU	100	100	80 HU
0		0	Window Level	0	0	Window Level
-100		-100	40 HU	-100	-100	35 HU
-200	-200	-200	-200
-300	-300	Window Width	-300
-400	-400	-400	1500 HU	-400
-500	-500	-500	Window Level	-500
-600	-600	-600	-500	-600
-700	-700	-700	-700
-800	-800	-800	-800
-900	-900	-900	-900
-1000	-1000	-1000	-1000

Figure 1.3.6

grey and white matter ranges from approx 22HU to 42HU, with cerebrospinal fluid measuring approximately 0HU. Thus a much narrower window must be selected to identify normal and abnormal intracranial anatomy.

Once the appropriate width of tissue HUs has been chosen, the central point of this width or level on the Hounsfield Scale needs to be selected. The window level to distinguish bony detail would therefore be at the central point or mean of the HU value of normal bone (approximately 400HU). Figure 1.3.6 indicates the most widely used window widths and levels for radiotherapy applications. Diagnostic colleagues may also utilise more specific windowing widths and levels for appreciation of other tissues such as the liver. It is important to appreciate that tissue types with Hounsfield Units falling outside the selected width and level will be either white or black, and thus lacking in detail.

If visual analysis is difficult due to ambient viewing conditions or inexperience, it is possible to acquire accurate digital measurements for each tissue type HU within the slice. Software on all scanners is configured to perform this function, and by comparing the digital measurements with HU guides such as Figure 1.3.5 tissue types can be established.

1.3.5 Using contrast

It is evident from Figure 1.3.5 that there are some tissue types that fall within a very narrow band of HU values, giving them a very similar appearance on images. If these tissues are in close proximity to one another, this similarity can make it impossible to distinguish between structures and demarcate borders. In radiotherapy, this is a particular challenge in centrally located disease where there may be lymph node involvement with a lack of discernable border between blood vessels, the gastrointestinal tract and possible lymphadenopathy.

These difficulties are common in centrally located bronchial tumours, lymphomas or pelvic tumours where regional iliac lymph chains may be affected.

In these cases, introduction of a contrast agent with a substantially different HU value can highlight different structures. This works best if the agent can be introduced into a vessel, usually in the circulatory or digestive system.

Intravenous contrast

Figures 1.3.7 and 1.3.8 demonstrate instances where vessel opacification is essential for accurate identification of centrally located lymphadenopathy adjacent to or encasing arterial vessel walls.

Figure 1.3.7 shows the arch of aorta (A) enhanced with intravenous (IV) contrast agent. Arterial opacification demonstrates aortic location with clear enlargement and compression of the aorta by adjacent lymph nodes (L).

Figure 1.3.8 shows iliac lymph node (L) involvement and adjacent iliac vessels (black arrow IV). The iliac vessels appear paler due to the high density contrast. This opacification allows the iliac vessels to be distinguished from the lymphadenopathy with ease.

Intracranial tumour demarcation is another invaluable use of an intravenous contrast agent. The breakdown in blood brain barrier and vascular nature of many

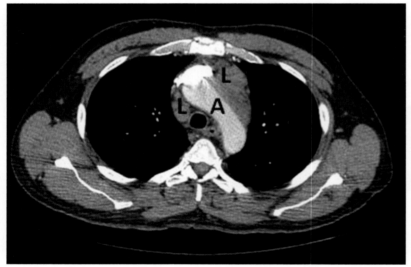

Figure 1.3.7

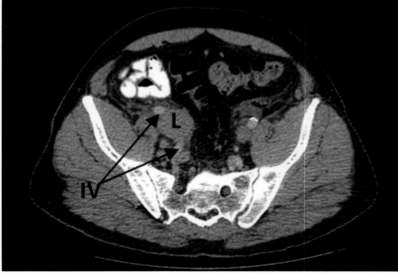

Figure 1.3.8

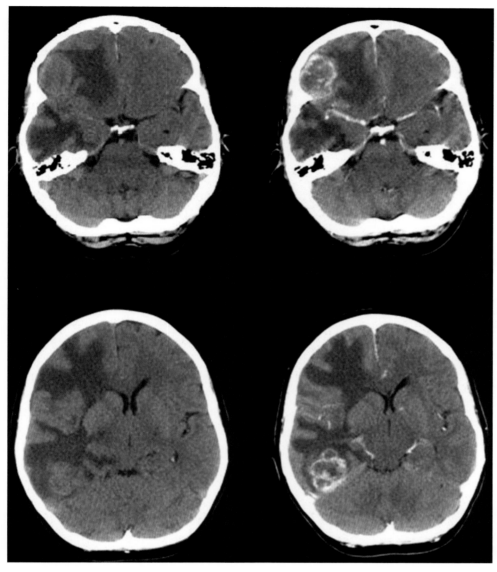

Figure 1.3.9

intracranial tumours lend themselves perfectly to increased detection with IV contrast. Figure 1.3.9 shows intracranial images taken of a patient with a primary lung tumour. The images on the left were taken without IV contrast and those on the right are the corresponding 'post IV contrast' images.

These images clearly show the benefit of IV contrast in intracranial imaging, with the contrast demarcating the evident metastatic deposits. The combination of reduced white matter attenuation caused by vasogenic oedema and the uptake of IV contrast within both metastases ensures that tumour size, location and boundary are all clearly visible.

It should be noted that IV contrast agents may be contraindicated in some patients. There is a recognised risk of inducing adverse reactions ranging from relatively minor side effects to severe anaphylaxis or renal failure. Patients with known allergies, asthma, impaired renal function or using specific diabetic medication may not be suitable for IV contrast use. It is advisable to check local policies prior to administration of any IV contrast agent.

Oral contrast

Similar CT densities of the gastrointestinal tract and adjacent organs and muscles often hamper clear demarcation of relevant anatomy and pathology. Thus many CT investigations of this area require introduction of oral contrast to distinguish between the bowel wall and adjacent anatomy. Some diagnostic examinations such as colonography or small bowel studies require the tract to be clear of any contents to allow clear luminal evaluation. Many other CT abdominal and pelvic examinations however do not require particular bowel preparation, other than recommendations to avoid solid foods for 3–4 hours prior to examination to ensure an empty stomach and duodenum. A low residue diet and particular rectal preparation may be required for some planning examinations in the pelvis. Different contrast agents are preferred for different parts of the gastrointestinal tract. These contrast agents are referred to as either positive or negative agents.

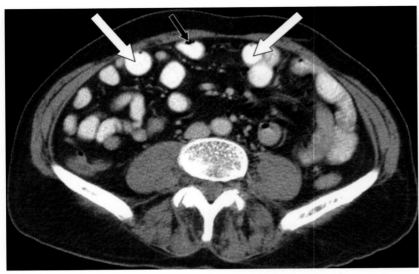

Figure 1.3.10

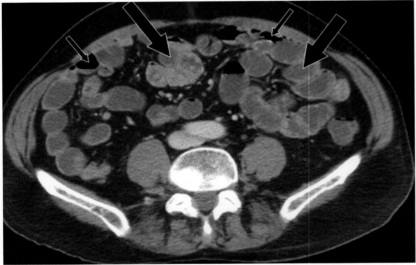

Figure 1.3.11

Positive agents such as a barium suspension or iodine-based solution are more dense than the soft tissue, and appear brighter on the CT images, as indicated by the white arrows in Figure 1.3.10. Barium suspension is routinely used for many examinations, but is contraindicated where perforation is suspected. Water-soluble iodine-based solutions are then used.

Negative agents such as water or air are less dense than soft tissues and appear darker on CT images, as indicated by the black arrows in Figure 1.3.11. The lumen of the oesophagus, stomach and small bowel are particularly well demonstrated with negative contrast agents. Figure 1.3.11 illustrates two types of negative contrast; the larger arrows indicate water introduced as a contrast agent prior to the scan and the smaller arrows point to air (also seen in Figure 1.3.10) already present within the small bowel. The air is also seen in small pockets above the water towards the anterior bowel wall, indicating that the patient is supine. Water is used to stage oesophagus, stomach, duodenum, jejunum and pancreas tumours.

Natural contrast agents have an important role to play, particularly in identification of abdominal structures. The presence of intra-abdominal fat assists greatly when assessing the small bowel and adjacent abdominal structures and often oral contrast agents are not required as the fat provides a natural inherent tissue density contrast. An increased amount of intra-abdominal fat is particularly noticeable in larger male patients where fat tends to be deposited within the abdominal cavity, as opposed to subcutaneously in some female patients.

1.3.6 Summarising CT Interpretation

Black usually indicates tissue types of low attenuation such as air, fat, or lung tissue. Above the diaphragm, air usually represents the respiratory tract and below the diaphragm it is more likely to be found in the digestive tract.

White usually indicates tissue types of high attenuation such as bone, cartilage or acute haemorrhage. It is always worth checking the presence or absence of contrast agent.

Grey usually indicates tissue types of medium attenuation such as organs, muscles, lymph tissue or body fluids. Where similar tissue types are hard to distinguish on images, scanner software tools can provide accurate digital HU measurements to assess tissue type.

Artificial enhancement of tumours, blood vessels, bowel, urinary bladder or digestive tract with contrast agents is invaluable to help delineate tissue types and determine tumour or organ borders.

Window width and level settings should be tailored to specific tissue types. As window width increases, image contrast decreases and vice versa. A range of window settings may be necessary for instances where multiple pathologies affect several tissue types within the CT slice. For example if a patient has a T2 N1 M1 lung tumour, it may be necessary to use the soft tissue window setting to visualise tumour and lymph nodes, and the lung window setting to demarcate tumour extension into the lung, as well as bone window settings to assess the extent of bony metastases.

1.4 Common CT Artefacts

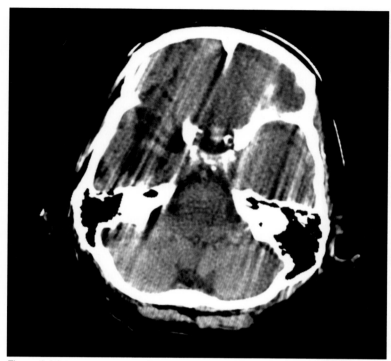

Figure 1.4.1

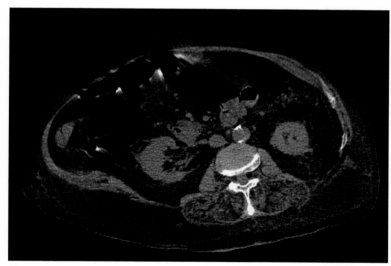

Figure 1.4.2

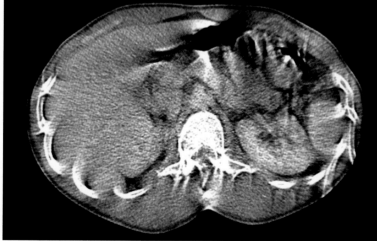

Figure 1.4.3

Accurate demarcation of cross-sectional anatomy relies upon the production of high quality images. An artefact is a distortion or misrepresentation of anatomy within the CT image, and can render subsequent image perception and CT density data incorrect. The resultant image will therefore display inaccurate CT numbers, so comparative measurement and assessment of tissue densities will be complicated by artefactual tissue attenuation values.

Artefacts can also distort or obscure the CT anatomy, giving rise to discrepancies in anatomical borders. Inaccurate demarcation of borders will inevitably lead to incorrect staging of disease progression or inaccurate outlining for radiotherapy planning, both vital to successful disease management.

When operating any CT system, it is essential to understand, recognise and be able to minimise many artefacts that can be generated, ensuring optimal image acquisition. Whilst it may be possible to minimise image noise and artefact during the imaging process, there are some image artefacts caused by the patient that are outside the control of even the most experienced radiographer. Patient respiratory motion is a typical example of this type of artefact. Many imaging techniques in both diagnostic and therapeutic radiography now use respiratory gated motion devices to reduce movement unsharpness and improve image resolution. Some common motion-induced artefacts can be seen in Figures 1.4.1 to 1.4.3. In Figure 1.4.1 there is a clear streak artefact caused by patient movement. This is masking oedema within the right temporal lobe. Figure 1.4.2 shows another streak artefact caused by respiration and high air/soft tissue interface in the bowel. In this case, the artefact is mimicking possible perforation and leakage of contrast agent. In Figure 1.4.3 the patient motion artefact is caused by respiration and coughing movement, causing 'ghosting' of soft tissues.

Whilst movement or patient motion artefacts are relatively straightforward to minimise by maximising patient comfort and making use of immobilisation devices, many radiographers can underestimate the value of a full, clear description of the examination and its relevance to subsequent treatment plans.

The presence of dense metallic objects such as prostheses, pacemakers, dental amalgam, metallic dentures or even hearing aids within the scan field of view will cause improper sampling of the surrounding tissue, as much of the x-ray beam will be absorbed. This gives rise to either a bright high attenuation stellate artefact surrounding the inhomogeneity or a black stellate signal loss area. This artefact also occurs when there is movement of two adjacent tissues of substantially different densities, e.g. skull vault and brain (as in Figure 1.4.1) or air and bowel (as in Figure 1.4.3) and can mimic or mask pathology.

The presence of large dense metallic objects within the scan field of view can have such an effect that the image quality and anatomical detail may be completely obscured. Accurate local diagnostic staging or planning can therefore be extremely compromised or impossible so, wherever possible, metallic objects should be removed from the area under investigation to improve image quality. Examples of frequently occurring artefacts are seen in Figures 1.4.4 to 1.4.6.

Figure 1.4.4 shows a metallic streak artefact caused by dental amalgam. In this patient, the artefact is masking tumour boundaries in the tongue and floor of mouth. Figure 1.4.5's metallic streak artefact is caused by bilateral hip prostheses, completely obscuring the prostate gland and its boundaries. In Figure 1.4.6 the metallic streak artefact is caused by a cardiac defibrillator which is obscuring the left breast region.

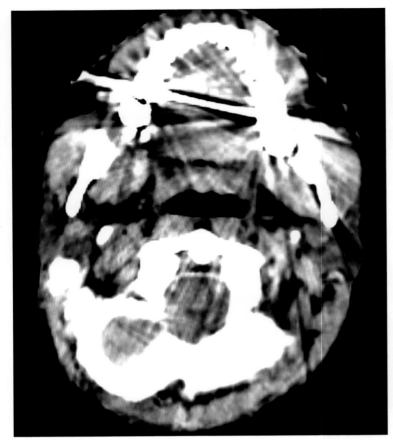

Figure 1.4.4

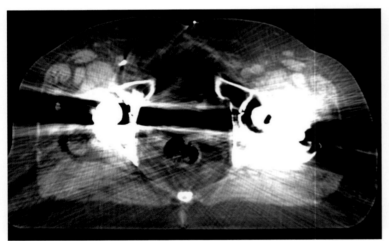

Figure 1.4.5

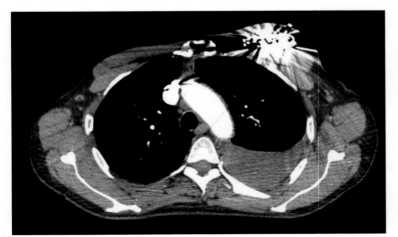

Figure 1.4.6

1.5 MRI Principles and Equipment: A brief introduction

Although CT remains the dominant imaging modality in radiotherapy planning, and indeed most of the images used within this book are CT based, increasing use of fused images for planning demands a rudimentary understanding of magnetic resonance imaging (MRI). Additionally, localised staging of many tumours including lung, rectum, cervix and brain now relies upon MRI to give detailed and accurate morphological data regarding spread or recurrence.

Two phrases are commonplace in the literature when describing MR images: 'Exquisite soft tissue differentiation' and 'Multiplanar acquisition'. Although CT is now capable of reconstructing images in multiple planes, enabling increased anatomical spatial awareness, MRI can demonstrate soft tissue detail that is far superior to CT. Not only can MRI produce images that will demonstrate two adjacent soft tissue types with amazing clarity dependent upon their chemical composition, but it also has the capability of displaying anatomical data in many forms, yielding greater diagnostic capability. Coupled with multiplanar acquisitions such as axial, coronal, sagittal and oblique plane imaging, MRI is a formidable imaging tool that is in great demand from a wide range of clinical specialities.

The principles underpinning the physics and equipment used are fabulously intricate and complex, so the reader will be relieved to discover that they are beyond the scope of this text. It is useful, however, to recognise the different appearances of MR images that are commonly utilised in radiotherapy. Many departments now also use MRI alongside CT images to outline disease borders prior to treatment and CT/MRI fusion is now an accepted technique for outlining many tumour types. Indeed MR and fused images are included within the intracranial section of this book. Fortunately many anatomical representations displayed in MRI sectional data are well recognised as many imaging planes are already familiar to current users of CT.

The 'exquisite soft tissue differentiation' is achieved when MRI interprets complex reactions between adjacent tissue types and changing magnetic fields to produce a wide range of tissue contrast types. MRI is capable of producing varied contrasts between differing tissue types, and several tissue contrasts or 'weighted' image sequences are commonly used during the same examination. Each different tissue weighting provides progressively increased sensitivity and specificity, and many examinations normally include at least two different weighted sequences.

Figures 1.5.1 to 1.5.3 indicate some of the different tissue contrasts or weightings commonly used. Diagnostic colleagues use MRI to stage many neoplasms including virtually all intracranial and head and neck, most pelvic, some breast, muscular and subcutaneous soft tissue and some primary bone tumours. Another area where MRI produces superior imaging is when assessing for secondary disease spread within the spine, investigating the possible level of any compressive spinal cord lesion.

MRI does not use any form of radiation and, magnetic safety queries aside, there are no known harmful effects of MRI imaging, provided the patient and scanning equipment are positioned correctly. MRI uses hydrogen, one of the fundamental building blocks found in abundance within the human body to help acquire images. Hydrogen is plentiful in water and lipids, and both are present in almost all body parts. Oedema surrounding neoplastic disease is therefore well visualised as it contains a high proportion of water molecules. IV contrast agents can also be utilised, increasing the sensitivity and specificity of the technique to display increased pathological detail. Areas that are bright on images are described as having a 'high signal' and conversely areas that are dark have a 'low signal'. Areas that display a grey shade are described as having 'intermediate signal'. The signal of each tissue type varies according to the contrast weighting of the particular sequence used. For example, a 'T1 weighted' image will demonstrate water as dark and therefore it has a low signal. On a 'T2 weighted' image, water will appear bright and is described as having a high signal. Examples of this are further described in Figures 1.5.1 to 1.5.3. Remember the appearance of water on a 'T1' image and a 'T2' image and you'll not go far wrong!

MRI does not come without its inherent limitations, however, and these shortcomings can preclude some patients from even entering the MRI imaging suite. MRI utilises a large superconducting magnet, typically of 1.5 Tesla, which essentially produces a massive magnetic field that increases exponentially closer to the magnet itself. This not only produces obvious risks to patients, relatives and staff with ferromagnetic implantable devices, but also requires the use of non-magnetic equipment within the room itself. Safety is of paramount importance, and must be adhered to at all times as the magnet itself is never turned off, even when the equipment is not being used.

Scanner technology requires many of the scanners to be a 'closed bore' or tunnel design and many patients find this environment claustrophobic and cannot tolerate the examination. However, as scanner technology progresses, many manufacturers are now engineering increasingly 'open' wider bore systems that many more patients can tolerate.

Safety and claustrophobia aside, MRI cannot 'see' some anatomical detail, and tissues containing very small quantities of hydrogen are virtually invisible on MRI. Therefore dense cortical bone and air will appear very dark on the images. Another consideration is the presence of metal objects within the field of view, which will cause loss of signal and image distortions as with CT. Dental amalgam can have a similar effect when imaging the mouth as it can in CT.

MRI, then, is not perfect, but does produce excellent-quality images, particularly where 'exquisite soft tissue differentiation' is required, and is a valuable imaging tool for localised staging of some diseases. In the foreseeable future, however, it will always be used alongside CT as a complementary modality to enhance many diagnostic and radiotherapy practices.

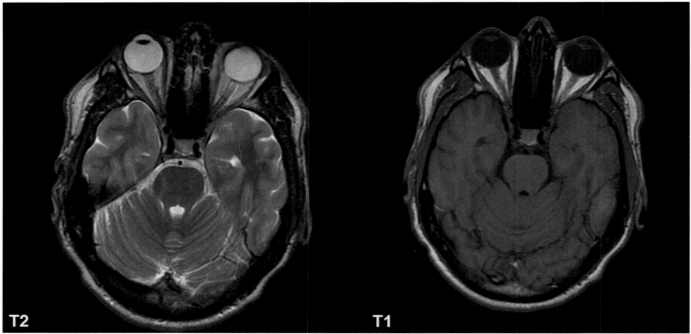

Figure 1.5.1

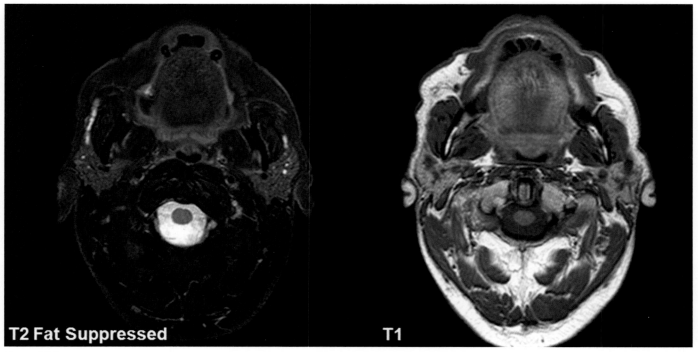

Figure 1.5.2

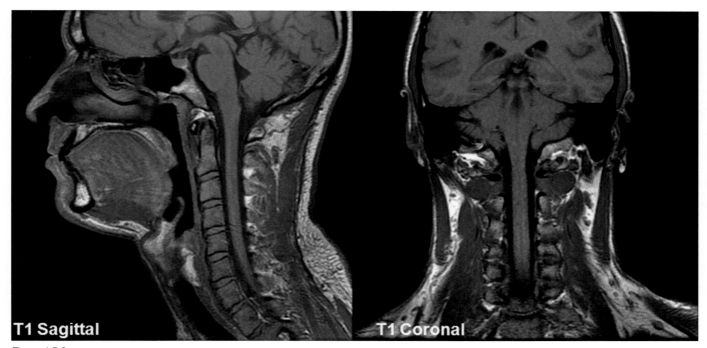

T1 Sagittal   T1 Coronal

Figure 1.5.3

Figure 1.5.1 shows a conventional T2 weighted image on the left. This has bright water (high signal) and hence bright CSF. It also has bright fat (high signal). On the right is the same patient imaged with a conventional T1 weighted image. This displays dark water (and CSF) and bright fat.

Figure 1.5.2 shows a conventional 'T2 Fat Suppressed' image on the left. This is a T2 image with adjusted contrast to remove all the high signals from the fat. There is bright fluid (a high signal from water) and dark fat (low signal). The fluid in the right parotid duct can be seen easily. Contrast this with the T1 image of the same patient seen on the right. This clearly has dark fluid (a low signal from water) and bright fat (high signal).

Figure 1.5.3 shows a T1 Sagittal midline image on the left. There is dark fluid (low signal) and bright fat (high signal). There is bright marrow in the mandible and dark air in the nasopharynx (low signal). On the right can be seen a T1 Coronal midline image. Thus there is a dark region in the petrous temporal bone due to the low signal of air and bone. It is probably worth revisiting this section after familiarisation with CT anatomy to try and identify these structures on MR.

Chapter 2
Pelvis and Abdomen

2.1 Musculoskeletal System

The bony pelvis comprises the sacrum and coccyx at the posterior with the innominate bones forming the lateral and anterior boundaries. Figure 2.1.1 illustrates the relationship between these bones. Each innominate bone is a fusion of three separate bones: the ilium (I), ischium (Is) and pubis (P). The superior and largest component is the ilium. Each ilium has a flared crest on the superior edge and a slightly concave inner surface known as the iliac fossa. The ilia intersect with the sacrum (S) via the sacroiliac joint. This extends for a considerable distance superior-inferior as well as anterior-posterior. The inferior of the ilium forms the superior of the acetabulum.

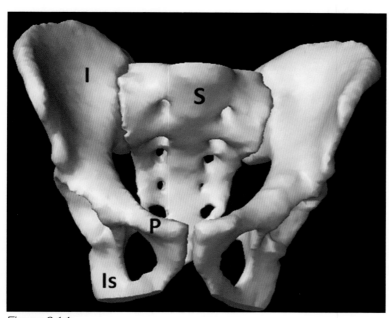

Figure 2.1.1

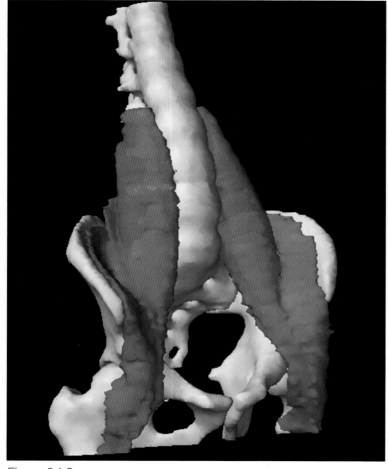

Figure 2.1.2

The acetabulum is the bowl-shaped depression that is the receptacle for the head of the femur. The inferior half of the acetabulum is formed by the ischium posteriorly and the pubis anteriorly. Figure 2.1.1 illustrates the relationship between the three components of the pelvic bones. An essential radiological feature of the pubic bones is the symphysis pubis, the anterior connection between the two rami. The other notable pelvic bony feature is the obturator foramen, which is the aperture formed by the arches of the pubis and the ischium. The skeletal system in the abdomen is much simpler, comprising the five lumbar vertebrae. On CT the wide nature of the vertebral bodies is evident as they are designed to support most of the body's weight.

The majority of the abdominal muscles are not immediately relevant in common radiotherapy practice since they rarely form target volumes or critical structures. Of note, however, are the paired psoas muscles lying parallel to the vertebral column, anteriorly and laterally, as shown in Figure 2.1.2. The psoas muscles are useful features to identify on CT since the ureters run anteriorly to them. They become wider as they descend the abdomen, joining the iliacus muscle, which covers the iliac fossae. At this point, they are known as the iliopsoas muscles. They then continue and reduce in size inferiorly until they reach the lesser trochanter of the femur.

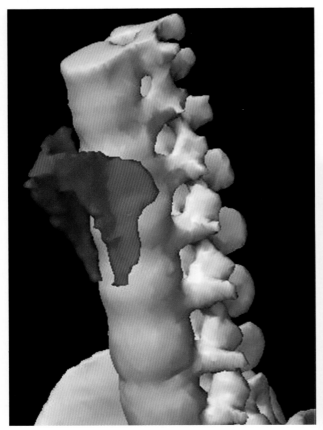

Figure 2.1.3

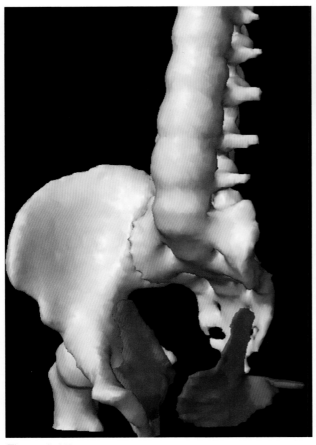

Figure 2.1.5

Towards the superior of the psoas muscles, they are joined by the crura of the diaphragm. The crura are shown extending towards the vertebral column in Figure 2.1.3. The diaphragm constitutes the boundary between thorax and abdomen and the two muscular 'crura', or legs, extend inferiorly along the spine to serve as anchors for the diaphragm. The retrocrural space between the crura and the vertebrae contains some important structures as will be seen later.

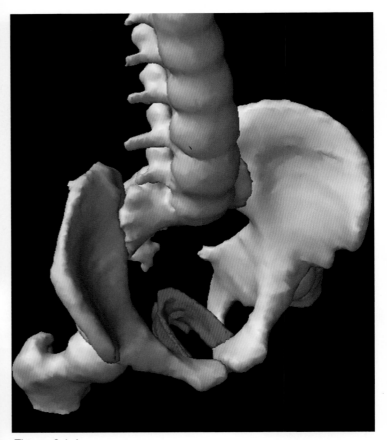

Figure 2.1.4

In the pelvis, some of the muscles should be identified to help distinguish them from other more relevant anatomy. The prime candidate for confusion is a collection of three flat muscles collectively known as the levator ani, as shown in Figure 2.1.4. This sheet runs from anterior to posterior, to form the inferior of the pelvis and thus provide support for the pelvic organs. In the male the proximity of the levator ani can cause confusion when attempting to delineate the inferior aspect of the prostate. Although not outlined in Figure 2.1.4, the levator ani muscle is connected to the coccyx by a fibrous band called the 'raphe'.

Further support for the pelvic organs is provided by the obturator muscles (Figure 2.1.5). They run along the lateral inner edge of the pelvis, covering the obturator foramina. They form the lateral support for the pelvic organs, forming a 'basket' shape with the levator ani muscle. The obturator internus are of note since they help denote the position of the obturator lymph nodes as will be seen later.

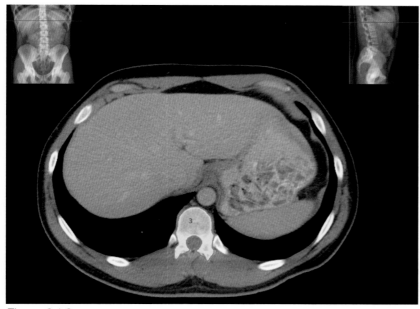

Figure 2.1.6

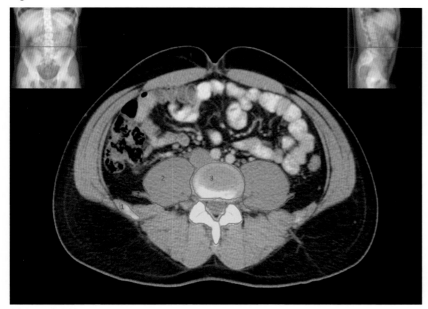

Figure 2.1.7

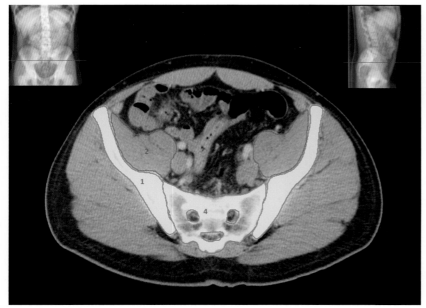

Figure 2.1.8

Figure 2.1.6 shows how the musculo-tendinous crura (7) of the diaphragm track posteriorly to meet the anterolateral surfaces of the upper lumbar vertebrae (3). The right crus is usually slightly thicker than the left and the crura in general are thickened anteriorly. The space behind the crura is known as the retrocrural space. It contains fatty adipose tissue in which several other higher attenuation smaller vessels and structures can be seen.

The thick psoas muscles (2) are seen in Figure 2.1.7 lateral to the lumbar vertebrae (3). These are occasionally split into psoas major and minor and are visible on most sections from the mid abdomen to the pelvis. They form part of the posterior abdominal wall and attach proximally to the lateral aspects of the lumbar vertebrae and intervertebral discs from T12 down to L5. They attach distally to the lesser trochanter of the femur. Although measuring about 45HU, similar to adjacent soft tissue structures, the psoas muscles are readily distinguishable on CT cross-section by the surrounding retroperitoneal adipose tissue (-65HU). The tip of the right iliac crest (1) is also seen on this image.

Figure 2.1.8 demonstrates the sharp contrast between the highly attenuating bone of the ilium (1) and the adjacent soft tissue structures, particularly at the cortex where bone density is greatest. The less dense 'cancellous' interior is a mixture of bone and fatty marrow organised in a 'trabecular' structure and thus appears less dense.

Within the sacrum (4) two sacral foraminae and the vertebral canal are seen. On axial section, the angle of the sacroiliac joints can be appreciated. Within the pelvis in Figure 2.1.8, the psoas muscle is joined by the iliacus muscle arising from the iliac fossa, to form the iliopsoas muscle (2).

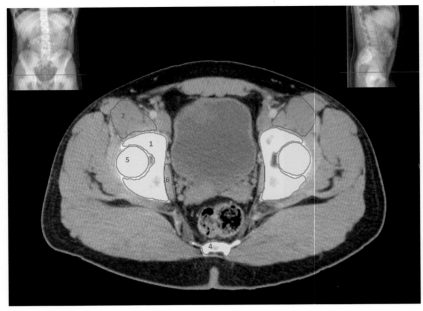

Figure 2.1.9

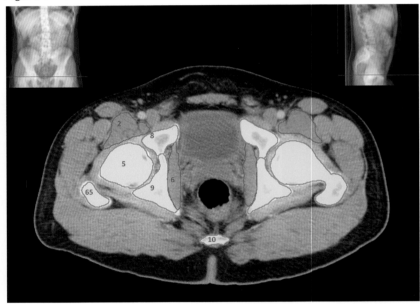

Figure 2.1.10

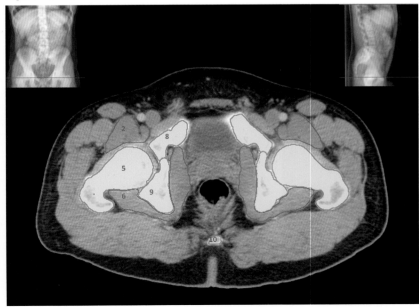

Figure 2.1.11

More inferiorly, in Figure 2.1.9, the iliopsoas (2) pierces the inguinal canal and is visible anterior to the ilium (1). Although rarely a site of primary pathological process, the psoas and iliopsoas muscles are both clinically and radiologically significant due to their proximity to the aorta, inferior vena cava, kidneys, ureters, digestive tract, pancreas, lymph nodes and spine. In cross-section, the femoral heads (5) appear round, located deep within each acetabulum formed by the ilium (1). The obturator internus muscle (6) is seen on the medial border of the ilium.

Figure 2.1.10 features more of the pelvic bones including the ischium (9) and pubis (8). The pubis (8) forms the anterior pillar of the acetabulum while the ischium (9) forms the posterior column. The obturator internus muscle (6) adjacent to the pelvic wall denotes the border of the pelvic brim forming the top of the funnel shaped pelvic diaphragm. Its internal borders, although sheathed in fascia, can be difficult to distinguish more inferiorly due to proximity to other pelvic soft tissues and levator ani muscle groups. The right greater trochanter (65) is apparently floating and not attached to the right femoral head (5). As with all structures, the viewer must scroll superior and inferior to fully appreciate the bony structure and components of the pelvis and hip joints.

In Figure 2.1.11 male pelvic structures are seen adjacent to the anterior 'belly' of the obturator internus muscle (6) where it attaches to the pubis (8). The muscle can be seen wrapping around the rear of the ischium (9) and inserting into the femur (5) at the medial greater trochanter surface. The inferior tip of the coccyx (10) is visible just anterior to the natal cleft.

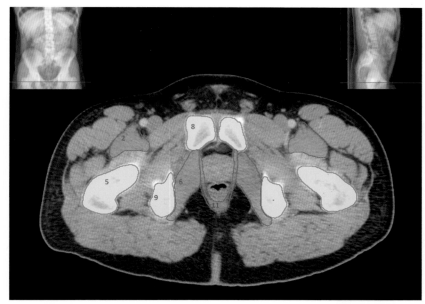

Figure 2.1.12

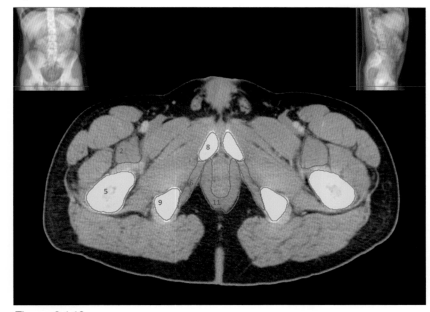

Figure 2.1.13

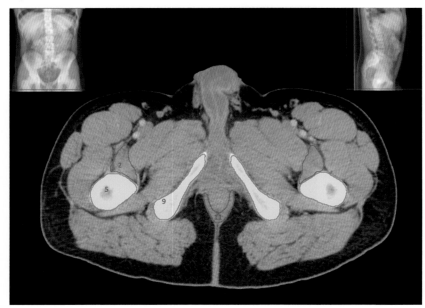

Figure 2.1.14

Figure 2.1.12 shows the levator ani (11), composed of the pubococcygeus, ilio-coccygeus and puborectalis muscles. The intimate relationship of this muscle to the rectum, internal pelvic organs and obturator internus muscle (6) is clear. The obturator internus (6) can be seen to bridge the obturator foramen between the pubis (8) and ischium (9).

With the exception of the bony pelvis and fat within the ischiorectal fossa, all other soft tissues are of similar density at about 40HU. This makes CT outlining of the prostatic apex, vagina and anus quite difficult. This is demonstrated in Figure 2.1.13 where potentially all soft tissues enclosed by the levator ani muscle group appear to form a single soft tissue mass, with few distinguishable markings or borders.

The levator ani muscle group (11) forms the base of the funnel shaped pelvic diaphragm closing the inferior pelvic aperture. The urogenital diaphragm, formed by a thin sheet of striated muscle, is located anterior to the levator ani muscle group. These muscles make soft tissue differentiation in the inferior pelvis particularly challenging in both males and females. This can be improved by supporting the axial CT sections with coronal section imaging using high resolution T2 MR. Central to Figure 2.1.14, the levator ani complex (11) intimately surrounds the anus. Fat within each ischiorectal and ischioanal fossa can be seen laterally to each ischium (9), separated centrally by the natal cleft. The shafts of the femora (5) lie laterally to this and the cancellous bony centres are clearly visible, surrounded by the higher density cortex.

2.2 Urinary System

The twin starting points of the urinary system are the kidneys, which are located at the rear of the abdomen, slightly anterior to the psoas muscles and lateral to the vertebral bodies. Each kidney is accompanied by an adrenal gland which is located superiorly and medially. These can be seen in Figure 2.2.1. Recall that the right kidney is the lower of the two due to the volume of liver above it.

Urine is produced in the kidneys by filtering out waste products from the bloodstream. The urine collects in the renal pelvis at the centre of the kidney. From here, the urine passes into the ureters. These are long and take an often tortuous route through the abdomen. It can be difficult to pick out the ureters on individual slices, especially with non-contrast images where they can mimic blood vessels. For much of the route, the ureters overlie the psoas muscles, being anterior and slightly medial to them. Figure 2.2.2 shows the ureters curving anteriorly before plunging posteriorly once they pass the fifth lumbar vertebra.

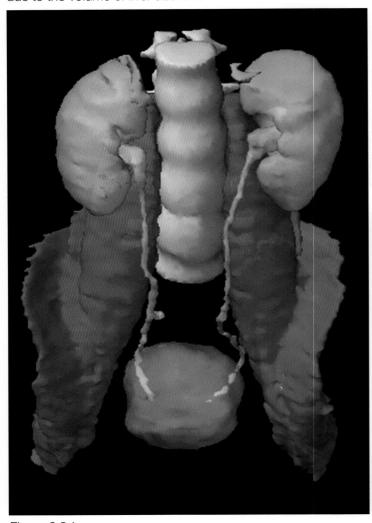

Figure 2.2.1

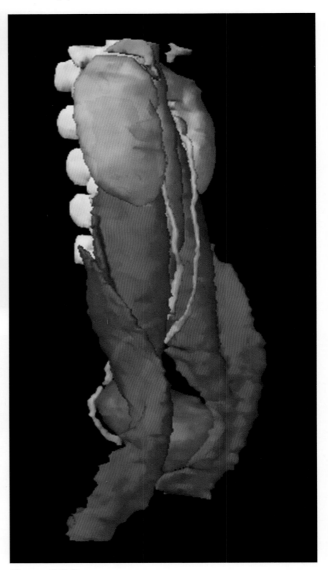

The final stage of the ureters' journey takes them around the posterior edge of the bladder towards the inferior 'trigone' area. The bladder is the main organ of interest with regard to radiotherapy in the urinary system. Since the bladder is essentially an elastic-walled bag of urine, it will deform readily around more solid anatomy adjacent to it. Thus it is not uncommon to find two or three separate 'bulges' of bladder appearing on CT slices around other structures. For some treatments such as prostate, it is common for the bladder to be maintained at full capacity and in these cases the pressure can give the bladder a more consistent shape, although the paler muscular wall stretches thin. For other treatments, such as to the bladder, voiding is encouraged before treatment or imaging. In these circumstances the muscular wall is much thicker but the shape and volume of the bladder can be surprisingly variable.

Figure 2.2.2

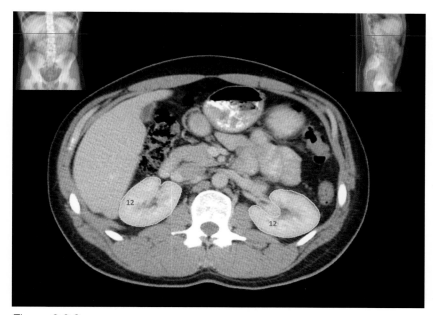

Figure 2.2.3

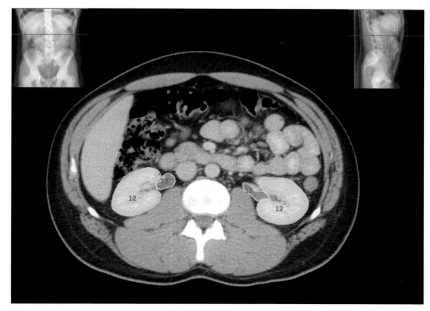

Figure 2.2.4

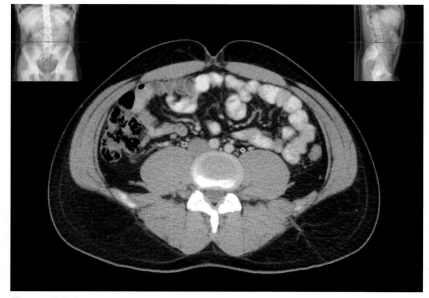

Figure 2.2.5

The kidneys (12) lie within the retroperitoneum lateral to the spine and psoas muscles. They can usually be found between T12 and L3, although this can vary with respiration and diaphragmatic motion.

Figure 2.2.3, at L2, shows the left renal hilum complete with renal arteries and veins. In Figure 2.2.4 at a slightly lower level, the ureters (13) have emerged from the renal pelvis.

Demarcation of the kidneys (12) (approx 30HU without IV contrast) is relatively straightforward due to the fibrous capsule and surrounding contrasting 'perinephric' fat. The thin layer of 'Gerota's' renal fascia can sometimes be seen surrounding the fat. The adrenal glands, not demonstrated here but discussed later, sit within Gerota's fascia, superior to the upper poles.

IV contrast enhances the renal cortex in Figure 2.2.4 with the cortical columns of Bertin separating the medulla into pyramid shaped segments. At the apex of each medullary pyramid, renal calyces form multiple funnel like structures that drain into the renal pelvis. Approximately 60–70 seconds after injection, the renal cortex will enhance (approximately 140HU) and then, minutes later, contrast will fill the renal calyces, renal pelvis, ureters and bladder.

Figure 2.2.5 illustrates the ureters. These are thin fibromuscular tubes of varying diameter (3–7mm). Localisation of the ureters can be complicated, particularly without IV contrast. It is, however, possible to delineate them on CT since they lie within fatty and connective tissues along their entire course. Care should be taken not to confuse ureters with small vessels or fatty stranding.

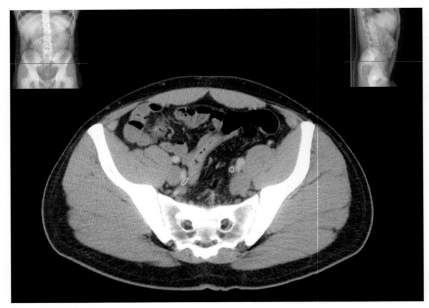

Figure 2.2.6

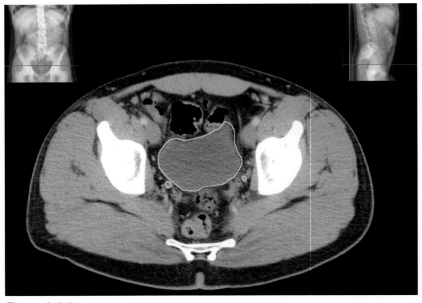

Figure 2.2.7

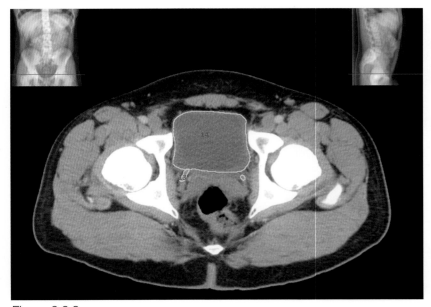

Figure 2.2.8

Ureters are best identified by tracking them inferiorly from the renal pelvis to the bladder. The ureters descend inferiorly and slightly medially from the renal pelvis, towards the anterior surface of the ipsilateral psoas muscle as seen in Figure 2.2.5.

Both ureters descend anterior to each psoas muscle until they cross the pelvic brim where they follow the path of the common iliac artery (Figure 2.2.6).

They then track posteriorly, crossing anterior to the external iliac artery before passing obliquely through the urinary bladder (14) wall posteriorly as seen in Figure 2.2.8. Any obstructive or compressive lesion at any point during the course of the ureter will cause dilation above it (hydro-ureter).

The urinary bladder (14) has variable appearances and position within the pelvis dependent upon the degree of filling. Partially distended bladders can be easily compressed by adjacent structures such as enlarged prostatic lesions, vaginal tumours, other pelvic masses or loops of sigmoid colon, as demonstrated in Figure 2.2.7, indenting the bladder's anterior right border. A prostatic or uterine fundus 'impression' is relatively normal. The partial volume effect is common where, due to its deformable nature, it may look as if bowel loops appear inside the urinary bladder.

When fully distended, the muscular wall should be uniform, smooth, free of calcification, and between 1mm and 3mm thick, measuring approximately 45HU.

After voiding, the urinary bladder walls will appear thicker, and more irregular. Pelvic irradiation will cause uniform inflamed thickening of the bladder wall that will be evident on follow-up planning CT.

2.3 Digestive System

The majority of the structures found in the abdomen are part of the digestive system and extend to the very inferior part of the pelvis. This section, therefore, features a large number of CT slices. Despite this, for much of the journey, the structure of the digestive system is fairly straightforward, consisting of a series of tubes.

Figure 2.3.1

Food enters the abdomen via the oesophagus before collecting in the stomach on the left hand side of the body, as seen in Figure 2.3.1. Like the bladder, the stomach is designed to enlarge to accommodate changes in capacity. Thus, unless the patient is undergoing strict dietary control, the stomach can exhibit a wide range of sizes. Immediately after a hearty meal, the stomach will have expanded inferiorly, anteriorly and medially, pushing other structures aside in order to accommodate its contents. On CT, the stomach contents can be seen to exhibit a horizontal fluid level.

After exiting the stomach, the digestive tract forms the duodenum and performs a tight U-turn (Figure 2.3.1), passing inferiorly and then medially to enter the jejunum. As it does so, it passes under the liver. The liver is a large solid structure dominating the right hand superior portion of the abdomen (Figure 2.3.2). It is the largest gland in the human body and is comprised of two main lobes, the small left lobe and the larger right lobe. The right lobe contains other much smaller lobes known as the caudate and quadrate lobe. The liver is not a major source of primary tumours but due to its rich blood supply it is a common site for metastatic deposits to grow. Sitting under the liver is the pear-shaped gall bladder which stores bile to assist with fat emulsification. Its fluid-filled nature means that on CT it can be readily identified as a darker, less dense structure.

The small intestine then curls round the head of the pancreas. The pancreas can be seen shaded orange in Figure 2.3.3 (from the superior) and Figure 2.3.4 (from the anterior). It lies across the upper abdomen with the tail on the left side, the body centrally placed and the head tucked into the curve of the duodenum. It lies against the spleen posterolaterally and the stomach superiorly.

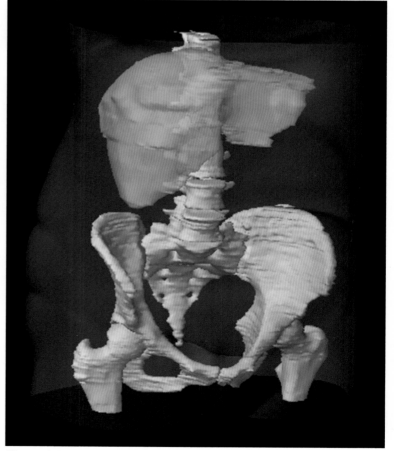

Figure 2.3.2

The small intestine is the next stage of the digestive tract and is a highly mobile structure. It has a sausage-like appearance on CT and can be distinguished from the large bowel by the lack of air in it. In the lower right of the abdomen, the small intestine connects to the large bowel via the ileocaecal valve. The large bowel starts with the caecum. This receives the small intestine contents and is situated in the inferior right hand side of the abdomen. Extending from the inferior part of the caecum is the small useless appendix, occasionally curling to resemble a pig's tail. The appendix can be seen in Figure 2.3.5 extending inferiorly and medially from the caecum. After exiting the caecum, the ascending colon passes superiorly until it reaches the liver. The colon can be identified by its characteristic appearance of interconnected rounded chambers called saccules.

The ascending colon then bends at the hepatic flexure to form the transverse colon. As the name suggests, the transverse colon moves transversely across the top of the abdomen. It does sag somewhat, however, and thus can loop a considerable distance inferiorly, occasionally causing confusion at lower slice levels as seen in Figure 2.3.6. However tortuous a route it takes, it approaches the spleen and the stomach and turns at the splenic flexure.

From this bend, the descending colon drops down the left hand side of the abdomen until it reaches the sigmoid flexure where it turns into the sigmoid colon as seen in Figure 2.3.7. The sigmoid colon is responsible for moving the intestinal contents from the left hand side of the body to the centrally and posteriorly placed rectum and it does this by forming a characteristic 'sigma' shape. The final bend in the digestive tract is the acutely angled rectosigmoid junction, marking the superior border of the rectum. It is important to identify this junction when outlining the rectum as a critical structure to ensure a clinically useful dose-volume histogram can be produced.

The rectum has a different appearance to the colon, lacking the saccules and forming a single large cavity (Figure 2.3.8). The variation in size and shape of the rectum is well-documented and a major cause of uncertainty in reproducibility of pelvic setups. The rectum curves along the anterior surface of the sacrum before moving slightly forward towards the centre of the pelvis. The rectum ends in the sphincter muscles of the anus. The anus is embedded in the levator ani muscle sheet and thus can be identified at the level where the levator ani widens on CT. This occurs because the levator ani is crossing at a more oblique angle along the width of the

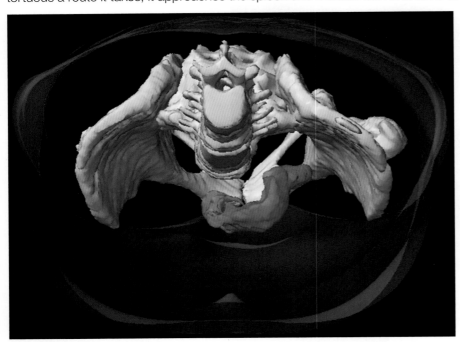

Figure 2.3.3

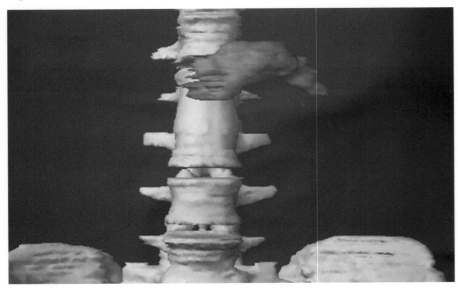

Figure 2.3.4

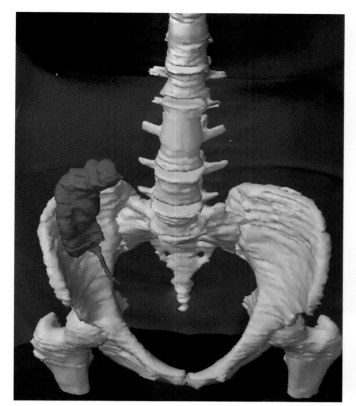

Figure 2.3.5

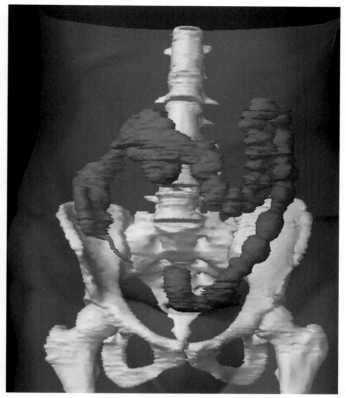

Figure 2.3.6

Figure 2.3.7

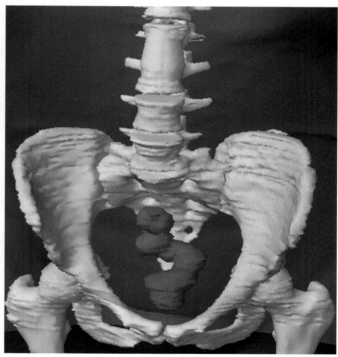

Figure 2.3.8

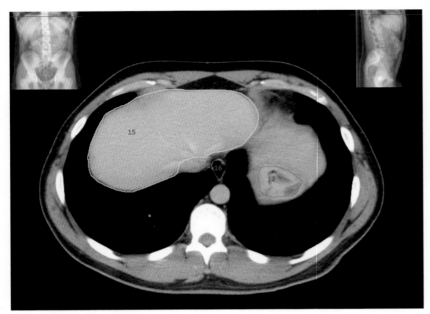

Figure 2.3.9

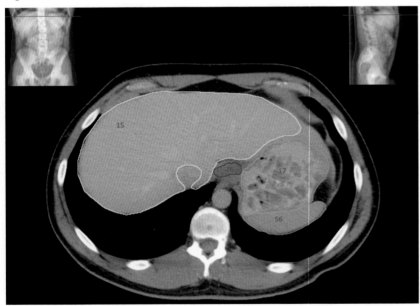

Figure 2.3.10

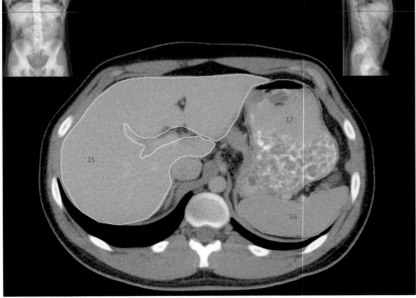

Figure 2.3.11

slice.

In Figure 2.3.9 at T11/12, structures within both the thoracic and upper abdominal cavities are present. In axial cross-section, the soft tissues of the thin muscular diaphragm (45HU) are poorly differentiated against the adjacent liver (15) and stomach wall (17). The crescent shaped lower lobes of each lung are clearly seen, visually very black and demonstrating few lung markings on this soft tissue window.

In the centre of Figure 2.3.9 immediately anterior to the aorta is a section of the distal third oesophagus (16). In this case it is slightly dilated with intraluminal air forming a natural inherent negative contrast agent. The thickness of a healthy oesophageal wall should not exceed 3mm when dilated. Wider circumferential dilatation is usually indicative of pathological or inflammatory process.

The oesophagus does thicken, however, as it passes through the diaphragmatic oesophageal hiatus to join the stomach (17) at the gastro-oesophageal junction (16 in Figure 2.3.10). This may mask the presence of small adenocarcinomas, although they are usually quite advanced and commonly demonstrate irregular luminal narrowing and wall thickening.

Water is also commonly utilised as a negative contrast agent when imaging the distal oesophagus and stomach to demonstrate wall thickening and irregularities. In radio-therapy, the stomach commonly contains partially digested food, as can be seen on Figures 2.3.10 to 2.3.14. The heavier stomach contents sink posteriorly, adjacent to the spleen (56) with fluid sitting on top. Fluid levels with a pocket of air/gas on top, as seen in Figures 2.3.11 to 2.3.14, make the stomach (17) readily distinguishable in many instances.

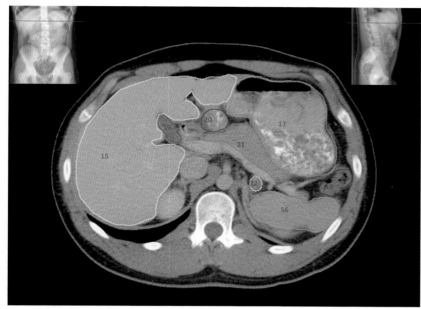

Figure 2.3.9

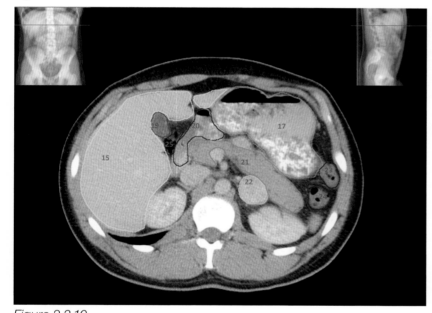

Figure 2.3.10

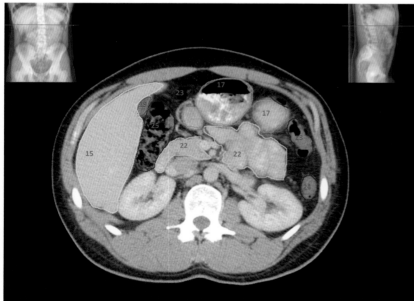

Figure 2.3.11

The pancreas (21) is level with L1/L2 and can be seen extending across the upper abdomen in Figures 2.3.12 and 2.3.13. Its 'head' sits right of midline within the curvature of the duodenum (20) while its body and tail extend to the left, posterior to the stomach and just anterior to the splenic vein. The CT appearance of the pancreas becomes less smooth and more lobulated with age, although increased fatty deposits make it easier to locate.

The liver (15) occupies a large part of the upper abdominal cavity in the right upper quadrant, as can be seen in Figures 2.3.9 to 2.3.16. The four lobes are divided by fissures meeting at the porta hepatis, where the portal vein enters the liver. The right lobe is the largest, occupying most of the right hand side. The left lobe, separated from the right by the falciform ligament, extends to the left across the midline in many instances. The caudate lobe is the smallest, and can be seen in Figure 2.3.11 immediately anterior to the inferior vena cava (IVC). Inferior to the caudate, the quadrate lobe lies behind the gall bladder.

The gall bladder (19) seen in Figures 2.3.12 to 2.3.14 indents onto the quadrate lobe and is dark due to the presence of biliary fluid. The visceral surface of the left lobe of the liver is in contact with the stomach (17), as seen in Figures 2.3.12 and 2.3.13.

Beyond the stomach, the remaining sections of the gastrointestinal tract can be seen on most cross-sections through the abdomen and pelvis, demonstrated in Figures 2.3.11 to 2.3.22.

The duodenum (20) appears in Figures 2.3.12 and 2.3.13, running from the gastric pylorus of the stomach to the proximal jejunum, forming a C-shape around the head of the pancreas (21). As it curves it passes the quadrate lobe of the liver (15), gall bladder (19) and hepatic flexure of the colon (25).

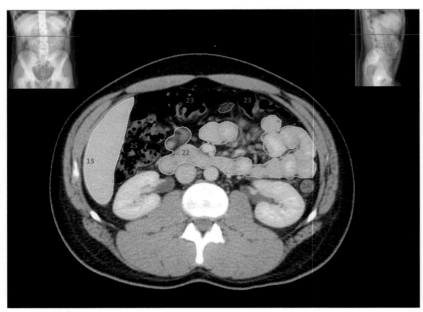

Figure 2.3.15

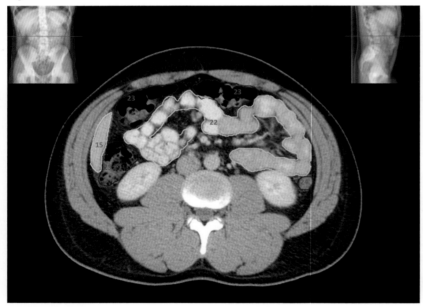

Figure 2.3.16

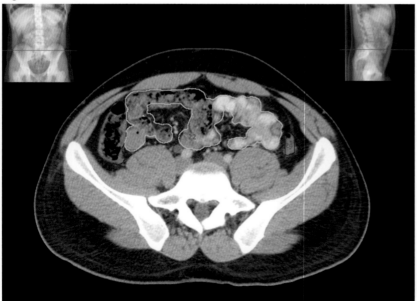

Figure 2.3.17

The remainder of the small bowel (22) is composed of jejunum and ileum. These can be seen folding and curving throughout the mid abdomen and pelvis within the peritoneum. As the small bowel is from 3 to 7 metres long, it appears on most abdominal CT sections as seen in Figures 2.3.14 to 2.3.19.

Generally, the loops of small bowel occupying the left mid abdomen can be identified as jejunum, and loops within the pelvis and right lower abdomen are the ileum. The jejunum is often empty as its Latin name suggests (*jejunus* means empty). Thus intraluminal detail can only be identified by CT contrast agents.

There are finer radiological identifiers, such as the high concentration of circular folds (*plicae circulares*) in the proximal jejunum. These increase intraluminal surface area and cause a 'feathered' appearance, particularly when positive oral contrast agent is used, as seen in Figures 2.3.14 and 2.3.15. The concentration of these folds gradually decreases along the length of the small bowel and they are absent at the terminal ileum.

The change in intraluminal CT appearance is evident in Figure 2.3.16 where there is a distinct difference between the much smoother appearances of the ileum to the right of midline, compared to that of the jejunum, left of midline. As the intraluminal contents are usually more fluid in consistency, any pockets of air will normally rise to the anterior aspect of the lumen, assuming the patient is supine, as can be seen clearly in Figures 2.3.18 and 2.3.19.

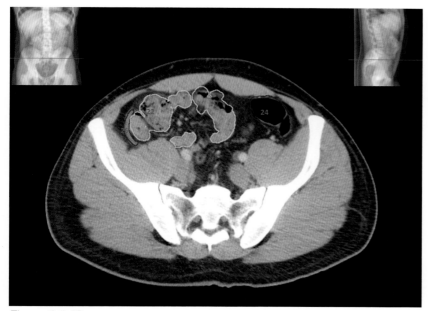

Figure 2.3.18

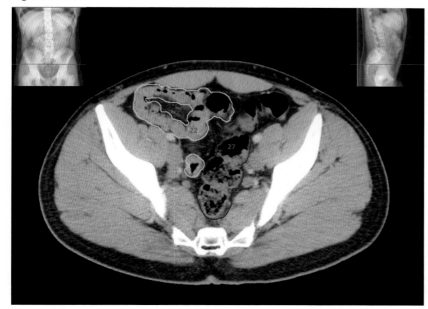

Figure 2.3.19

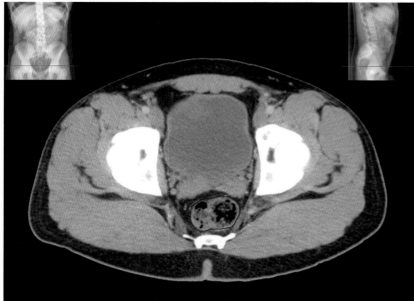

Figure 2.3.20

The large bowel or 'colon' can also be seen throughout the abdomen and continues into the pelvis. It can be traced through Figures 2.3.11 to 2.3.22 (18, 23, 24, 25, 27, 28 and 66). The CT appearances of the colon can be distinguished from loops of the small bowel by larger folds and the presence of intraluminal gas within solid faecal matter.

The colon usually follows a relatively simple and less tortuous route when compared to the small bowel. The ascending colon rises on the right (25) before turning at the hepatic flexure (61). The transverse colon (23) crosses the abdomen to the left then turns at the splenic flexure (18) to form the descending colon (24) dropping down the left side.

After the sigmoid flexure, the sigmoid colon (27) curls around into the pelvis before forming the rectum (28) and anus (29). It is useful to follow this route superior and inferior on contiguous CT slices when attempting to visualise the different parts of the colon. To trace the path of the colon, it is often easier to start at the rectum (28 in Figure 2.3.20). The rectum may be easier to locate on axial CT slices than the caecum (66 in Figure 2.3.17).

Figure 2.3.20 shows the rectum quite loaded with faecal matter and gas. Surrounding the rectum, the dark layer of fat within the perirectal fascia provides a boundary between the rectum and adjacent structures. Scrolling superiorly from the rectum, the sigmoid colon (27 in Figure 2.3.19) extends anteriorly across the left piriformis and iliopsoas muscles and iliac vessels towards the left anterior abdominal wall. The descending colon, surrounded by fat (24 in Figures 2.3.13 to 2.3.17) can be traced up from the pelvic brim to the splenic flexure (18 in Figure 2.3.12).

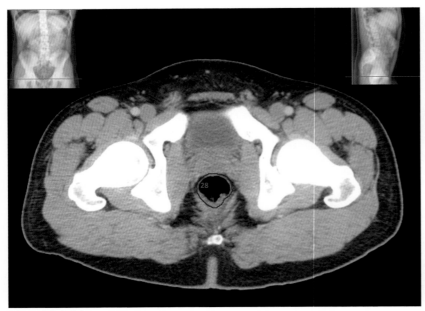

Figure 2.3.21

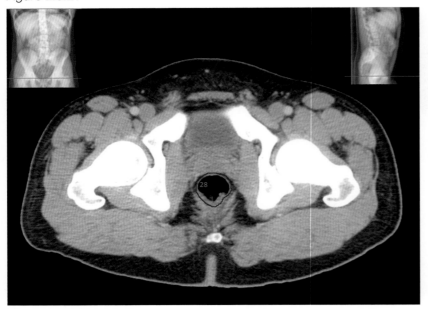

Figure 2.3.22

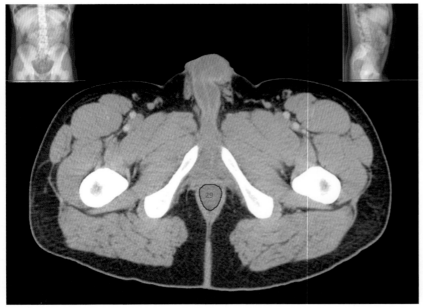

Figure 2.3.23

At this point it is important to scroll inferiorly and superiorly to trace the transverse colon (23) to the right, posterior to the anterior abdominal wall. The path of the transverse colon is quite tortuous as it often sags inferiorly. At the hepatic flexure the ascending colon (25) can be traced inferiorly down to the blind ended caecum (66 in Figure 2.3.17) at the ileocaecal valve. The vermiform appendix (26) can be seen lateral to the caecum, in the right iliac fossa.

Returning to the rectum, in Figure 2.3.21 the rectum (28) has a large pocket of intraluminal gas visible. This is clearly pushing the other pelvic organs anteriorly, demonstrating the difficulty presented by variable rectal volume when attempting to localise target positions.

The walls of the rectum should be about 5mm thick. Posteriorly to the rectal wall can be seen the striations of the coccygeus muscle (part of the levator ani complex). These lie within the ischiorectal fossae and extend laterally to the lateral pelvis walls. They should not be confused for rectal wall.

In Figure 2.3.22, the muscular walls of the anus (29) can be seen centrally, surrounded by the levator ani complex.

2.4 Male Reproductive System

From a radiotherapy perspective, the CT anatomy of the male external genitalia is of little interest as it is rarely computer-planned and the structures are readily visible to the naked eye. The prevalence of tumours arising in the prostate and seminal vesicles, however, makes an understanding of CT anatomy of the internal male reproductive system increasingly important.

The essential function of the internal reproductive system of the male is to produce and combine the various ingredients of semen. Sperm cells are transported inside the body from the testes via the vasa deferentia. These paired tubes run up the outside of the pelvic wall inside the spermatic cord along with the testicular artery and vein. They then penetrate the abdominal muscles through the inguinal canal and leave the spermatic cord. Figure 2.4.1 shows how the spermatic cords are thicker than the vasa deferentia. Each vas deferens then loops its way posteriorly, curving over the top of the bladder as seen in Figure 2.4.1. They then descend the posterior wall of the bladder and approach each other, widening out to form an 'ampulla' each.

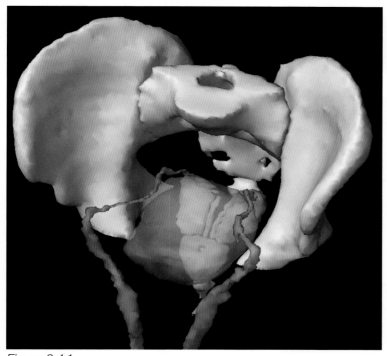

Figure 2.4.1

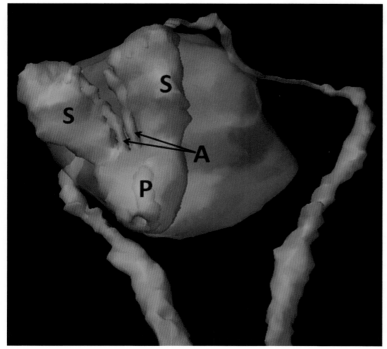

Figure 2.4.2

The main component of semen is seminal fluid, which is produced and stored in the seminal vesicles. They are long feathery structures that extend superiorly and slightly laterally along the posterior wall of the bladder and are a common site for spread of prostate tumours. The seminal vesicles (S) and ampullae (A) join up superior to the prostate (P) as seen in a view from the inferior and posterior in Figure 2.4.2. Together they form the ejaculatory ducts which then descend to penetrate the prostate gland.

The prostate gland sits under the bladder encircling the urethra and is the size and shape of a walnut. It is responsible for adding prostatic fluid to the sperm and seminal fluid. The ejaculatory ducts carry the fluid anteriorly to join the urethra inside the prostate.

The urethra then exits the prostate gland, passes through the small and often indistinguishable bulbourethral or 'Cowper's' gland for its final ingredients and then passes down the penis superiorly to the penile bulb. The penile bulb is the proximal section of the penis between the two roots of penis.

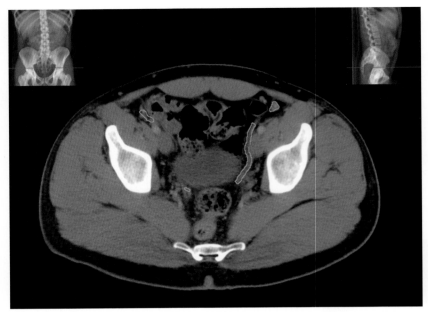

Figure 2.4.3

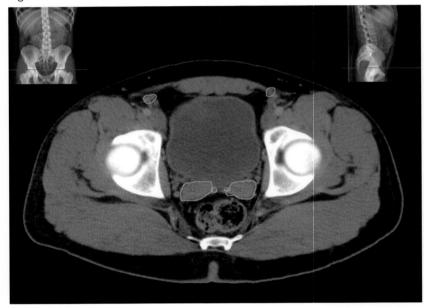

Figure 2.4.4

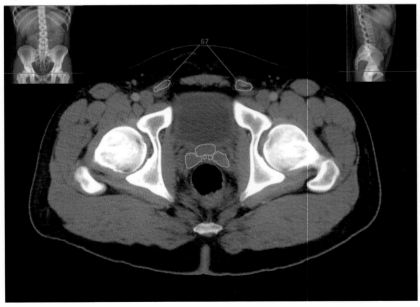

Figure 2.4.5

Figure 2.4.3 shows the vasa deferentia (30). They are a pair of 3–5mm thick muscular tubes following a tortuous route from the testes to a dilated ampulla at the base of the seminal vesicles (31 in Figure 2.4.4). As such, they can be quite difficult to locate and track along their course. Knowledge of their course and adjacent anatomy can help the viewer track them, and as with all tubular structures on CT, it is essential to view contiguous slices superiorly and inferiorly along their course.

Each vas deferens (30) ascends from the scrotum, within the spermatic cord (67), external to the pelvic cavity, seen on Figures 2.4.5 to 2.4.10. The spermatic cord is a little easier to localise, since it is larger and contains the vas deferens, testicular artery, vein, lymphatic ducts, nerves and surrounding fatty tissues.

Passing through the inguinal canal, as seen in Figure 2.4.4, the vasa deferentia leave the spermatic cords and enter the pelvic cavity. From here, they cross over the external iliac vessels and between the supero-lateral borders of the bladder and the lateral pelvic wall. This section of the left ductus is seen in Figure 2.4.3 (30).

The duct then crosses the posterolateral angle of the bladder, traverses the ureter, and can be seen in Figure 2.4.4 medial to the seminal vesicles (31). At this point, the vasa deferentia are easier to demarcate due to ampullary dilatation.

Figure 2.4.5 shows the paired seminal vesicles (31) located between the base of the urinary bladder and the rectum. These are lobulated soft tissue structures and are not fixed. They can appear asymmetrical, but tend to resemble a bow-tie extending either side of the vasa deferentia ampullae, as seen in Figure 2.4.4.

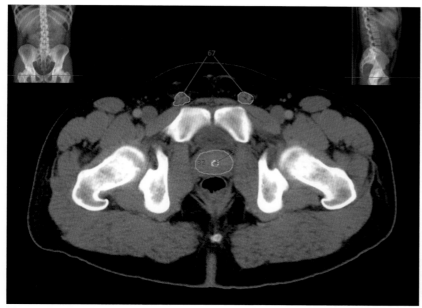

Figure 2.4.6

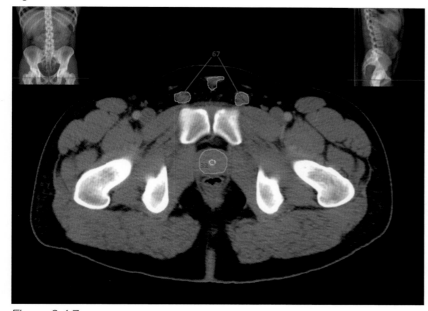

Figure 2.4.7

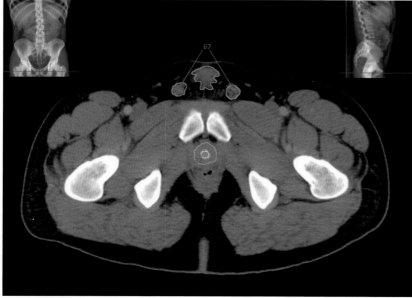

Figure 2.4.8

There is a thin surrounding layer of fat that helps to define the borders of the seminal vesicles. This is useful when assessing infiltrative tumour progression from adjacent organs. Spread of tumour infiltration from the prostate can be quite difficult to assess on CT when relying on changes in HU, but it can make the seminal vesicles appear increasingly bulky or asymmetrical.

More inferiorly, the prostate gland (32) can be seen in Figures 2.4.6 to 2.4.8. Sitting inferior to the neck of the urinary bladder and level with the symphysis pubis, the prostate encloses the urethra (33). It is pyramidal in shape, with its base in contact with the bladder and apex resting on the pelvic floor muscles. A normal prostate measures around 40mm LR, 30mm AP and 50mm SI. The size of the gland is dependent on age and after 45 years gland enlargement is not uncommon. As a consequence, the gland often indents into the bladder.

On CT, the prostate appears relatively homogeneous, with a soft tissue density of approximately 50HU. The prostate's zonal anatomy is often indistinguishable. Prostatic secretions can sometimes cause flecks of calcification within the gland. Ring-like calcifications are occasionally seen, although these tend to be associated with previous infection. The borders of the healthy gland are smooth and can be well demarcated in some individuals by surrounding fat deposits. The prostate is also surrounded by a rich plexus of vessels and nerves. Anteriorly, this is termed 'the anterior plexus of Santorini'. Posterolaterally (at 5 and 7 o'clock positions) this plexus is known as the neurovascular bundles. This periprostatic plexus can cause confusion when attempting to identify and outline the inferior border of the gland. Calcified 'phleboliths' within these venous vessels peripheral to the gland can help to identify the capsule.

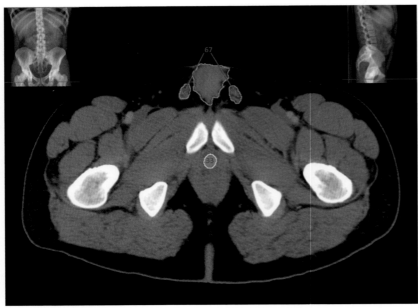

Figure 2.4.9

Figures 2.4.6 to 2.4.7 illustrate how close the prostate lateral border is to the obturator internus muscles. More inferiorly in Figures 2.4.8 and 2.4.9, the levator ani complex obscures the border. Posteriorly, the borders of the gland may be equally as difficult to assess as the rectum can be very close to the peripheral zone, separated only by minimal fat planes and perirectal fascia. In Figures 2.4.6 to 2.4.8 the fat plane separating the prostatic pseudo capsule and the rectum is well demonstrated. Localisation of the anterior border is relatively less complicated due to loose areolar tissues within the retropubic space. Recognition of the prostate outline can therefore be particularly difficult, and it is essential that thin CT sections are utilised here to minimise partial volume effects from the gland and adjacent structures.

Inferiorly, the root of the penis (35) is seen in Figure 2.4.10. The crura of the corpus cavernosum run along the internal aspect of the ischial tuberosities. These can be clearly seen converging anteriorly at the root of the penis (35). Medial to these roots can be seen the bulb of the penis (34). This is the proximal end of the corpus spongiosum of the penis.

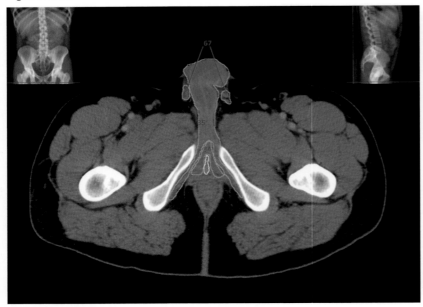

Figure 2.4.10

2.5 Female Reproductive System

The female reproductive system comprises structures for producing ova as well as enabling their fertilisation and subsequent development. Ova are produced in the follicles of the two ovaries. These are paired organs about the size and shape of olives (O in Figures 2.5.1 and 2.5.2). They are situated laterally to the uterus (U) and connected to it via the fallopian tubes. The ovaries have a distinctive appearance on CT with follicles being visible and a fluid-filled low density interior.

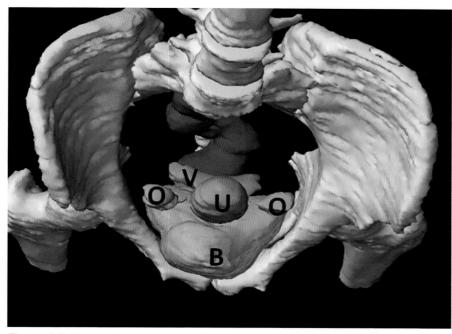

Figure 2.5.1

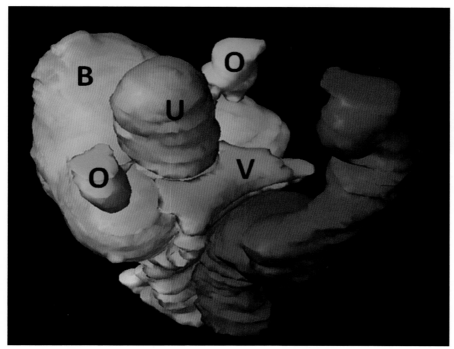

Figure 2.5.2

The uterus is a large pear-shaped organ that is usually situated superiorly to the bladder (B), extending anteriorly. In some cases the uterus is retroverted and falls towards the posterior part of the pelvic cavity. The ovaries and uterus are supported by ligaments and the uterus is covered in a multitude of supportive tissues called the parametrium. This sometimes makes the border hard to delineate on CT. The uterus comprises a thick muscular wall (myometrium) enclosing a central cavity (endometrium). The endometrium can usually be seen on CT as a thin fluid-filled cavity.

The opening from the uterus comprises a fairly thick ring called the cervix that curves from a horizontal opening (internal os) down to a more inferior exit, the external os. The external os connects with the vaginal vault. This is the expanded superior portion of the vagina. The vagina (V) is a collapsible muscular tube that is sandwiched between the rectum and the bladder or urethra. It can be seen in Figure 2.5.2 from a left-posterior view with the expanded vault of vagina leading to the cervix. On CT, the vagina has a flat appearance in an anterior-posterior direction while extending laterally.

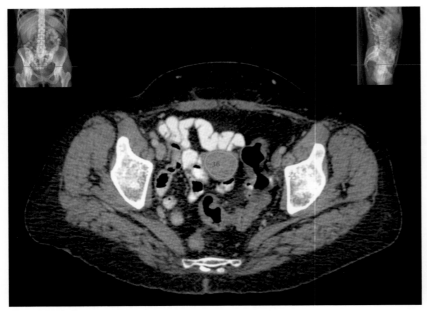

Figure 2.5.3

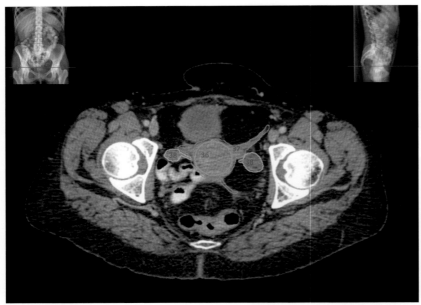

Figure 2.5.4

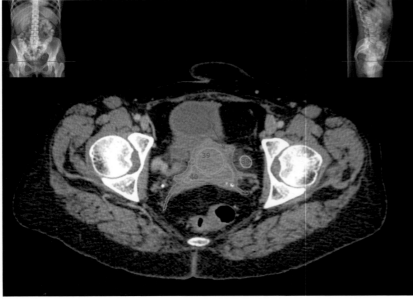

Figure 2.5.5

The CT appearances of the uterine body (36) can be extremely variable. Its position, size, shape and tissue density can vary with degree of urinary bladder filling, age, hormonal status and presence of uterine leiomyoma or other disease processes. The reader should also be prepared for the possibilities of anteversion, neutral alignment or retroversion. In most cases, the uterus rests on and indents the superior aspect of the urinary bladder. When full, however, the urinary bladder will tilt the uterus superiorly and posteriorly into a near vertical plane and CT sections will therefore be along the short axis of the fundus, as demonstrated in Figure 2.5.3. In this plane, the cross-sectional diameter should be no greater than 50mm in a patient of reproductive age. On a non-contrast CT examination, the endometrial/myometrial interface is difficult to appreciate, unless the uterine cavity contains fluid. The myometrium is composed of dense muscular fibres and measures 70HU. The uterine cavity measures less depending upon the amount and type of fluid within.

Figure 2.5.4 shows the smooth body of the uterus (36) immediately posterior to the urinary bladder with a barely visible vesico-uterine pouch between. Directly posterior to the uterus is the perirectal fascia and loops of small bowel are seen to the right. Fluid is occasionally seen in the recto-uterine pouch (of Douglas).

The slightly irregular boundaries of the broad ligament can be seen surrounding the body of the uterus, and the round ligament (37) is well demonstrated on the left. Its broad base at the uterus tapers off as it extends to the inguinal canal. Either side of the uterus, both ovaries (38) are seen, with suspensory ligament just visualised on the right. The ovaries may have uniform soft tissue density but may also contain multiple cystic areas associated with follicular development.

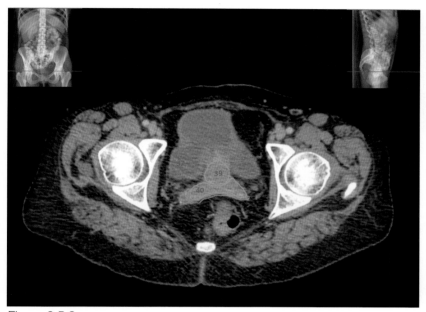

Figure 2.5.6

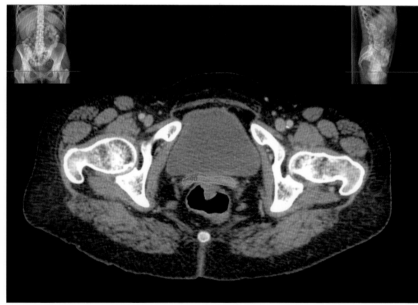

Figure 2.5.7

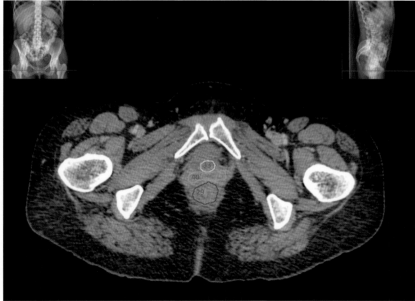

Figure 2.5.8

Figure 2.5.5 shows how the fatty tissue surrounding the left ovary (38) and cervix (39) is infiltrated with loose strands of fibrous tissue and small parametrial vessels. This can complicate demarcation of the ureters, which lie directly posterior to each ovary. Strands of the sacrouterine ligament can be seen extending laterally and posteriorly towards the sacrum on the right.

Both Figures 2.5.5 and 2.5.6 show the dense cervix (39) indenting into the urinary bladder anteriorly and anterior vaginal fornices (40) posteriorly. Lateral to the vagina, soft tissue stranding from the uterovaginal plexus of nerves and vessels causes the surrounding fatty tissues to appear unclear and of mixed attenuation. At this level both ureters pass approximately 1–2cm lateral to the cervix and are surrounded by a discrete border of fat.

Figure 2.5.7 demonstrates how the soft tissue vagina (40) is flattened between the posterior wall of the urinary bladder and the perirectal fascia and rectum. The rectum is clearly visible posterior to the vagina as it contains rectal gas (-1000HU).

The lumen of the vagina is usually indistinguishable, although it can also sometimes contain air. Occasionally some imaging centres prefer the use of tampon insertion to enhance visualisation of the vaginal lumen.

The ureters lie 1cm laterally to the vagina. Strands of the levator ani muscles are also visible more posteriorly within the fat of the ischiorectal fossae.

Inferiorly in Figure 2.5.8, the boundaries of the urethra (33), vagina (40) and anus (29) are difficult to distinguish, and are bordered laterally by the levator ani muscle complex. Lateral to this, the triangular, fatty ischioanal fossae are well demarcated.

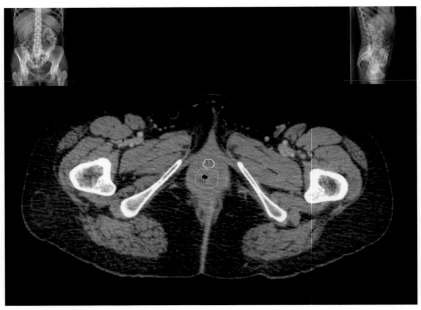

Figure 2.5.9

Figure 2.5.9, at the level of the ischial tuberosities, illustrates the clitoral crura extending anteriorly and medially from the ischia. These converge at the clitoris superficial to subcutaneous fatty tissue of the mons pubis.

Air is seen within the vaginal orifice (40), posterior to the urethra (33). The levator ani muscle complex lies intimately in contact with the lateral vaginal walls. Posterior to the vaginal orifice, the inferior borders of the anus are just visible, surrounded by the external anal sphincter. The natal cleft extends posteriorly, separating the ischioanal fossae.

2.6 Circulatory System

The circulatory system in the abdomen and pelvis is of interest to the therapy radiographer since the major lymph node groups in these regions are located near and named after the main vessels. The major vessels carrying blood to and from the abdomen are the abdominal aorta and the inferior vena cava (IVC). Figure 2.6.1 illustrates the blood supply with red and blue representing the arteries and veins respectively. The descending abdominal aorta penetrates the diaphragm from the thorax slightly anterior and to the left of the vertebral column and remains there as it descends. It is accompanied by the IVC which is anterior and to the right of it. The IVC passes through the liver at the superior extent of the abdomen and can be difficult to distinguish on CT without the aid of contrast. The other major blood vessel penetrating the liver is the hepatic portal vein that carries nutrient-rich blood from the digestive system to the liver for processing. This is formed by the junction of the superior mesenteric vein and splenic vein.

As the aorta descends, branches emerge to supply the various organs of the region. The first major branch is the coeliac artery at about T12, followed by the superior mesenteric artery at L1 and the two relatively large renal arteries just below it. Further small branches such as the inferior mesenteric artery follow until the aorta bifurcates into the common iliac arteries at about L4.

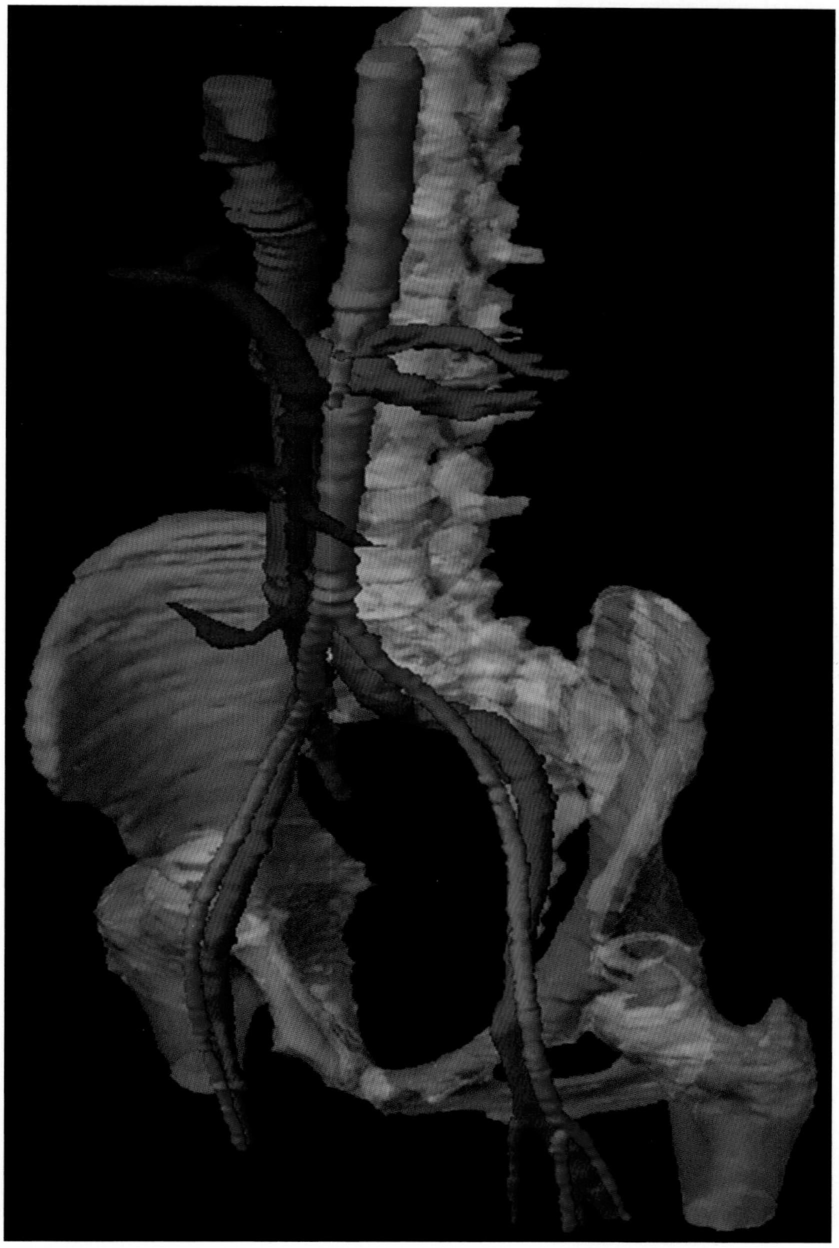

The common iliac arteries move laterally as they descend until they each bifurcate into internal and external iliac arteries. The small internal iliac arteries supply the pelvic organs and soon split into small structures that are tricky to spot on CT. The larger external iliac arteries move anteriorly and laterally before changing into the femoral arteries.

Venous drainage follows the arterial supply, with femoral veins becoming external iliac veins before joining the internal iliac veins to form the common iliac veins then the IVC. The bifurcation points of arteries do not always match the confluence points of their corresponding veins. In particular, the aorta bifurcation is usually at L4 and the vena cava confluence is usually at L5.

Figure 2.6.1

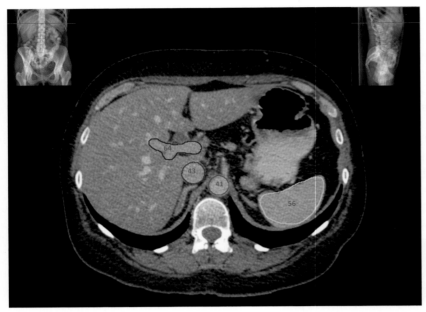

Figure 2.6.2

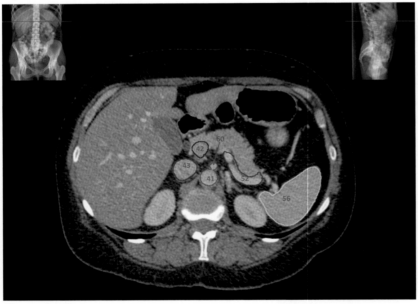

Figure 2.6.3

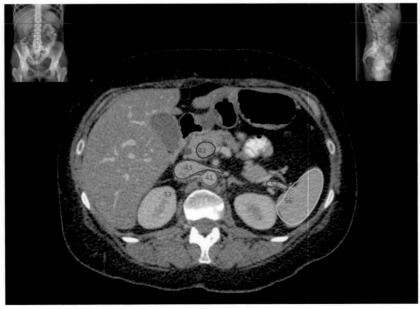

Figure 2.6.4

Directly anterior to the vertebral body of T11/T12, and very slightly left of midline, the well demarcated descending aorta (41) is seen in Figure 2.6.2. The IVC (43) is also seen anterior to the right crus. In this image, it has a similar rounded cross-sectional appearance as the aorta. However, it should be noted that the IVC may change appearance depending upon intra-abdominal pressure, and may appear flattened in full inspiration or rounded in expiration.

The aorta has higher intra-luminal pressure and retains a circular cross-section. The aorta is commonly found to the left of midline, and IVC to the right.

Directly posterior to the right crus (and right of the aorta) can be found the azygos vein and thoracic duct. Posterior to the left crus (and left of the aorta) runs the hemi-azygos vein. This retrocrural space is also important as it is a common site for lymphadenopathy. Care must be taken to view contiguous slices superior and inferior to avoid confusing dilated azygos or hemi-azygos veins for something more sinister.

The hepatic portal vein (64) is seen penetrating the liver in Figure 2.6.2. This is formed by the superior mesenteric vein (42) and the splenic vein (52) seen in Figure 2.6.3. The superior mesenteric vein is visualised here in cross-section, while the splenic vein is cut through longitudinally as it runs medially along the posterior surface of the pancreas from the spleen (56).

Figure 2.6.4 shows branches leaving and joining the main vessels. The left renal vein is joining the IVC (43) and the right renal artery (53) is leaving the abdominal aorta (41). As branches remove blood from the abdominal aorta (41) it decreases in diameter as it extends inferiorly.

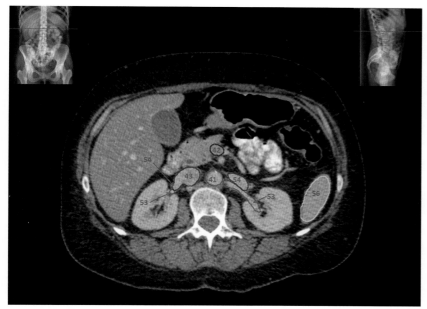

Figure 2.6.5

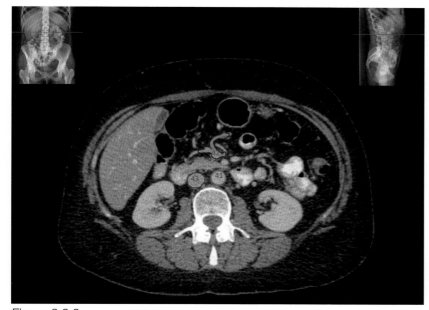

Figure 2.6.6

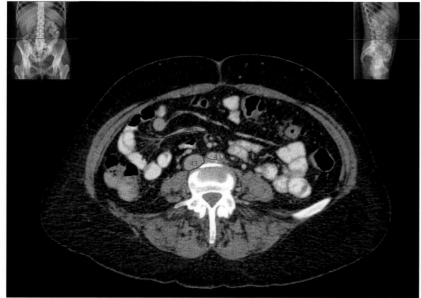

Figure 2.6.7

In Figure 2.6.5 the aorta (41) lies just anterior to the vertebral body of L2, slightly to the left of midline. Immediately posterior to the aorta lie two small ovoid soft tissue structures. These are the lower portions of the diaphragmatic crura, and again must be tracked on contiguous slices to avoid any confusion with para-aortic lymph nodes.

Also in Figure 2.6.5, the left renal artery (53) can be seen extending to the hilum of the left kidney from the aorta. This is asymmetrical due to the difference in level between the two kidneys. The level at which the right kidney appears varies due to the mass of the liver.

A small section of the right renal artery is seen immediately posterior to the right renal vein (54) as it exits the IVC (43). The left renal vein (54) runs directly anterior to the left renal artery (53) from the hilum of the left kidney, passing anterior to the aorta (41).

Care must be taken when viewing the IVC (43) following IV contrast agent. In early phase imaging, contrast enhanced blood flowing from kidneys into the renal veins and into the IVC travels cranially along the lateral aspects of the IVC lumen. This can mimic an IVC obstruction.

Branches of the superior mesenteric vein (42) are seen within the intra-abdominal fat in Figure 2.6.6. These strands collect nutrient-rich blood from the digestive system and connect together to form the hepatic portal system that returns the blood via the liver.

Figure 2.6.7 illustrates a partial voluming effect between the vertebral bodies of L4 and the intervertebral disc. Anterior to the vertebral body, the aorta (41) has a flattened and ovoid appearance. This is due to the aorta bifurcating into the common iliac arteries (44) as seen in Figure 2.6.8.

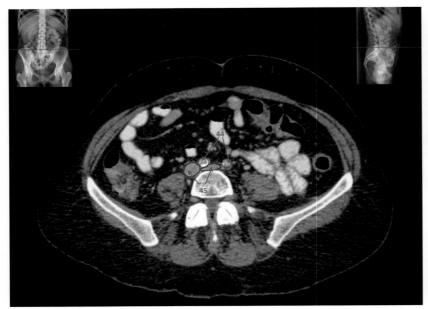

Figure 2.6.8

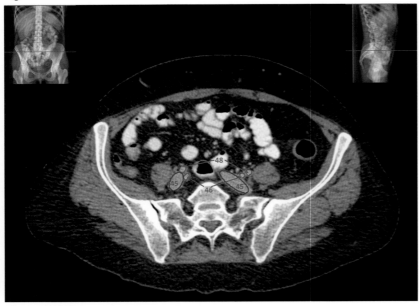

Figure 2.6.9

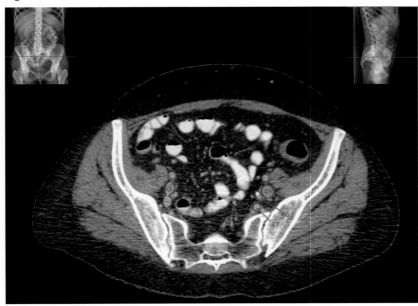

Figure 2.6.10

In Figure 2.6.7, the IVC (43) is still a single vessel and the confluence of the common iliac veins (45) does not appear until the slightly inferior Figure 2.6.8 image at the level of L5. In this image the left common iliac vein (45) crosses beneath the right iliac artery (44).

A clear understanding of vascular anatomy is extremely useful when attempting to locate associated para vascular pelvic lymphatic stations.

A thin fat plane surrounding the vessels usually helps delineate vessel borders. However fat plane obliteration caused by disease progression may mask the vessel wall and cause difficulties with demarcation. The following guidelines should assist with this:

• Always track superior and inferior on contiguous slices from the abdominal aorta and IVC to confirm the tubular nature of vessels.

• All vessels reduce in cross-sectional diameter as they extend more inferiorly into the pelvis.

• Arterial and venous vessels are always paired as they extend through the pelvis.

• High attenuation circumferential calcification within the arterial walls can often be seen. This is normally only found in the walls of arterial vessels as seen in the right common iliac artery (44) in Figure 2.6.8.

• In the absence of calcification or fat planes, consider utilising IV contrast with early phase imaging.

• Although it may vary, the arterial iliac and femoral vessels (44, 46 and 48) tend to be anterior and slightly lateral to their respective venous vessels (45, 47 and 49) as seen in Figures 2.6.8 to 2.6.10.

• Arteries tend to be round in cross-section and veins tend to be ovoid and slightly flattened, as can be seen throughout the body. However, care must be taken in the pelvis due to the obliquity of the external iliac vessels (48). Axial CT sections through the pelvis will give these arteries an ovoid appearance in cross-section.

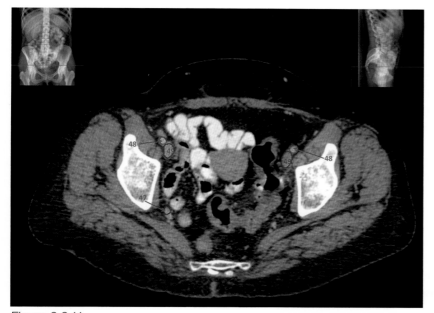

Figure 2.6.11

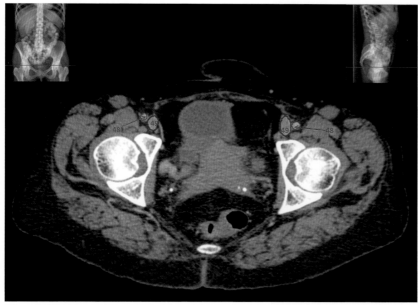

Figure 2.6.12

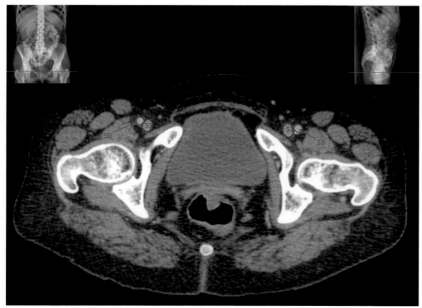

Figure 2.6.13

Figure 2.6.11 shows the internal iliac vessels (47) just medial to the ilium and superior attachment of internal obturator muscle. Inferiorly from here, the internal iliac vessels are small and quite difficult to track, following a relatively tortuous path to supply the various pelvic viscera.

The external iliac vessels (48 and 49) are larger and thus relatively easy to track throughout the pelvis into the femora. Figures 2.6.11 and 2.6.12 show the external iliac vessels tracking anteriorly and laterally. The surrounding intra-pelvic fatty tissue assists clear localisation and demarcation of the vasculature, even on the right side on Figure 2.6.11 where loops of small bowel are in close proximity.

When the external iliac vessels pass through the anterior abdominal wall they are referred to as the femoral artery and veins as they are no longer intra-pelvic structures. It is at this transition that they can be seen in Figure 2.6.12, level with the acetabulum. Anterior to the pubis, the femoral artery is externally palpable and is recognised by its pulsatile movement.

Figure 2.6.13 illustrates how the femoral vessels are surrounded by subcutaneous fat. The artery is noticeably smaller and rounder in cross-section. There are other smaller vessels branching off the external iliac vessels anterior to the femoral vessels. Although not always readily visible, it is also possible to visualise the femoral nerve in cross-section in close proximity to the femoral artery.

2.7 Lymphatic System

Although identification of lymph nodes is not within the daily remit of most radiotherapy practice, it is becoming increasingly important to understand their approximate position. Lymph nodes are distributed along the vascular vessels and are commonly named after them or after other adjacent structures. Figure 2.7.1 illustrates the pelvic and abdominal nodes. The superior nodes of the long chain along the aorta and IVC are the retrocrural group (68). Below these can be seen the superior mesenteric (69) and the pre and para-aortic nodes (70). As the aorta bifurcates, the nodal groups also split into the common iliac nodes (71). Below these are the external iliac (72) and the small internal iliac node chains (75). Further posterior can be found the sacral (73) and pararectal nodes (74). The interior of the pelvis is served by various nodes such as the parauterine, or paravesicular. Lateral to these can be found the obturator nodes (76) lying in a notch on the medial surface of the pubis behind the obturator internus muscle. The most superficial nodes are the inguinals (77). Although not illustrated, it is often possible to visualise the cysterna chyli on CT. It is about 6mm wide and 60mm long and located anterior to L1 and L2. It lies adjacent to the aorta and posterior to the crus of the right hemi-diaphragm. Beyond the retrocrural space, the cysterna chyli drains into the thoracic duct.

Normal abdominal and pelvic lymph nodes range from 0.5 to 11mm in size, and are often detected on CT, particularly when thin slices are utilised. It can be difficult to differentiate internal structure using CT; therefore the primary indicator of nodal abnormality will be an increase in size, particularly in their short axis. Different nodal regions have different size nodes so it is important to understand both location and variations in normal size.

The following CT sections highlight the positions of the major nodal groups relevant to radiotherapy in cross-section. An indication of their normal size and the structures that they drain is also given.

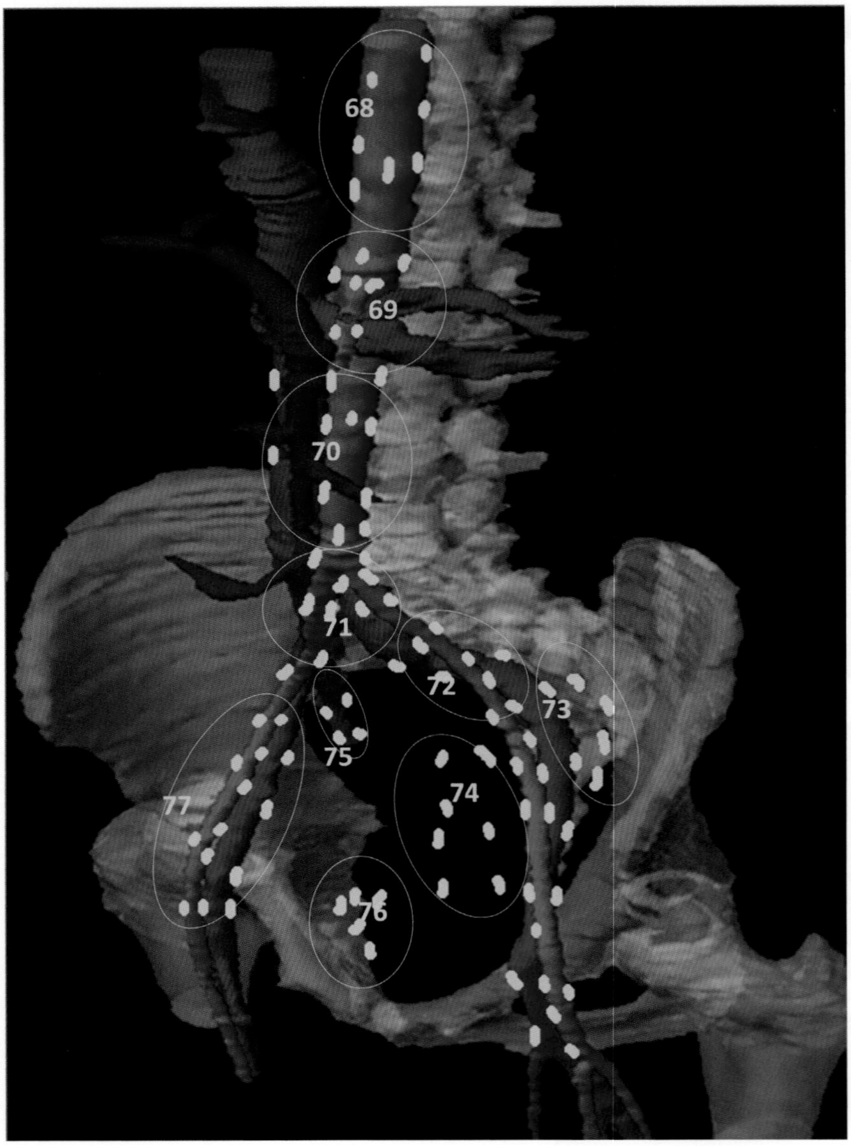

Figure 2.7.1

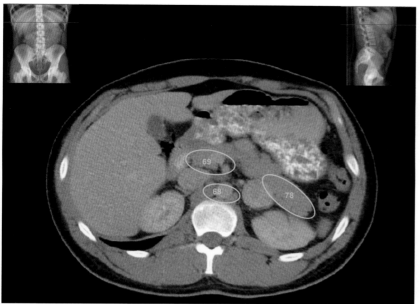

Figure 2.7.2

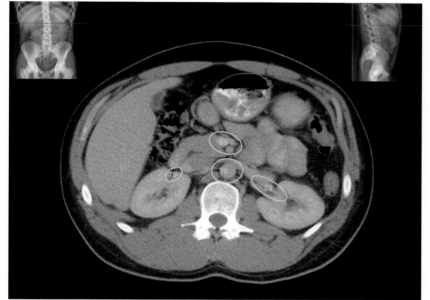

Figure 2.7.3

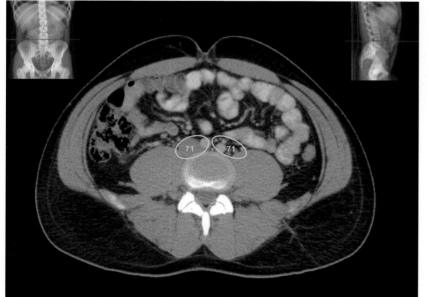

Figure 2.7.4

Figure 2.7.2 is at the level of L1.

68. Retrocrural nodes (≤6mm). Drain lungs and pleura.

69. Superior mesenteric nodes (≤10mm). Drain small and large bowel. There are over 100 mesenteric lymph nodes throughout the mesentery.

78. Pancreaticosplenic nodes (≤10mm). Drain lymphoma, leukaemia, small intestine, ascending and transverse colon.

Figure 2.7.3 is at the level of L2.

70. Lumbar/Para-aortic nodes (≤11mm). Drain ovary, testes, uterus, kidney and prostate.

69. Superior mesenteric nodes (≤10mm). Drain small and large bowel.

79. Renal lymph nodes (≤9mm). Drain kidneys, ovaries, testes.

Figure 2.7.4 is at the level of L4/L5.

71. Common iliac nodes (≤9mm). Drain rectum, prostate. Grouped in medial, lateral and intermediate chains.

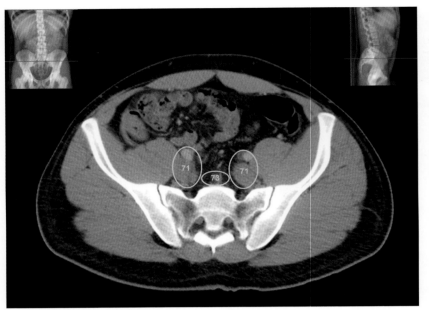

Figure 2.7.5

Figure 2.7.5 is at the mid-sacral level.

71. Common iliac nodes (≤9mm). Drain rectum, prostate. Grouped in medial, lateral and intermediate chains.

73. Sacral lymph nodes (≤7mm). Drain posterior pelvic organs. Part of the internal iliac group, running along the median and lateral sacral vessels.

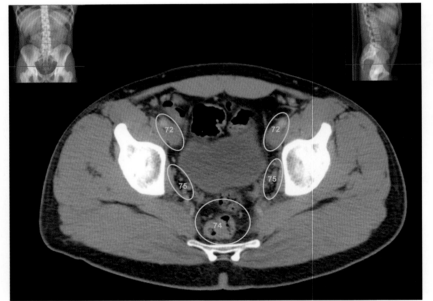

Figure 2.7.6

Figure 2.7.6 is at the lower sacral level.

72. External iliac nodes (≤10mm). Drain bladder, prostate, proximal vagina, uterus, ovary.

74. Pararectal nodes. Drain the rectum. Adjacent to the rectal wall within the perirectal fascia.

75. Internal iliac nodes (≤7mm). Drain most pelvic organs.

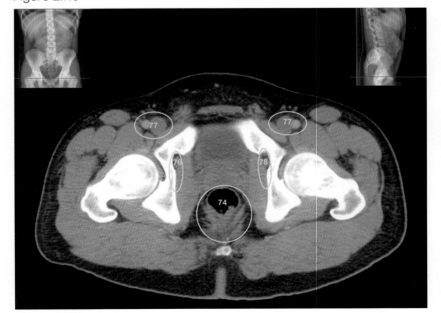

Figure 2.7.7

Figure 2.7.7 is at mid-acetabular level.

74. Pararectal nodes. Drain the rectum. Adjacent to the rectal wall within the perirectal fascia.

76. Obturator nodes (≤7mm). Drain prostate, bladder and cervix. Present in the 'obturator notch' just lateral to the obturator internus muscle.

77. Inguinal nodes (≤10mm). Drain vulva, distal vaginal, distal rectum, anus and penis.

2.8 Male Pelvis and Abdomen Fully Labelled CT Scans

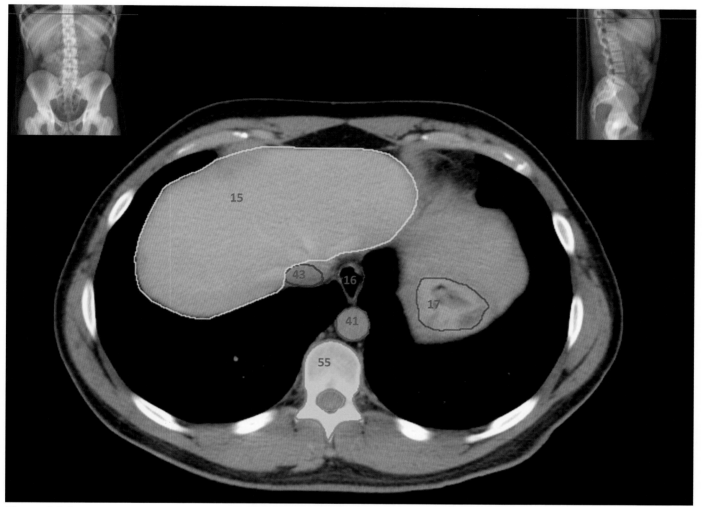

Figure 2.8.1

15. Liver
16. Oesophagus
17. Stomach
41. Descending Abdominal Aorta
43. Inferior Vena Cava
55. Thoracic Vertebra

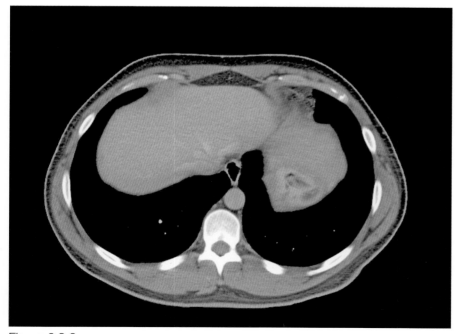

Figure 2.8.2

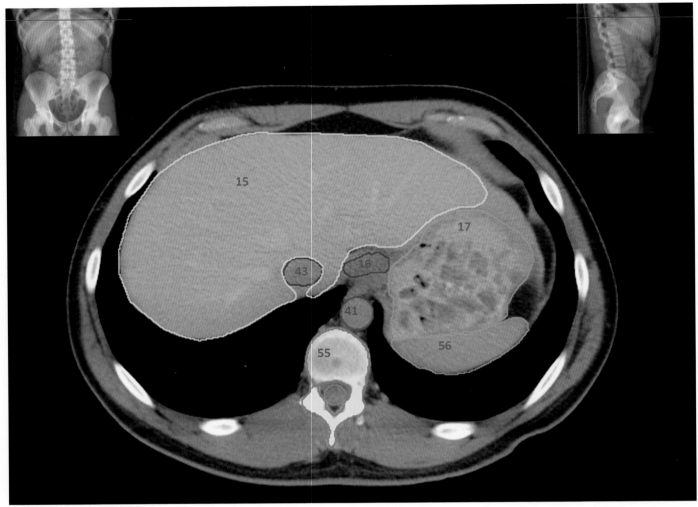

Figure 2.8.3

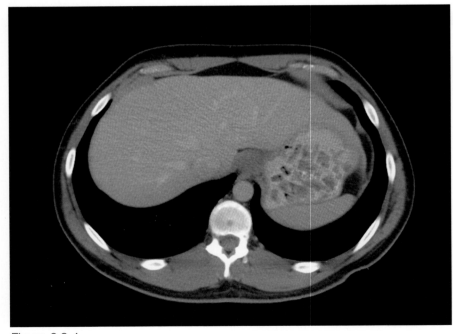

15. Liver
16. Oesophagus
17. Stomach
41. Descending Abdominal Aorta
43. Inferior Vena Cava
55. Thoracic Vertebra
56. Spleen

Figure 2.8.4

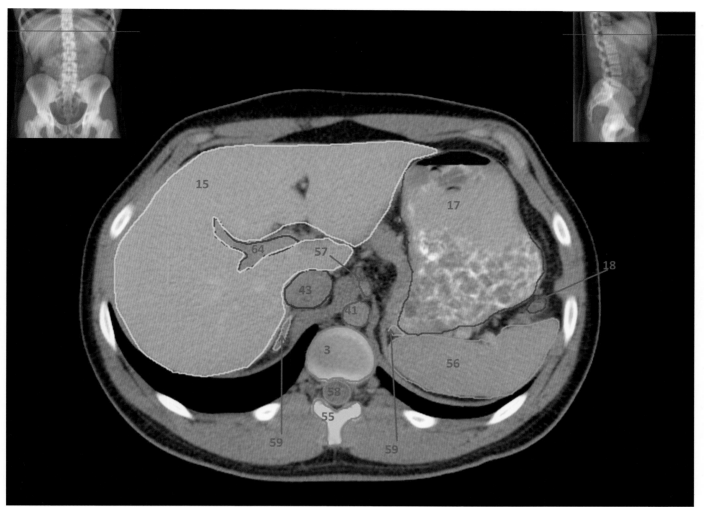

Figure 2.8.5

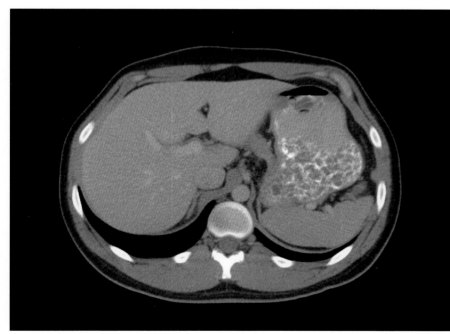

Figure 2.8.6

3. Lumbar Vertebrae
15. Liver
17. Stomach
18. Splenic Flexure
41. Descending Abdominal Aorta
43. Inferior Vena Cava
55. Thoracic Vertebra
56. Spleen
57. Coeliac Artery
58. Spinal Cord
59. Adrenal Gland
64. Hepatic Portal Vein

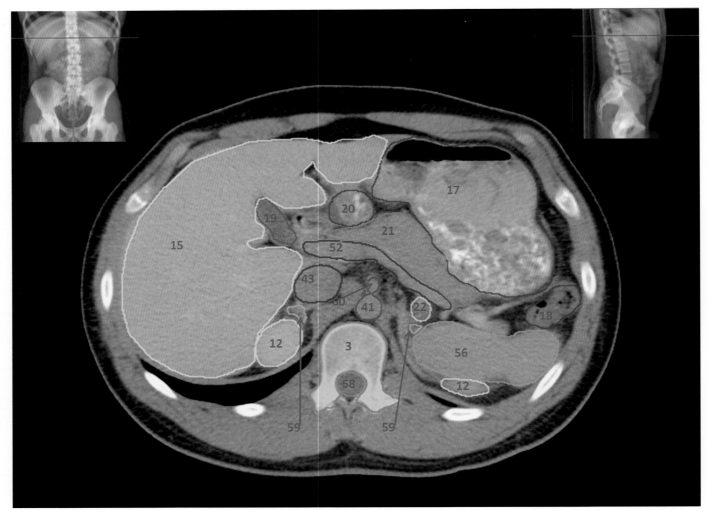

Figure 2.8.7

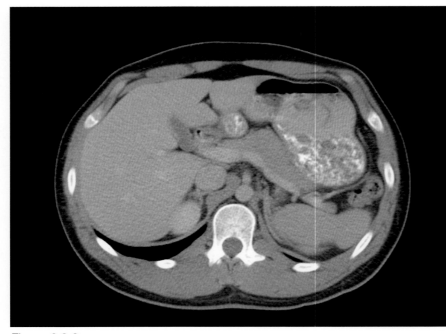

Figure 2.8.8

3. Lumbar Vertebra
12. Kidney
15. Liver
17. Stomach
18. Splenic Flexure
19. Gall Bladder
20. Duodenum
21. Pancreas
22. Small Bowel
41. Descending Abdominal Aorta
43. Inferior Vena Cava
52. Splenic Vein
56. Spleen
58. Spinal Cord
59. Adrenal Gland
60. Superior Mesenteric Artery

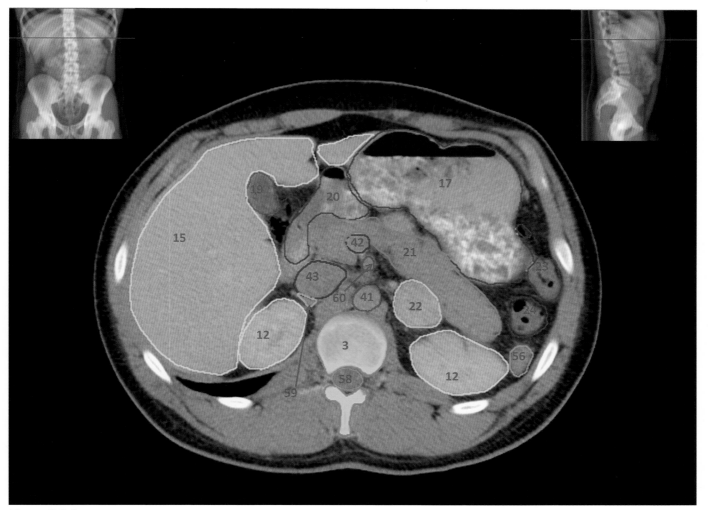

Figure 2.8.9

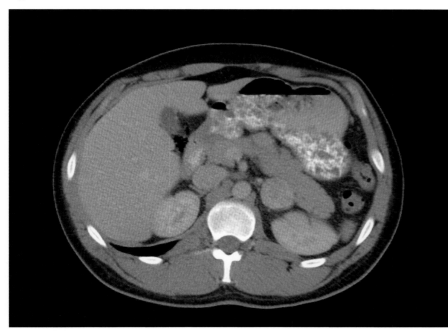

Figure 2.8.10

3. Lumbar Vertebra
12. Kidney
15. Liver
17. Stomach
19. Gall Bladder
20. Duodenum
21. Pancreas
22. Small Bowel
23. Transverse Colon
24. Descending Colon
41. Descending Abdominal Aorta
42. Superior Mesenteric Vein
43. Inferior Vena Cava
56. Spleen
58. Spinal Cord
59. Adrenal Gland
60. Superior Mesenteric Artery

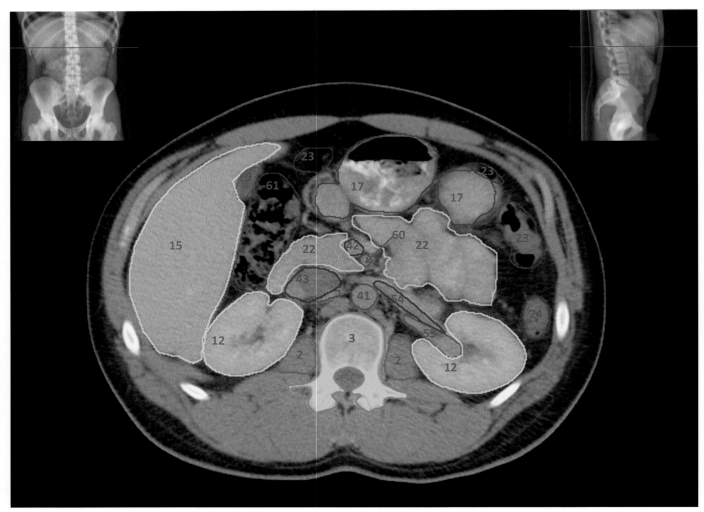

Figure 2.8.11

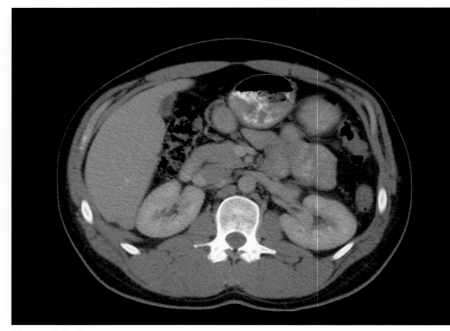

Figure 2.8.12

2. Psoas Muscle
3. Lumbar Vertebra
12. Kidney
15. Liver
17. Stomach
19. Gall Bladder
22. Small Bowel
23. Transverse Colon
24. Descending Colon
41. Descending Abdominal Aorta
42. Superior Mesenteric Vein
43. Inferior Vena Cava
53. Renal Artery
54. Renal Vein
60. Superior Mesenteric Artery
61. Hepatic Flexure

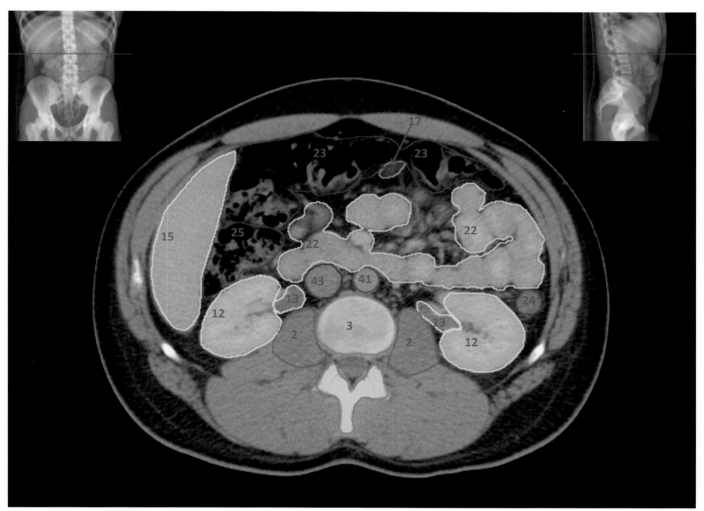

Figure 2.8.13

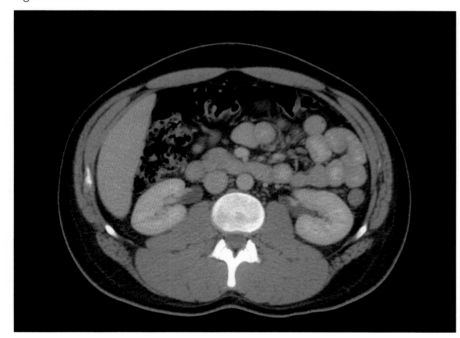

Figure 2.8.14

2. Psoas Muscle
3. Lumbar Vertebra
12. Kidney
13. Ureter
15. Liver
17. Stomach
22. Small Bowel
23. Transverse Colon
24. Descending Colon
25. Ascending Colon
41. Descending Abdominal Aorta
43. Inferior Vena Cava

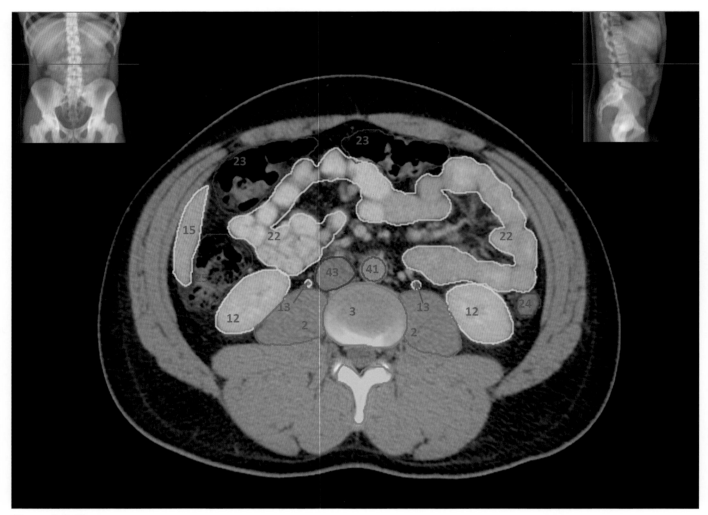

Figure 2.8.15

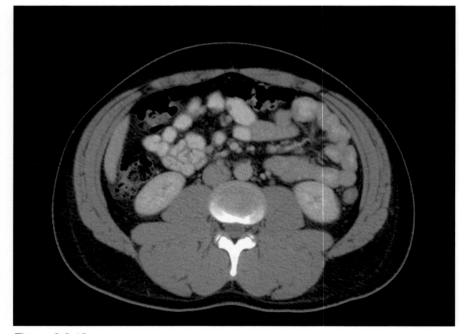

Figure 2.8.16

2. Psoas Muscle
3. Lumbar Vertebra
12. Kidney
13. Ureter
15. Liver
22. Small Bowel
23. Transverse Colon
24. Descending Colon
25. Ascending Colon
41. Descending Abdominal Aorta
43. Inferior Vena Cava

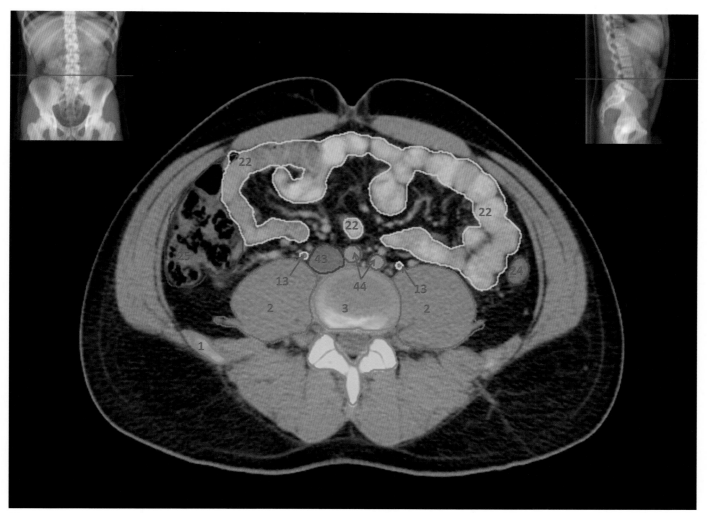

Figure 2.8.17

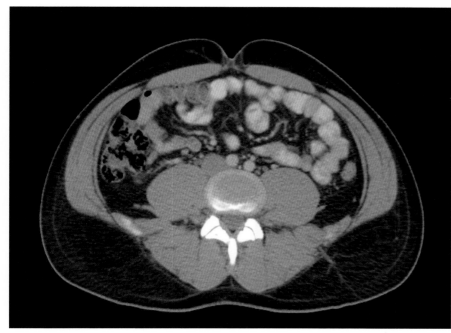

1. Ilium (Crest)
2. Psoas Muscle
3. Lumbar Vertebra
13. Ureter
22. Small Bowel
24. Descending Colon
25. Ascending Colon
44. Common Iliac Artery
43. Inferior Vena Cava

Figure 2.8.18

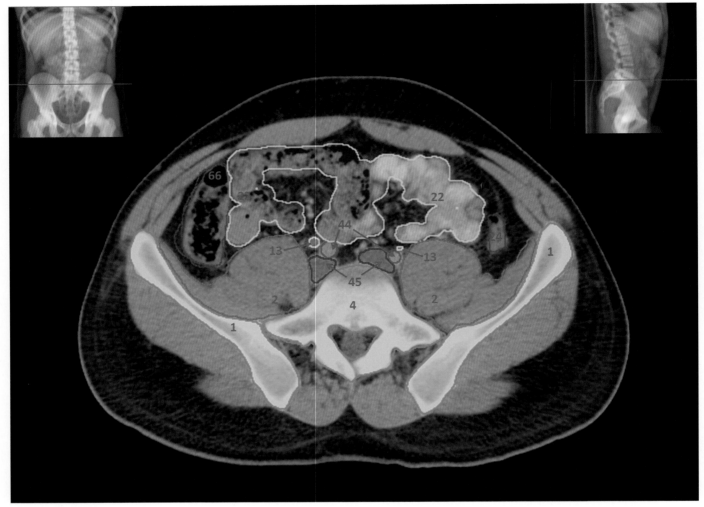

Figure 2.8.19

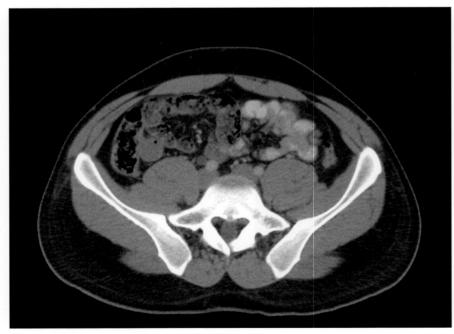

Figure 2.8.20

1. Ilium
2. Psoas Muscle
4. Sacrum
13. Ureter
22. Small Bowel
24. Descending Colon
44. Common Iliac Artery
45. Common Iliac Vein
66. Caecum

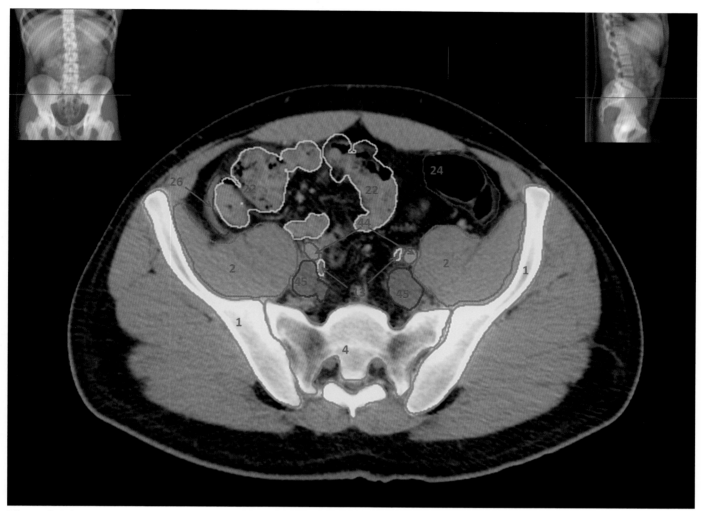

Figure 2.8.21

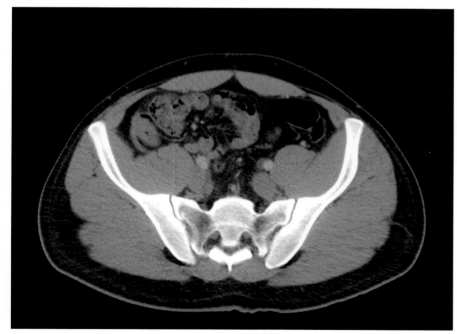

1. Ilium
2. Psoas Muscle
4. Sacrum
13. Ureter
22. Small Bowel
24. Descending Colon
26. Appendix
44. Common Iliac Artery
45. Common Iliac Vein

Figure 2.8.22

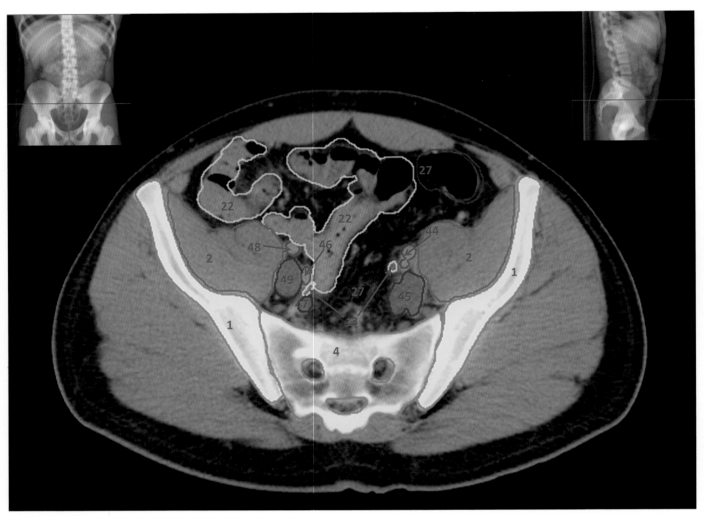

Figure 2.8.23

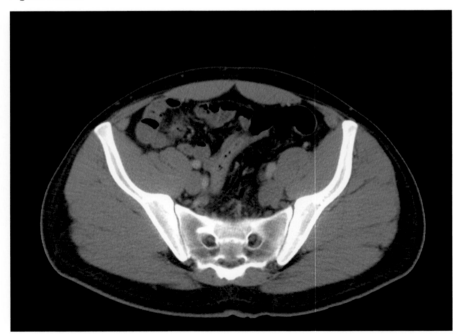

1. Ilium
2. Psoas Muscle
4. Sacrum
13. Ureter
22. Small Bowel
27. Sigmoid Colon
44. Common Iliac Artery
45. Common Iliac Vein
46. Internal Iliac Artery
47. Internal Iliac Vein
48. External Iliac Artery
49. External Iliac Vein

Figure 2.8.24

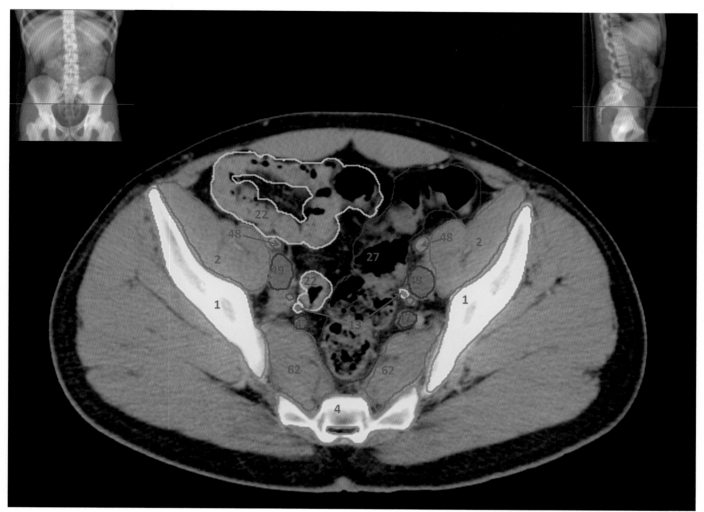

Figure 2.8.25

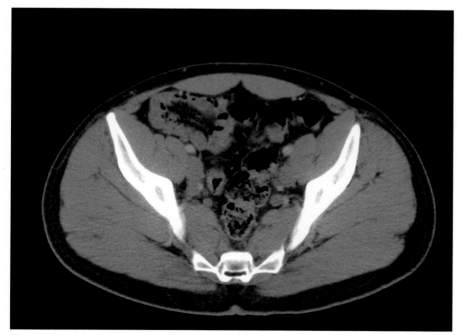

1. Ilium
2. Psoas Muscle
4. Sacrum
13. Ureter
22. Small Bowel
27. Sigmoid Colon
47. Internal Iliac Vein
48. External Iliac Artery
49. External Iliac Vein
62. Piriformis Muscle

Figure 2.8.26

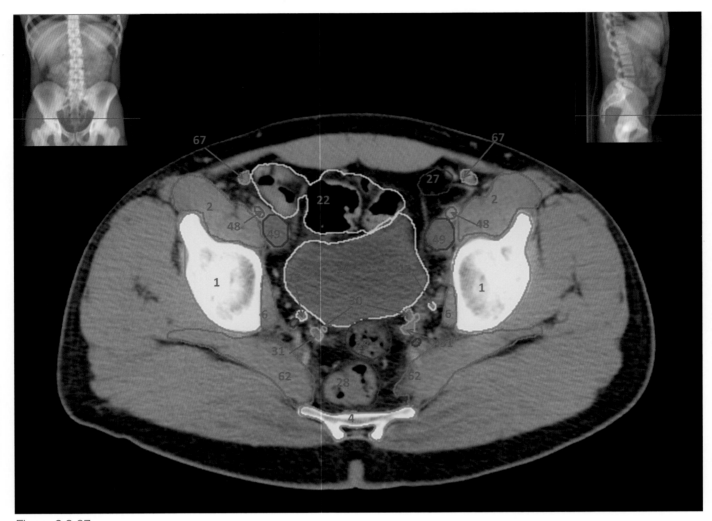

Figure 2.8.27

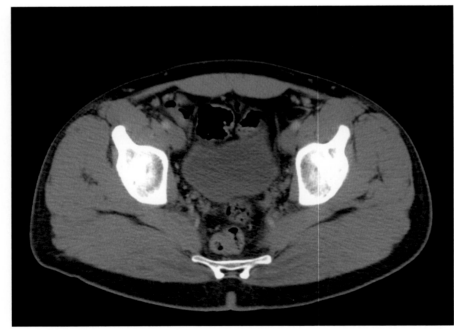

Figure 2.8.28

1. Ilium
2. Psoas Muscle
4. Sacrum
6. Obturator Internus Muscle
13. Ureter
14. Bladder
22. Small Bowel
27. Sigmoid Colon
28. Rectum
30. Vas Deferens
31. Seminal Vesicles
48. External Iliac Artery
49. External Iliac Vein
62. Piriformis Muscle
67. Spermatic Cord

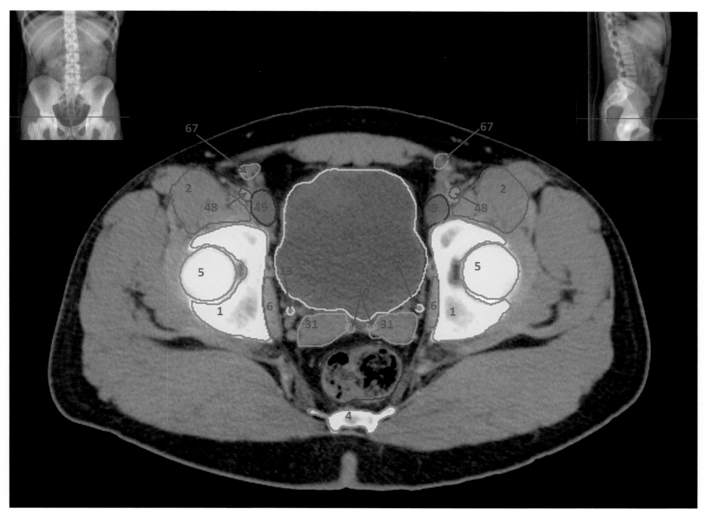

Figure 2.8.29

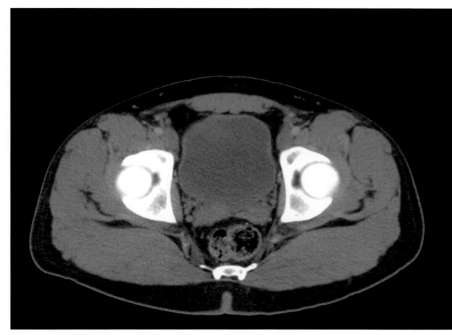

Figure 2.8.30

1. Ilium
2. Psoas Muscle
4. Sacrum
5. Femoral Head
6. Obturator Internus Muscle
13. Ureter
14. Bladder
28. Rectum
30. Vas Deferens
31. Seminal Vesicles
48. External Iliac Artery
49. External Iliac Vein
67. Spermatic Cord

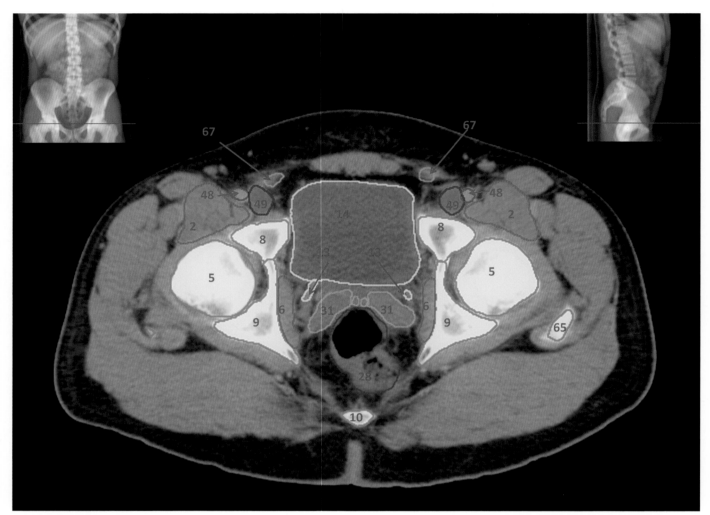

Figure 2.8.31

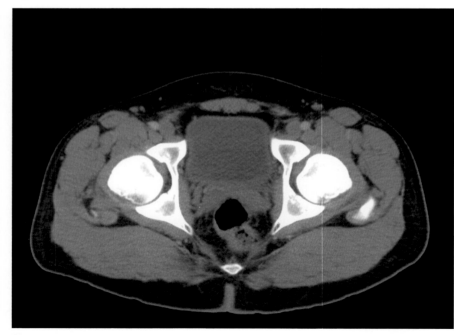

Figure 2.8.32

2. Psoas Muscle
5. Femoral Head
6. Obturator Internus Muscle
8. Pubis
9. Ischium
10. Coccyx
13. Ureter
14. Bladder
28. Rectum
31. Seminal Vesicles
48. External Iliac Artery
49. External Iliac Vein
65. Greater Trochanter
67. Spermatic Cord

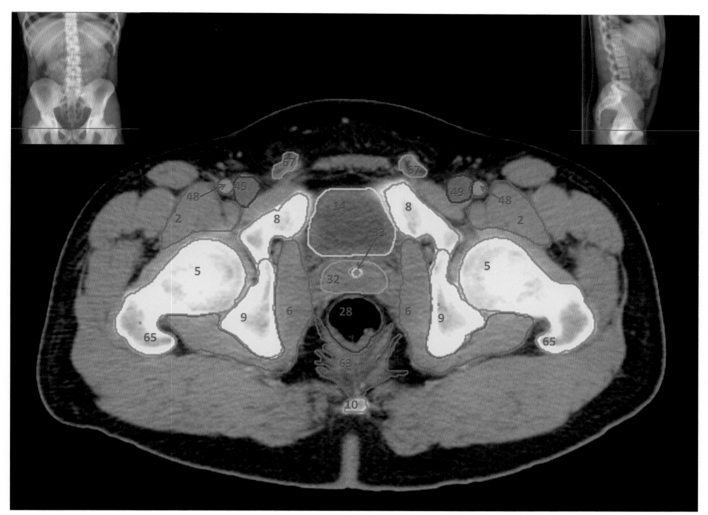

Figure 2.8.33

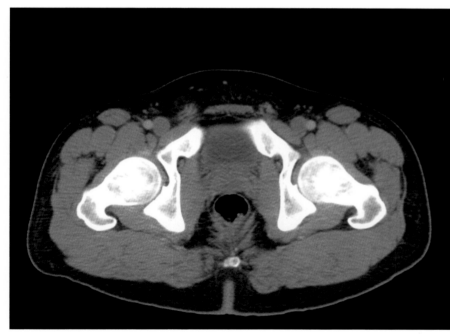

Figure 2.8.34

2. Psoas Muscle
5. Femoral Head
6. Obturator Internus Muscle
8. Pubis
9. Ischium
10. Coccyx
14. Bladder
28. Rectum
32. Prostate
33. Urethra
48. External Iliac Artery
49. External Iliac Vein
63. Coccygeus Muscle
65. Greater Trochanter
67. Spermatic Cord

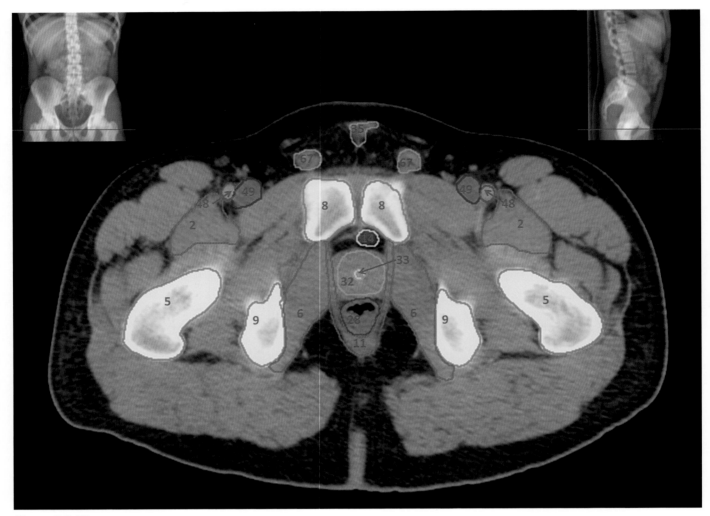

Figure 2.8.35

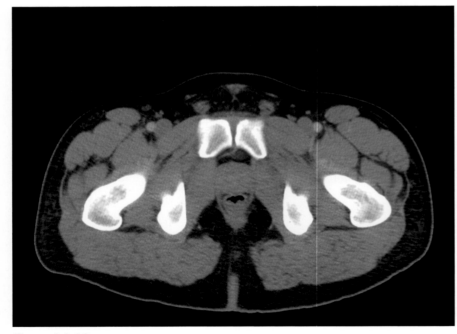

2. Psoas Muscle
5. Femur
6. Obturator Internus Muscle
8. Pubis
9. Ischium
11. Levator Ani Muscle
14. Bladder
28. Rectum
32. Prostate
33. Urethra
35. Penis
48. External Iliac Artery
49. External Iliac Vein
67. Spermatic Cord

Figure 2.8.36

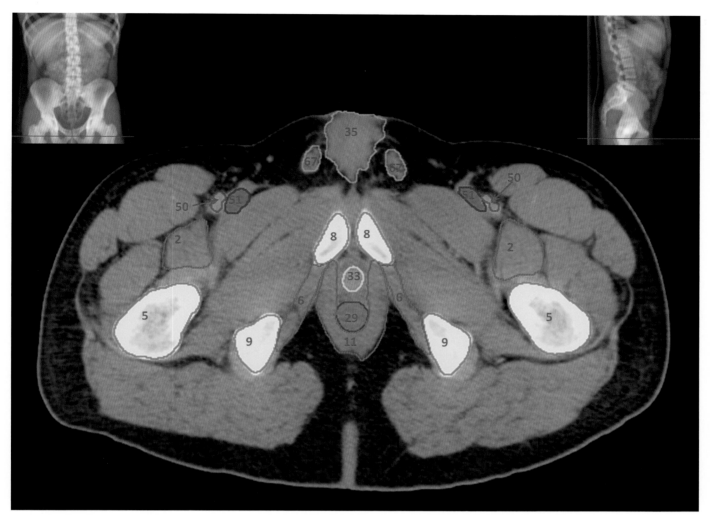

Figure 2.8.37

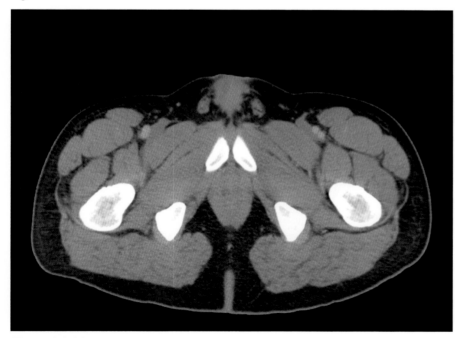

2. Psoas Muscle
5. Femur
6. Obturator Internus Muscle
8. Pubis
9. Ischium
11. Levator Ani Muscle
29. Anus
33. Urethra
35. Penis
50. Femoral Artery
51. Femoral Vein
67. Spermatic Cord

Figure 2.8.38

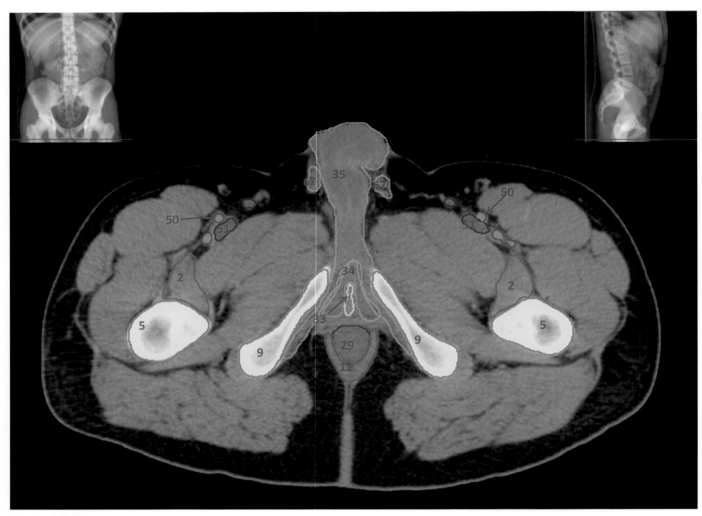

Figure 2.8.39

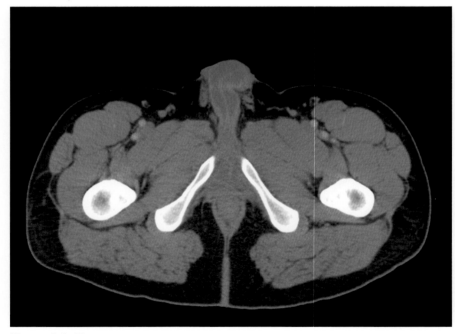

Figure 2.8.40

2. Psoas Muscle
5. Femur
9. Ischium
11. Levator Ani Muscle
29. Anus
33. Urethra
34. Penile Bulb
35. Penis
50. Femoral Artery
51. Femoral Vein
67. Spermatic Cord

2.9 Female Pelvis and Abdomen Fully Labelled CT Scans

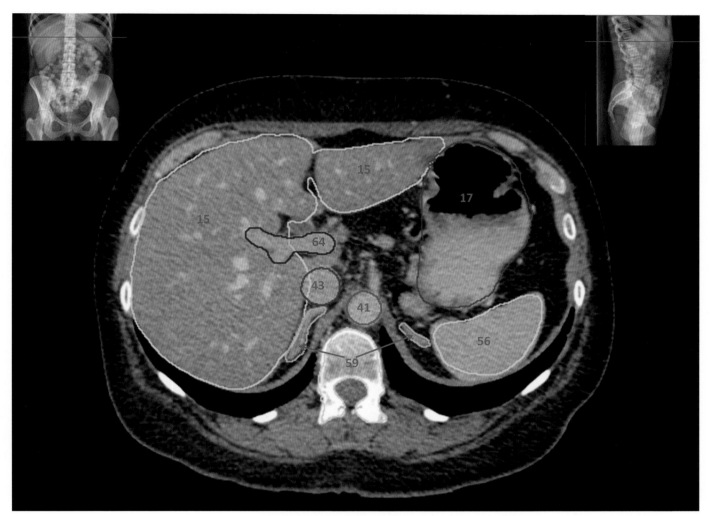

Figure 2.9.1

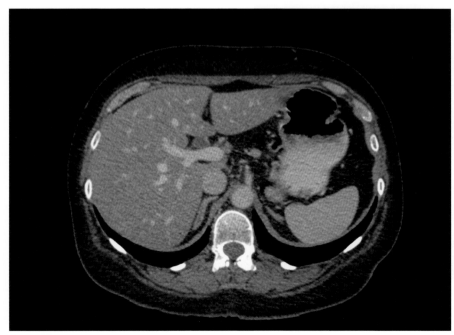

15. Liver
17. Stomach
41. Descending Abdominal Aorta
43. Inferior Vena Cava
56. Spleen
59. Adrenal Gland
64. Hepatic Portal Vein

Figure 2.9.2

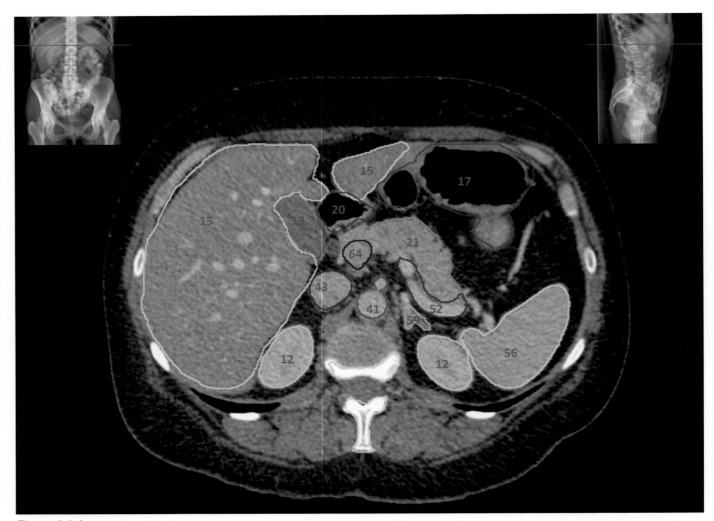

Figure 2.9.3

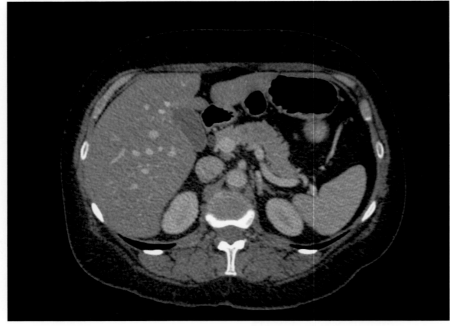

Figure 2.9.4

12. Kidney
15. Liver
17. Stomach
19. Gall Bladder
20. Duodenum
21. Pancreas
41. Descending Abdominal Aorta
43. Inferior Vena Cava
52. Splenic Vein
56. Spleen
59. Adrenal Gland
64. Hepatic Portal Vein

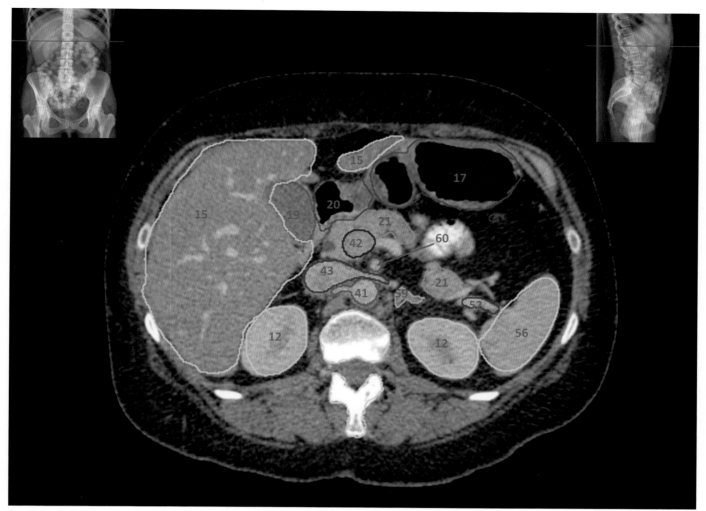

Figure 2.9.5

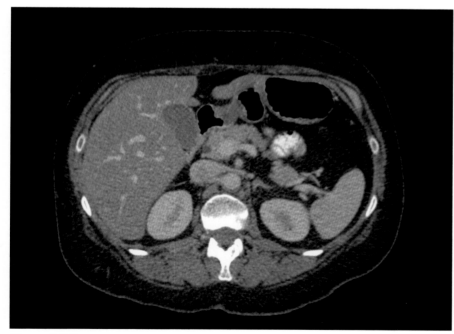

Figure 2.9.6

12. Kidney
15. Stomach
17. Liver
19. Gall Bladder
20. Duodenum
21. Pancreas
41. Descending Abdominal Aorta
42. Superior Mesenteric Vein
43. Inferior Vena Cava
52. Splenic Vein
56. Spleen
59. Adrenal Gland
60. Superior Mesenteric Artery

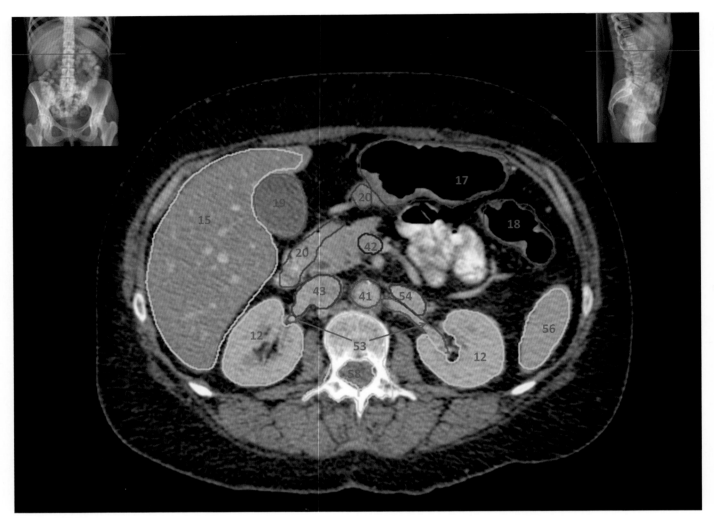

Figure 2.9.7

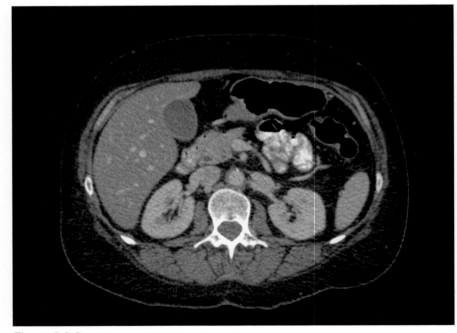

Figure 2.9.8

12. Kidney
15. Liver
17. Stomach
18. Splenic Flexure
19. Gall Bladder
20. Duodenum
41. Descending Abdominal Aorta
42. Superior Mesenteric Vein
43. Inferior Vena Cava
53. Renal Artery
54. Renal Vein
56. Spleen
58. Spinal Cord

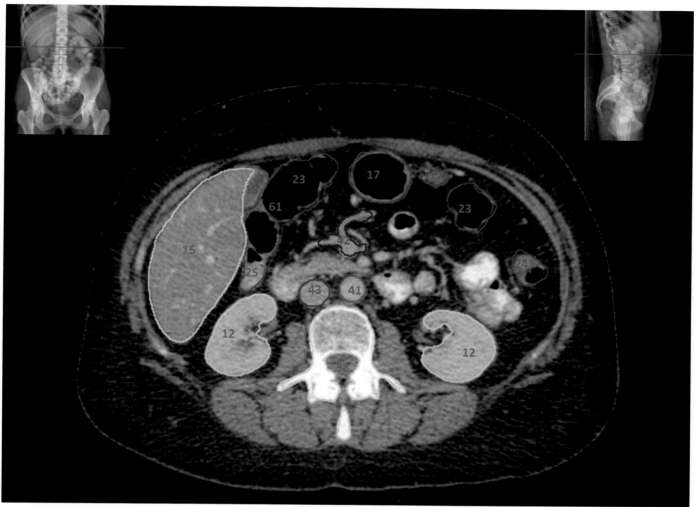

Figure 2.9.9

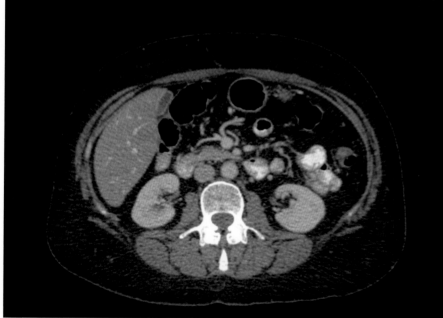

Figure 2.9.10

12. Kidney
15. Liver
17. Stomach
19. Gall Bladder
23. Transverse Colon
24. Descending Colon
25. Ascending Colon
41. Descending Abdominal Aorta
42. Superior Mesenteric Vein
43. Inferior Vena Cava
58. Spinal Cord
61. Hepatic Flexure

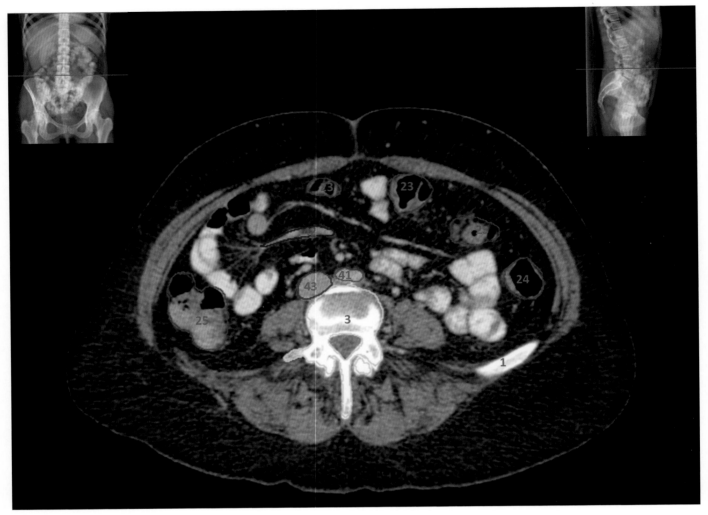

Figure 2.9.11

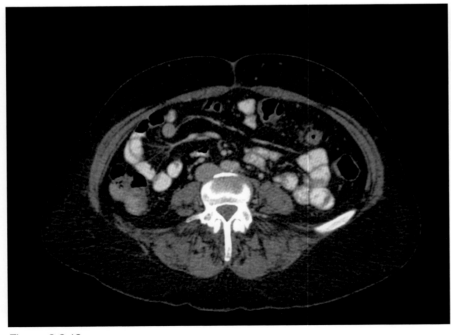

Figure 2.9.12

3. Lumbar Vertebra
23. Transverse Colon
24. Descending Colon
25. Ascending Colon
41. Descending Abdominal Aorta
42. Superior Mesenteric Vein
43. Inferior Vena Cava

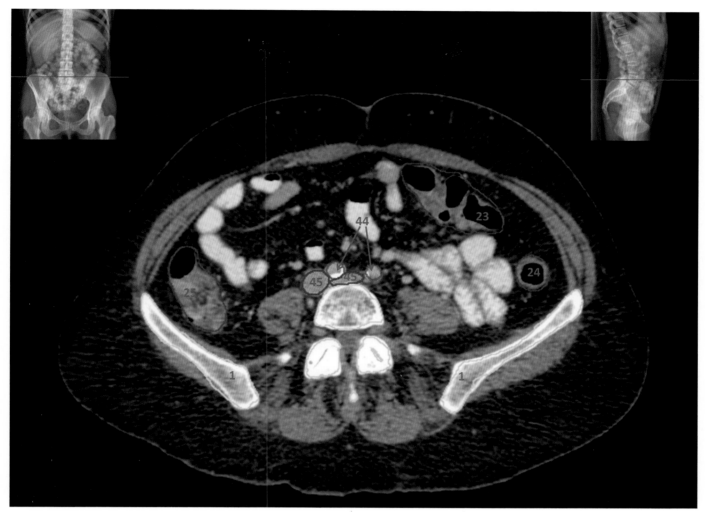

Figure 2.9.13

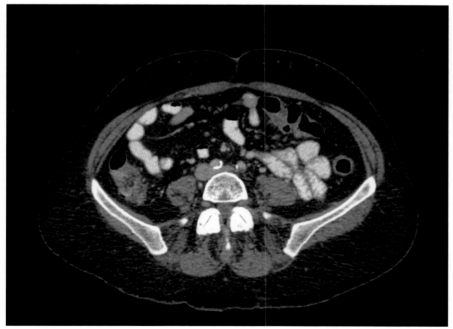

Figure 2.9.14

1. Ilium
23. Transverse Colon
24. Descending Colon
25. Ascending Colon
44. Common Iliac Artery
45. Common Iliac Vein

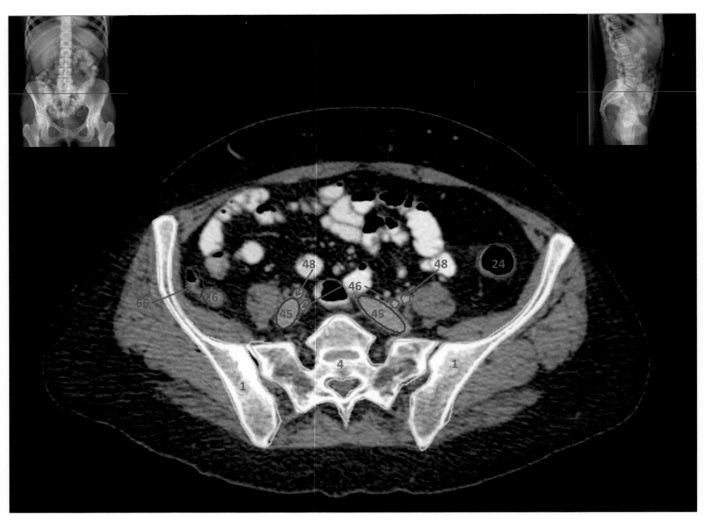

Figure 2.9.15

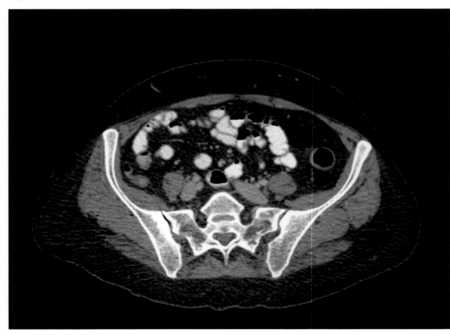

Figure 2.9.16

1. Ilium
4. Sacrum
24. Descending Colon
26. Appendix
45. Common Iliac Vein
46. Internal Iliac Artery
48. External Iliac Artery
66. Caecum

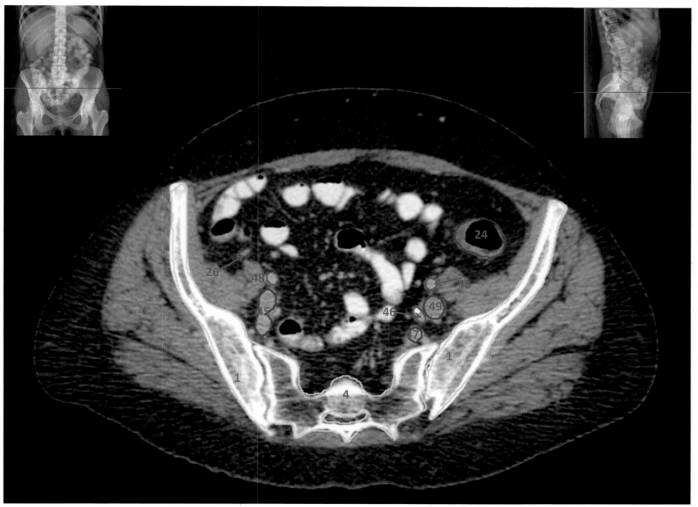

Figure 2.9.17

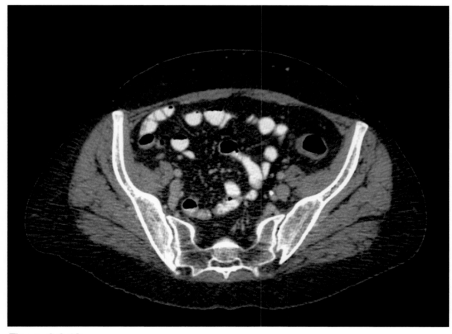

Figure 2.9.18

1. Ilium
4. Sacrum
24. Descending Colon
26. Appendix
45. Common Iliac Vein
46. Internal Iliac Artery
47. Internal Iliac Vein
48. External Iliac Artery
49. External Iliac Vein

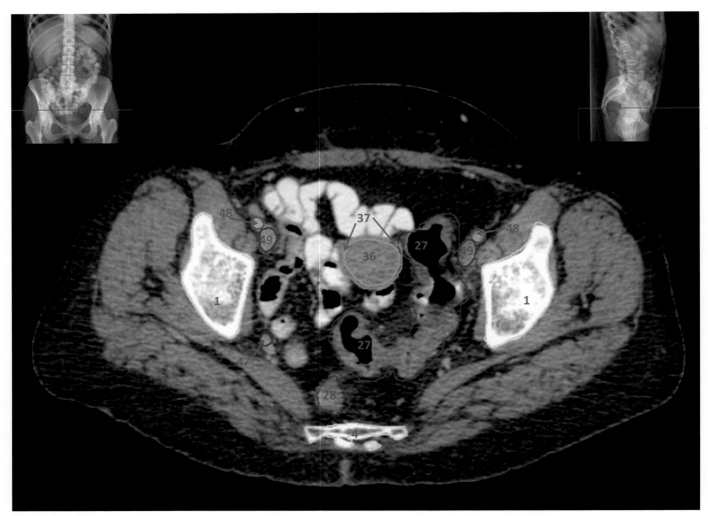

Figure 2.9.19

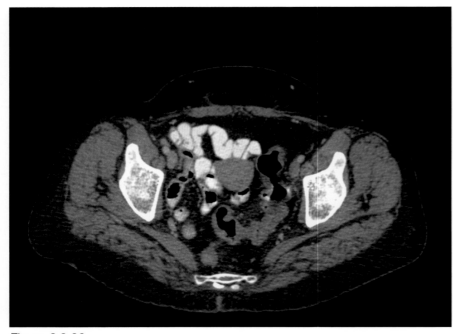

Figure 2.9.20

1. Ilium
4. Sacrum
27. Sigmoid Colon
28. Rectum
36. Uterus
37. Ligaments
47. Internal Iliac Vein
48. External Iliac Artery
49. External Iliac Vein

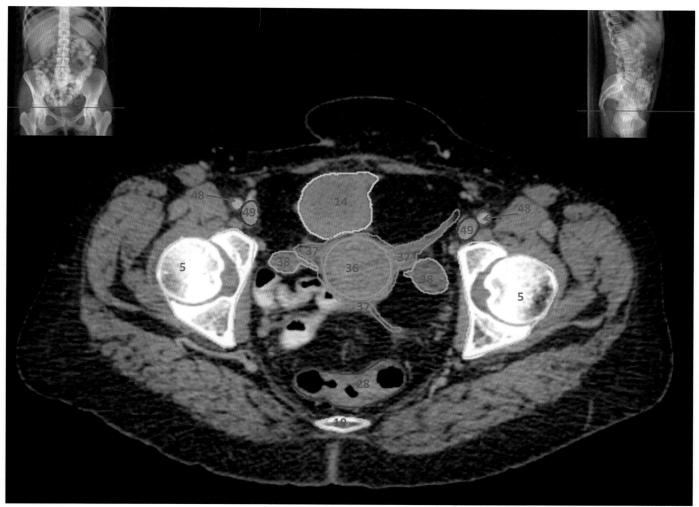

Figure 2.9.21

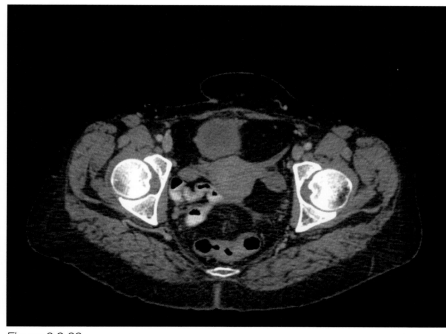

Figure 2.9.22

5. Femur
10. Coccyx
14. Bladder
28. Rectum
36. Uterus
37. Ligaments
38. Ovary
48. External Iliac Artery
49. External Iliac Vein

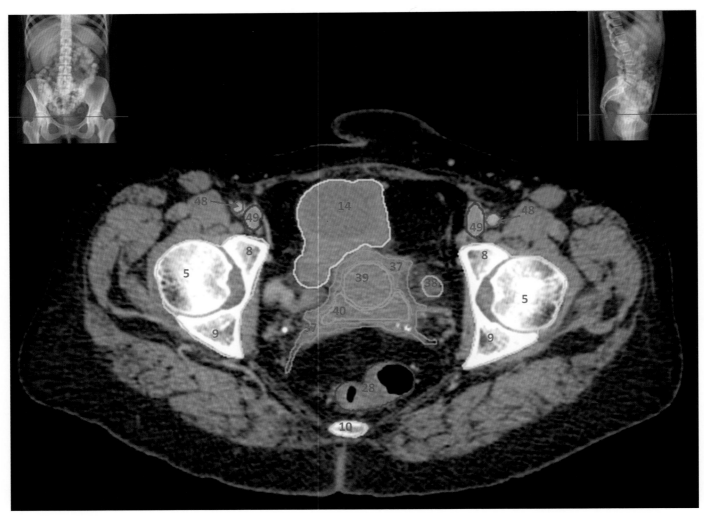

Figure 2.9.23

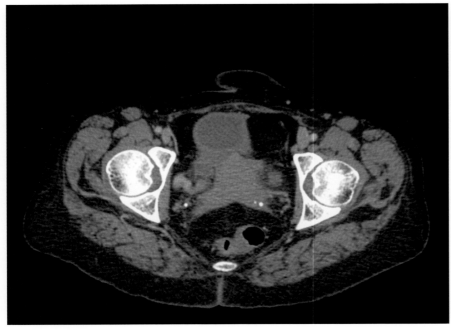

Figure 2.9.24

5. Femur
8. Pubis
9. Ischium
10. Coccyx
14. Bladder
28. Rectum
37. Ligaments
38. Ovary
39. Cervix
40. Vagina
48. External Iliac Artery
49. External Iliac Vein

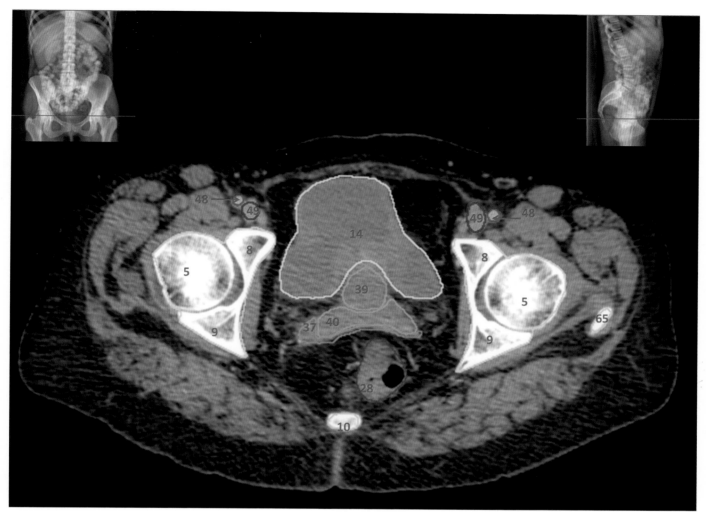

Figure 2.9.25

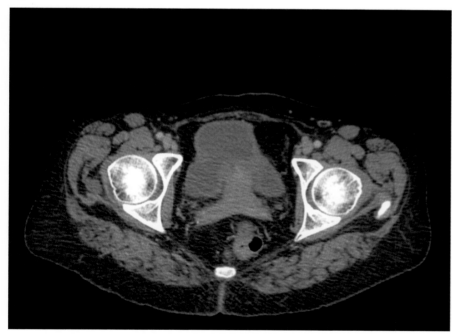

Figure 2.9.26

5. Femur
8. Pubis
9. Ischium
10. Coccyx
14. Bladder
28. Rectum
37. Ligaments
39. Cervix
40. Vagina
48. External Iliac Artery
49. External Iliac Vein
65. Greater Trochanter

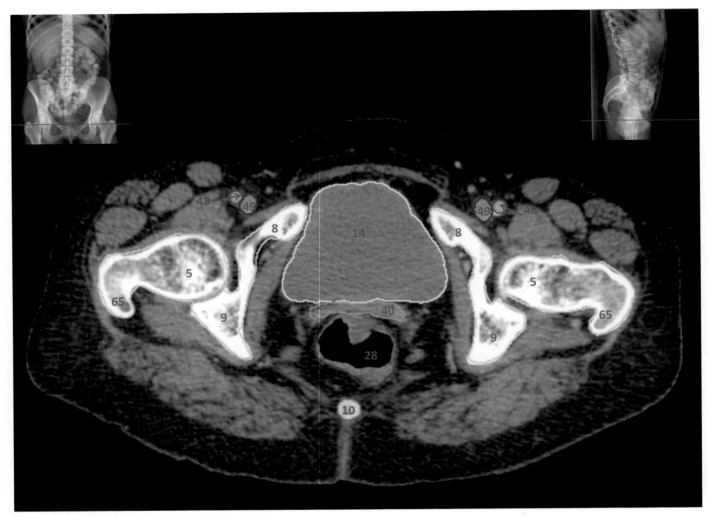

Figure 2.9.27

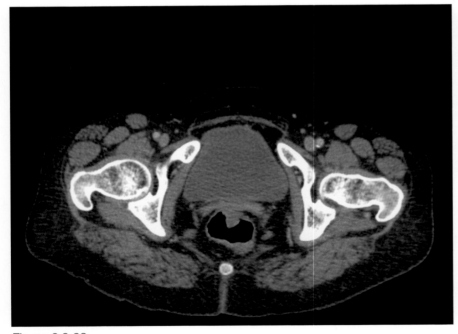

Figure 2.9.28

5. Femur
8. Pubis
9. Ischium
10. Coccyx
14. Bladder
28. Rectum
40. Vagina
48. External Iliac Artery
49. External Iliac Vein
65. Greater Trochanter

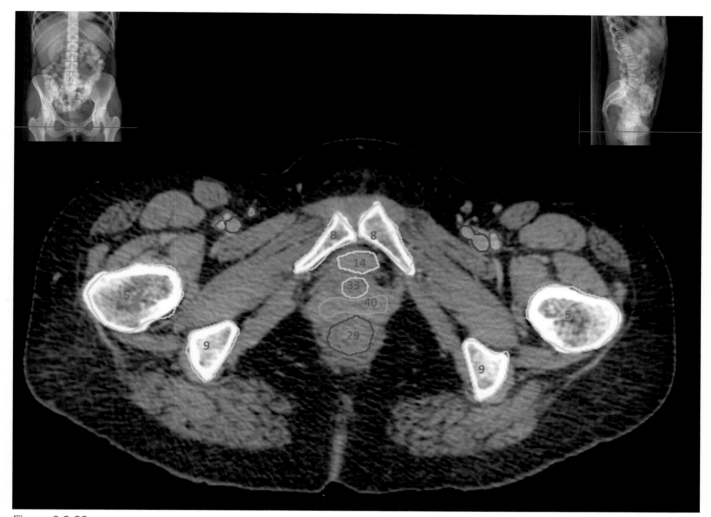

Figure 2.9.29

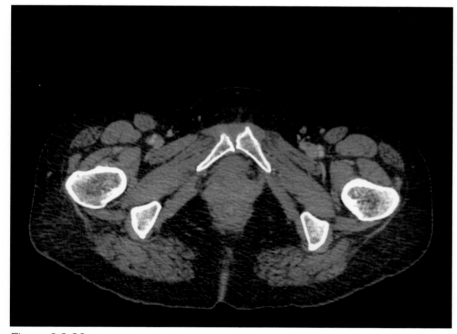

5. Femur
8. Pubis
9. Ischium
14. Bladder
29. Anus
33. Urethra
40. Vagina

Figure 2.9.30

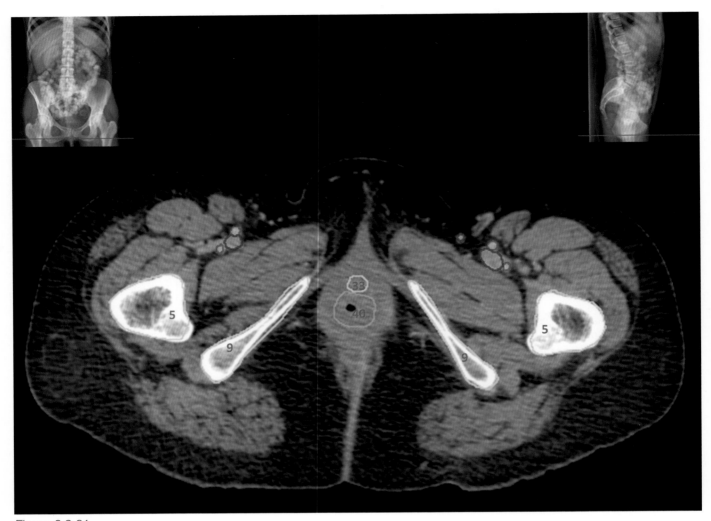

Figure 2.9.31

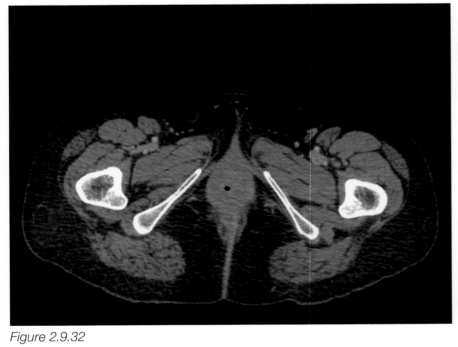

Figure 2.9.32

5. Femur
9. Ischium
33. Urethra
40. Vagina

2.10 Common Pelvis and Abdomen Tumour Pathology CT Appearance

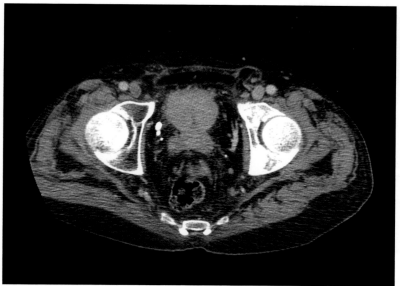

Figure 2.10.1

Prostate

Figure 2.10.1 clearly shows an enlarged prostate with solid-looking seminal vesicles, indicating proximal involvement. This is common since 75% of prostate tumours arise in the posterior of the gland. There is evidence of internal iliac nodal involvement on the right. The clearly defined borders of the prostate suggest that the capsule has remained intact and there is no evidence of spread to the lateral pelvic wall.

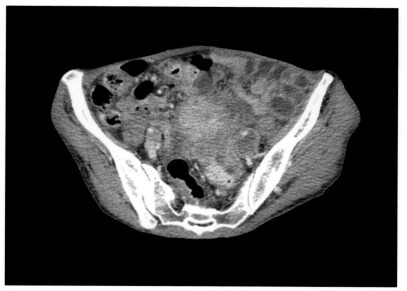

Figure 2.10.2

Cervix

The relative paucity of adipose tissue in Figure 2.10.2 makes demarcation of pelvic structures challenging. This cervix tumour has spread locally to involve the vault of vagina. Cervical tumours can be exophytic and bulky or infiltrative as in this image. Further spread can involve the parametrium. Lymphatic spread is via the obturator, internal and external iliac nodes to the common iliac nodes.

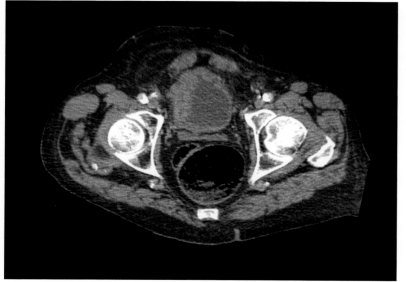

Figure 2.10.3

Bladder

Transitional cell carcinoma tumours of the bladder are often multi-focal and pedunculated (on a stalk). In this patient, Figure 2.10.3 shows a thickened irregular right lateral bladder wall protruding into the bladder lumen delineated by the lower density urine within. The tumour has extended beyond the bladder muscular wall limits and there is some posterior extension with a suggestion of spread including the right seminal vesicle.

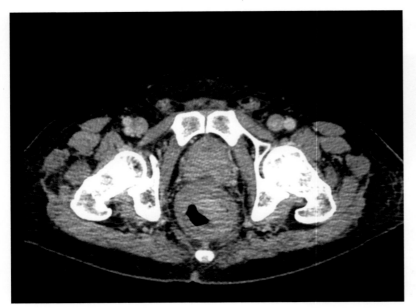

Figure 2.10.4

Rectum

Figure 2.10.4 demonstrates the typical thickened wall of a rectal adenocarcinoma. This can be easily judged by comparing it with Figure 2.10.1. The tumour has involved most of the rectal circumference. The border between the rectum and prostate is difficult to distinguish. The rich lymphatic plexus surrounding the rectum within the pararectal fascia is often affected.

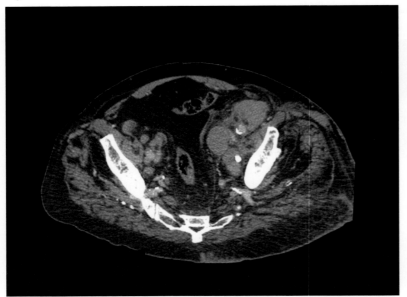

Figure 2.10.5

External iliac nodes

In Figure 2.10.5, the external iliac nodes on the left hand side are hugely involved. On the right hand side there is evidence of internal and external iliac node involvement although the individual masses are not as sizeable. Without the administration of IV contrast, it would be difficult to distinguish vessels from surrounding adjacent lymphadenopathy.

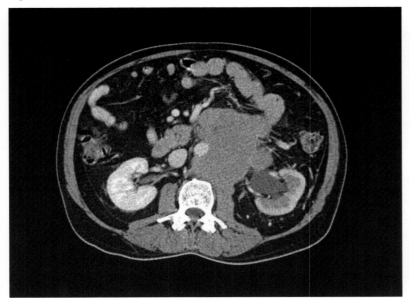

Figure 2.10.6

Para-aortic nodes

This large soft tissue mass in the centre of Figure 2.10.6 comprises a coalescence of para-aortic nodes from a seminoma surrounding the aorta. Compression of the left ureter has caused hydro-ureter and hydronephrosis and urine is clearly visible in the renal pelvis. The cortex of the left kidney is less opacified than the right, suggesting reduced renal function on the left. IV contrast in the aorta highlights its position in relation to the lymph mass.

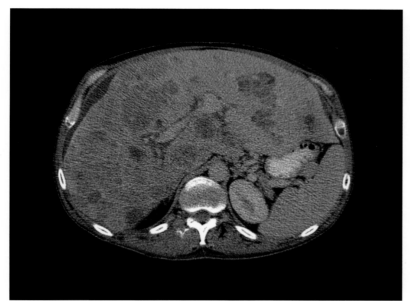

Figure 2.10.7

Liver metastases

Figure 2.10.7 shows an enlarged liver (hepatomegaly) with multiple areas of low attenuation. Some of these metastatic deposits are well-defined while others have indistinct borders. Most liver metastases have a poor blood supply so can be easily distinguished from an enhanced liver following IV contrast administration, particularly at arterial and late (equilibrium) phases.

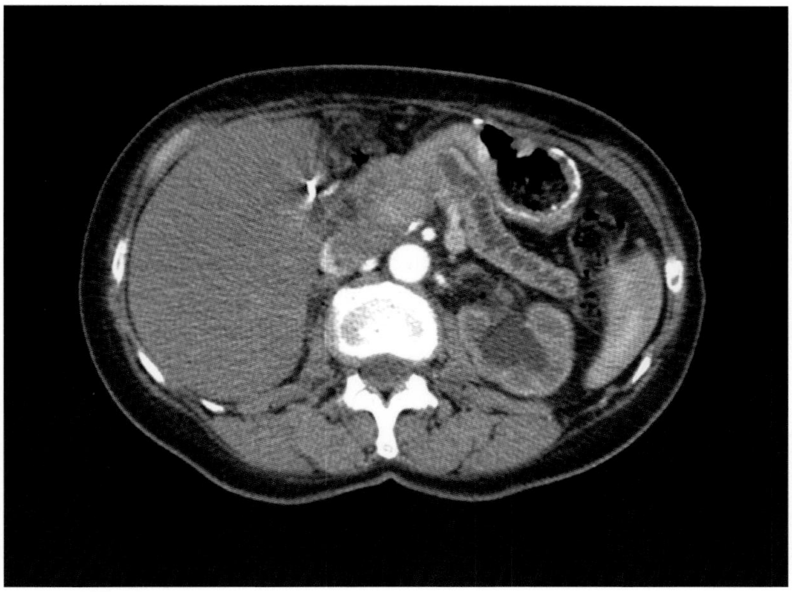

Pancreas

Figure 2.10.8 shows a bulky mass with reduced attenuation in the head of the pancreas as it curves round the hepatic portal vein. There is dilatation of the pancreatic duct within the body and tail of pancreas, suggestive of pancreatic ductal obstruction by the mass. There is also suggestion of distant ureteric compression as the left kidney is demonstrating early signs of hydronephrosis with urine build-up in the renal hilum.

Figure 2.10.8

Bone metastases

Bone metastases can have a variety of appearances on CT depending on whether they are osteolytic (destroying bone) or sclerotic. Figure 2.10.9 illustrates the mixed nature of this pathology. The right ilium shows a less dense osteolytic area behind the iliac fossa containing a high density sclerotic deposit. Elsewhere, the whole ilium has a mottled appearance, especially when contrasted with Figure 2.10.2.

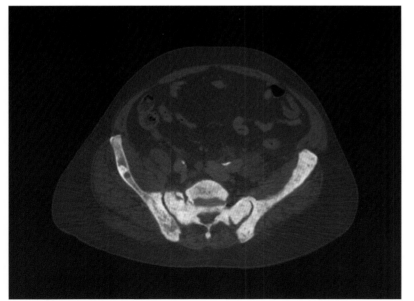

Figure 2.10.9

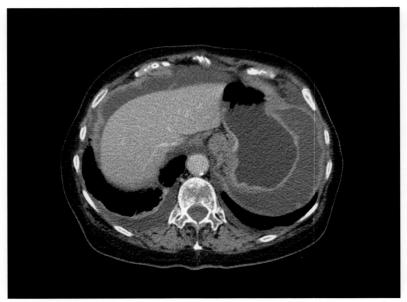

Figure 2.10.10

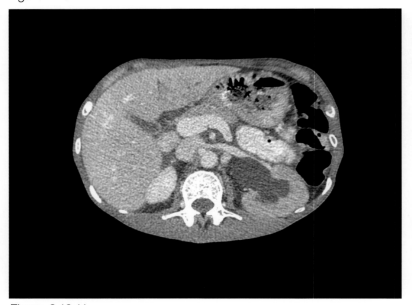

Figure 2.10.11

Stomach

Gastric carcinoma typically presents on CT as a diffuse, thickened, irregular intraluminal mass. It is vital for accurate CT localised staging to ensure the patient drinks approximately 500–600ml of water immediately prior to CT acquisition. The water provides a negative low density contrast and also distends the healthy gastric wall. Any irregular luminal areas will be evident, as is demonstrated in Figure 2.10.10 at the gastro-oesophageal junction. There are also considerable intra-abdominal ascitic fluid collections.

Hydronephrosis

In Figure 2.10.11, a left sided bladder wall tumour has occluded the left ureteric orifice, limiting the flow of urine into the bladder from the left. This has caused dilatation of the left ureter, hydro-ureter and distension of the renal collecting systems, hydronephrosis. The cortical excretional phase of the left kidney is also slower than the right, suggestive of impaired renal function on the left.

2.11 Self-Test Questions: Male Pelvis and Abdomen

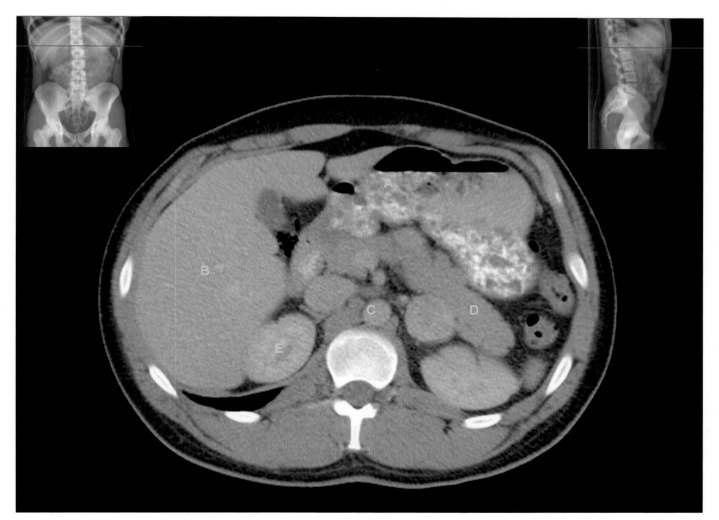

Figure 2.11.1

A

B

C

D

E

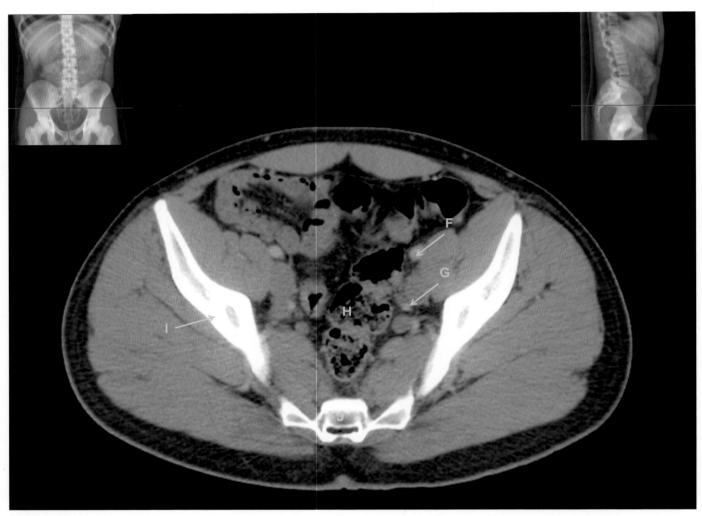

Figure 2.11.2

F

G

H

I

J

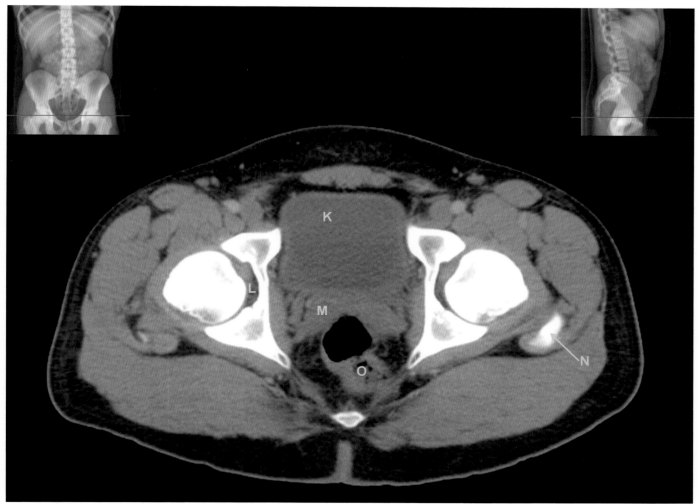

Figure 2.11.3

K

L

M

N

O

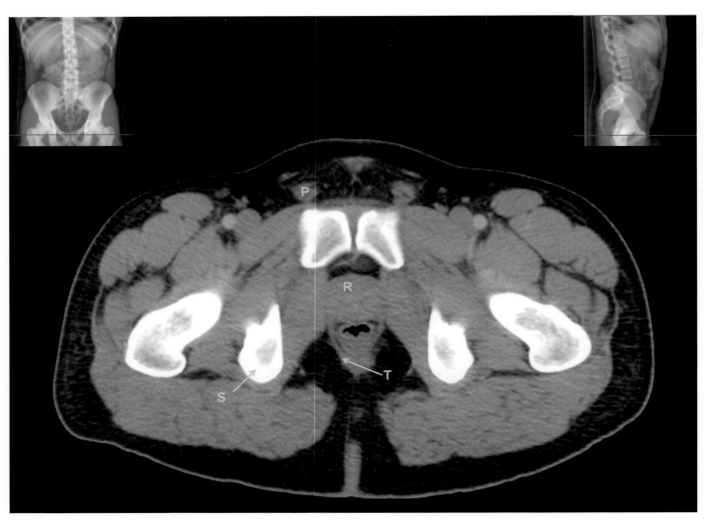

Figure 2.11.4

P

Q

R

S

T

Self-Test Questions: Female Pelvis and Abdomen

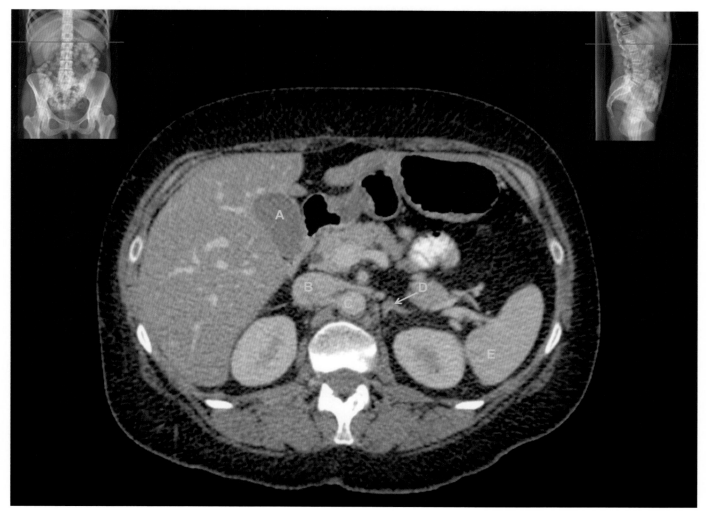

Figure 2.11.5

A

B

C

D

E

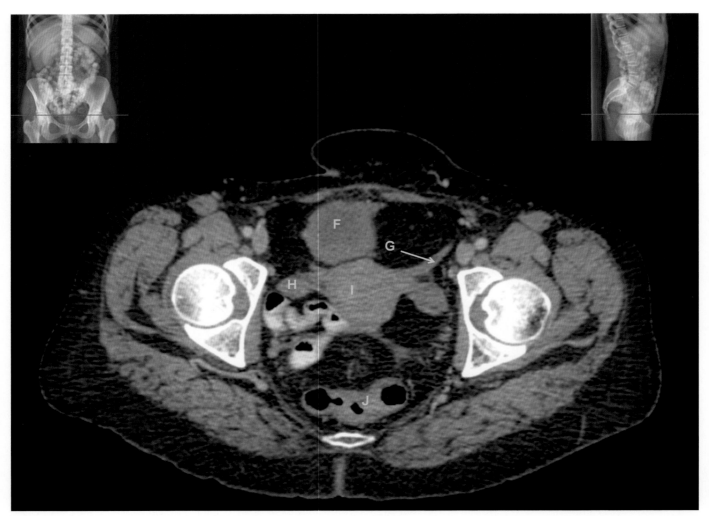

Figure 2.11.6

F

G

H

I

J

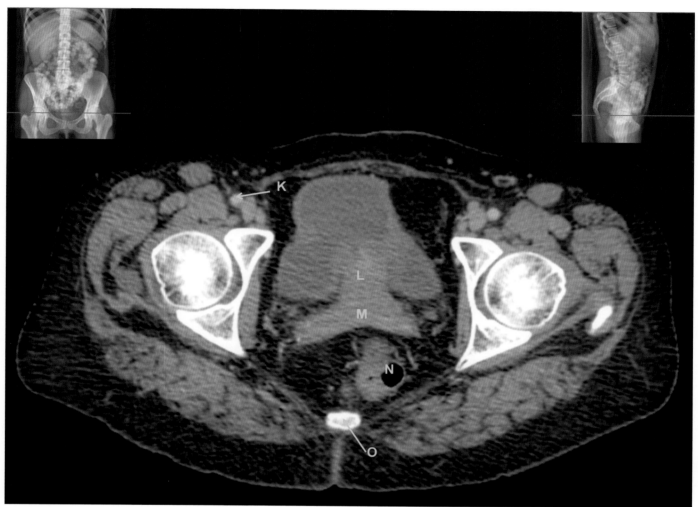

Figure 2.11.7

K

L

M

N

O

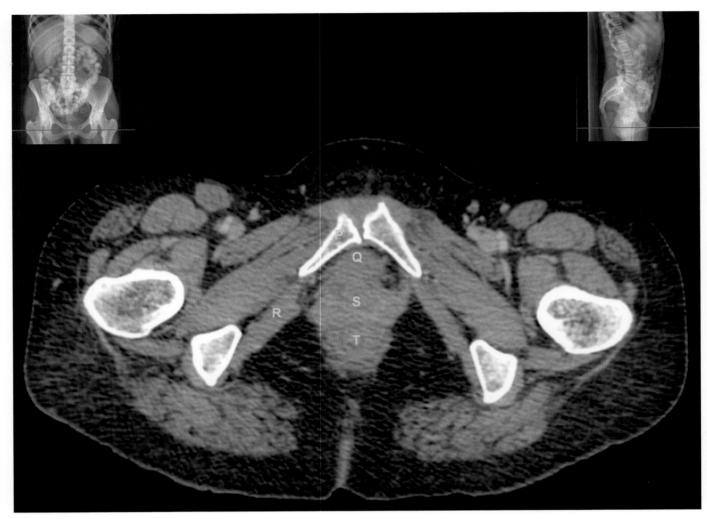

Figure 2.11.8

P

Q

R

S

T

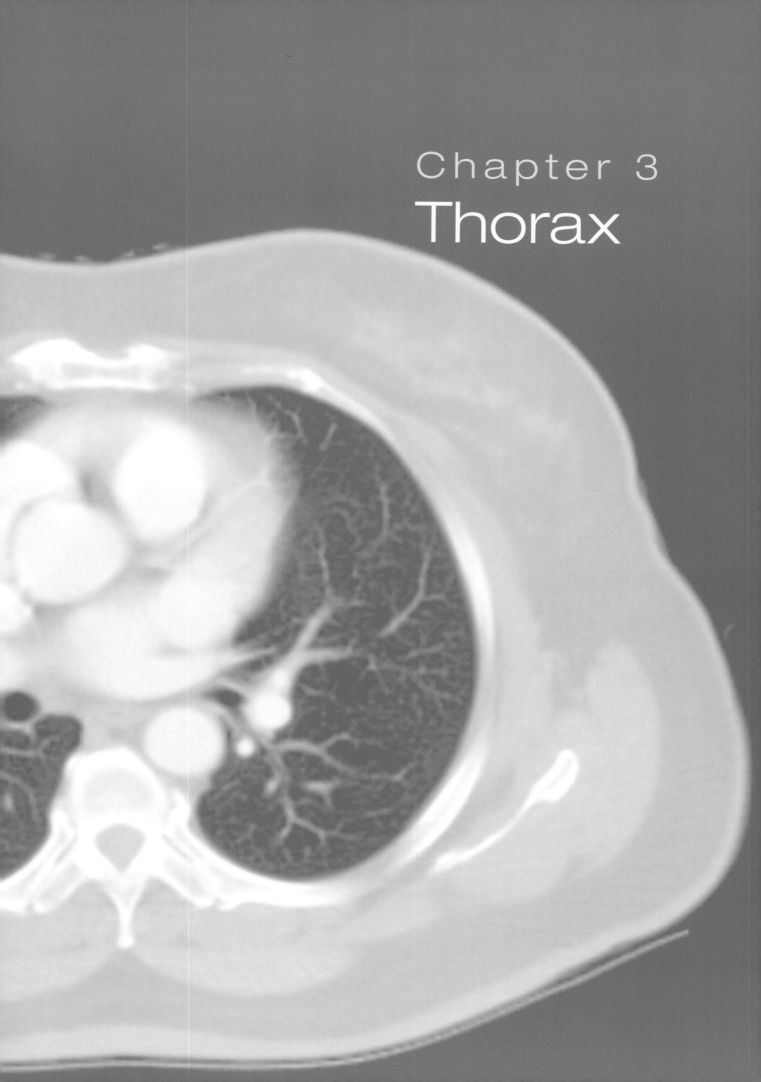

Chapter 3
Thorax

3.1 Musculoskeletal System

The skeletal system in the thorax is designed to produce a resizable framework within which the lungs can expand and contract while retaining protection. The thoracic cage is sealed inferiorly by the muscular sheet of the diaphragm. The superior aspect of the cage is relatively small and bounded by the highly curved upper ribs and the clavicles (C) joining the sternum (St) as seen in Figure 3.1.1. Additional support is provided by the vertebral column (V) posteriorly and the scapula (Sc) supero-posteriorly. Anteriorly, the sternum protects the thorax. The superior of the sternum forms the suprasternal notch with the heads of the clavicles. Inferiorly, the sternum tapers to a point known as the xiphoid process, or xiphisternum. On CT, the bony detail is not of major interest but the difference between thoracic and lumbar vertebrae should be noted, in particular the facets for attachment of the ribs.

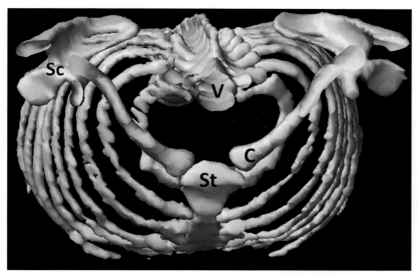

Figure 3.1.1

Although there are many thoracic muscles, for radiotherapy purposes these are of little direct interest. The pectoralis muscles, however, should be identified in order to help determine the posterior border of the breast tissue and some lymph node groups. Figure 3.1.2 shows how the pectoralis major muscles cover the superior portion of the chest, connecting the sternum and clavicle with the greater tubercle of the humerus. Underneath this lies the smaller pectoralis minor muscle that connects the third, fourth and fifth ribs to the scapula.

The other muscle of note in the thorax is the diaphragm. This domed muscle flattens when tensed to expand the thorax. It can be seen on lower thorax CT scans as a thin sheet separating the lungs from the abdominal contents. It is particularly thick at the medial and posterior region near the vertebrae. It is attached to the vertebral column by two crura (one per side). These have already been identified in Chapter 2.

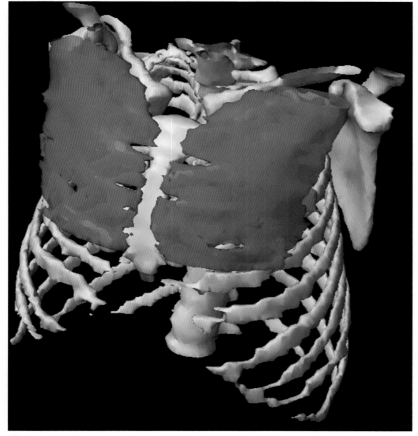

Figure 3.1.2

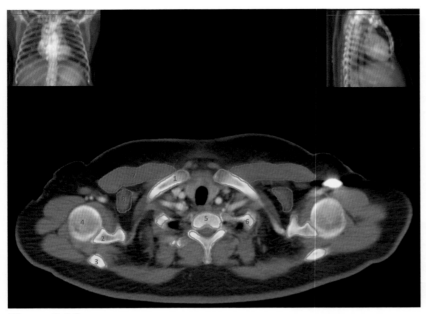

Figure 3.1.3

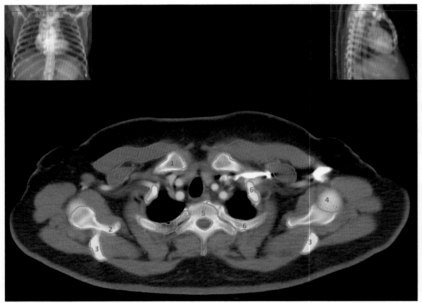

Figure 3.1.4

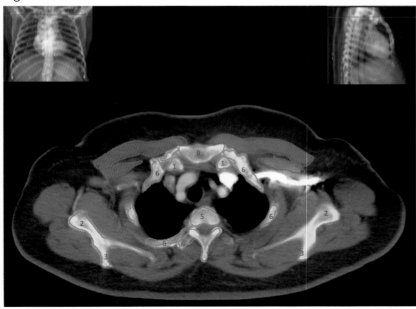

Figure 3.1.5

Figures 3.1.3 to 3.1.5 show the superior of the thoracic cage formed by the clavicle (1), scapula (2) and upper thoracic ribs (6). In Figure 3.1.3, at about T1, the superior spine of scapula (3) can be seen posteriorly. Laterally to the scapula can be seen the head of humerus (4).

Anteriorly lie the pectoralis muscle group (7 and 8). Symmetry of these muscles is dependent upon the choice of immobilisation position adopted. If both arms are raised above the head, the lateral bulk of both pectoralis muscles will be extended and stretched superiorly and will be symmetrical; however muscle bulk appearances will differ if one arm is raised and the other remains at rest by the patient's torso.

Each pectoralis major muscle (7) spans a relatively large proportion of the upper thorax. These paired fan-shaped muscles cross the superior anterior chest wall from the sternum (9) and inferior clavicles (1) to the greater tubercle of each humerus (4).

Demarcation between the pectoralis major (7) and pectoralis minor (8) is aided by a fat plane between them. Level II interpectoral lymph nodes (Rotter's) may be present within this fat plane and can reduce interpectoral fat plane perception, but any resulting asymmetry will be apparent when both sides are compared.

The pectoralis minor muscles are the smaller of the two groups as their name suggests. They lie inferior to pectoralis major and slightly laterally and span the gap from the third, fourth and fifth ribs to the coracoid process of each scapula.

The fat border between the muscle and deep breast fibroglandular tissue is discernable in Figure 3.1.6. Although superior demarcation of local invasion of underlying musculature is best demonstrated by contrast and fat suppression MRI imaging, the fat plane between the breast glandular tissue and pectoralis major muscle can be clearly seen at this level.

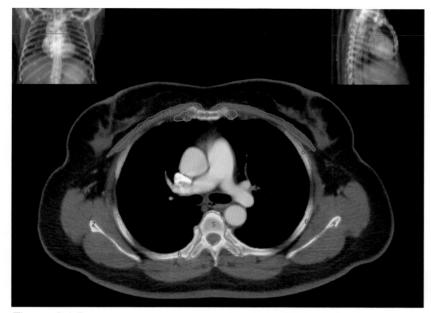

Figure 3.1.6

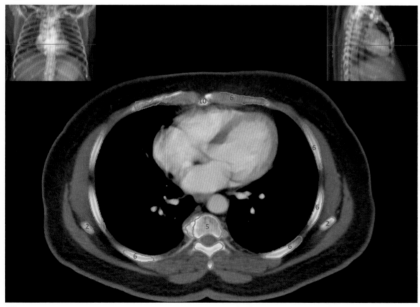

Figure 3.1.7

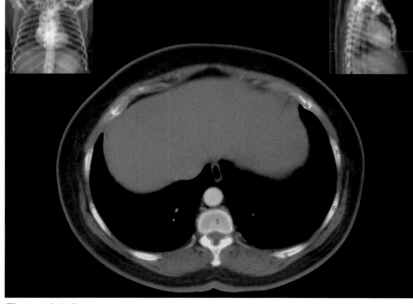

Figure 3.1.8

In Figure 3.1.6, the scapulae have a particularly thin cross-section. As both arms are raised above the patient's head the scapulae rotate and appear to extend slightly laterally. The normal bony thoracic skeleton will have smooth contours and be symmetrical, providing both arms are either positioned above the head, or down by the torso. Like all skeletal bones there is a high natural contrast between the soft tissue and sternum (9), ribs (6) and spine (5). There are also often calcification deposits present within the costal cartilages, particularly close to the sternum (9). Figure 3.1.7 illustrates the inferior aspects of the scapulae (2) and the xiphisternum (10) at the inferior of the sternum.

Figure 3.1.8, at T11 level, demonstrates the junction between the thoracic and abdominal spaces, which are separated by the diaphragm. The diaphragm is a thin domed sheet of muscle, and should be of regular width with no contour abnormalities. It can be difficult to visualise due to its relatively thin nature and proximity to abdominal soft tissue structures. This is simplified by adjacent intra-abdominal fat deposits, although these may not be apparent above the liver on the right hemi-diaphragm.

Cordlike thickening of the paravertebral muscle fibres is sometimes visualised on forced inspiration and crura can be clearly visualised on lower images. Retrocrural evaluation is vital for determining the presence of lymphadenopathy.

The spine should be viewed on bony window settings to assess for metastatic deposits. These are frequently involved in destructive processes in the laminae and vertebral bodies (5). Solitary fractures at atypical locations, such as upper and mid thoracic regions, should be treated as suspicious of metastatic disease. The spinal canal should also be examined for soft tissue extension into the canal and cord.

3.2 Digestive System

After the complexity and diversity of the digestive system in the abdomen and pelvis, the reader will be relieved by the simplicity of the thoracic digestive system. This comprises the thin collapsible muscular tube of the oesophagus. The small cross-section, frequent lack of lumen and absence of surrounding fat often make the oesophagus hard to spot on CT, despite it being a relatively common treatment site. The oesophagus tends to be divided into three distinct sections: an upper, middle and lower third. The cervical section starts at the lower posterior hypopharynx, becomes the thoracic oesophagus to drop through the mediastinum and pierces the diaphragm as the abdominal oesophagus to join the stomach. It can be located for much of its upper course by an understanding of its position posterior to the trachea. In Figure 3.2.1 the brown oesophagus hugs the posterior border of the green trachea. Below the bifurcation, it descends in roughly the same position, moving slightly left and anteriorly towards the stomach before penetrating the diaphragm through the oesophageal hiatus at about T10.

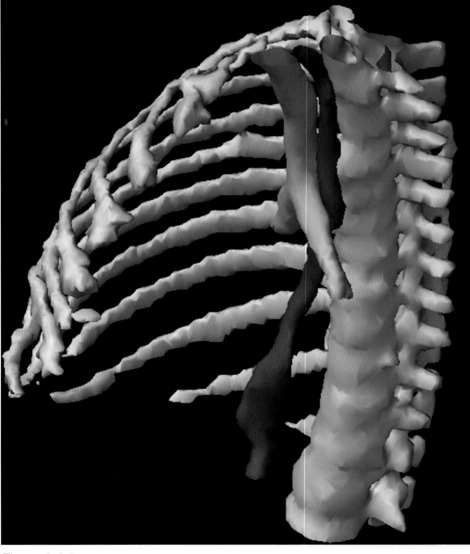

Figure 3.2.1

The upper thoracic oesophagus (11) extends from the level of the suprasternal notch to the tracheal bifurcation as seen in Figure 3.2.2. The upper oesophagus can be difficult to visualise on non-contrast CT by the inexperienced viewer due to the relatively small cross-section and irregular shape. Occasional lack of clear surrounding fat and incomplete distension also further complicate clear demarcation.

Localisation can be aided by considering a few simple guidelines. Normally the oesophagus is located in the midline, although lateral displacement is possible. The usual position is posterior to the flat portion of the trachea and anterior to the thoracic vertebral bodies as seen in the enlarged Figure 3.2.2.

The wall thickness should be relatively uniform along its length. Areas of thickening of more than 3–5mm and prestenotic dilation are indicative of disease. Intraluminal air or well timed administration of intraluminal CT contrast can help visualisation of the lumen and wall thickening. This patient's lumen can clearly be seen in the enlarged Figures 3.2.3 and 3.2.4. IV contrast agent will help delineate adjacent vascular structures and the oesophagus will be seen in between the azygos vein and aorta. The mid-thoracic portion behind the heart is very close to the left atrium, and can sometimes be poorly visualised due to cardiac motion.

Inferior to this level, the path of the oesophagus moves anterior until it reaches the diaphragm. The inferior portion of the oesophagus continues beyond the oesophageal hiatus in the diaphragm until it joins the gastric fundus.

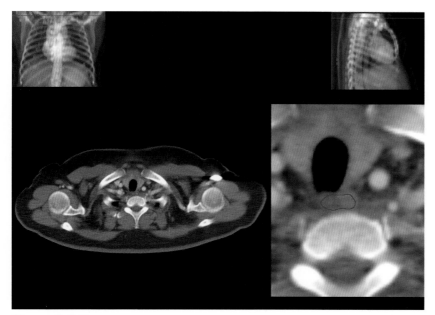

Figure 3.2.2

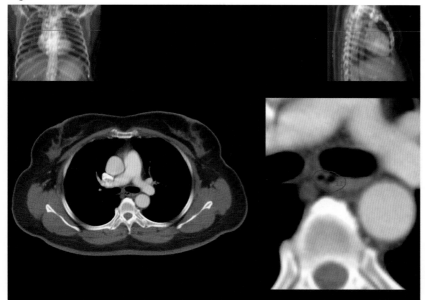

Figure 3.2.3

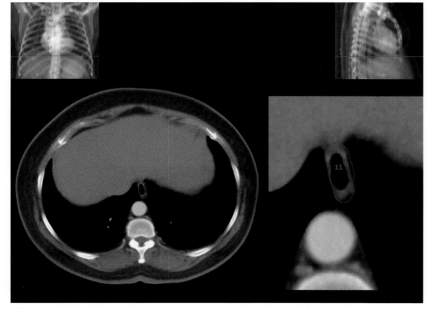

Figure 3.2.4

3.3 Respiratory System

The respiratory system comprises most of the bulk of structures within the thoracic cage and is designed to enable gaseous exchange by expanding to draw in fresh air and then contracting to expel used air. The inlet for the air is the trachea which has a horseshoe-shaped appearance in cross-section. The trachea is held open by almost complete rings of cartilage. The rings are open at the posterior of the trachea, causing a flattened posterior wall and the characteristic shape on CT. This structure allows for passage of food through the adjacent oesophagus without the rings impeding its progress.

The trachea splits into two bronchi and these then conduct the air to the paired lungs. The left bronchus supplies a reduced volume of inferior lung tissue due to the position of the heart so tends to take a more horizontal approach than the right bronchus. On CT, this manifests itself by a more oval cross-section than the circular appearance of the right bronchus.

The lungs themselves are spongy in nature and thus differ from the air tubes, which are hollow air-filled structures. This difference is apparent when 'lung' window settings are used. On 'soft tissue' settings, both lung and air tubes appear black.

As previously mentioned, the heart occludes much of the left side of the thorax and this means that the lungs are asymmetrical in structure and size. The left lung has an upper and lower lobe whereas the right has an upper, lower and middle lobe. These terms are somewhat misleading as Figure 3.3.1 demonstrates. The anterior of the upper lobes (light green) can be seen to extend to the inferior part of the thorax. Additionally, the posterior upper lobes (mid green) extend superiorly almost to the lung apices. This can cause confusion if a lower lobe tumour is reported yet appears to be in the superior part of the thoracic cage.

The lobes are separated by fissures. These fissures are occasionally visible on CT, but are also identifiable by the relative paucity of vessels within the lung at the edges of the lobes. On the medial aspect of each lung can be found the hilum, where the various tubes, such as the bronchi, nerves and pulmonary vessels, enter and leave the lungs.

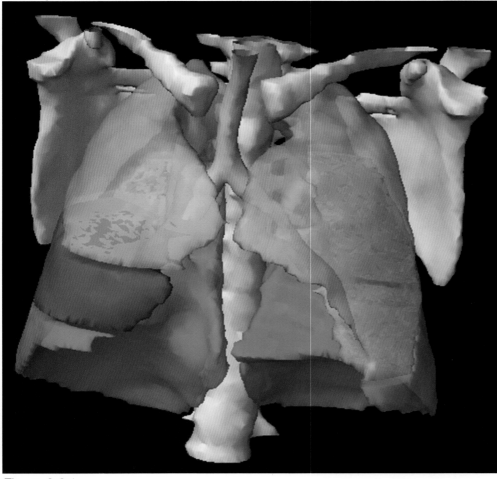

Figure 3.3.1

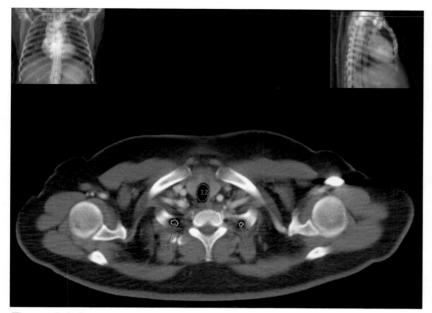

At the level of the sternal notch the most visible part of the respiratory system is the trachea (12). This structure is easily recognisable on CT by its distinctive horseshoe appearance. It contains air with HU of -1000 and is black in appearance on all window width and level settings as seen in Figure 3.3.3. At this level the trachea is partially enclosed by the thyroid gland lobes (laterally) and isthmus (anteriorly). The tracheal cartilages may also contain calcified deposits in some patients. The tips of the lung apices are also just visible here (13 and 14).

Figure 3.3.2

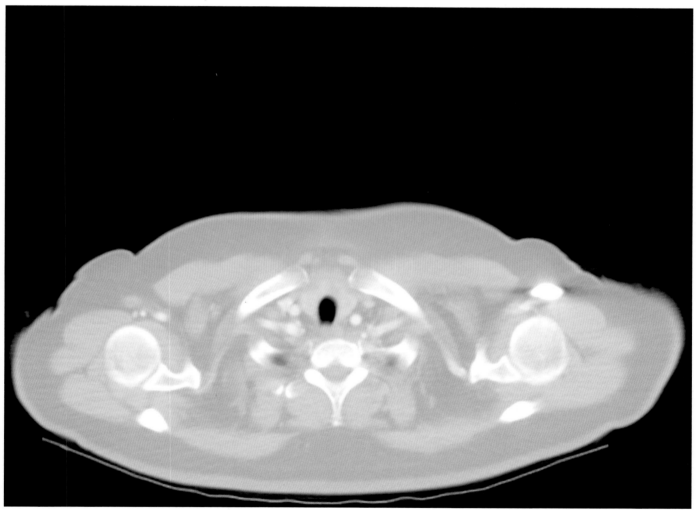

Figure 3.3.3

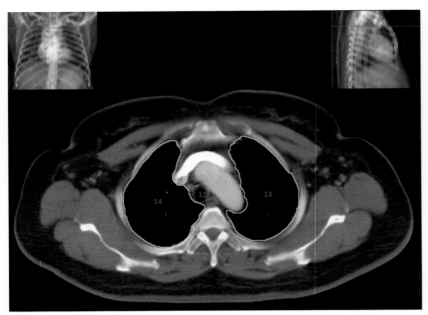

Figure 3.3.4

Within the superior mediastinum, Figures 3.3.4 and 3.3.5 show that the trachea (12) varies considerably in cross-sectional shape, and is not always midline. Here it deviates slightly to the right due to the location of the aortic arch. Here, the trachea has a rounded cross-section, but is still easily identifiable as it contains air. The borders of the lung segments are not easily discerned without in-depth knowledge of bronchopulmonary segments. Apical zones of upper lobes of both lungs (13 and 14) are also visible; both are well aerated and are adjacent to the chest walls. The difference in density between air in the trachea and lung tissue can be noted on Figure 3.3.5.

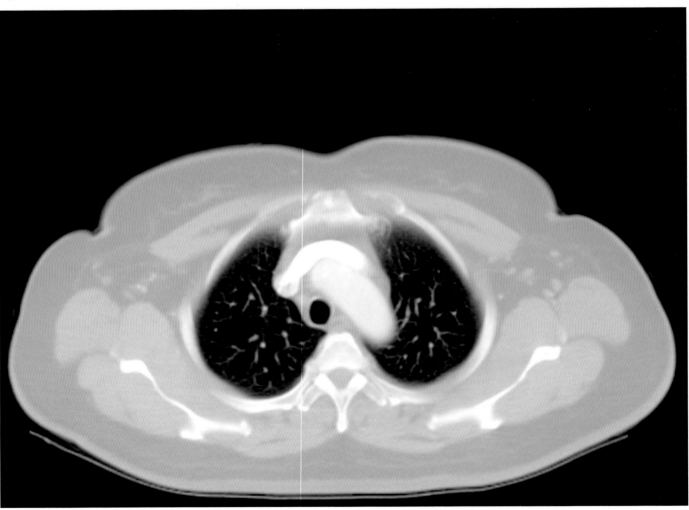

Figure 3.3.5

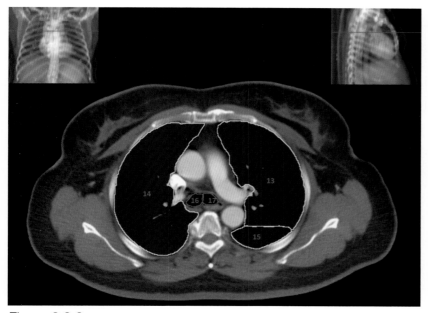

Figure 3.3.6

Still within the superior mediastinum, at T4/5, the trachea has bifurcated into the right (16) and left (17) main bronchi. Both are air-containing structures anterior to the vertebral body, and slightly to the right of centre. The fissures dividing the lungs into lobes can sometimes be seen on thin slices through the lung. Anterior segments of lower lobes of right (14) and left (13) lungs as well as superior segment of left lung (15) are seen. Figure 3.3.7 shows how the pulmonary vessels and bronchi separate further and reduce in size and accompany each other to the periphery. This is termed the bronchial tree.

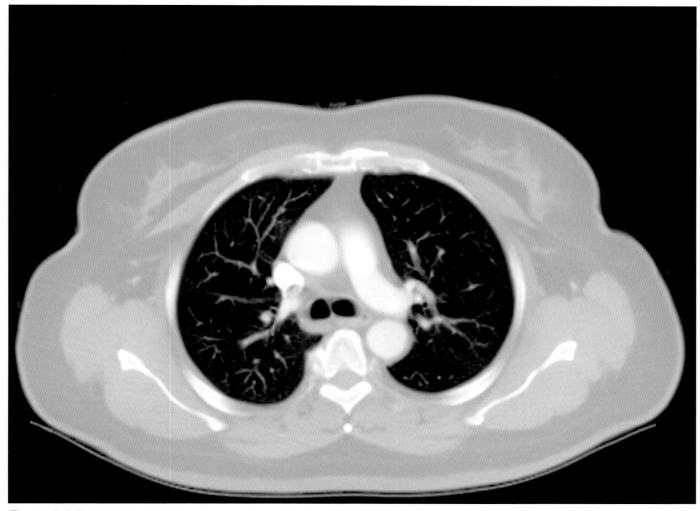

Figure 3.3.7

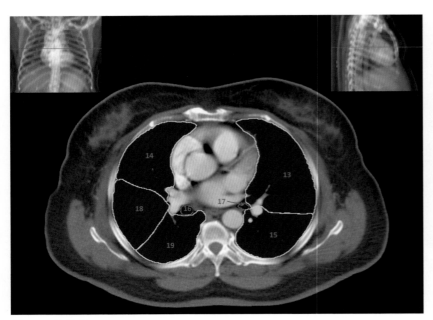

In Figures 3.3.8 and 3.3.9, the two main bronchi have further subdivided into the right lower lobe bronchus (16) and left lower lobe bronchus (17). Using lung window settings, it is possible to visualise individual lobes within the lungs as seen on the left in Figure 3.3.9. Lobar segmentation is more complex and might not be apparent on slices thicker than 5mm but may be visualised by following branches of the pulmonary veins. The right lower lobe (19), middle lobe (18) and upper lobe (14) are easily identified. The left lower lobe (15) and upper lobe (13) can also be seen.

Figure 3.3.8

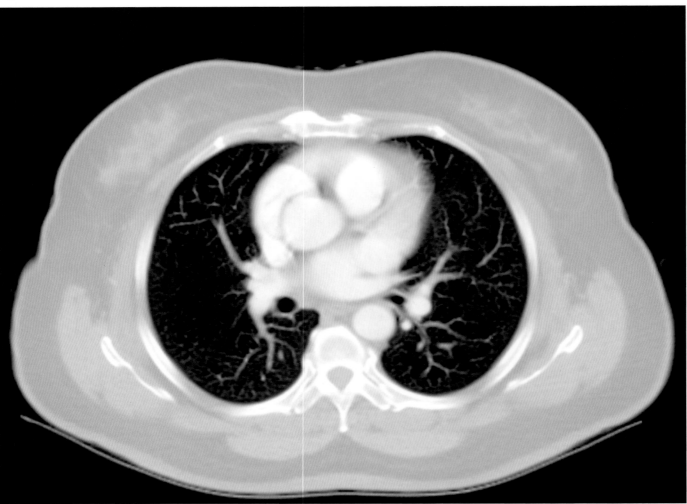

Figure 3.3.9

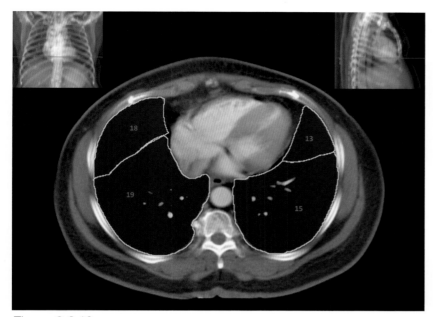

Figures 3.3.10 and 3.3.11 show the middle (18) and lower (19) lobes of the right lung as well as the upper (13) and lower (15) lobes of the left lung. As the pulmonary vessels and branches of the bronchial tree extend deeper into the lungs, they become too small to visualise on soft tissue settings, although they are visible in Figure 3.3.11 due to their high inherent contrast.

An osteophyte on the vertebral body is slightly displacing the medial aspect of the lower lobe of the right lung. These osteophytes are normally due to degenerative spondylosis and are often seen on the lateral and anterior aspects of the thoracic vertebral bodies.

Figure 3.3.10

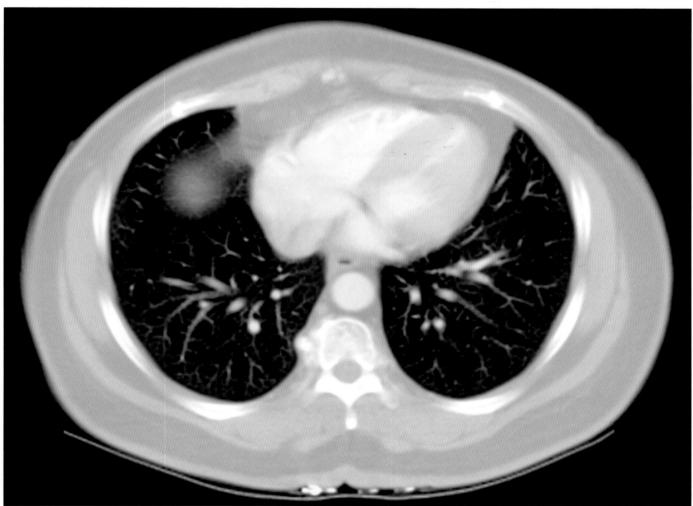

Figure 3.3.11

3.4 Cardiovascular System

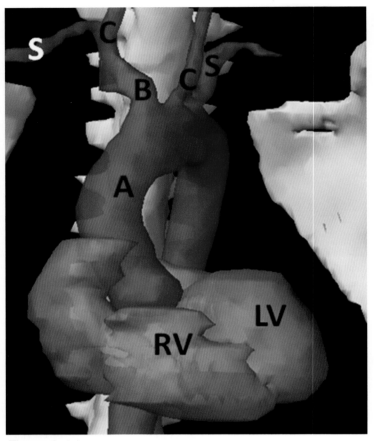

Figure 3.4.1

Although some aspects of the cardiovascular system represent a challenge to CT interpretation, it is rare that the therapy radiographer is required to identify specific elements of it. An understanding of the location of the main vessels and structures will, however, enable abnormalities to be spotted, lymph node regions to be identified and assist with general orientation.

The heart operates as a fluid pump with two main pumping chambers (the ventricles) and two ante-chambers (the atria) that collect blood for pumping. Figure 3.4.1 illustrates the main exit route of blood from the heart. Blood exits the left ventricle (LV) to the main arteries via the ascending aorta (A). This arches superiorly and posteriorly before descending slightly anteriorly and to the left of the vertebral column.

The first few branches off the aorta are of some interest. The very first are the tiny coronary arteries that supply the heart muscle itself. After that comes the brachiocephalic artery (B). This is an unpaired artery that is necessary due to the left hand position of the heart and carries blood to the right hand side of the thorax. It then

branches into the right subclavian (S) and common carotid (C) arteries. The subclavian arteries duck under the clavicles to supply the arms while the carotids ascend to supply the head and neck.

The left common carotid (C) and subclavian (S) arteries are the next two main arteries emerging directly from the aorta and do not require a brachiocephalic artery to link them to it. After the arch, the aorta plunges inferiorly with only a few branches emerging from it, such as the bronchial arteries that supply the lungs with oxygenated blood. Most of the major arterial branching occurs after the aorta has penetrated the diaphragm as seen in the previous chapter.

The deoxygenated blood from the body returns via the venous system to either the superior or inferior vena cava. The superior vena cava (SVC) returns blood from the head and neck and is fed by left and right brachiocephalic veins. Unlike the corresponding arterial supply, these are paired structures and are in turn supplied by the jugular and subclavian veins. Figure 3.4.2 shows the jugular (J) and

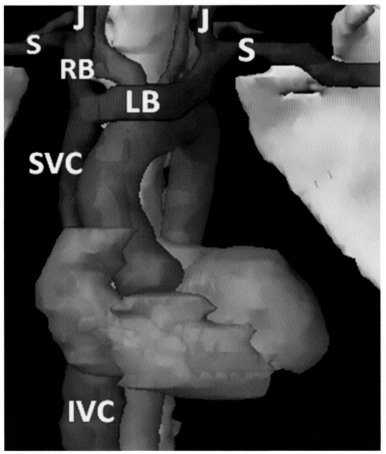

Figure 3.4.2

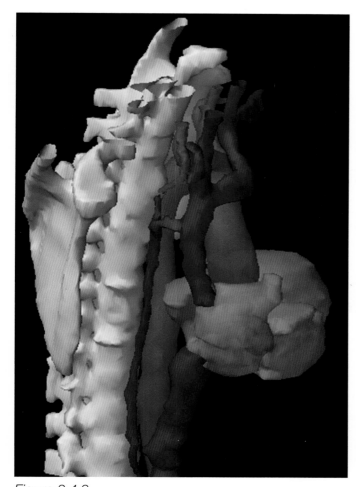

Figure 3.4.3

subclavian (S) veins on each side joining to form the right and left brachiocephalic veins (RB and LB). These then combine to form the relatively short SVC. The IVC collects most of the blood from the lower body and can be seen slightly anterior and to the right of the aorta as it rises through the thorax. Some blood is also returned via the smaller azygos and hemi-azygos veins which run anteriorly to the vertebral column and connect the superior and inferior venae cavae.

The veins all empty into the right atrium as seen in Figures 3.4.2 (anterior view) and 3.4.3 (lateral view). The azygos vein can be seen clearly in Figure 3.4.3 as the smaller vein posterior to the venae cavae and aorta.

The right atrium pumps the deoxygenated blood into the right ventricle and blood passes from here into the pulmonary trunk. This is a short vessel that runs posteriorly before splitting into the left and right main pulmonary arteries. Figure 3.4.4 illustrates the pulmonary trunk (P) emerging from the right ventricle at the anterior of the body, passing posteriorly and then bifurcating into the left and right pulmonary arteries (LPA and RPA).

After penetrating the lungs at the hilum, the pulmonary arteries branch dramatically to perfuse the lungs. After gaseous exchange has occurred, the

oxygenated blood is gathered into the four pulmonary veins. Each lobe has a corresponding pulmonary vein apart from the right middle and upper lobes, which both drain into a single vein. The pulmonary veins leave the hilum and empty into the left atrium. They can be seen on CT inferiorly to the pulmonary arteries and posteriorly to the atria. From the left atrium, the oxygenated blood is pumped to the left ventricle ready for the circulatory cycle to begin again.

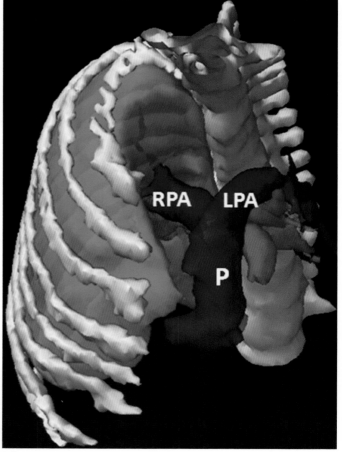

Figure 3.4.4

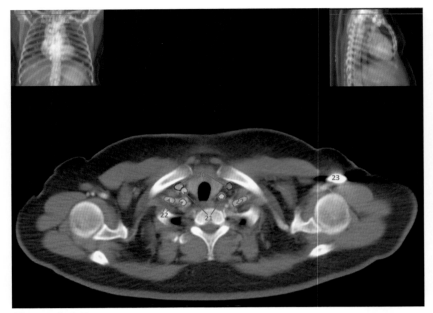

Figure 3.4.5

At the thoracic inlet several vessels can be visualised, especially with the aid of IV contrast agent. Depending upon the timing of the injection and scan acquisition, the opacity of the different vessels can vary. This area is conventionally scanned 25–30 seconds from the start of injection, typically injected at 3ml/second. This allows the IV contrast to circulate and mix through the cardiopulmonary system, and enter the aorta. Figure 3.4.5 shows some contrast still entering the system via the subclavian vein (23). This is quite dense as it has not yet mixed and become more diluted with blood within the cardiopulmonary system.

In Figure 3.4.5, lateral to the trachea, lie the common carotid arteries (21), medial and posterior to the internal jugular veins (20). Asymmetry of jugular veins is relatively common, and as such has very little pathological significance. The subclavian arteries (22) can be seen extending towards each axilla.

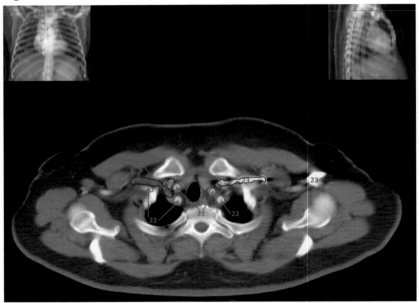

Figure 3.4.6

Figure 3.4.6 demonstrates both subclavian arteries (22). On the right can also be seen the subclavian vein (23). Both common carotid arteries (21) are visible lateral to the trachea. Behind the head of the clavicle is the right internal jugular vein (20) adjacent to the right common carotid artery and subclavian vein.

Slightly more inferiorly in Figure 3.4.7, the jugular and subclavian veins have converged into the right (25) and left (23) brachiocephalic veins. The effect of contrast within the left brachiocephalic vein can be noted when compared with the appearance of the right vein.

Paired subclavian veins and arteries can be seen in longitudinal section posterior to the pectoralis minor, although the high level of contrast on the left (23) obscures details. These vessels are usually easily identified due to the surrounding axillary fatty tissue.

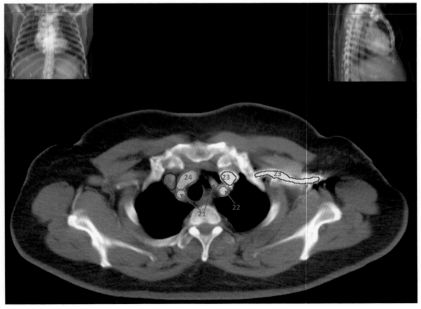

Figure 3.4.7

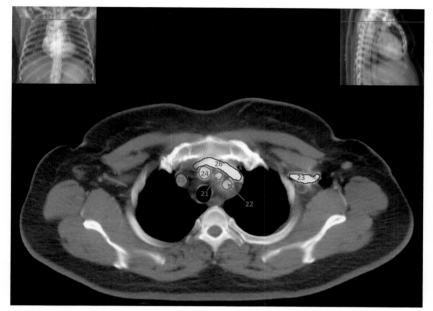

Figure 3.4.8

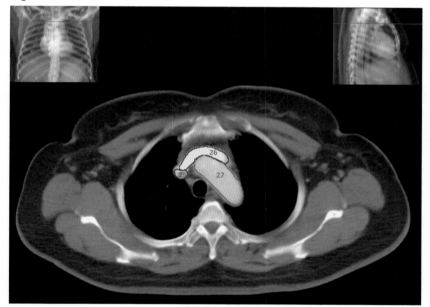

Figure 3.4.9

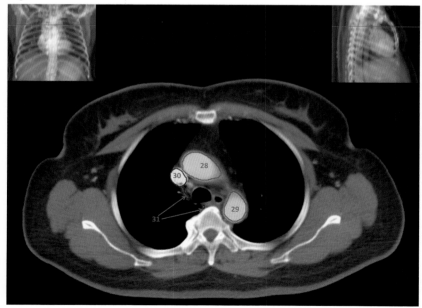

Figure 3.4.10

At this level (T2/T3) in Figure 3.4.8 the left subclavian vein (23) is still visible, posterior to the left pectoralis minor. Within the superior mediastinum, the vessels are fewer and more easily distinguished. There are three main arteries here, and two main veins. There is just one brachiocephalic artery (24). This is the first main vessel arising from the arch of the aorta. The next major branch is the left common carotid artery (21) and then left subclavian artery (22). The two brachiocephalic veins appear slightly different at this level, as the longer left vein (26) extends across the mediastinum towards the right vein (25). They will meet inferiorly to form the SVC.

In Figure 3.4.9 the arch of aorta (27) is visible curving posteriorly and laterally within the mediastinum. The left brachio-cephalic vein (26) can be seen extending around the anterior aspect of the arch of aorta and converging with the right brachiocephalic vein (25) in order to form the SVC (30 in Figure 3.4.10). The trachea and oesophagus can be seen medial to the aortic arch.

Figure 3.4.10 is at a level just inferior to the aortic arch (about T4/T5) so both the ascending (28) and descending (29) thoracic aorta can be identified. The SVC (30) is lateral to the ascending aorta, and is relatively radio-opaque due to a higher concentration of contrast. The aorta usually has a diameter less than 4cm. Any increase could suggest aneurysm, infiltration or adjacent disease processes.

The azygos vein (31) is arching over the root of the right lung, adjacent to the trachea. The azygos vein, if particularly bulky, can sometimes be mistaken for para-aortic lymph nodes.

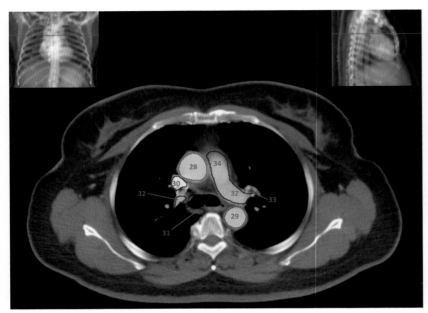

Figure 3.4.11

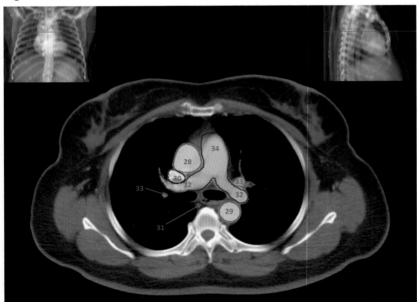

Figure 3.4.12

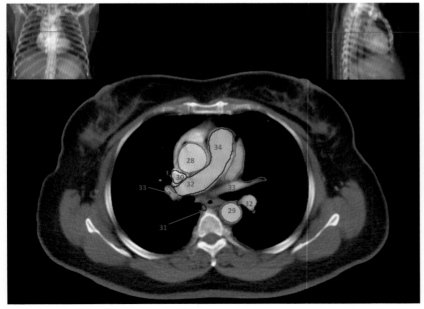

Figure 3.4.13

Medial to the ascending aorta (28), the main pulmonary trunk (34) arises and passes posteriorly. It then bifurcates and in Figure 3.4.11 the left main pulmonary artery (32) extends into the hilum of the left lung. Just anterior to this are smaller pulmonary vessels (33). Slightly inferior, in Figure 3.4.12, a further subdivision of a right pulmonary vein (33) can be seen. The descending thoracic aorta (29) is clearly visible on both these images posterior to the left main pulmonary artery.

Between the ascending aorta (28) and bifurcation of trachea (carina) is the 'aortopulmonary window' which contains mediastinal lymph nodes. Any diseased lymph nodes may also be seen inferior to the carina and visualisation of these is made easier by the presence of mediastinal fat. The SVC (30) can be seen adjacent to the ascending aorta (28). It is much smaller than the aorta since it only contains blood from tissue superior to the heart.

Although veins are composed of the same three layers as arteries, the walls are much thinner, lack the internal elastic membranes and are subject to reduced internal pressures. As a consequence, veins can be deformed or compressed by neighbouring structures. In these images this is illustrated by the SVC's flattened borders adjacent to the ascending aorta and right main pulmonary artery. This is also evident throughout the body.

Figure 3.4.12 shows the bifurcation of the main pulmonary trunk (34) into the right and left main pulmonary arteries (32). Slightly inferiorly in Figure 3.4.13 the pulmonary veins (33) exit the hilum. The azygos vein (31) is seen running alongside the oesophagus. Care must be taken not to mistake a bulky azygos vein for oesophageal borders.

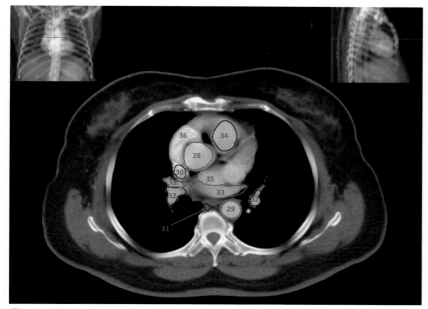

Figure 3.4.14

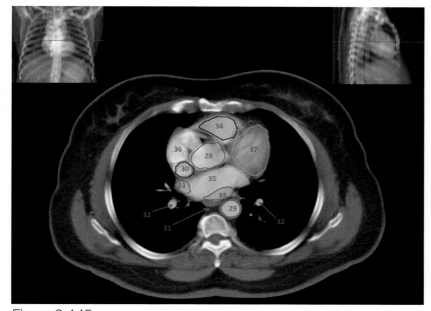

Figure 3.4.15

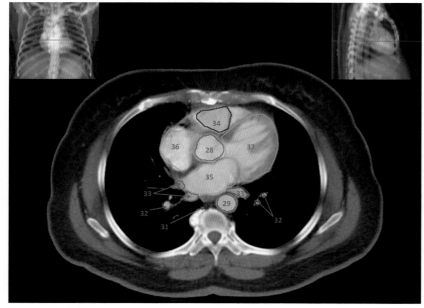

Figure 3.4.16

Figure 3.4.14 (at about T7/8) is inferior to the lung hilar regions although branches of the pulmonary veins (33) and arteries (32) can still be seen. Using these soft tissue window settings it is quite difficult to see the inferior lobar bronchi but they lie slightly medial to each pulmonary vein.

Adjacent and slightly to the left of the spine runs the descending aorta (29), characteristically round in cross-section and apparent on all sections below T4. On the opposite side of the vertebral column runs the azygos vein (31) immediately posterior to the oesophagus. This is visible until its origin close to the diaphragm at the junction of the right ascending lumbar and subcostal veins.

Figure 3.4.15 cuts through the anterior mediastinum and the superior sections of the heart can be seen. The root of the ascending aorta (28) is central to the origin of the pulmonary trunk (34) and the SVC (30). The right atrium (36) is visible surrounded by the SVC (30), root of aorta (28) and pulmonary trunk (34). The left atrium (35) is the most posterior of the chambers, lying between the root of ascending aorta (28) and the descending aorta (29).

Forming the left border of the heart is the left ventricle (37). Of note are the striated patterns caused by the rough 'trabeculae carneae' of the thick muscle. The stranded appearances in Figure 3.4.16 are caused by the papillary muscles within the heart.

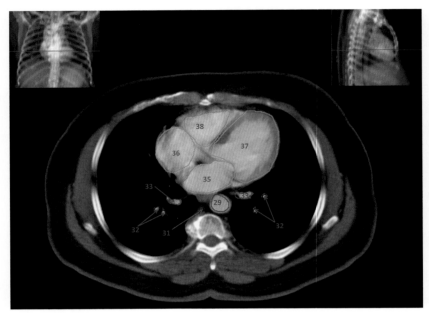

Figure 3.4.17

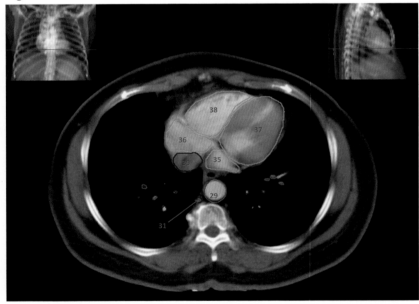

Figure 3.4.18

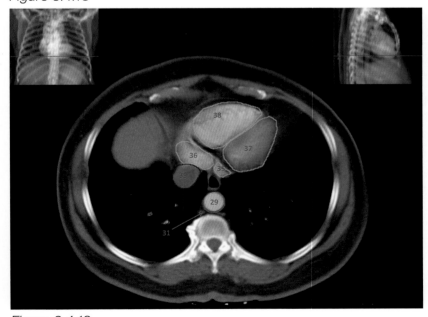

Figure 3.4.19

Figure 3.4.17 clearly shows cardiac orientation within the mediastinum as well as all four chambers. The heart is roughly conical and sits slightly obliquely within the mediastinum. Its 'apex' is formed by the left ventricle (37) and points anteriorly, inferiorly and to the left. Opposite to the apex is the flattened 'base' of the heart which is formed by the right (36) and left (35) atria.

The anterior surface is formed by the right ventricle (38) and anterior aspect of the left ventricle (37) and sits immediately posterior to the sternum. The space between the sternum and anterior border of the heart is known as the anterior mediastinum, while the space behind the heart is known as the posterior mediastinum. Within the posterior mediastinum can be seen the descending aorta (29), azygos vein (31) and oesophagus.

The right border is made up of the walls of the right (36) and left (35) atria. The left border comprising the walls of the left ventricle (37) and atrium (35) is sometimes referred to as the pulmonary border.

Notice on these images how the thickness of the chamber walls varies, corresponding to the workload and functionality of each chamber. By far the thickest wall belongs to the left ventricle (37). Separating the two ventricles is the intraventricular septum. This normally demonstrates a slight convexity towards the right due to the greater mass and internal ventricular pressure of the left ventricle.

Demarcation of the relatively small and tortuous coronary arteries can be difficult due to heart movement and the relatively thick slices used in radiotherapy CT. Figure 3.4.20 is a diagnostic cardiac gated image of the heart and demonstrates arterial vascular anatomy of the heart. Although this level of clarity will not be visible on many planning techniques, this image will help the reader understand the vascular morphology of the heart and anterior mediastinum. This is particularly relevant when planning breast fields. The left coronary artery bifurcates into the left circumflex and left anterior descending arteries. The location of the latter (LAD) is of most significance when considering left breast radiotherapy as it can often be included in the treatment fields, together with the internal thoracic arteries and veins (mammary vessels). The LAD runs over the left ventricle and anterior to the intraventricular septum on the surface of the heart. Both pairs of the internal thoracic vessels descend either side and anterior to the heart, directly posterior to the costal cartilages fixed to the sternum.

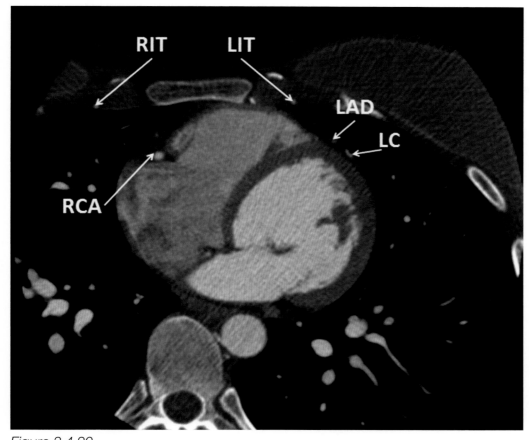

Figure 3.4.20

3.5 Lymphatic System

The thorax is the site of the culmination of lymphatic drainage and contains the major lymphatic vessels. Lymph from below the diaphragm rises through the thoracic duct. As it does so, it collects lymph from the left hand side of the thorax. Lymph from the left hand side of the head and neck also empties into the upper part of the thoracic duct. The thoracic duct, although relatively small, can occasionally be seen on CT and is located between the aorta and the azygos vein. Lymph from the right hand side of the body above the diaphragm drains into a different vessel known as the right lymphatic duct. Both lymph vessels return the collected fluid to the circulatory system via the subclavian veins just before they are joined by the jugular veins.

Rouvière's description of nodal distribution and classification is well recognised and commonplace in many texts. It classifies thoracic nodes into parietal or visceral. Parietal nodes drain structures of the chest wall and are found external to the pleura. These include the internal mammary, intercostal, pericardial and diaphragmatic groups. These can be seen in Figure 3.5.1. Visceral nodes are contained within the mediastinum or hila of the lungs. These include the hilar, carinal, paratracheal, and tracheobronchial. These can be seen in Figure 3.5.2.

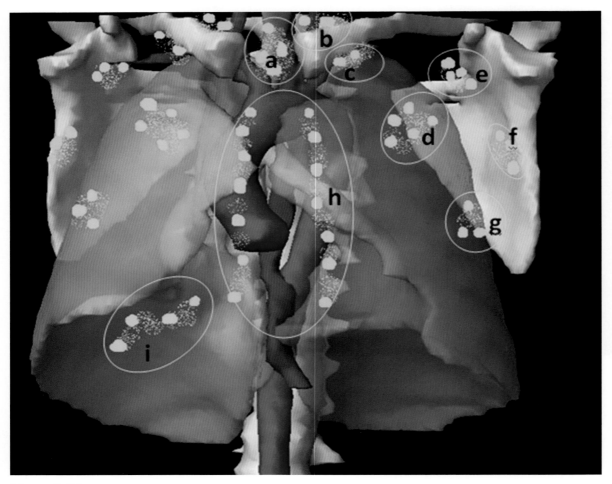

Figure 3.5.1

Parietal Nodes
a) Anterior cervical
b) Supraclavicular
c) Subclavicular
d) Interpectoral (Rotter's)
e) Deep axillary
f) Superficial axillary
g) Paramammary
h) Parasternal/Internal mammary
i) Infraphrenic

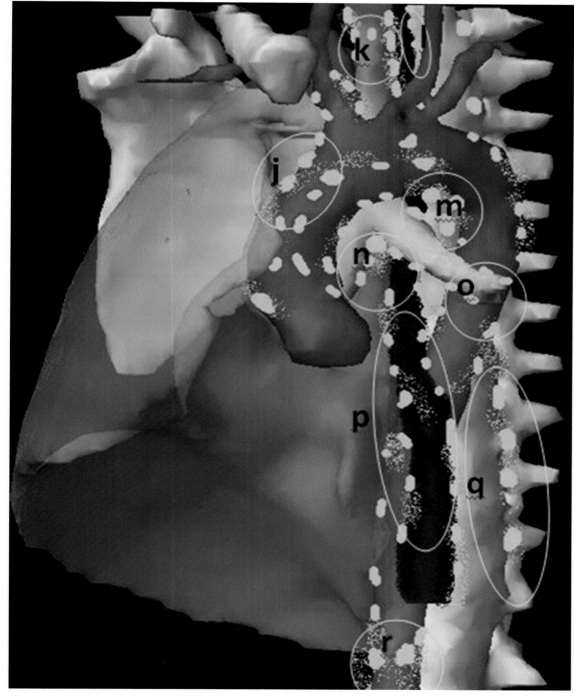

Figure 3.5.2

Visceral Nodes

j) Para-aortic

k) Paratracheal

l) Upper para-oesophageal

m) Aorticopulmonary

n) Sub-carinal

o) Hilar lymph

p) Mid para-oesophageal

q) Para-vertebral

r) Retrocrural

With specific reference to lung cancer TNM staging, more complex maps of nodal stations using systematic nodal nomenclature are used to accurately gauge sentinel node location and lymph drainage routes. These nodal maps enable understanding of the disease process and offer a valuable prognostic indicator. Following a study of resected histopathological specimens in relation to the bronchial tree in 100 patients, Naruke (1967) provided the first well recognised map of thoracic nodes for use in TNM staging. Since then, however, a variety of other nodal maps have been developed, including that of the American Thoracic Society (1983), and Mountain-Dresler (1997). As a consequence, there has been an absence of a universally accepted map of thoracic nodal stations, leading to varied observational and surgical differences. The International Association for the Study of Lung Cancer (IASLC) has now developed a combined system as depicted in Figure 3.5.3. This will hopefully provide a universally recognised system to help standardise TNM staging in lung cancer. As well as describing the adjacent anatomical nodal nomenclature, this map also divides the nodal stations into localised zones; Supraclavicular, Upper, AP, Subcarinal, Lower, Hilar, Interlobar and Peripheral zones. It is important to note that the numbers used in Figure 3.5.3 refer to the accepted labels for these nodes arising from this mapping system. Thus they do not match the numbers used elsewhere in this text.

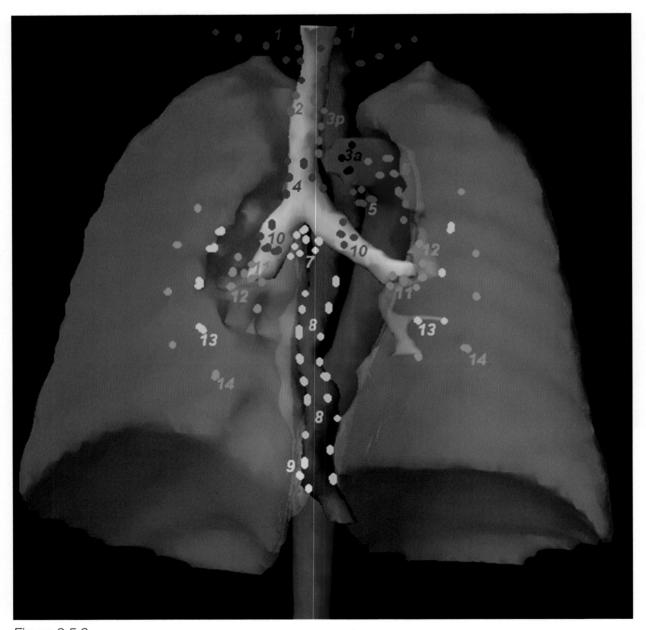

Figure 3.5.3

Figure 3.5.3

1. Lower Cervical, supraclavicular and sternal notch – Supraclavicular zone
2. Upper Paratracheal – Upper zone
3. 3a – Prevascular – Upper zone
3. 3p – Retrotracheal – Upper zone
4. Lower Paratracheal – Upper zone
5. Subaortic – AP zone
6. Para-aortic – AP zone
7. Subcarinal – Subcarinal zone
8. Para-oesophageal – Lower zone
9. Pulmonary ligament – Lower zone
10. Hilar – Hilar zone
11. Interlobar – Interlobar zone
12. Lobar – Peripheral zone
13. Segmental – Peripheral zone
14. Subsegmental – Peripheral zone

Assessment of thoracic lymph nodes using CT provides invaluable inform-ation relating to location, size and characterisation. CT usually demon-strates a normal lymph node as a rounded or oval soft tissue mass (45HU). Surrounding fat planes and occasional small deposits of adipose tissue at the hilum enable localisation of nodal groups relatively easily using thin-slice CT. However, paucity of mediastinal fat or coalescence of enlarged nodes can hinder accurate assessment of lymph node or disease borders. In this case IV contrast agents can help to demonstrate adjacent vessel borders. It is important to scroll through adjacent slices in non-IV contrast studies to distinguish between nodal enlargement and vasculature. This potential confusion often necessitates the use of IV contrast agent for many staging CT examinations in the thorax.

The size of normal lymph nodes can vary throughout the thorax from ≤7mm (such as hilar) to 11mm (such as sub-carinal) when measured across the short axis. Lymph node size alone should not be used as a predictor of significant disease. It is quite possible in pathologies such as bronchogenic carcinoma to demonstrate normal sized lymph nodes on CT, and conversely it is also possible to discover enlarged lymph nodes with no evidence of significant disease. CT appearance is also an important consideration when assessing lymphadenopathy. There may be enlargement of isolated nodes, coalescence of groups of adjacent nodes or there may also be diffuse infiltration from diseased nodes into adjacent mediastinal adipose tissues, reducing the normal fat/soft tissue differential.

CT attenuation within the lymph node is of value too, and while diseased thoracic nodes may demonstrate normal soft tissue patterns on CT, necrotic lymph nodes may be of low attenuation (usually metastases from lung carcinoma, seminoma or lymphoma). There are also disease processes that cause calcification to be deposited in thoracic lymph nodes (such as infectious granulomatous diseases, TB and Hodgkin's disease post treatment). Some nodes can also increase in CT attenuation following IV contrast (usually metastases).

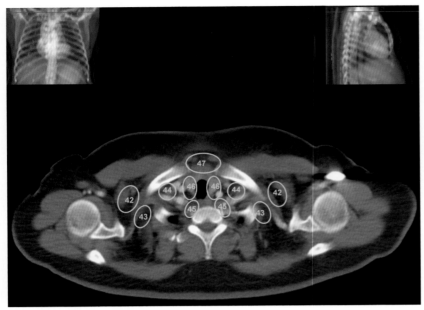

Figure 3.5.4

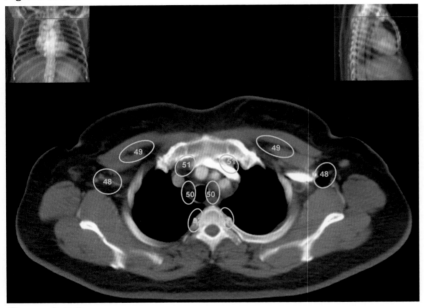

Figure 3.5.5

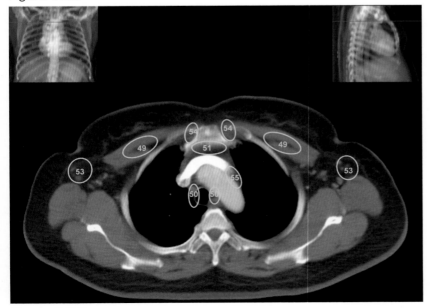

Figure 3.5.6

Figure 3.5.4 shows the lymph node groups visible at the thoracic outlet. Some of the most commonly irradiated nodes in radiotherapy are the supraclavicular (42), renowned as common routes of spread for head and neck and breast tumours. On the other side of the clavicles can be seen the infraclavicular (43) nodes. The jugular chain (44) lies among the larger blood vessels in this region. The para-oesophageal (45) and paratracheal (46) chains of nodes run vertically along their related structures. The most inferior of the anterior cervical nodes (47) lie in the suprasternal notch.

In Figure 3.5.5 (at about the level of T2), the paratracheal and para-oesophageal nodes (50) are closely entwined. In this region, the deep axillary lymph nodes (48) can also be seen. Another common site for lymph node involvement from breast tumours, it can be seen that there is plenty of room for growth in the fatty spaces of the axilla. Anterior and medial to these are the interpectoral nodes (49). These are also known as 'Rotter's nodes'. The anterior mediastinal nodes (51) lie just posterior to the sternum.

Figure 3.5.6 is taken at the level of the aortic arch and the most superior of the para-aortic nodes (55) lie just next to the arch itself. The paratracheal and para-oesophageal (50) chains are still closely connected. The anterior mediastinal nodes (51) have now been joined by the parasternal (54) or 'internal mammary chain'. This is another potential route of spread for breast tumours.

Rotter's nodes (49) maintain their position between the pectoralis muscles while the superficial axillary nodes (53) are lateral.

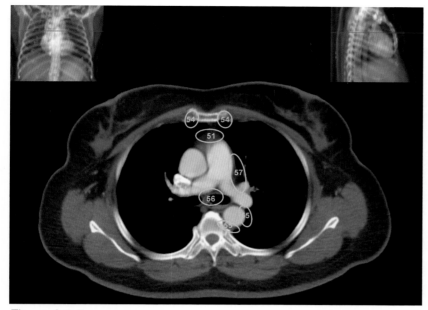

Figure 3.5.7

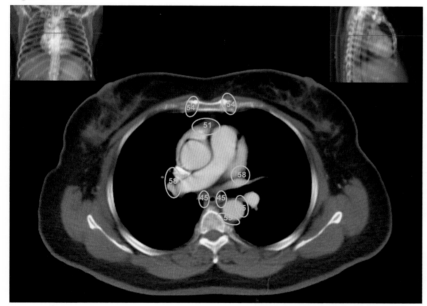

Figure 3.5.8

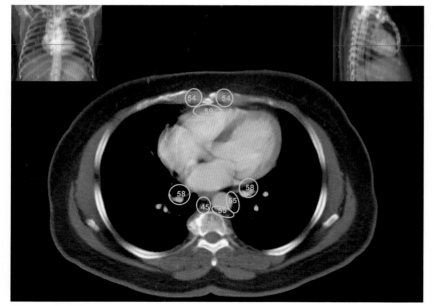

Figure 3.5.9

Figure 3.5.7 is at the level of the bifurcation of the trachea (about T6) and the two main bronchi can be seen easily. Between the two bronchi lie the subcarinal nodes (56). The internal mammary chain (54) and anterior mediastinal (51) nodes enclose the sternum. Lymph nodes in the aorticopulmonary window (57) lie along the left pulmonary artery and the para-aortic nodes (55) accompany the descending thoracic aorta.

At the slightly lower level of Figure 3.5.8, many of the same nodes are still present in similar positions. The internal mammary chain (54), anterior mediastinal (51) and para-aortic nodes (55) have not changed much. This level features the hilum of the lungs, however, and the bronchopulmonary, or 'hilar' nodes (58) have appeared. The para-oesophageal chain (45) continues, now without its accompanying paratracheal nodes.

Figure 3.5.9 again features many of these node groups at a lower level. The hilar (58), para-oesophageal (45), para-aortic (55) and parasternal (54) are all still present. The anterior mediastinal nodes have been replaced by the precardial nodes (59). Below this level the parasternal (internal mammary chain) connects to the diaphragmatic nodes that are situated just behind the xiphoid process.

3.6 Full Thoracic CT

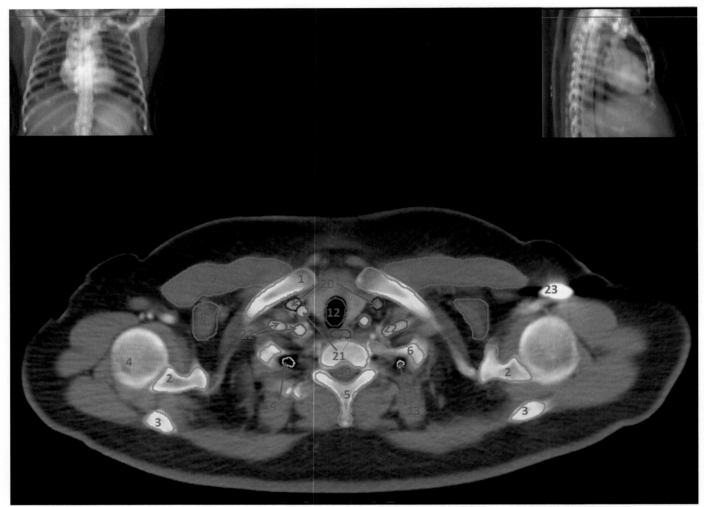

Figure 3.6.1

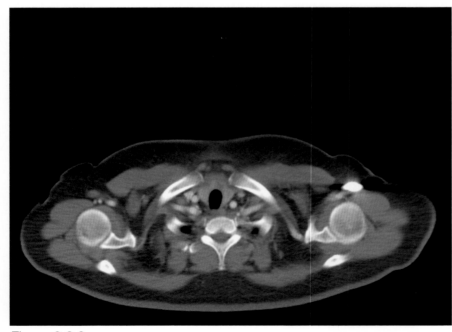

1. Clavicle
2. Scapula
3. Spine of Scapula
4. Head of Humerus
5. Thoracic Vertebra
6. Rib
7. Pectoralis Major Muscle
8. Pectoralis Minor Muscle
11. Oesophagus
12. Trachea
13. Upper Lobe of Left Lung
14. Upper Lobe of Right Lung
20. Jugular Vein
21. Carotid Artery
22. Subclavian Artery
23. Subclavian Vein

Figure 3.6.2

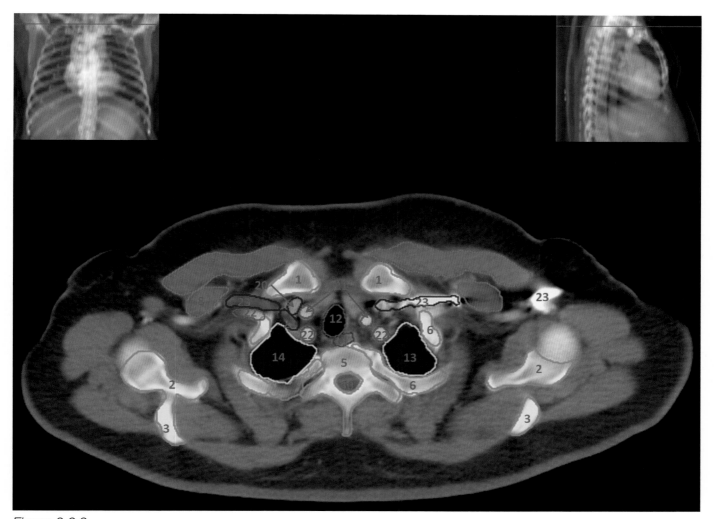

Figure 3.6.3

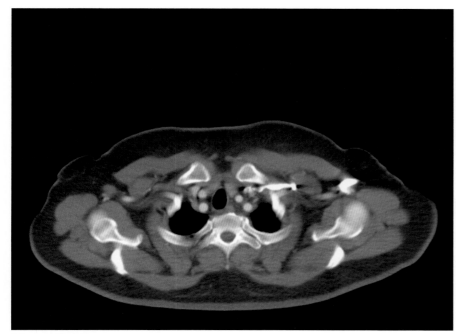

Figure 3.6.4

1. Clavicle
2. Scapula
3. Spine of Scapula
5. Thoracic Vertebra
6. Rib
7. Pectoralis Major Muscle
8. Pectoralis Minor Muscle
11. Oesophagus
12. Trachea
13. Upper Lobe of Left Lung
14. Upper Lobe of Right Lung
20. Jugular Vein
21. Carotid Artery
22. Subclavian Artery
23. Subclavian Vein
40. Spinal Cord

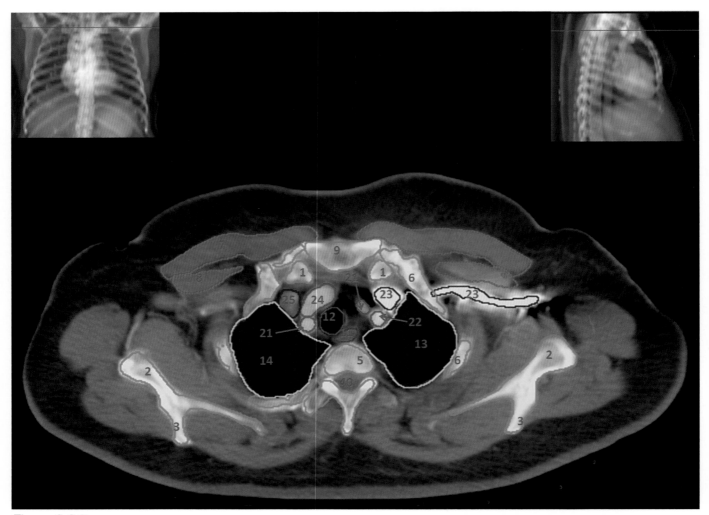

Figure 3.6.5

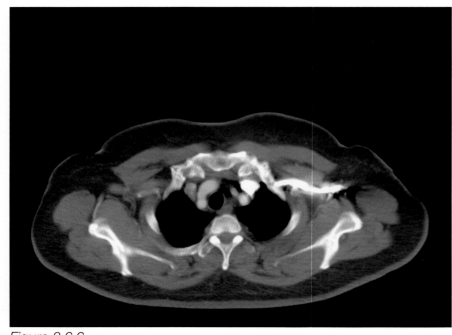

Figure 3.6.6

1. Clavicle
2. Scapula
3. Spine of Scapula
5. Thoracic Vertebra
6. Rib
7. Pectoralis Major Muscle
8. Pectoralis Minor Muscle
9. Sternum
11. Oesophagus
12. Trachea
13. Upper Lobe of Left Lung
14. Upper Lobe of Right Lung
21. Carotid Artery
22. Subclavian Artery
23. Subclavian Vein
24. Brachiocephalic Artery
25. Right Brachiocephalic Vein
40. Spinal Cord

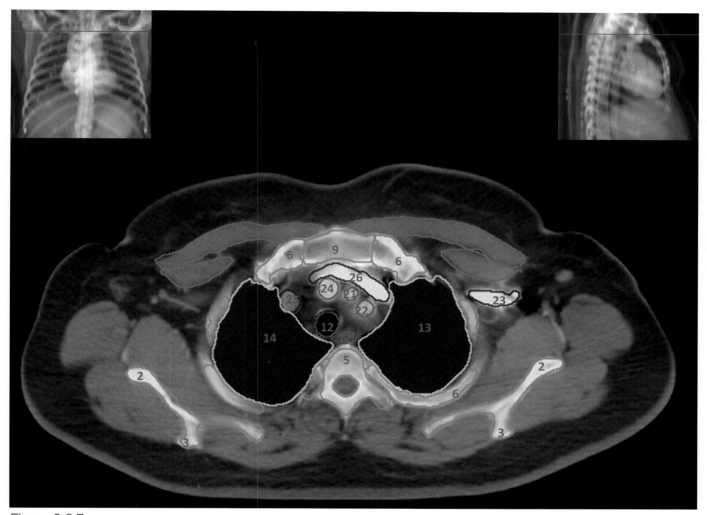

Figure 3.6.7

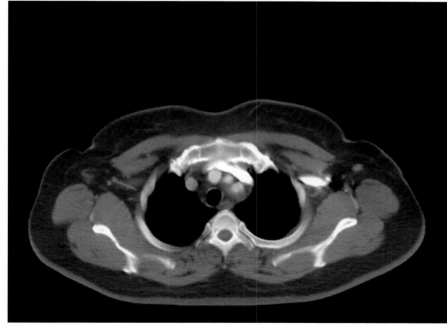

Figure 3.6.8

2. Scapula
3. Spine of Scapula
5. Thoracic Vertebra
6. Rib
7. Pectoralis Major Muscle
8. Pectoralis Minor Muscle
9. Sternum
11. Oesophagus
12. Trachea
13. Upper Lobe of Left Lung
14. Upper Lobe of Right Lung
21. Carotid Artery
22. Subclavian Artery
23. Subclavian Vein
24. Brachiocephalic Artery
25. Right Brachiocephalic Vein
26. Left Brachiocephalic Vein
40. Spinal Cord

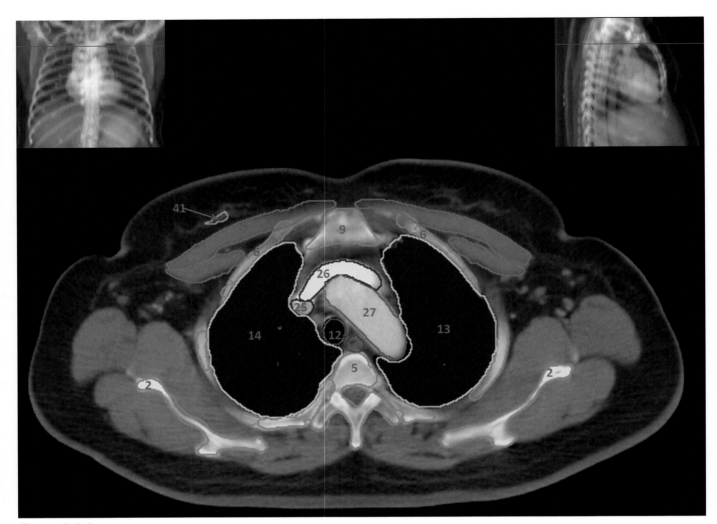

Figure 3.6.9

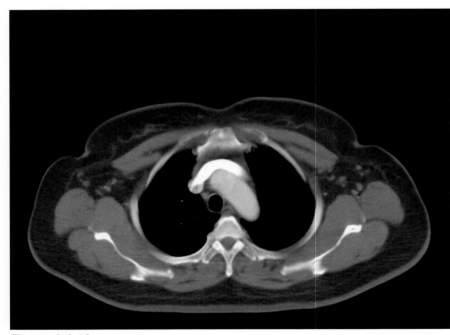

Figure 3.6.10

2. Scapula
5. Thoracic Vertebra
6. Rib
7. Pectoralis Major Muscle
8. Pectoralis Minor Muscle
9. Sternum
11. Oesophagus
12. Trachea
13. Upper Lobe of Left Lung
14. Upper Lobe of Right Lung
25. Right Brachiocephalic Vein
26. Left Brachiocephalic Vein
27. Arch of Aorta
40. Spinal Cord
41. Glandular Tissue of Breast

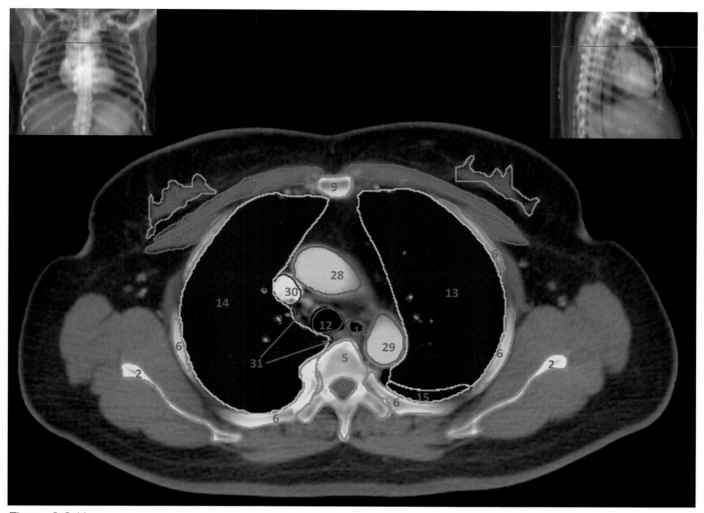

Figure 3.6.11

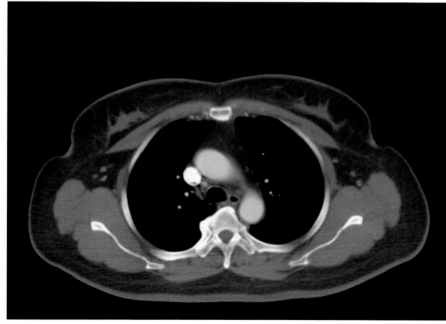

Figure 3.6.12

2. Scapula
5. Thoracic Vertebra
6. Rib
7. Pectoralis Major Muscle
8. Pectoralis Minor Muscle
9. Sternum
11. Oesophagus
12. Trachea
13. Upper Lobe of Left Lung
14. Upper Lobe of Right Lung
15. Lower Lobe of Left Lung
28. Ascending Thoracic Aorta
29. Descending Thoracic Aorta
30. Superior Vena Cava
31. Azygos Vein
40. Spinal Cord
41. Glandular Tissue of Breast

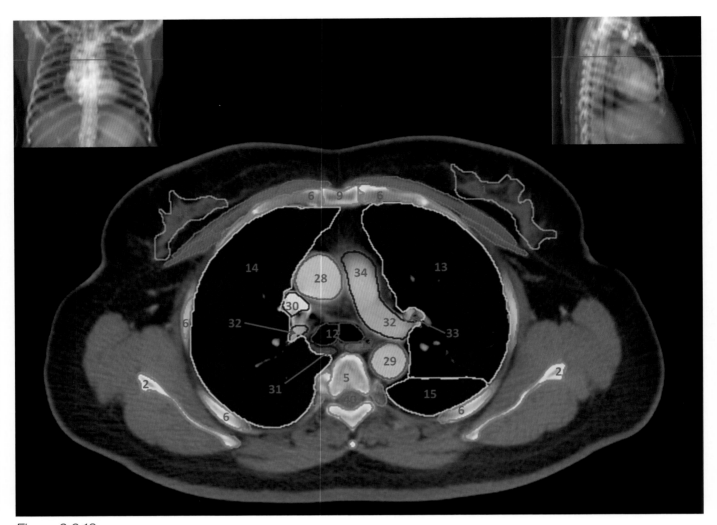

Figure 3.6.13

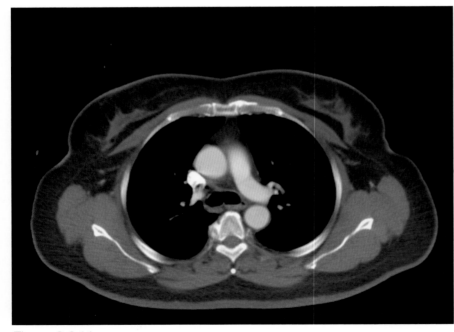

Figure 3.6.14

2. Scapula
5. Thoracic Vertebra
6. Rib
7. Pectoralis Major Muscle
8. Pectoralis Minor Muscle
9. Sternum
11. Oesophagus
12. Bifurcation of Trachea
13. Upper Lobe of Left Lung
14. Upper Lobe of Right Lung
15. Lower Lobe of Left Lung
28. Ascending Thoracic Aorta
29. Descending Thoracic Aorta
30. Superior Vena Cava
31. Azygos Vein
32. Pulmonary Artery
33. Pulmonary Vein
34. Pulmonary Trunk
40. Spinal Cord
41. Glandular Tissue of Breast

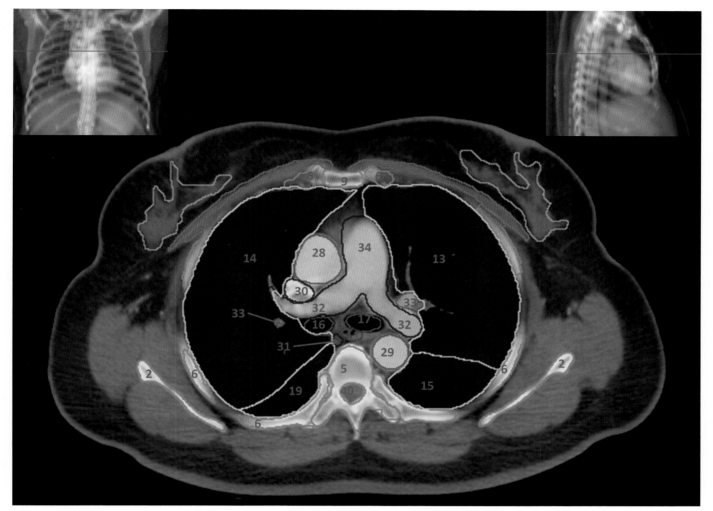

Figure 3.6.15

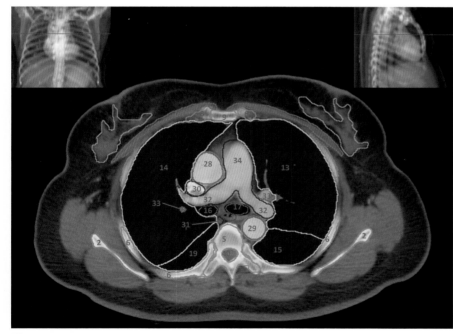

Figure 3.6.16

2. Scapula
5. Thoracic Vertebra
6. Rib
7. Pectoralis Major Muscle
8. Pectoralis Minor Muscle
9. Sternum
11. Oesophagus
13. Upper Lobe of Left Lung
14. Upper Lobe of Right Lung
15. Lower Lobe of Left Lung
16. Right Main Bronchus
17. Left Main Bronchus
19. Lower Lobe of Right Lung
28. Ascending Thoracic Aorta
29. Descending Thoracic Aorta
30. Superior Vena Cava
31. Azygos Vein
32. Pulmonary Artery
33. Pulmonary Vein
34. Pulmonary Trunk
40. Spinal Cord
41. Glandular Tissue of Breast

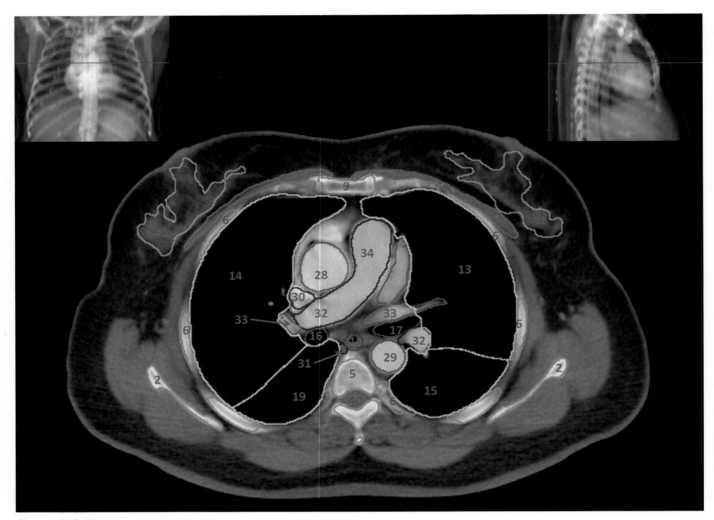

Figure 3.6.17

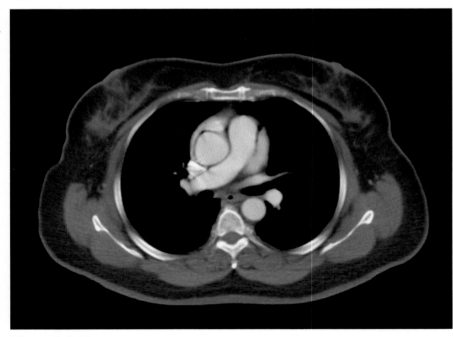

Figure 3.6.18

2. Scapula
5. Thoracic Vertebra
6. Rib
7. Pectoralis Major Muscle
9. Sternum
11. Oesophagus
13. Upper Lobe of Left Lung
14. Upper Lobe of Right Lung
15. Lower Lobe of Left Lung
16. Right Main Bronchus
17. Left Main Bronchus
19. Lower Lobe of Right Lung
28. Ascending Thoracic Aorta
29. Descending Thoracic Aorta
30. Superior Vena Cava
31. Azygos Vein
32. Pulmonary Artery
33. Pulmonary Vein
34. Pulmonary Trunk
40. Spinal Cord
41. Glandular Tissue of Breast

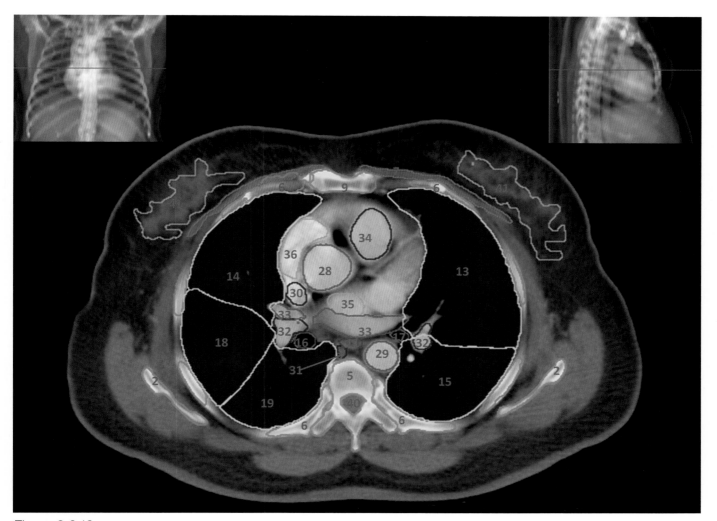

Figure 3.6.19

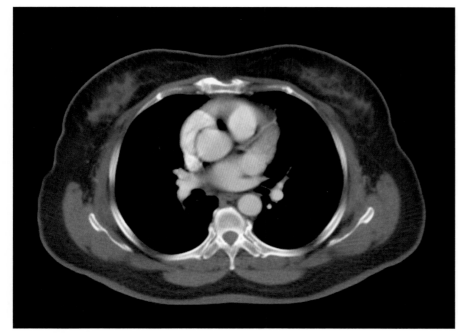

Figure 3.6.20

2. Scapula
5. Thoracic Vertebra
6. Rib
7. Pectoralis Major Muscle
9. Sternum
11. Oesophagus
13. Upper Lobe of Left Lung
14. Upper Lobe of Right Lung
15. Lower Lobe of Left Lung
16. Right Main Bronchus
17. Left Main Bronchus
18. Middle Lobe of Right Lung
19. Lower Lobe of Right Lung
28. Ascending Thoracic Aorta
29. Descending Thoracic Aorta
30. Superior Vena Cava
31. Azygos Vein
32. Pulmonary Artery
33. Pulmonary Vein
34. Pulmonary Trunk
35. Left Atrium
36. Right Atrium
40. Spinal Cord
41. Glandular Tissue of Breast

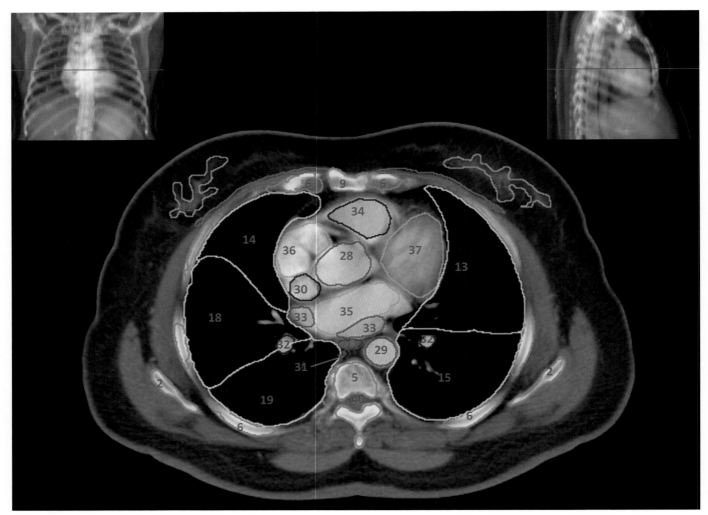

Figure 3.6.21

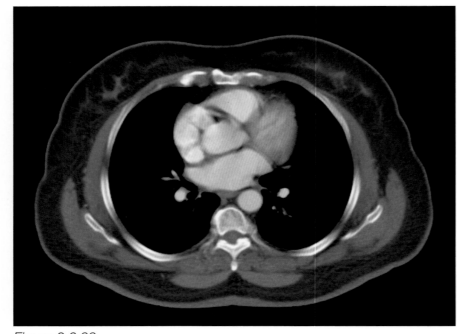

Figure 3.6.22

2. Scapula
5. Thoracic Vertebra
6. Rib
7. Pectoralis Major Muscle
9. Sternum
11. Oesophagus
13. Upper Lobe of Left Lung
14. Upper Lobe of Right Lung
15. Lower Lobe of Left Lung
18. Middle Lobe of Right Lung
19. Lower Lobe of Right Lung
28. Ascending Thoracic Aorta
29. Descending Thoracic Aorta
30. Superior Vena Cava
31. Azygos Vein
32. Pulmonary Artery
33. Pulmonary Vein
34. Pulmonary Trunk
35. Left Atrium
36. Right Atrium
37. Left Ventricle
40. Spinal Cord
41. Glandular Tissue of Breast

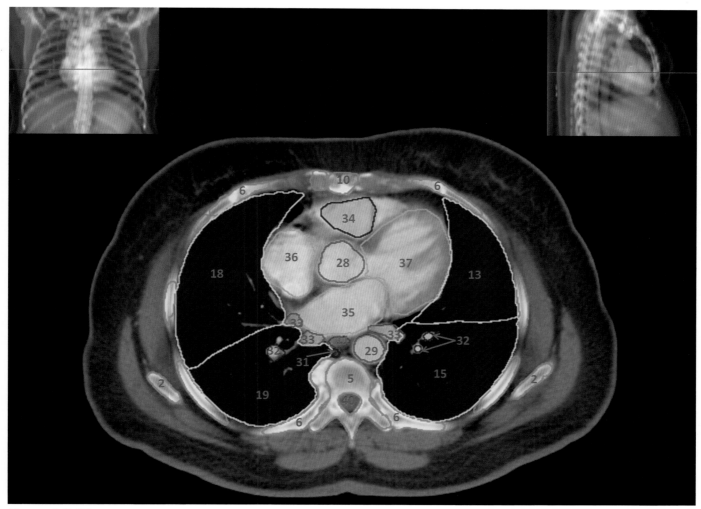

Figure 3.6.23

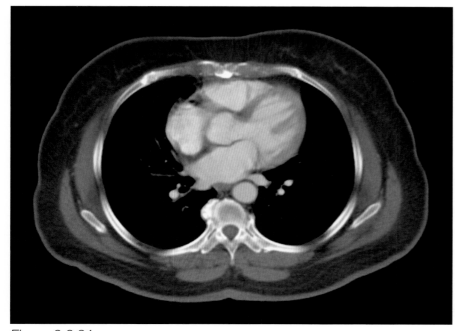

Figure 3.6.24

2. Scapula
5. Thoracic Vertebra
6. Rib
10. Xiphoid Process
11. Oesophagus
13. Upper Lobe of Left Lung
15. Lower Lobe of Left Lung
18. Middle Lobe of Right Lung
19. Lower Lobe of Right Lung
28. Ascending Thoracic Aorta
29. Descending Thoracic Aorta
31. Azygos Vein
32. Pulmonary Artery
33. Pulmonary Vein
34. Pulmonary Trunk
35. Left Atrium
36. Right Atrium
37. Left Ventricle
40. Spinal Cord

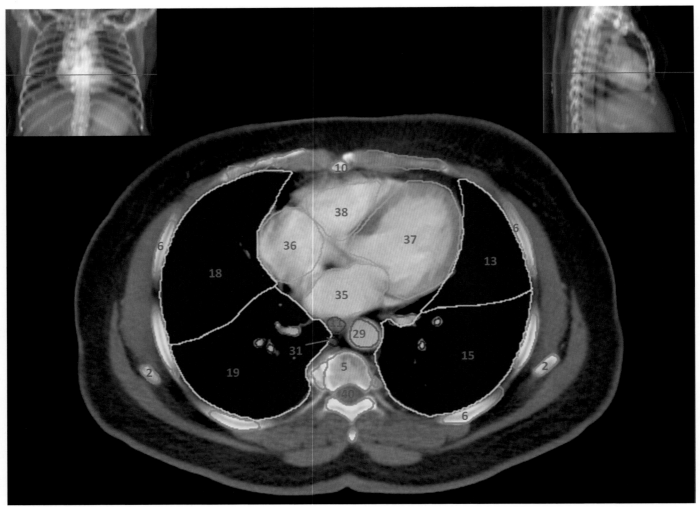

Figure 3.6.25

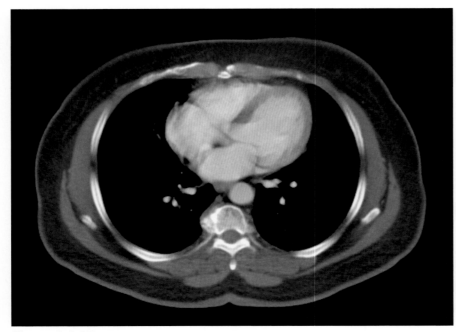

Figure 3.6.26

2. Scapula
5. Thoracic Vertebra
6. Rib
10. Xiphoid Process
11. Oesophagus
13. Upper Lobe of Left Lung
15. Lower Lobe of Left Lung
18. Middle Lobe of Right Lung
19. Lower Lobe of Right Lung
29. Descending Thoracic Aorta
31. Azygos Vein
35. Left Atrium
36. Right Atrium
37. Left Ventricle
38. Right Ventricle
40. Spinal Cord

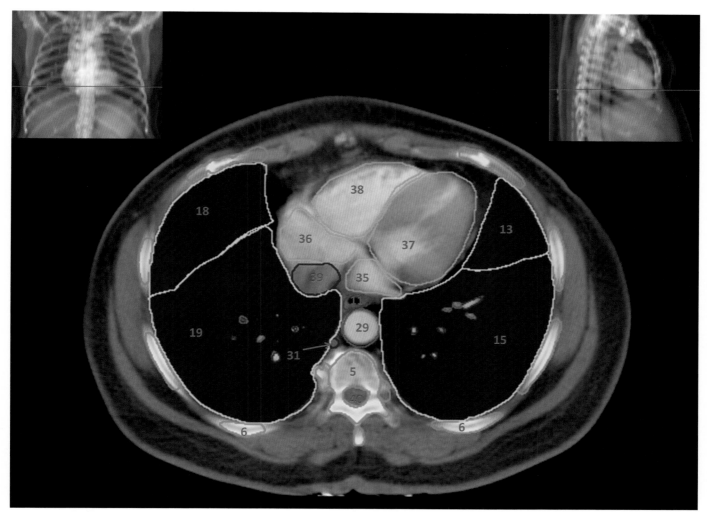

Figure 3.6.27

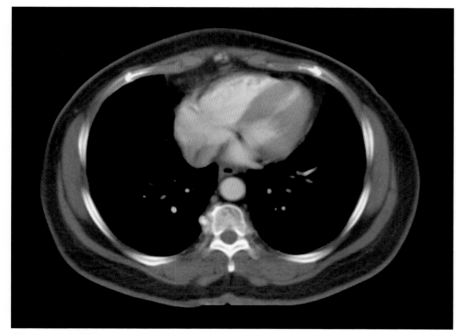

Figure 3.6.28

5. Thoracic Vertebra
6. Rib
11. Oesophagus
13. Upper Lobe of Left Lung
15. Lower Lobe of Left Lung
18. Middle Lobe of Right Lung
19. Lower Lobe of Right Lung
29. Descending Thoracic Aorta
31. Azygos Vein
35. Left Atrium
36. Right Atrium
37. Left Ventricle
38. Right Ventricle
39. Inferior Vena Cava
40. Spinal Cord

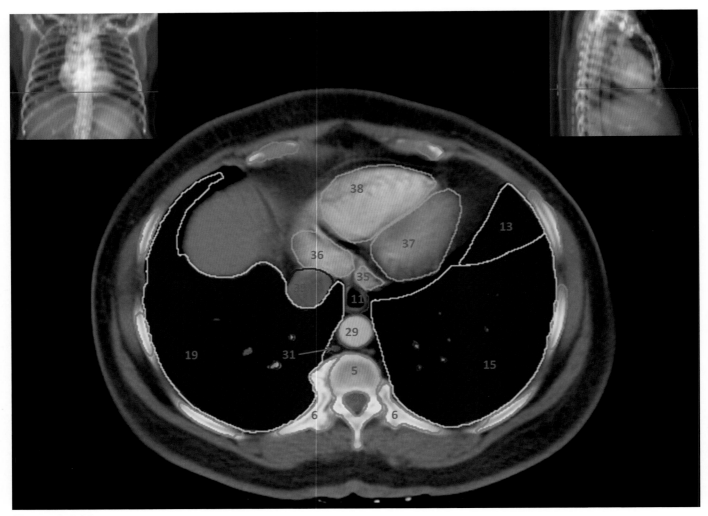

Figure 3.6.29

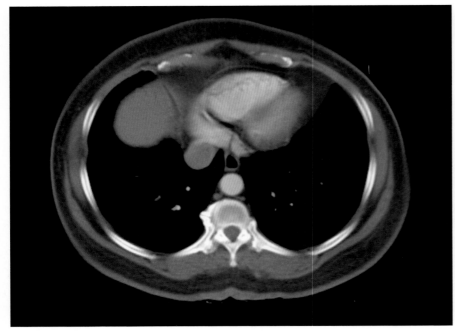

Figure 3.6.30

5. Thoracic Vertebra
6. Rib
11. Oesophagus
13. Upper Lobe of Left Lung
15. Lower Lobe of Left Lung
19. Lower Lobe of Right Lung
29. Descending Thoracic Aorta
31. Azygos Vein
35. Left Atrium
36. Right Atrium
37. Left Ventricle
38. Right Ventricle
39. Inferior Vena Cava
40. Spinal Cord

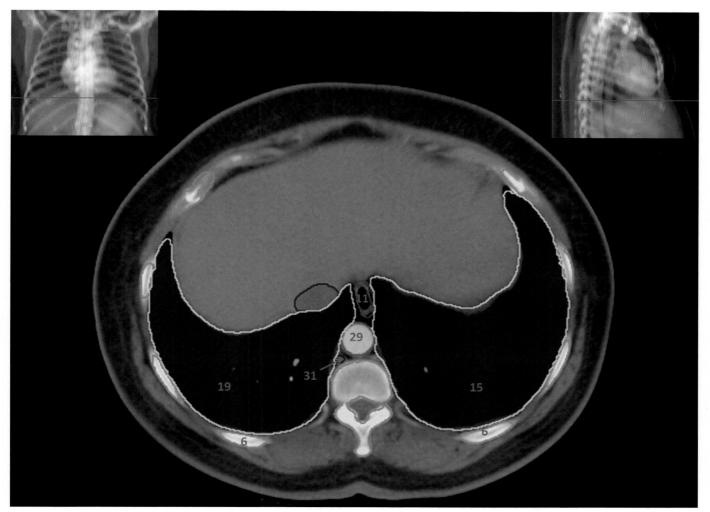

Figure 3.6.31

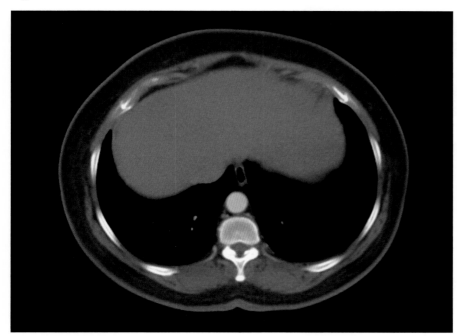

Figure 3.6.32

6. Rib
11. Oesophagus
15. Lower Lobe of Left Lung
19. Lower Lobe of Right Lung
29. Descending Thoracic Aorta
31. Azygos Vein
39. Inferior Vena Cava
40. Spinal Cord

3.7 Common Thoracic Tumour Pathology CT Appearance

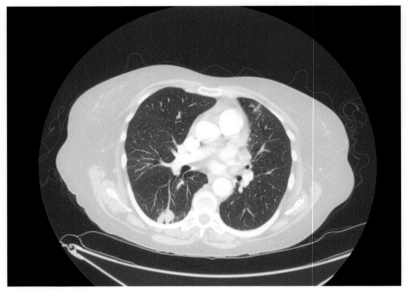

Figure 3.7.1

Small cell lung

The lung window settings used in Figure 3.7.1 highlight a small cell lung tumour in the posterior aspect of the right lung. This tumour is in the right lower lobe; the dark band representing the fissure between lower and middle lobe is clearly visible.

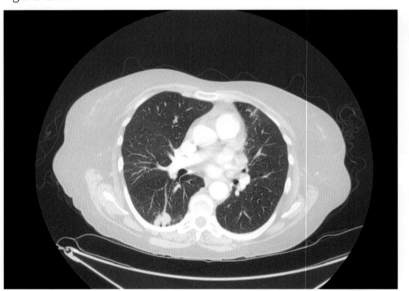

Figure 3.7.2

Non small cell

Bronchogenic carcinomas arise from the tissues of the bronchial tree. Figure 3.7.2 depicts a large mass in the left lung that is encasing the pulmonary trunk and left pulmonary artery. Posteriorly the lung can be seen to be separated from the chest wall when compared to the right lung, indicating pleural effusion.

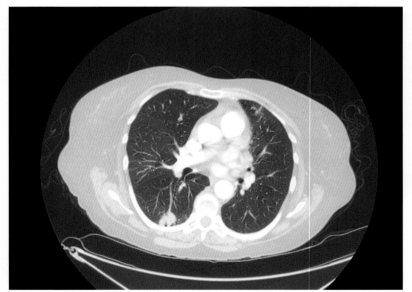

Figure 3.7.3

Mesothelioma

Figure 3.7.3 demonstrates a pleural based thickening encasing the whole of the right lung. There is also an associated large pleural effusion, readily identifiable by the uniform hypodense appearance of the pleural fluid. There are also flecks of calcification present within the pleura, consistent with asbestos exposure. The right thoracic cavity has a smaller volume than the left as the pleura has contracted. These are typical appearances consistent with a mesothelioma.

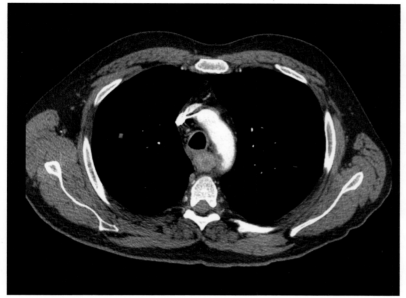

Figure 3.7.4

Mid oesophagus

Although the oesophagus can be difficult to spot when the lumen is collapsed or occluded, the circular mass posterior and left of the trachea in Figure 3.7.4 is clearly visible. An oesophageal wall thickness greater than 5mm is abnormal and, in this image, a thick circumferential growth is visible. The potential for mediastinal or tracheal involvement can be appreciated. IV contrast in the posterior arch of aorta shows how dangerous this can be.

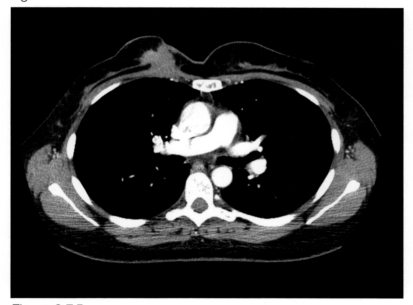

Figure 3.7.5

Lower oesophagus

The fluid in the stomach in Figure 3.7.5 highlights the thickened gastro-oesophageal junction. The mass anterior to the crura suggests a tumour of the lower third oesophagus. Adenocarcinoma is commonly associated with tumours of the lower third of the oesophagus.

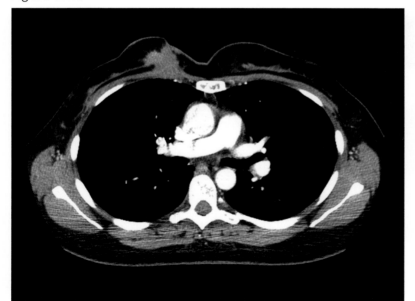

Figure 3.7.6

Breast

Figure 3.7.6 illustrates a right sided breast tumour that has extended anteriorly to involve the subcutaneous tissue. It has also spread posteriorly to invade the pectoralis muscle group of the chest wall. The mass is spiculated and thin strands of tumour tissue extend into the surrounding fatty tissues. The effect of this growth on the patient contour is particularly evident in this image.

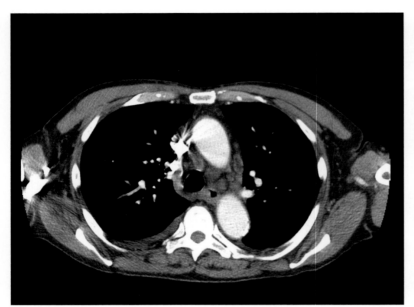

Figure 3.7.7

Mediastinal nodes

Multiple mediastinal nodes can be identified in Figure 3.7.7. When comparing this image with the normal anatomy at this level in Figure 3.6.12 the paratracheal, para-oesophageal and para-aortic nodes are clearly enlarged. Anteriorly to the ascending aorta can be seen the anterior mediastinal nodes.

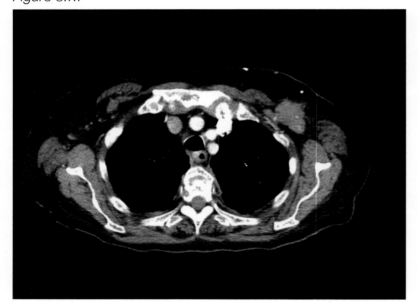

Figure 3.7.8

Axillary nodes

The enlarged axillary node is clearly visible on the left of Figure 3.7.8. This patient has left sided breast carcinoma.

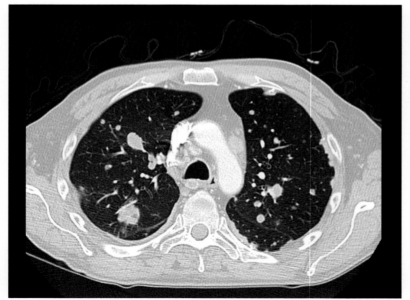

Figure 3.7.9

Lung metastases

The lung window settings in Figure 3.7.9 highlight the multiple pulmonary metastases scattered throughout both lungs. Although not always necessary for peripheral lesions, the use of IV contrast can help to distinguish between metastatic deposits and the higher attenuating pulmonary vessels. These can also be identified by tracking on adjacent images.

3.8 Self-Test Questions: Thorax

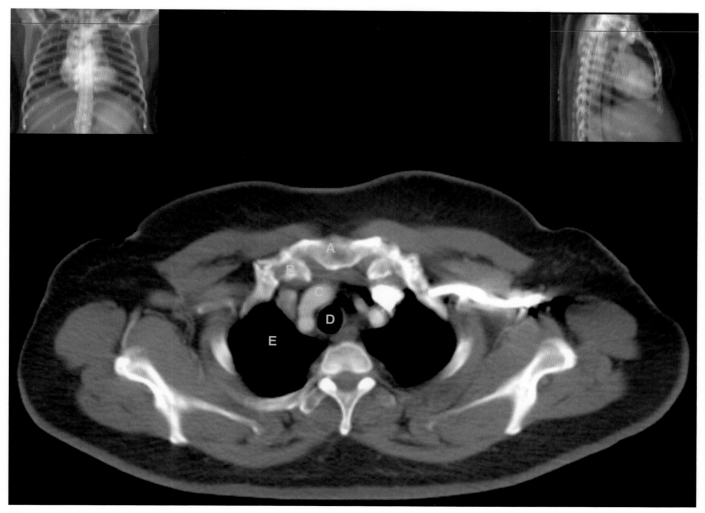

Figure 3.8.1

A

B

C

D

E

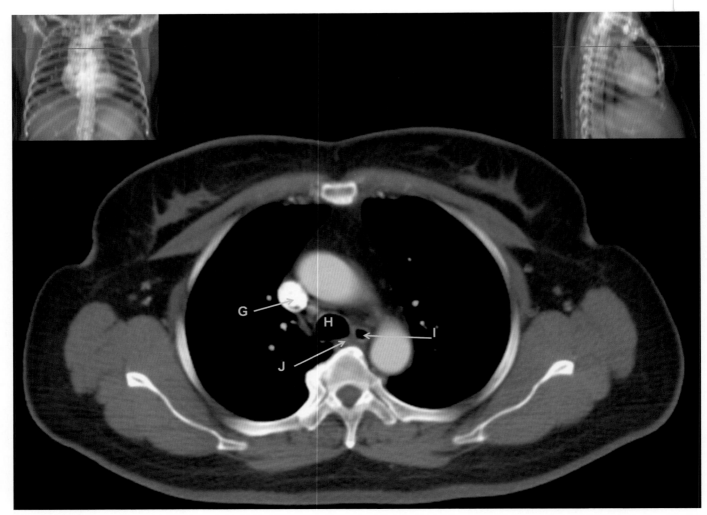

Figure 3.8.2

F

G

H

I

J

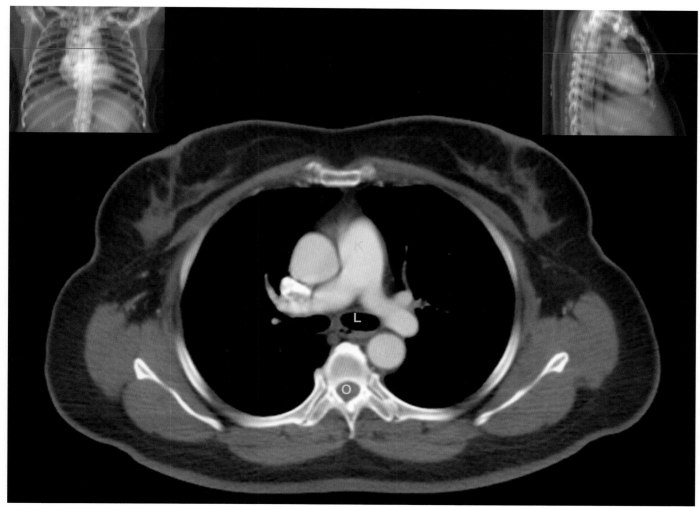

Figure 3.8.3

K

L

M

N

O

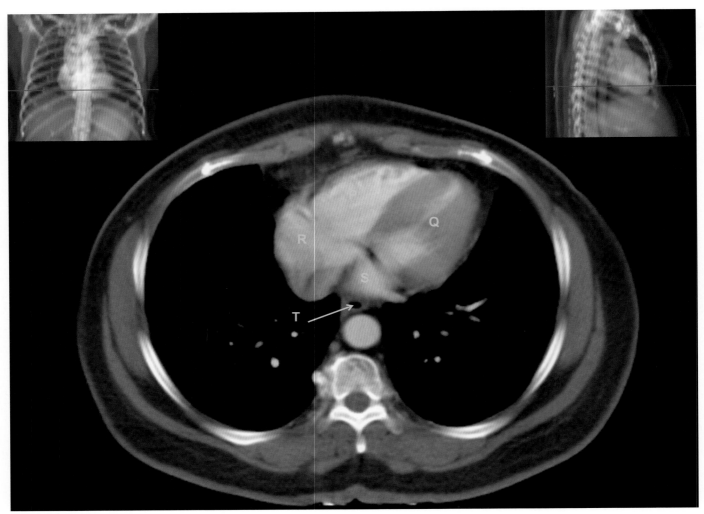

Figure 3.8.4

P

Q

R

S

T

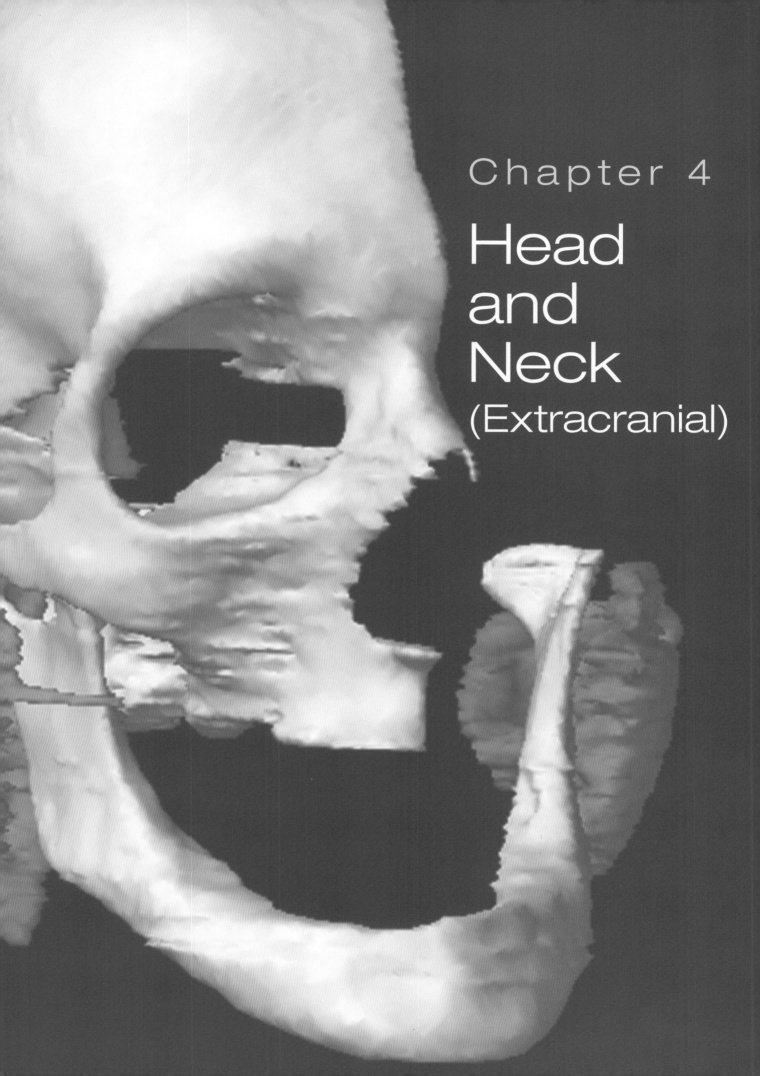

Chapter 4

Head
and
Neck
(Extracranial)

4.1 Musculoskeletal System

Although there are a large number of small bones in the head and neck region, it is not necessary for the therapy radiographer to be able to identify them all on CT. The bones can be considered as three main groups: the skull, hyoid bone and cervical vertebrae. The skull is made of 28 bones grouped as either cranial bones that form the chambers holding the brain or as facial bones. Although normal CT does not demarcate the individual bones well, an understanding of the general whereabouts and appearance of a few key bones is useful for radiotherapy practice.

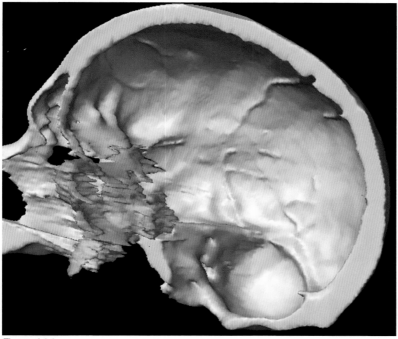

Figure 4.1.1

One of the most useful bones to identify is the keystone of the skull: the sphenoid bone, as shown in Figure 4.1.1. This sits in the middle of the skull, forming essential parts of the cranium and allowing for connection of key facial bones too. Amongst its many features are grooves for the carotid arteries and optic nerves, the pituitary fossa, roof of the nasopharynx, support for the brain stem and the large sphenoid sinus (S in Figure 4.1.2). The sphenoid sinus occupies the midline superior to the pharynx and curves up both anteriorly and posteriorly to the pituitary fossa. There are two superior projections of the sphenoid: the anterior and posterior clinoid processes and these form the anterior and posterior walls of the pituitary fossa.

There are several other sinuses in the skull as shown in Figure 4.1.2 in green. The maxillary sinuses (M) on either side of the nasal cavity sit in the maxillae. The frontal sinus (F) is situated medially and superiorly to the orbits in the frontal bone. The ethmoid sinus (E) or 'labyrinth' runs between these three above the nasal cavity and between the orbits. These sinuses are important navigational landmarks in CT anatomy.

There are other air-filled cavities in the skull. The main structures of the hearing apparatus are located in passageways in the petrous ridge of the temporal bone. At the inferior part of the skull, the mastoid processes are formed from the occipital bones and can be easily palpated posteriorly to the inferior of the pinna. These processes contain air cells to help lighten the skull and are easily identified by their bubbly appearance on CT.

The mandible is a separate bone to the skull, featuring a vertical arm 'ramus' on each side and the curving 'body' forming the lower jaw. It connects to the skull via the temporomandibular joint between the posterior part of the superior ramus and the temporal bone. See Figure 4.1.3. This joint allows the mandible to pivot during

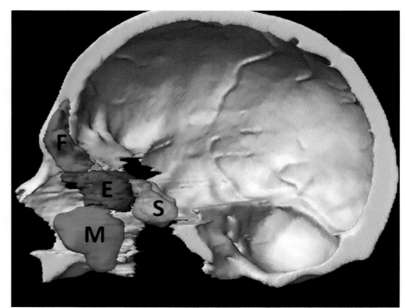

Figure 4.1.2

mastication or speech. Anterior to the joint, the mandible ramus has a slight superior protrusion called the coronoid process that can be seen to disappear behind the zygomatic arch. This appears on CT as an island of bone surrounded by soft tissue and should be noted to avoid confusion.

The other separate bone in the head and neck region is the hyoid bone, seen in Figure 4.1.3 between the mandible and the spinal column. This small horseshoe-shaped bone is found superiorly to the larynx and allows for attachment of both larynx cartilages and tongue muscles. It is unique in the body since it does not articulate with any other bones.

There are seven cervical vertebrae, as seen curving under the skull in Figure 4.1.3. These are smaller than the other vertebrae in the body since they bear less weight. They are also characterised by the presence of 'transverse foraminae', which are small holes lateral and slightly anterior to the vertebral bodies. The foraminae can be seen in Figure 4.1.4 and form a passageway for the vertebral arteries that help supply the brain with blood. The first and second cervical vertebrae (Figure 4.1.5) are atypical in appearance, to allow rotation of the head. The first cervical vertebra is named 'the atlas' after the Greek Titan Atlas who bore the world on his shoulders. It has a small body and mainly comprises an anterior and posterior arch, making it resemble a ring.

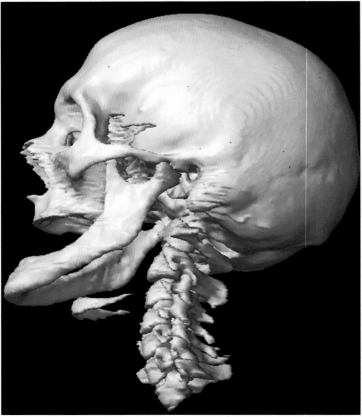

Figure 4.1.3

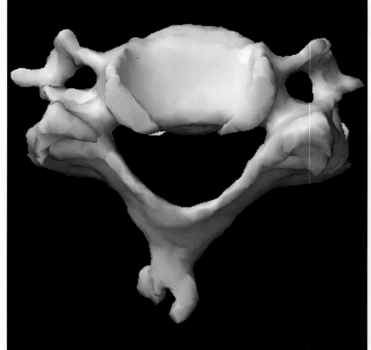

Figure 4.1.4

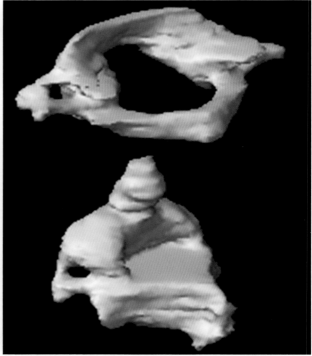

Figure 4.1.5

The second cervical vertebra is known as 'the axis' and it features a long 'odontoid process' or 'dens' that penetrates superiorly through the atlas, enabling rotation.

For radiotherapy purposes, the muscles of the head and neck mainly have value in terms of locating other more relevant structures. The long twisted journey of the sternocleidomastoid muscle is a prime example, as shown in Figure 4.1.6. Each one starts at the sternum and the clavicle at the anterior of the body and travels superiorly, laterally and posteriorly to meet the ipsilateral mastoid process. It is of value since, for much of its length it overlies the carotid sheath containing the carotid artery, jugular vein and jugular lymph node chain.

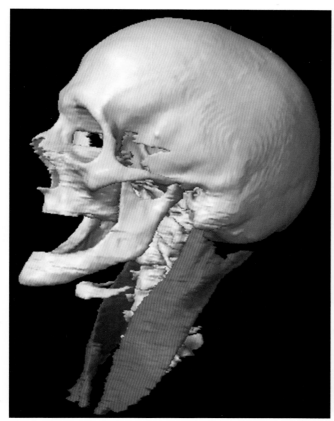

Figure 4.1.6

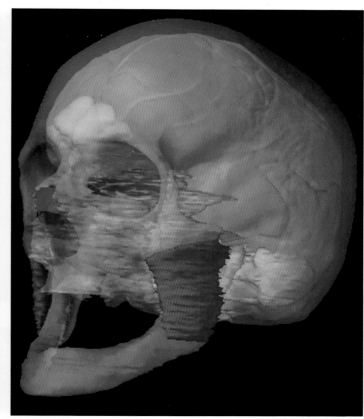

Figure 4.1.7

The other important muscle to be aware of is the masseter muscle, as seen in Figure 4.1.7. This lies along the lateral side of the mandibular ramus and, along with the pterygoid muscle medially to the ramus, helps with mastication. It is important to identify this muscle since the parotid gland overlies it and distinguishing between the two structures is vital.

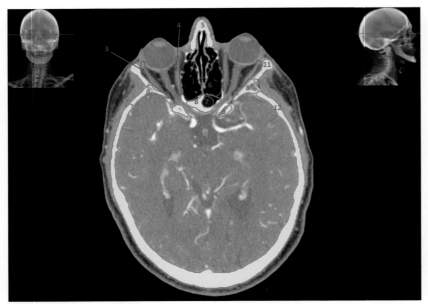

Figure 4.1.8

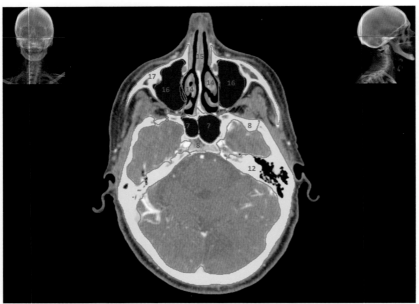

Figure 4.1.9

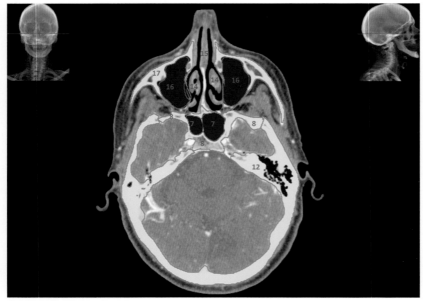

Figure 4.1.10

When viewing CT images within the head and neck, it should be noted that the region includes a wide range of CT tissue densities, from air passages to bony structures. This can make it difficult to select windows to view all tissue densities. Soft tissue window settings are probably the best, although bone or even 'neuro' windows may be useful.

It should also be noted that above the hyoid most structures are symmetrical (assuming positioning is accurate); asymmetry is usually a sign of pathological process or disease.

In Figure 4.1.8 the nasal bones (5) can be seen immediately anterior to the nasal cavity. Lateral to the nasal cavity are the cells of the air-containing ethmoid labyrinth (6). The ethmoid air cells form a honeycomb labyrinth of 3–18 air pockets per side, each separated by a thin layer of bone covered with a very thin layer of soft tissue mucosal lining. Separating the orbital cavities from the ethmoid labyrinth are thin bony walls called the lamina papyracea which form the medial orbital walls along with the lacrimal bones. The lateral orbital walls are formed by the sphenoid (8) and the zygoma (11). The orbital globes are clearly seen at the base of each orbital cavity. The densities of sclera, vitreous fluid and lens are clearly visualised.

Either side of the orbital globes, two of the four main rectus muscles are seen. The medial (4) and lateral rectus (3) along with the superior, inferior (13 in Figure 4.1.9), and oblique muscles are responsible for eye movements. The four larger rectus muscles enlarge with thyroid orbitopathy resulting in the characteristic staring of the eyes (Thyroid eye disease). The optic nerve extends centrally from the posterior aspect of the globe towards the apex of the cavity by the posterior wall of the sphenoid sinus (8). In Figures 4.1.9 and 4.1.10 the nasal cavity is clearly divided by the central nasal septum (15) and more lateral conchae (14).

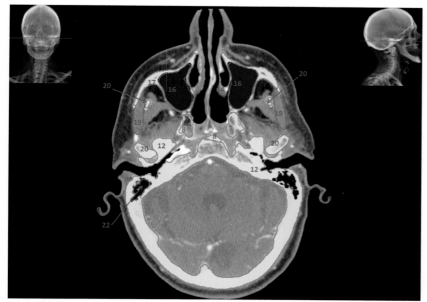

Figure 4.1.11

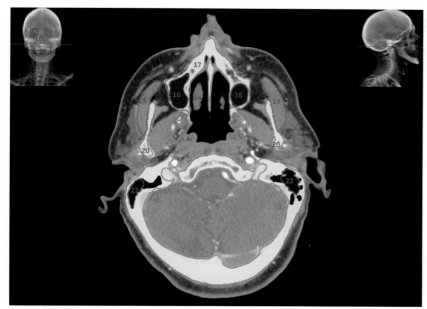

Figure 4.1.12

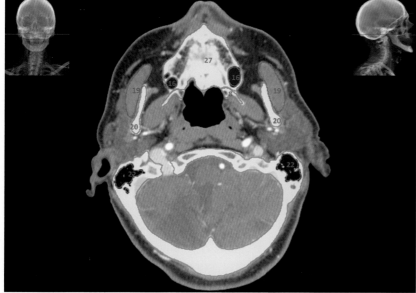

Figure 4.1.13

The masseter (19) in Figures 4.1.11 to 4.1.17 originates from the zygomatic arch and extends superficially over the ramus of the mandible (20). The muscle is commonly ovoid in shape in cross-section, but can be rounder and enlarged, associated with benign muscle hypertrophy, linked with excessive chewing and teeth grinding. Relevant neighbouring structures, posterior and lateral to the masseter muscles, are the parotid glands, discussed below. The hinged temporomandibular joint is seen in Figure 4.1.11 where the head of the mandible (20) can be seen articulating with the temporal bone (12).

The air-containing cavities within the head and neck may appear quite similar since many are surrounded by high density bone and filled with low density air. Although similar in appearance, some are part of the paranasal sinuses, some are cavities linked to external orifices (ears, nose and mouth) and some are seemingly closed cavities within bony structures.

These cavities normally contain air and have a high inherent contrast to the surrounding bone, making them relatively easy to locate on CT. However, these cavities may contain fluid or soft tissues associated with sinus disease, infective or infiltrative processes. The paranasal sinuses (16) are visualised in Figures 4.1.8 to 4.1.13, and are all actually extensions of the respiratory part of the nasal cavity. The development of infection or tumour within the sinus cavities can spread relatively easily through the air filled spaces and along their adjoining openings, occasionally into neighbouring sinus cavities. All the paranasal sinuses are normally well aerated with relatively smooth wall contours and are all linked via various openings. Some of these are poorly located, such as the hiatus semilunaris. High up in the maxillary sinuses (16) on their medial wall, these allow drainage into the nasal cavity only when the sinus is nearly full with the head erect.

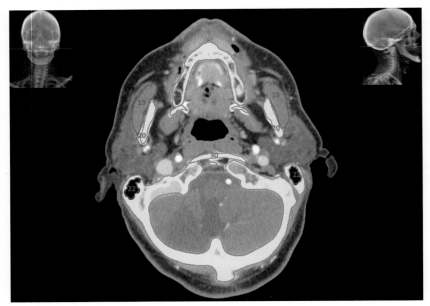

Figure 4.1.14

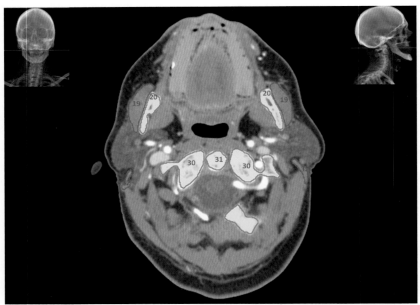

Figure 4.1.15

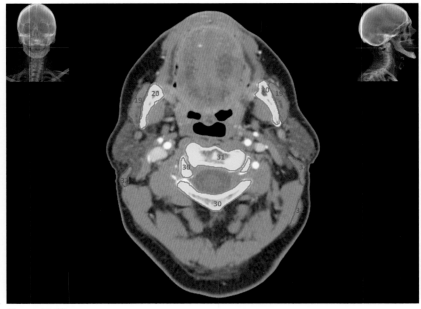

Figure 4.1.16

There are corresponding named sinus cavities within the frontal, ethmoid (6), sphenoid (7) and maxillary (16) bones as seen in Figures 4.1.8 to 4.1.13. Directly posterior to the ethmoid labyrinth, the paired sphenoid sinuses (7) are seen within the body of the sphenoid bone (8). Each sinus is likely to show asymmetry, as seen in Figure 4.1.10, where the left sphenoid sinus is considerably larger than the right. The thin bony midline septum may also be deviated left or right. The sphenoid sinuses and bone are located centrally within the skull base, and are adjacent to several important structures.

The pituitary gland, carotid canal and foramen lacerum (carrying the internal carotid arteries) are all located very close to the sphenoid sinus. Tumours infiltrating the sphenoid bone will have obvious complications during treatment. The maxillary sinuses or 'antra' (16) are two relatively symmetrical and large pyramidal shaped cavities within the maxillary bones (17 in Figures 4.1.10 to 4.1.13). The floor of each maxillary sinus is formed by the alveolar recesses in the hard palate (27) and it is not uncommon to see roots of molar teeth extending into the sinuses, covered only by a thin layer of bone and mucosal lining.

The nasal cavity (18) links the external nares to the roof of the mouth. It is divided into two by the nasal septum (15) as seen in Figures 4.1.8 to 4.1.12. The septum has thin cartilaginous and bony sections formed by the perpendicular ethmoid plate, vomer and septal cartilage. Either side of the nasal septum in Figures 4.1.9 to 4.1.13 can be seen the nasal conchae (14). The thick lining of the nasal conchae causes them to enhance vividly following the injection of IV contrast agents. Figures 4.1.10 to 4.1.14 show the mastoid air cells (22) within the otherwise very dense petrous temporal bones (12). The sternocleidomastoid muscle (32 in Figures 4.1.15 and 4.1.16) attaches to the lateral surface of the mastoid process and adjacent occipital bone.

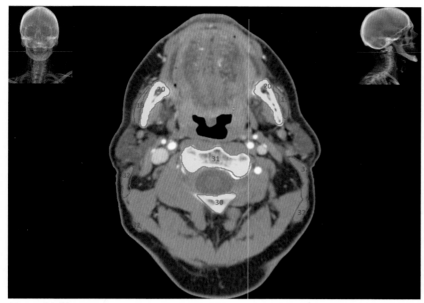

Figure 4.1.17

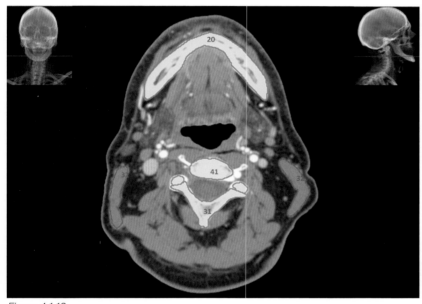

Figure 4.1.18

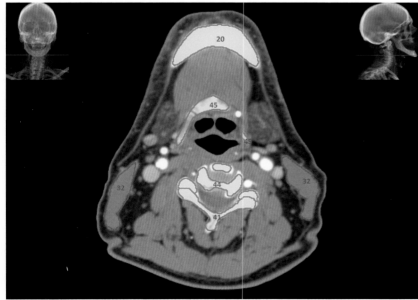

Figure 4.1.19

The masseter muscle (19) is relatively small in cross-section in Figure 4.1.17, as many of its fibres have inserted slightly superiorly on the ramus of the mandible (20). The mandible (20) is seen in Figures 4.1.11 to 4.1.19. In many patients there are teeth sited in the alveolar sockets; however the frequent presence of very dense amalgam dental fillings causes considerable streak artefacts across the adjacent soft tissues. These artefacts are described in more detail in the introduction (pages 13–15). The edentulous (toothless) patient selected to illustrate this text was specifically selected, as once their false teeth had been removed prior to imaging, there would be little or no imaging artefacts present in the oral cavity. This does make illustration of normal teeth slightly difficult, but does illustrate normal soft tissue CT anatomy which can be applied in clinical practice. It should be noted, however, that in the edentulous mandible the alveolar sockets will become absorbed over time, and several years after the teeth have been removed most of the alveolar bone and processes will be entirely reabsorbed. This will give the body of the mandible a narrower profile.

In Figure 4.1.11 medial to the masseter muscle (19) can be seen the mandibular coronoid processes, separated from the temporomandibular joint by a gap called the mandibular notch. Below the notch, in Figure 4.1.12, the superior aspect of each ramus can be seen in cross-section tapering from the neck of the mandible. At the angle of the mandible in Figure 4.1.17, the mandible curves anteriorly to form the body and recognisable horseshoe shape as seen in Figure 4.1.18. The hyoid bone (45) is seen in Figures 4.1.19 and 4.1.20. The hyoid, along with the mandible and styloid processes attaches to muscles from the floor of the mouth, tongue and larynx inferiorly. The hyoid has a body anteriorly and both lesser and greater horns or cornu projecting posteriorly.

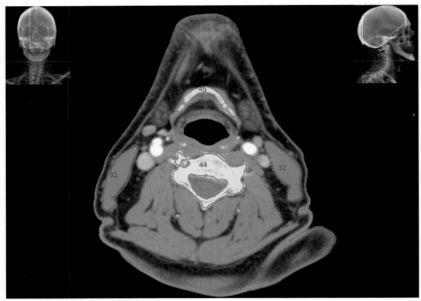

Figure 4.1.20

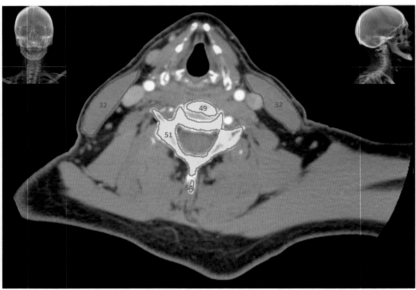

Figure 4.1.21

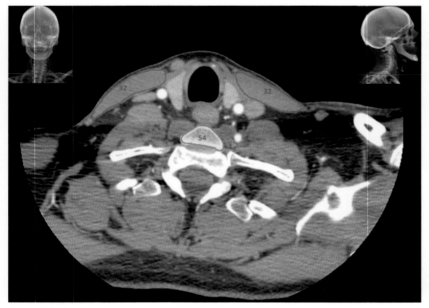

Figure 4.1.22

The bony structure of the cervical spine can be seen in Figures 4.1.14 to 4.1.22. Depending upon the degree of cervical flexion and gantry angulation, there may well be sections of multiple cervical vertebrae included in the scan plane and it may be difficult to recognise specific vertebral levels. The viewer should scroll through contiguous images following the path of the cervical spine, perform sagittal reformats or use planning software to plot reference lines on the scout view. Elements of C1 and C2 are quite recognisable, as seen in Figure 4.1.15. The lateral masses of C1 (30) can be seen either side of the odontoid process of C2 (31). The left vertebral artery is clearly seen within the transverse process of C1 (30). This is not clearly demonstrated on the right, and there is also partial voluming of the occipital bone on the left. Slightly inferiorly in Figure 4.1.16, the posterior arch of C1 can be seen (30) posterior to the larger body of C2 (31).

The sternocleidomastoid muscle (32) is a key landmark in the neck. It divides the neck diagonally into the anterior and posterior cervical triangles. These regions are used for descriptive purposes when indicating clinical anatomy and disease spread. The sternocleidomastoid muscle is a broad strap muscle and attaches inferiorly to the anterior surface of the manubrium of the sternum and superior surface of the medial third of the clavicle. From here, the muscle flattens and ascends slightly obliquely, as can be seen in Figures 4.1.20 to 4.1.22. Deep to the muscle is the carotid sheath anteriorly. As the muscle ascends further in Figures 4.1.17 to 4.1.19, it flattens and twists its axis, and ascends parallel to the lateral aspect of the neck at approximately C4/5.

4.2 Digestive System

The digestive system starts with the oral cavity and for much of radiotherapy practice this will either be of little relevance or will be filled with a mouth bite. The large genioglossus muscle (tongue) fills most of the cavity normally. It is bounded superiorly by the hard palate anteriorly and then the sloping roof of the soft palate posteriorly. It is in this region that food receives secretions of saliva from three paired glands as seen in Figure 4.2.1.

The parotid glands (P) are the largest and are located laterally to the masseter muscle and anterior to the pinna. They curve round to penetrate surprisingly deep behind the posterior of the mandibular rami. The parotid

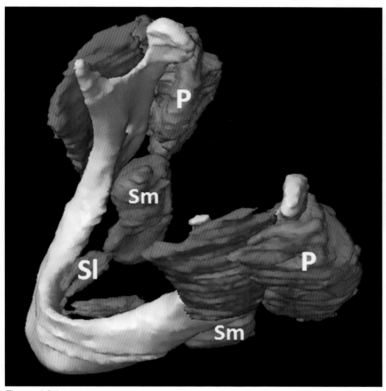

Figure 4.2.1

('Stenson's') duct can just be seen extending anteriorly along the masseter muscle. The salivary glands are lobulated and contain fluid; thus on CT they have a reduced density and characteristic 'bubbly' appearance. The submandibular glands (Sm) are the next largest glands and are located behind and under the angle of mandible. Although the parotid gland is the largest, it only accounts for approximately 25% of total salivary volume and the submandibular glands account for 60% to 65%. The final salivary glands are the small sublingual glands (SI) found just behind the mandible in the anterior floor of mouth. They lack the obvious shapes of the other salivary glands, forming a small horseshoe shape at the anterior of the floor of mouth.

Localisation of the salivary glands on CT may be quite difficult for the relatively inexperienced viewer, yet is of great clinical importance when considering treatment fields for some head and neck cancers. It is well documented that irradiating the salivary glands produces a range of acute and chronic complications, such as xerostomia where salivary flow can be compromised following radiotherapy. Here are several hints to help localise the salivary glands on CT:

- CT density

Typically, the parotid glands are composed of fatty glandular tissue and demonstrate an intermediate CT density between that of fat and muscle, approximately -5HU. The submandibular glands have a slightly higher density than the parotid glands. The parotid gland has a slightly inhomogeneous appearance. Gland density is age dependent; the parotid gland may be isodense with adjacent muscle tissues in children and young adults. Age related changes bring about a significant fall in gland density due to an increase in fibro-fatty glandular and adipose tissue. The reduced density does have the advantage of improving border demarcation.

- Position

The salivary glands, although capsulated, are relatively pliable and are easily displaced by adjacent abnormalities or more rigid structures. Each of the three glands is usually paired, and displays symmetry, although the parotid gland may be more irregular, with accessory glands along the parotid duct.

- Appearance

It is not uncommon to see calcified deposits ('calculi') in the parotid and submandibular glands. Multiple dilated ducts may be seen in the presence of glandular abnormalities. Radiation can induce a range of changes within the parotid glands. These may be transient or chronic, and most patients will have chronic changes above 30–40Gy. Glandular swelling will be evident in the acute phase due to leakage from damaged endothelial linings. There will be diffuse heterogeneous enhancement following IV contrast. Fibrosis and atrophy occur in the chronic stage, and the gland will demonstrate higher CT density and reduced volume.

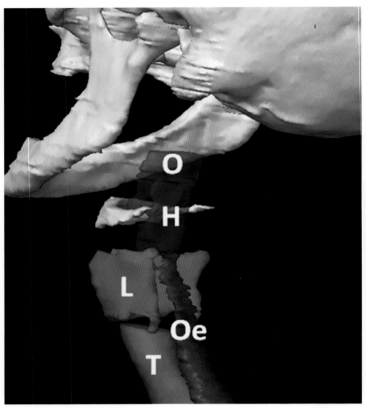

Figure 4.2.2

Figure 4.2.2 shows the next stage of the digestive system. After the oral cavity, the digestive tract passes the pointed tip of the soft palate, known as the uvula and continues into the oropharynx (O). The oropharynx is the shortest part of the pharynx and leads inferiorly to the hypopharynx (H) at the level of the epiglottis. The epiglottis is part of the larynx and serves to direct air and food into the larynx and oesophagus respectively. It can be seen that the oropharynx is located behind the mandible body and the hypopharynx behind the hyoid bone. From the posterior part of the hypopharynx, the digestive system continues into the oesophagus (Oe) which runs behind the larynx (L) and then behind the trachea (T) in the thorax.

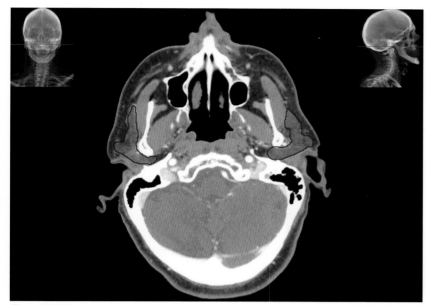

Figure 4.2.3

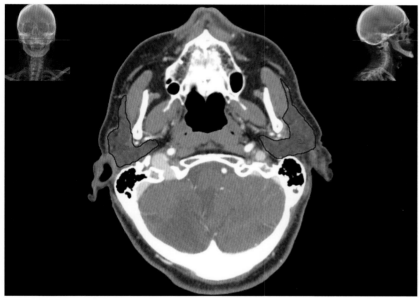

Figure 4.2.4

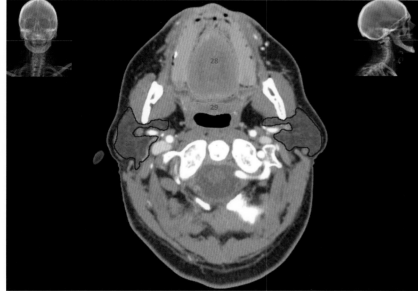

Figure 4.2.5

Figure 4.2.3 is a CT section just inferior to the temporomandibular joints. The parotid gland (21) is seen wedged between the ramus of the mandible, masseter muscle and ear. As with many structures within the body, its name describes its location (*para* – near or around and *otis* – ear). The parotid gland is visible in Figures 4.2.3 to 4.2.6. The parotid has two lobes: superficial and deep. The larger superficial lobe extends irregularly and overlaps the posterior part of the masseter muscle and the majority of the mandibular ramus. The deep lobe extends behind the ramus of the mandible, enclosing the retromandibular vein and branches of the external carotid artery. The tip of the deep lobe extends medially to the fatty parapharyngeal space seen in Figure 4.2.5. Of clinical interest, it should be noted that there are approximately 20 intraparotid lymph nodes that are first order drainage for the external auditory canal, pinna and surrounding adjacent scalp.

The left parotid duct can be seen crossing the superficial aspect of the masseter muscle in Figure 4.2.4. The duct tapers off and narrows as it leaves the anterior edge of the gland. The duct is not as well demarcated on the right, as accessory portions of the parotid gland are seen to extend across the right masseter muscle. This is a common finding, and these accessory parotid glands may well appear to be completely separate to the gland itself, but will still be associated with the duct.

Figure 4.2.5 demonstrates how the deep lobe extends posterior and medial to the mandibular ramus. A finger-like projection of the gland extends posterior to the ramus of the mandible. The tongue (28) can be seen occupying the oral cavity, surrounded by the horseshoe shaped gums. The soft palate (29) is seen draping over the posterior dorsal aspect of the tongue.

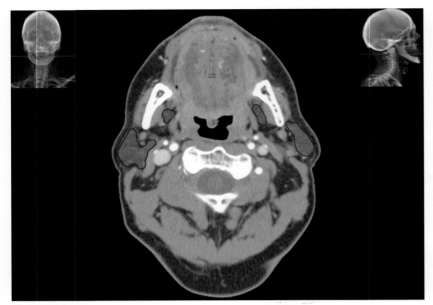

Figure 4.2.6

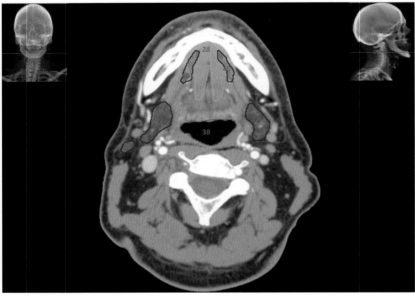

Figure 4.2.7

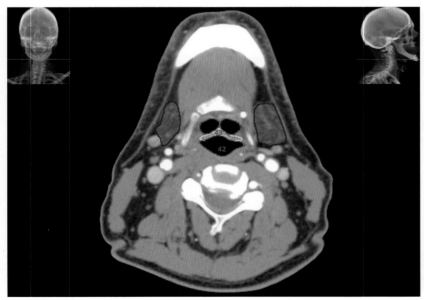

Figure 4.2.8

Figure 4.2.6 shows the small grape-like appearance of the uvula (37), which hangs off the inferior aspect of the soft palate into the oropharynx. Figure 4.2.7 demonstrates the base of the tongue (28) in the floor of the mouth. The tongue is divided by the median septum, separating symmetrical halves, and also has a base, body and apex. The median septum can be seen in Figure 4.2.6 as a faint soft tissue line running centrally along the tongue. This division is also seen in Figure 4.2.7, where each side of the genioglossus muscle is separated by the lingual septum.

Both sublingual glands (40) can be seen in Figure 4.2.7. These paired salivary glands can be relatively difficult to demarcate on CT since they are not capsulated. The submandibular glands (39) however are much larger and can be seen in Figures 4.2.6 to 4.2.9. The corresponding greater horn of the hyoid bone is medial to each gland, separated by a thin fat plane.

Demarcation of the submandibular (Wharton's) duct is difficult on CT as it has a relatively tortuous route from its anterior aspect to either side of the lingual frenulum. The duct is approximately 50mm long, similar to the parotid duct, but is much smaller in calibre. Due to the lengthy and tortuous nature of the duct, the submandibular gland commonly displays salivary calculi. This is of clinical relevance, as an obstructed and enlarged submandibular gland may also mimic the appearance of a large malignant lymph node or primary carcinoma. Associated lymph nodes may be partially embedded within the gland laterally, or lie lateral to the gland.

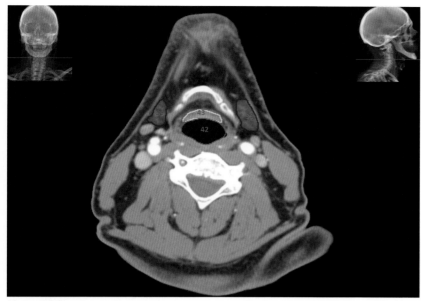

Figure 4.2.9

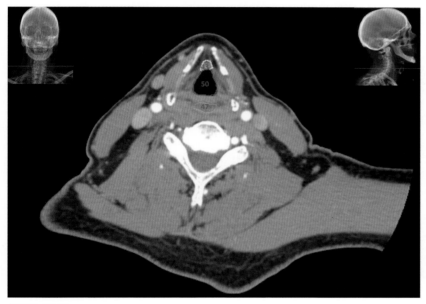

Figure 4.2.10

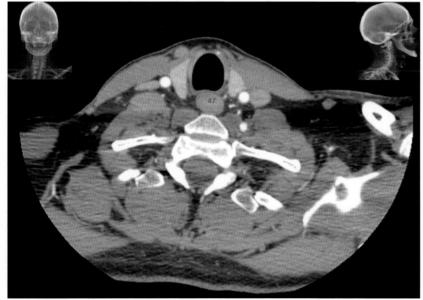

Figure 4.2.11

Below the oropharynx (38) can be seen the hypopharynx (42) in Figures 4.2.8 and 4.2.9. Air within the lumen enables the epiglottis (43) to be clearly visualised. The leaf shaped epiglottic cartilage (43) projects from the posterior surface of the thyroid cartilage superiorly into the oropharynx. The epiglottis is suspended from the body of the hyoid bone by the hyoepiglottic ligament in the midline. This ligament is covered by a thin mucous membrane called the glossoepiglottic fold and together they can be seen in Figure 4.2.8. The two smaller air-filled spaces anterior to the epiglottis are the valleculae, which are essentially two small depressions either side of the glossoepiglottic fold.

The inferior stalk of the epiglottis (43) is seen just anterior to the larynx (50) in Figure 4.2.10. At this level (about C6) it is difficult to fully demarcate the boundaries of the origin of the cervical oesophagus (47). The oesophagus sits between the posterior of the larynx (50) and the inferior constrictor muscle of the pharynx.

More inferiorly, in Figure 4.2.11, the oeso- phagus is more clearly defined. It is larger in cross-section and the muscular external borders are well demarcated against the lower density surrounding fatty tissues. From this level, the oesophagus occupies its well recognised course slightly to the left of midline, anterior to the vertebral bodies, and behind the trachea. There is normally a thin fat plane separating the flattened posterior border of the trachea and the anterior of the oesophagus, called the tracheoesophageal groove. This contains loose adipose connective tissues, the recurrent laryngeal nerve and some paratracheal lymph nodes. The parathyroid glands are also situated laterally within the tracheoesophageal groove.

4.3 Respiratory System

In terms of anatomical description of the upper respiratory tract, the anatomy is subdivided into nasal cavity, nasopharynx, oral cavity, oropharynx and hypopharynx. Anatomy and pathology is also described as being either supra or infra hyoid. Some texts refer to the anatomy as the aerodigestive tract. Air enters the respiratory system via the nostrils (the external nares) and passes to the nasal cavity. This is bisected by the nasal septum and further subdivided by the curtain-like nasal conchae (or turbinate bones). These have a rich blood supply and are hairy so act as both radiators to warm the air and filters to extract particles.

At the posterior of the nasal cavity through the internal nares lies the nasopharynx. The long tube of the nasopharynx extends from the inferior of the sphenoid bone down to the oropharynx at the level of the soft palate. The nasopharynx can be seen in green in Figure 4.3.1 behind the pink nasal conchae leading down to the larynx.

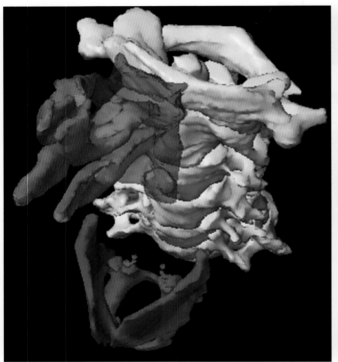
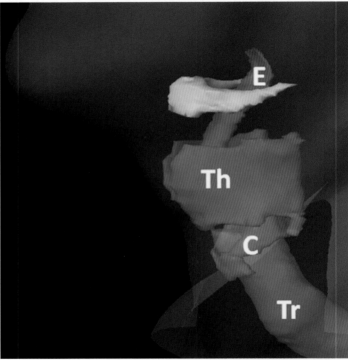

Figure 4.3.1   Figure 4.3.2

From this point, the respiratory passage is shared with the digestive tract through the oropharynx and hypopharynx until the epiglottis is reached, as seen in Figure 4.3.2. The epiglottis (E) is a leaf-shaped piece of cartilage that is technically part of the larynx. It serves to direct air into the larynx for most of the time but during the swallowing reflex it directs food and drink into the oesophagus.

The larynx is a cartilaginous structure formed from three large pieces of cartilage and three small paired cartilages. The largest part of the larynx is formed by the thyroid cartilages (Th). These form the side walls and anterior of the larynx and form an inverted V-shape in cross-section. The superior anterior region of the thyroid cartilage is notched and the prominence of this structure is commonly known as the Adam's Apple. For clinical descriptive purposes, the larynx is divided into three distinct areas: the supraglottis, glottis and subglottis. The supraglottis extends from the tip of the epiglottis to the laryngeal ventricles. It is a relatively large area of the larynx and contains the epiglottis, pre-epiglottic fat, false vocal cords and arytenoid cartilages. The glottis is the central section of the larynx containing only the true vocal cords, responsible for the origins of voice production. The subglottis extends from the inferior surface of the true vocal cords to the inferior edge of the ring-shaped cricoid cartilage (C). Extending inferiorly from this is the trachea (Tr). Other smaller paired cartilages can be found at the posterior of the larynx. These are the arytenoids, the horn-shaped cuneiform and tiny corniculate cartilages.

Although not part of the respiratory system the thyroid gland is physically close to the larynx so will be mentioned briefly at this point. Responsible for regulation of metabolism, it lies inferior and anterior to the thyroid cartilage. It consists of two lobes connected by an 'isthmus'. The upper lobe on each side is considerably

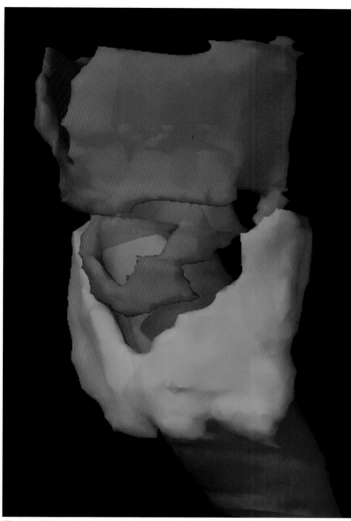

Figure 4.3.3

longer than the lower lobe, giving the thyroid gland a shape like an inflated rugby post as seen in Figure 4.3.3. The thyroid gland enhances strongly with iodine-based contrast on CT due to its natural absorption of iodine.

When viewing the respiratory system within the head and neck, it is important to remember the wide range of tissue densities within the whole series of images. By its very nature, the respiratory tract should be well aerated, allowing the passage of air in and out of the lungs, and therefore full of air. Air will always appear black irrespective of window settings. In many instances in the presence of tumour pathology, the aerated spaces may be either compressed or infiltrated by soft tissue masses. There may be relatively unchecked spread of disease within and along the linings of aerated cavities as there are few boundaries to impede disease progression.

Within the head and neck region there are other air-containing cavities adjacent to and linked via various openings. The paranasal sinuses, described in section 4.1, are extensions of the respiratory part of the nasal cavity, and are adjacent to both the nasal cavity and nasopharynx. Although linked, it is important to be able to distinguish between the adjacent aerated cavities. Poor image resolution and perception, predominantly affected by reconstruction algorithm, slice thickness and window settings can make some of the bony boundaries very difficult to appreciate. This is demonstrated in Figure 4.3.4 where it is difficult to demarcate the lateral wall of the left nasal cavity. The thin bony walls separating the sinus and nasal cavity appear to be missing. When trying to demarcate such fine structures in the head and neck, it is vitally important to view the images using bone and lung windows as well as soft tissue window settings, using the thinnest slices possible. The soft tissue windows used in Figures 4.3.4 to 4.3.12 enable high image contrast and most of the structures within the upper respiratory tract are well demarcated.

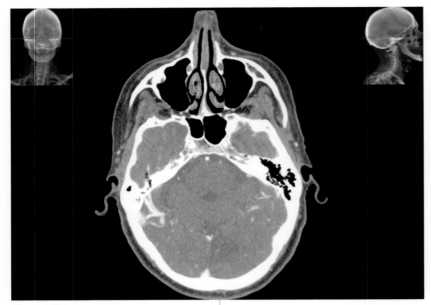

Figure 4.3.4

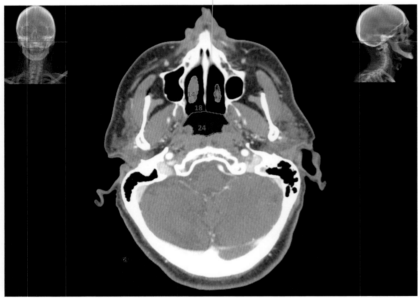

Figure 4.3.5

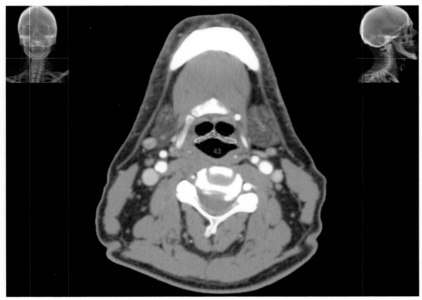

Figure 4.3.6

The nasal septum bisects the nasal cavity in the midline, as seen in Figure 4.3.4. The septal cartilage and perpendicular bony plate of the ethmoid are clearly visible. As mentioned in previous chapters, anatomy within the suprahyoid region tends to be symmetrical, left and right, simplifying recognition of abnormalities. However, it is certainly not unusual to see a deviated nasal septum, occasionally congenital or commonly attributed to previous nasal trauma.

The nasal conchae (14) are seen either side of the septum. These hang down from the lateral nasal walls forming scroll-like shapes, and project medially and inferiorly. The paired superior, middle and inferior nasal conchae have a rich arterial supply and plentiful venous drainage. As a consequence, nasally inhaled air passing over them is warmed. Radiologically, this is noticeable after administration of IV contrast agent when the nasal mucosa surrounding the conchae enhance vividly.

Posterior to the nasal cavity (18) the naso-pharynx (24) is seen in Figure 4.3.5. There are no physical boundaries between the nasal cavity and nasopharynx. Within the lateral walls of the nasopharynx in Figure 4.3.5 can be seen the torus tubularis. They are small, rounded soft tissue structures, just posterior to a V-shaped indentation on the lateral nasopharyngeal wall. The indentations are the pharyngeal openings to the pharyngotympanic (auditory or Eustachian) tube. The torus tubularis is the cartilaginous hood that projects over the opening to the pharyngotympanic duct.

Figure 4.3.6 demonstrates the hypo-pharynx (42) level with the body of the hyoid bone. The inferior aspects of the hyoid bone suspend the larynx by the thyrohyoid membrane.

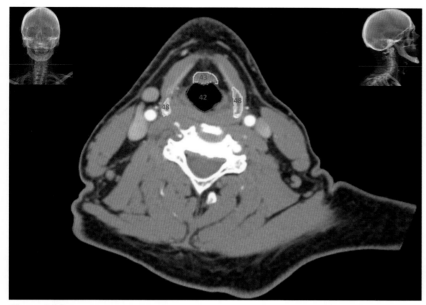

Figure 4.3.7

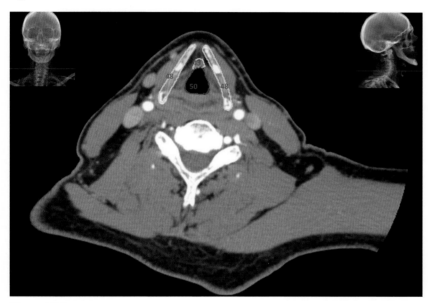

Figure 4.3.8

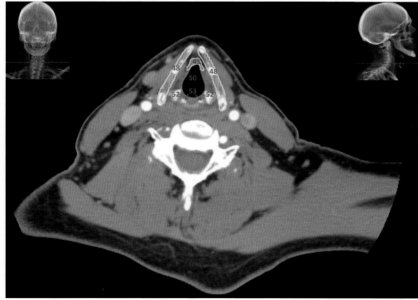

Figure 4.3.9

Figure 4.3.7 shows the air filled hypopharynx (42) posteriorly to the stalk of the epiglottis (43). The laminae of the thyroid cartilages (48) are well demonstrated in Figure 4.3.8. The laminae are essentially two quadrilateral cartilaginous plates, with projections extending from the posterior corners. These are the superior and inferior thyroid cornuae or horns. The laminae (Latin – thin plates) converge and are fused anteriorly at the laryngeal prominence in the midline. They are not totally fused anteriorly and in Figures 4.3.8 and 4.3.9 there is a gap or notch. This is called the thyroid notch, and when viewed anteriorly it forms a V-shaped groove.

There are flecks of calcification within the thyroid cartilages (48) in Figures 4.3.7 to 4.3.10. All the cartilages within the larynx are composed of hyaline cartilage and normally undergo some sort of calcification or endochondral ossification. Not all of the cartilages calcify simultaneously, and this process can vary with age and gender. Calcification is usually evident in the paired arytenoid cartilages (52) by the third decade, and the whole of the thyroid cartilage usually demonstrates some level of calcification by the seventh decade. However, this is less extensive in females where calcification is minimal in the anterior aspects of the thyroid gland. This is radiologically significant as many aspects of the laryngeal cartilages are evident on CT without IV contrast, and can also be well demarcated even on plain film imaging.

Whilst the thyroid cartilage covers the anterolateral aspects of the glottis, the cricoid (55) cartilage (from the Greek for ring) encircles the subglottic area. The 'band' of the ring faces anteriorly, as seen in Figures 4.3.10 and 4.3.11. It is much broader posteriorly. The vocal cords are level with the superior aspect of the cricoid cartilage.

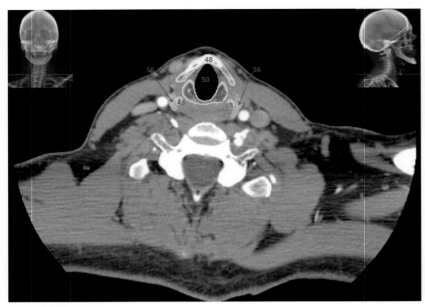

Figure 4.3.10

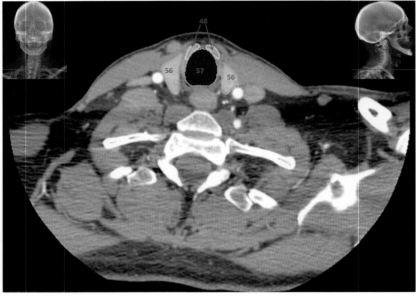

Figure 4.3.11

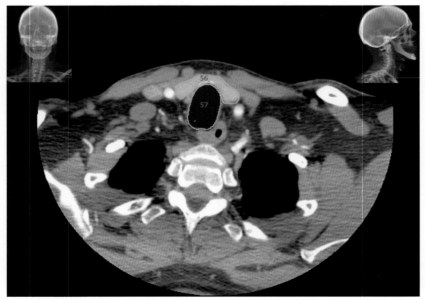

Figure 4.3.12

In Figure 4.3.11 the trachea (57) is suspended from the inferior aspect of the cricoid cartilage by the cricotracheal ligament, which is difficult to appreciate in cross-section. Although not part of the respiratory system, the thyroid gland (56) can be seen in Figures 4.3.10 to 4.3.11, adjacent to the trachea. The thyroid is of clinical significance due to its location within the visceral space and likely subsequent mass affect on the trachea and airways following any degree of enlargement.

The thyroid gland is surrounded by a thin fibrous capsule, which is in turn covered by a superficial layer of the deep cervical fascia, which adheres to the trachea. The gland is also normally quite mobile, and moves superiorly with the larynx during swallowing.

The gland is located inferior to the larynx, and has two relatively large lobes, left and right. The pear shaped lobes extend either side of the trachea (57) as seen in Figure 4.3.11. The lobes and thin 'isthmus' of glandular tissue crossing anterior to the trachea can be seen in Figure 4.3.12.

The thyroid gland itself normally appears as a smooth soft tissue structure, appearing slightly hyperdense to the surrounding soft tissues because of the relatively high iodine content (approximately 65HU). The thyroid gland is also highly vascularised, receiving almost 80 to 120ml of blood per minute from the superior and inferior thyroid arteries, and as such, following IV contrast agent, the gland will enhance vividly. The gland should normally be heterogeneous, but may display a cystic, solid, haemorrhagic or calcified appearance, particularly if the gland is enlarged due to goitre.

4.4 Circulatory System

In Chapter 3, it was explained how the first main arteries originating from the aorta are the brachiocephalic (which bifurcates into the right subclavian and right common carotid) and the left common carotid and left subclavian arteries. The main vascular supply to the head and neck arises from the common carotid (C) and vertebral (V) arteries. Both vertebral arteries are the first main vessel branching off each subclavian (S) vessel. The vertebral artery makes its way to the cervical vertebrae and ascends through the transverse foraminae, as seen in Figure 4.4.1. It then bends over the atlas and enters the skull through the foramen magnum.

The common carotid artery winds its way towards the central base of skull, bifurcating at approximately C3/C4 into the internal (IC) and external (EC) carotid arteries. Of the two, the internal carotid is larger in lumen. The internal carotid artery is destined for the brain and penetrates the skull through the sphenoid bone. The external carotid supplies the extracranial tissues and splits into smaller branches to supply the facial structures. Deoxygenated blood from intracranial structures exits the skull via the internal jugular vein. This accompanies the internal carotid artery inside the carotid sheath. Extracranial drainage passes into a number of veins including the external, posterior and anterior jugulars which ultimately drain into the subclavian veins.

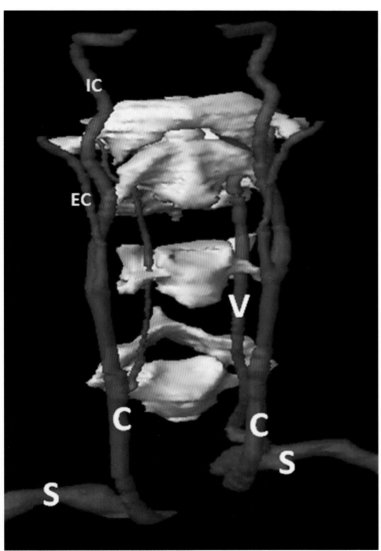

Figure 4.4.1

Demarcation of vessels and their boundaries can be difficult on a non-contrast CT examination, particularly in the head and neck region as there are so many other adjacent supporting structures. The CT density of unopacified vessels is approximately 55HU, and this is similar to an adjacent muscle, or lymphadenopathy (approximately 45). This is compounded when using relatively wide soft tissue window settings to help visualise a wider tissue range in the neck, and adjustments in window settings may have to be made to track unopacified vessels. Fat deposits in spaces surrounding the head and neck vasculature, common in the infra-hyoid region, provide fat planes of reduced CT density (approximately -65HU), that can enable clear demarcation of the vessels.

The common carotid artery and internal jugular veins are enclosed within the carotid sheath, a tubular fascia extending from the base of the skull to the root of the neck. The presence of the carotid sheath assists in image interpretation since the carotid artery and internal jugular veins will always be close neighbours. Also there may be atherosclerotic deposits of dense calcification (carotid plaques) within the arterial walls and particularly around the carotid bifurcation, increasing the detectability of vessels on non-contrast scans. Although the presence of carotid plaques limits the accuracy of diagnostic imaging by obscuring the level of carotid artery stenosis, it is beneficial on radiotherapy planning scans. The tissue density of the affected vascular wall is increased by approximately 250HU, and therefore inherent tissue contrast between that and neighbouring structures is greatly increased. Contrast enhanced scans of the head and neck region are a preferred option, as a well timed bolus of IV contrast agent will opacify both arterial and venous vasculature. The location of vessel walls and adjacent disease will be well demonstrated.

There are other pitfalls in assessing head and neck vasculature, even following the administration of IV contrast agent:

• **Movement unsharpness:** Should the patient swallow during image acquisition, the anatomical boundaries of structures close to the larynx may be blurred. During swallowing the larynx elevates and all adjacent anatomy will move medially and or laterally, causing movement unsharpness artefact on the image.

• **Abnormal appearances:** It is not uncommon to see one internal jugular vein that is larger than the other. This is usually of little clinical significance and is an incidental finding in most cases. Another incidental finding of little clinical significance is a tortuous carotid vessel. These vessels may be deviated medially, in close proximity to the pyriform recesses and thyroid cartilage.

• **Contrast layering in the internal jugular vein:** This, again, is not an uncommon finding and usually occurs on the same side as the injection site, early on in the injection phase, giving the appearance of an unusual filling defect. There is a small amount of retrograde filling in the internal jugular vein, and the contrast tends to sit in the posterior aspect of the vein lumen, with a definite 'fluid level' appearance. If the same area is re-scanned 60 seconds later, the contrast will have washed out and the filling defect artefact will disappear.

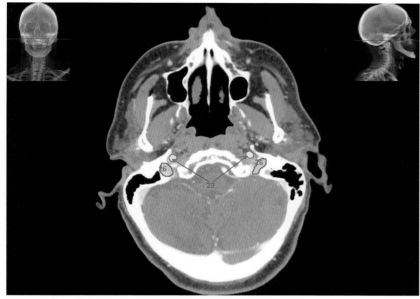

Figure 4.4.2

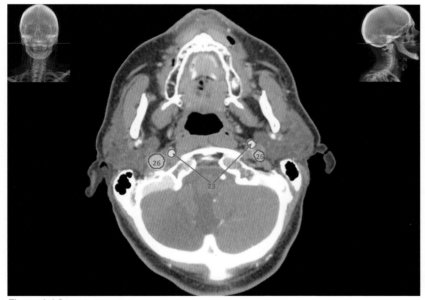

Figure 4.4.3

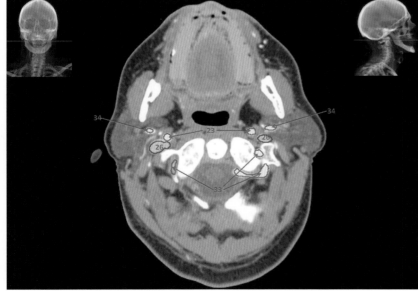

Figure 4.4.4

Figure 4.4.2 shows the internal carotid arteries (23) and internal jugular veins (26) in close proximity to the base of the skull. The arteries appear much brighter on the images compared to the veins, indicating a relatively early (arterial) phase acquisition. The approximate timing of this group of images would be 15–20 seconds post-injection.

In Figures 4.4.2 and 4.4.3 the intracranial section of the left vertebral artery is well demonstrated compared to the right vertebral artery. When progressing inferiorly, the right vertebral artery can be seen to be stenotic throughout its entire course, corroborating the narrowed intracranial section.

In Figure 4.4.3 both internal carotid arteries (23) and internal jugular veins (26) are well demarcated. It is just possible to distinguish the carotid sheath surrounding both paired vessels. The deep retromandibular portions of both parotid glands are lateral to the carotid sheaths.

The transverse foraminae of C1 can be seen within the transverse processes in Figure 4.4.4. The vertebral arteries (33) at this point follow a complex route into the cranium. They ascend out of the foraminae, fold posteriorly over the transverse process and then curl medially over the superior aspect of the lateral arch. The vessel then twists and ascends superiorly through the foramen magnum into the cranial cavity.

Maxillary branches of the external carotid arteries (34) are seen in Figures 4.4.4 and 4.4.5, just medial to the retromandibular portion of the parotid gland. These vessels are both well demarcated and have associated maxillary veins in close proximity, although they are difficult to identify because of poor opacification. Each internal jugular vein lies just laterally to their corresponding artery. This positional relationship continues inferiorly into the root of the neck.

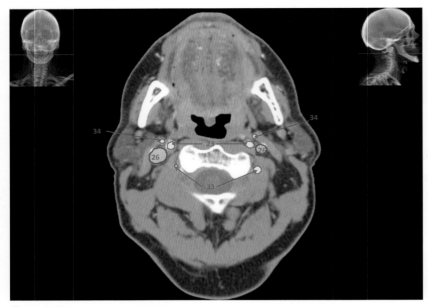

Figure 4.4.5

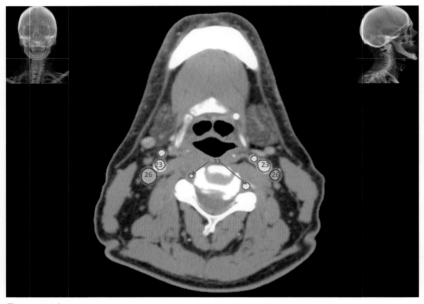

Figure 4.4.6

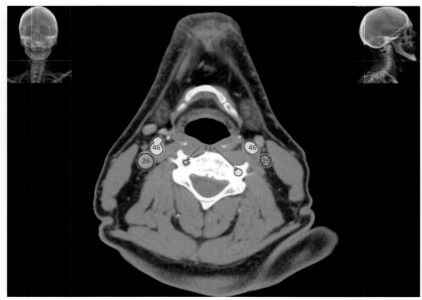

Figure 4.4.7

In Figure 4.4.6, approximately 20mm anterior to the right internal jugular vein, a small ovoid soft tissue structure can be seen in the fatty tissues in contact with the posterior aspect of the right submandibular gland. This could be an enlarged submandibular lymph node. However, tracking this structure superiorly and inferiorly suggests it is a tubular structure. This is the right external jugular vein. The corresponding vessel can be seen on the left, but is slightly smaller in cross-section. It is not unusual to see dominant vessels such as this. The external jugular vein descends obliquely across the sternocleidomastoid muscle until it empties into the subclavian vein.

Figures 4.4.6 and 4.4.7 depict the carotid bifurcation. In Figure 4.4.6 there are two carotid vessels; the larger, more posterior vessel is the internal carotid artery (23) and the smaller vessel is the external carotid artery. Figure 4.4.7 shows a single common carotid vessel (46), indicating that the vessel has not yet bifurcated. On the right, the external and internal carotid arteries can be seen at the point of bifurcation. From their origins from the brachiocephalic on the right and arch of aorta on the left, there are no branches off the common carotid arteries.

Localisation of the carotid and jugular vessels within the carotid sheath is useful in understanding adjacent lymphatic nodal groups. Many of the deep nodal groups descend close to the carotid sheath, close to the internal jugular vein, and are named relative to their position, as seen in the next section. This deep nodal chain runs along the length of the internal jugular vein, deep to the sternocleidomastoid muscle. There is also a smaller corresponding superficial nodal chain associated with the external jugular vein, running along the vein, superficial to the sternocleidomastoid muscle.

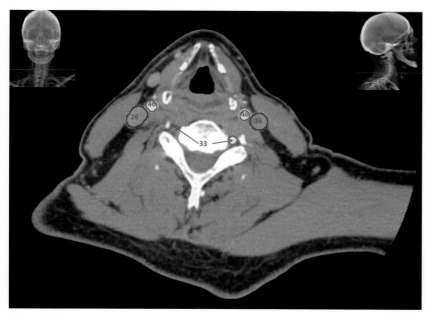

Figure 4.4.8

In Figure 4.4.8 the carotid sheath can be identified in the fat plane medial to the sternocleidomastoid muscle. This contains the common carotid artery (46) and the jugular vein (26). The vertebral arteries (33) are continuing their journey alongside the vertebral bodies. In this patient, the right vertebral artery is still considerably constricted compared to the left. Below this level, the circulatory system maintains the same arrangement until the brachiocephalic artery and veins are reached, as seen in Chapter 3.

4.5 Lymphatic System

As with elsewhere in the body, the main lymph vessels and nodes follow the circulatory system. Thus in the head and neck most of the superficial lymph nodes drain into the internal jugular node chain. Lymph from anterior structures such as the oral cavity, tonsils and tongue drains via submental and submandibular nodes to the more superior jugulodigastric node group and then down the internal jugular lymph chain. The middle internal jugular nodes receive lymph from the pharynx and larynx. The inferior internal jugular nodes drain the lower pharynx, larynx, thyroid and oesophagus. The internal jugular chain runs from the base of the skull down to the supraclavicular node group.

The head and neck nodes are divided into superficial, shown on Figure 4.5.2, and deep, shown on Figure 4.5.3. These nodal chains are further subdivided into six main levels or classifications recognised within oncology, as shown in Figure 4.5.1.

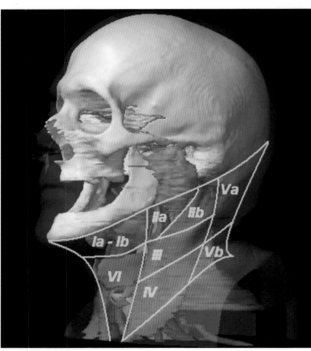

Figure 4.5.1

Level Ia (submental) and **Level Ib** (submandibular). Location: Floor of the mouth

Level IIa (jugulodigastric) and **IIb** (superior internal jugular). Location: Deep and adjacent to upper aspect of sternocleidomastoid muscle. Extend from skull base to hyoid bone.

Level III (middle internal jugular). Location: Adjacent to middle aspect of sternocleidomastoid muscle.

Level IV (lower internal jugular). Location: Adjacent to lower aspect of sterno-cleidomastoid muscle. Levels II, III and IV form the 'anterior triangle'.

Levels Va and **Vb** (upper, middle and lower spinal accessory). Location: Deep to the posterior aspects of the sternocleidomastoid muscle. Form the posterior triangle.

Level VI (parapharyngeal, paratracheal and pretracheal). Location: Within the visceral space.

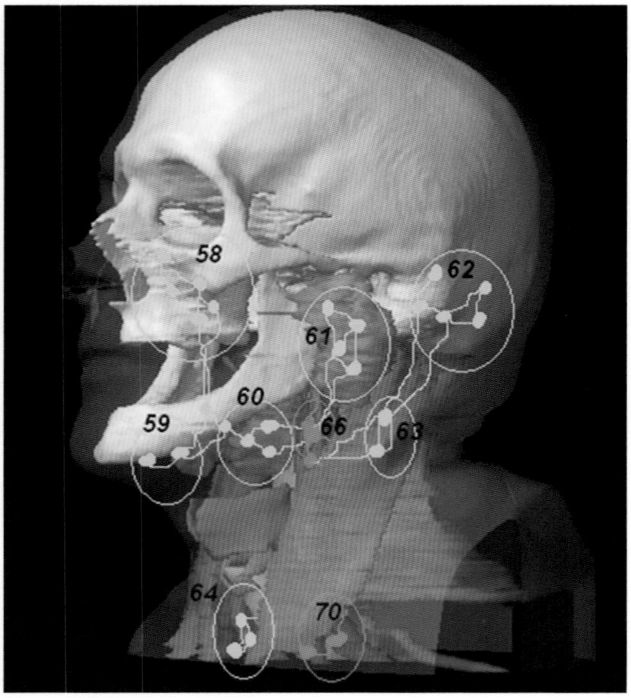

Superficial Cervical Lymph Nodes

58. Facial
59. Submental (Level Ia)
60. Submandibular (Level Ib)
61. Superficial parotid
62. Auricular and occipital (Level Va)
63. External jugular (Level III)
64. Visceral (prelaryngeal and pretracheal) (Level VI)
66. Jugulodigastric (Deep Level IIa)
70. Inferior internal jugular (Deep Level IV)

Figure 4.5.2

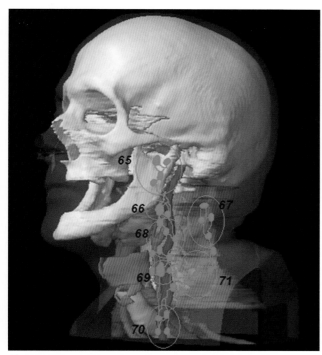

Figure 4.5.3

Deep Cervical Lymph Nodes

65. Deep parotid
66. Jugulodigastric (Level IIa)
67. Spinal accessory (Level Va and Vb)
68. Superior internal jugular (Level IIa and IIb)
69. Middle internal jugular (Jugulo-omohyoid) (Level III)
70. Inferior internal jugular (Level IV)
71. Supra and transverse clavicular

The other lymphatic structures to be found in the head and neck are the masses of lymphoid tissue known as the tonsils. These form Waldeyer's ring and lie in three distinct groups: the palatine, lingual and pharyngeal tonsils. Figure 4.5.4 illustrates the tonsil positions (in orange) in relation to the tongue (pink) and the pharynx (green). The rounded palatine tonsils (Pa) are the most easily seen and are located laterally to the uvula in the walls of the oropharynx. The lingual tonsils (Li) are less well-structured and lie across the base of the tongue (T). The pharyngeal tonsils (Ph) lie in the posterior roof of the nasopharynx.

Of the body's approximate 800–850 lymph nodes, 300 are located within the relatively small head and neck region, making high resolution CT imaging an essential tool for nodal imaging. Most diagnostic centres prefer to use multi planar and multi sequence MRI techniques to accurately stage local disease and nodal involvement so it is unlikely that comparative high resolution sub mm diagnostic CT images will be available, although many CT systems have this capability.

Axial imaging through the head and neck reveals a circular 'lymphoid collar' of nodal tissue encircling the head and neck with superficial and deep nodal chains connected to form a relatively complex system of drainage. The fatty space deep to the sternocleidomastoid muscle and within the paraspinal space provides excellent inherent contrast for clear demarcation of nodes within the internal jugular and accessory spinal chains. However, in patients of low body mass or where obliteration of anatomical boundaries has been caused by disease progression, CT interpretation can be quite challenging. This is particularly noticeable on non-contrast CT examinations, so many centres routinely utilise a relatively late IV contrast enhanced technique.

The relatively complex anatomical relationships between the various structures require the use of all the images within the CT volume and careful tracking from superior to inferior and back again, following the anticipated locations of both superficial and

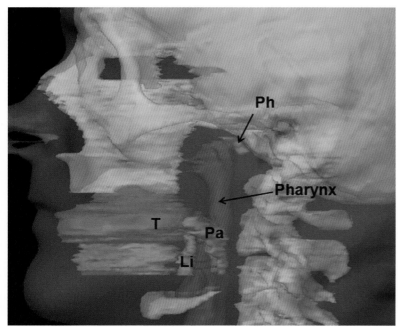

Figure 4.5.4

177

deep nodal chains. It is important to recognise that most cervical nodes drain lymph from ipsilateral locations. There are some exceptions however. Nodes associated with the floor of the mouth may receive lymph from both ipsilateral and contralateral aspects. Lymph from the midline sections of the tongue and tongue base may also drain into contralateral nodes via a complex array of afferent vessels.

It is therefore important to recognise that specific tumour sites within the head and neck, particularly oropharyngeal tumours, will have their own characteristic pattern of lymphatic involvement. With the exception of lymphoma, nodal involvement of the lower internal jugular and spinal accessory chains is indicative of further disease progression as this demonstrates sequential nodal spread. Lymphoma can also arise in the head and neck region, where Hodgkin's disease typically affects the nodes at levels III, IV and V. Affected nodes are commonly multiple and rounded but may be unilateral or bilateral. Extra-nodal lymphatic tissue within Waldeyer's ring is regularly affected in Non-Hodgkin's lymphoma.

Lymph nodes in the head and neck are assessed on CT by similar criteria to the rest of the body, whereby nodal appearance is a useful indicator of disease. In most cases, normal lymph nodes are not well visualised on CT, but should be slightly ovoid in cross-section, and demonstrate a relatively homogeneous CT density with a slightly fatty hilum. Size, shape, multiplicity, location, possible coalescence and CT density are all significant prognostic indicators of disease. Many patients will have nodes in the upper deep cervical chain with diffuse enlargement caused by repeated oral or upper respiratory tract infections that are unrelated to metastatic spread. Although a few discrete nodes such as the jugulodigastric (sentinel node) normally measure up to 15mm, lymph nodes demonstrated over 10mm in high risk patients should be considered abnormal or diseased. As well as being enlarged, diseased nodes may demonstrate a low density central area indicative of metastatic tumour necrosis or, conversely, affected nodes may all demonstrate homogenous CT density, as seen in lymphoma.

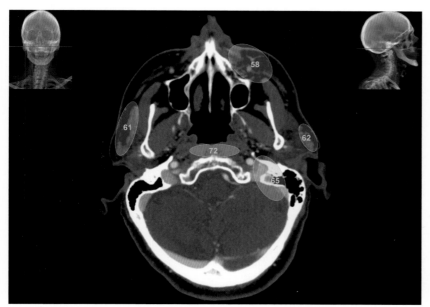

Figure 4.5.5

Figure 4.5.5 shows the location of lymph nodes level with the pharyngotympanic tube (auditory canal).

58. Left facial

61. Right superficial parotid

62. Left auricular (Level Va)

65. Deep parotid

72. Retropharyngeal

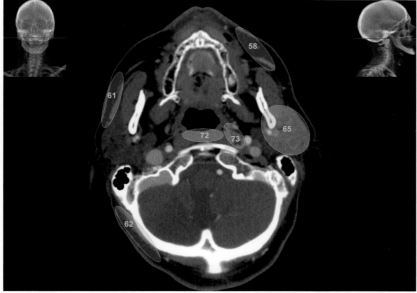

Figure 4.5.6

Figure 4.5.6 shows the location of lymph nodes level with the alveolar process of the maxilla and nasopharynx.

58. Left facial

61. Right superficial parotid

62. Right occipital (Level Va)

65. Left deep parotid (there are two groups: 20–30 nodes are embedded within the gland tissue itself and there is also a group of deeper nodes medial to the retromandibular parotid lobe)

72. Retropharyngeal

73. Left node of Rouvière

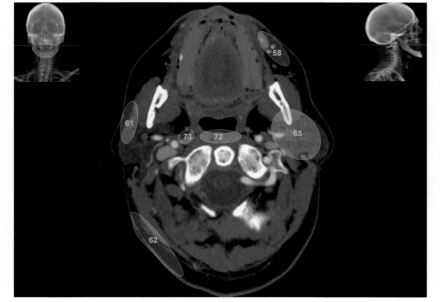

Figure 4.5.7

Figure 4.5.7 shows the location of lymph nodes level with the tongue and oropharynx.

58. Left facial

61. Right superficial parotid

62. Right occipital

65. Left deep parotid

72. Retropharyngeal

73. Right node of Rouvière

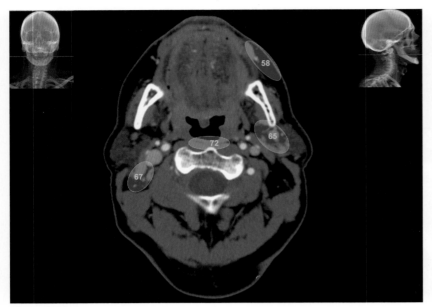

Figure 4.5.8

Figure 4.5.8 shows the location of lymph nodes level with the tongue and oropharynx, just inferior to Figure 4.5.7.

58. Left facial

65. Left deep parotid

67. Right spinal accessory (Level Va)

72. Retropharyngeal

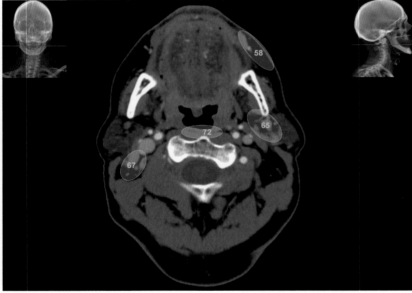

Figure 4.5.9

Figure 4.5.9 shows the location of lymph nodes level with cervical vertebra C3 and the submandibular glands.

59. Left submental (Level Ia)

60. Right submandibular (Level Ib)

63. Left external jugular (Level III)

66. Right jugulodigastric (Sentinel) (Level IIa)

67. Right spinal accessory (Level Va)

68. Superior internal jugular (Level IIa)

72. Retropharyngeal

74. Nuchal

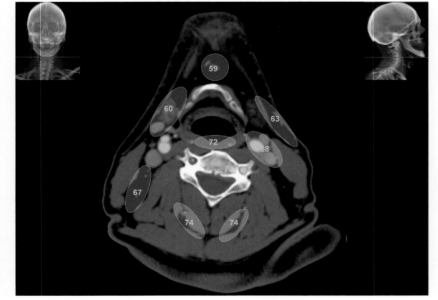

Figure 4.5.10

Figure 4.5.10 shows the location of lymph nodes level with cervical vertebra C4 and body of the hyoid bone.

59. Submental (Level Ia)

60. Right submandibular (Level Ib)

63. Left external jugular (Level III)

67. Right spinal accessory (Level Va)

68. Superior internal jugular (Level IIa)

72. Retropharyngeal

74. Nuchal

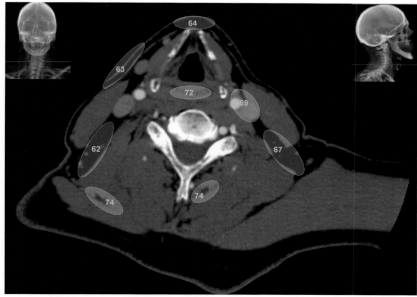

Figure 4.5.11

Figure 4.5.11 shows the location of lymph nodes level with cervical vertebra C5, just superior to the glottis.

63. Right external jugular (Level III)

64. Visceral (Level VI)

67. Spinal accessory (Level Vb)

69. Left middle jugular chain (Level IIa)

72. Retropharyngeal

74. Right and left nuchal

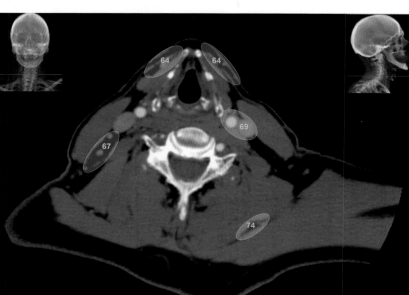

Figure 4.5.12

Figure 4.5.12 shows the location of lymph nodes level with the inferior aspect of cervical vertebra C5 and the glottis.

64. Visceral (Level VI)

67. Right spinal accessory (Level Vb)

69. Left middle internal jugular (Level III)

74. Left nuchal

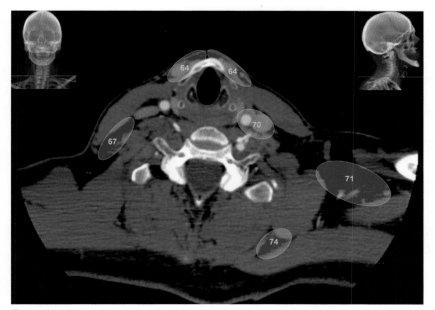

Figure 4.5.13

Figure 4.5.13 shows the location of lymph nodes level with the inferior aspect of cervical vertebra 6 and the cricoid cartilage.

64. Visceral (Level VI)

67. Right spinal accessory (Level Vb)

70. Left inferior internal jugular (Level IV)

71. Left supraclavicular

74. Left nuchal

4.6 Deep Spaces

Three-dimensional understanding of the deep cervical fascial boundaries and spaces within has been expanded upon by the use of CT and MRI in recent years. The patterns of spread of infection and tumour growth within these deep spaces are now diagnostically supported with CT and MRI, rather than the surgeon's knife. Infection and tumour spread tends to be concentrated along any free space that exists between fascial planes and structures. Thus from a radiotherapy perspective it can be seen that an understanding of these deep spaces can help identify main routes of local spread. The deep spaces are divided into supra- and infrahyoid regions, as indicated in Figure 4.6.1. An in-depth description of the spaces is beyond the scope of this text and readers seeking more detailed information are directed to relevant texts in the bibliography.

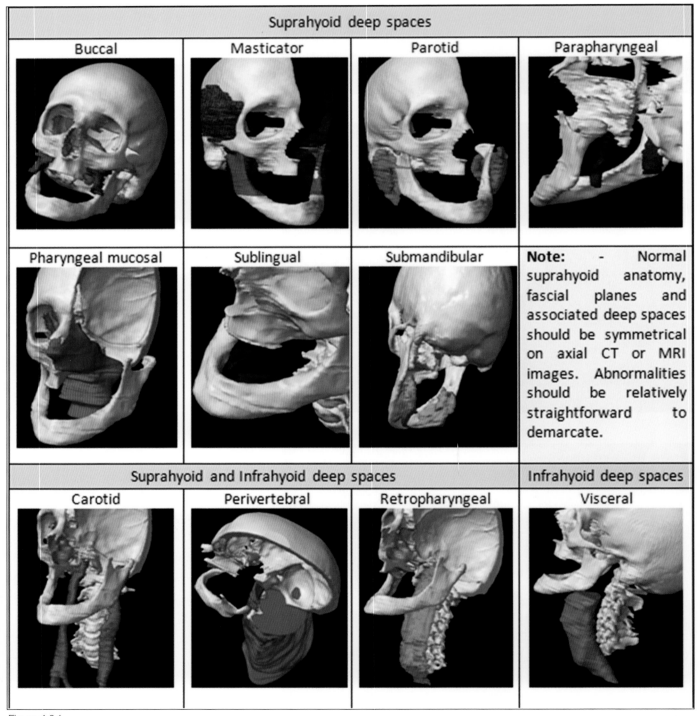

Figure 4.6.1

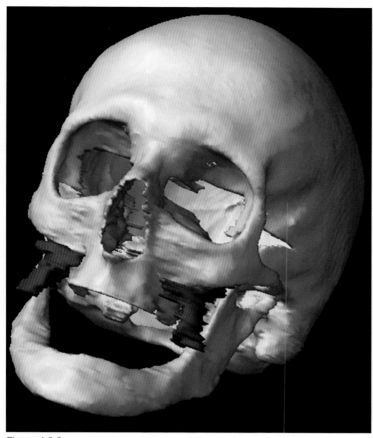

Figure 4.6.2

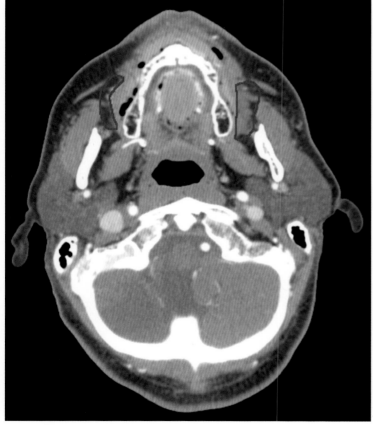

Figure 4.6.3

4.6.1 Buccal Space

The buccal spaces are paired and suprahyoid. As seen in Figure 4.6.3, the buccal space is predominantly filled with adipose tissue called the buccal fat pad. The space extends medially between the maxillary sinuses and mandibular rami and is poorly compartmentalised. Its boundaries are the buccinator muscle medially, superficial facial muscles laterally and anterior aspect of the parotid gland and medial pterygoid muscle posteriorly. Fat within the buccal space communicates with fat in the masticator space as seen later. The parotid duct crosses the space as it bends medially to pass through the buccinator muscle and into the mouth. This divides the space up into anterior and posterior sections. Radiologically, the fat within the posterior section has consistently lower attenuation than in the anterior buccal space.

Clinical implications

The buccal space is poorly compartmentalised, particularly in superior, inferior and posterior directions. This facilitates the spread of pathology to and from the buccal space, particularly from the parotid gland into the oral cavity. The parotid duct, accessory parotid glands, minor salivary glands, buccal arteries, facial vein, buccal lymph nodes and channels and branches of the facial and mandibular nerve all pass through the buccal space.

Tumour pathology

Pathology from adjacent spaces, parotid and oral tumours can spread into the buccal space. The commonest buccal tumours are squamous cell lesions within buccal lymph nodes and lymph channels related to adjacent spaces. Other tumours are related to structures contained within the space such as minor salivary gland tumours, pleomorphic adenomas, and acinic cell carcinomas. Other rarer lesions are connective, neural, muscular and lymphatic in origin.

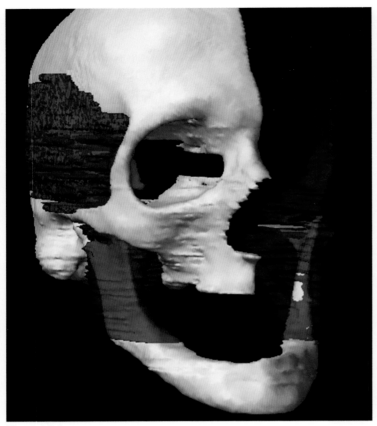

Figure 4.6.4

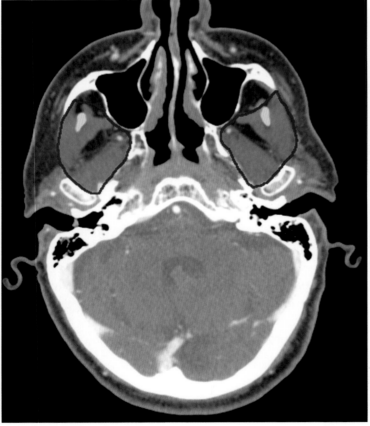

Figure 4.6.5

4.6.2 Masticator Space

The masticator spaces are paired, suprahyoid and enclose the muscles of mastication. The muscles included are the masseter, medial and lateral pterygoid and temporalis. The masticator space can be divided into two smaller sections, supra and infrazygomatic masticator spaces, as seen in Figure 4.6.4. The borders of the supra-zygomatic space can be quite variable, yet extend to include the whole of the temporalis muscle and its attachments to the high parietal calvarium. More inferiorly, below the zygomatic arch, the inferior borders of the infrazygomatic masticator space are the angle of the mandible inferiorly, zygomatic arch superolaterally, attachments of the pterygoid muscles, and base of the skull superomedially around the infratemporal fossa. The masticator space is within the superficial layer of the deep cervical fascia; however, there is no horizontal fascia separating the two smaller spaces. The buccal space lies anteriorly.

Clinical implications

At the superomedial margin, the masticator space borders the base of the skull, up to and including the lateral pterygoid plate of the sphenoid and crossing the foramen ovale. Retrograde perineural spread of disease from the masticator space into the cranium is possible. Tumour infiltration along the mandibular nerve may cause trismus, spasm of the masticator muscle.

Tumour pathology

Tumours from salivary glands, nasopharynx, oropharynx and oral cavity have great potential to extend into the masticator space. Tumours originating from within the masticator space tend to be sarcoma based.

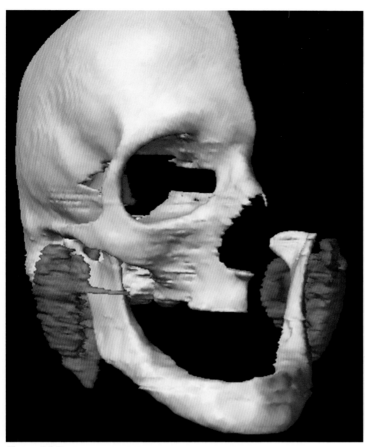

Figure 4.6.6

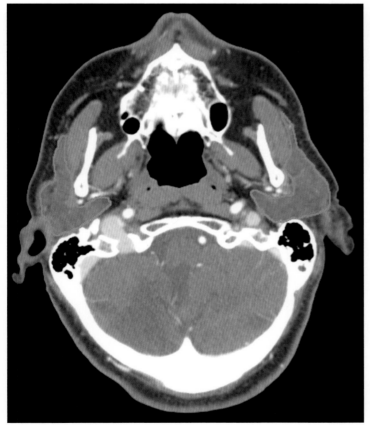

Figure 4.6.7

4.6.3 Parotid Space

The parotid spaces are paired, suprahyoid and essentially enclose the parotid glands. The parotid space extends from the pinna posteriorly to the anterior borders adjacent to and occasionally over the masseter muscle. The parotid space can extend inferiorly beyond the angle of the mandible to the platysma muscle (just under the skin surface). The deep retromandibular parotid lobe extends medially adjacent to the fatty parapharyngeal space. Like the parotid gland, the space is divided into superficial and deep parotid spaces by the location of the extracranial portion of the facial nerve. As mentioned previously, it is extremely difficult to see this on normal CT scans; however, as the nerve runs lateral to the retromandibular vein, the location of the nerve can be approximated. The parotid space is enclosed by the superficial layer of the deep cervical fascia.

Clinical implications

Due to relatively late embryological encapsulation of the parotid gland, this space includes 20–30 intraparotid lymph nodes. Other structures enclosed within the parotid space are the retromandibular vein, maxillary branch of the external carotid artery, extracranial portion of the facial nerve and the proximal parotid duct.

Tumour pathology

Parotid tumours include Warthin's tumour, mucoepidermoid carcinoma, adenocarcinoma, adenoid cystic carcinoma and more commonly benign mixed tumours.

Non-Hodgkin's lymphoma (primary and metastatic) is also found. The encapsulated lymph nodes are the first level drainage from the scalp, deep face and external auditory canal. As the facial nerve passes through the parotid space, neural based tumours may also be present.

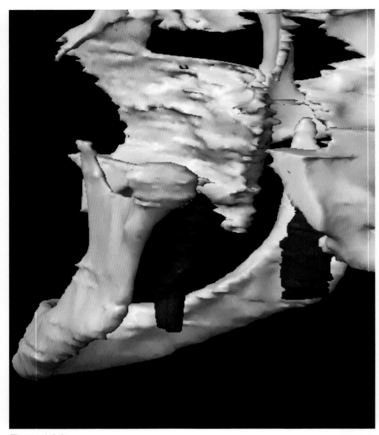

Figure 4.6.8

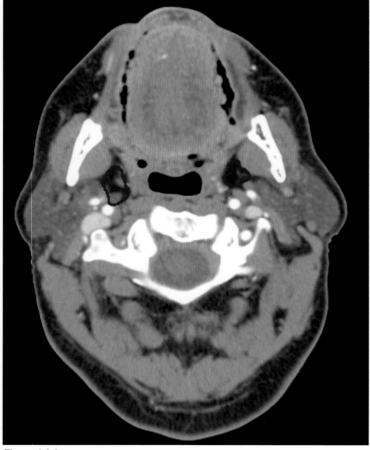

Figure 4.6.9

4.6.4 Parapharyngeal Space

The paired, suprahyoid parapharyngeal spaces are relatively vertical tubular structures. They are filled with adipose tissue and are centrally sandwiched between other vital deep spaces, either side of the pharynx. The parapharyngeal space extends from the base of the skull superiorly to the submandibular space inferiorly. It borders the masticator space anteriorly, the parotid space laterally, perivertebral space and carotid spaces posteriorly and pharyngeal mucosal space medially. An understanding of the adjacent spaces will aid localisation of the parapharyngeal space. Being composed mainly of adipose tissue, it is relatively easy to locate on CT with a lower attenuation (-65HU).

Clinical implications

The space contains adipose tissue, small vessels, small branches of the mandibular division of the trigeminal nerve and very little else. There are no fascial planes separating the space superoinferiorly and therefore disease can spread relatively easily through the loose connective tissue. Sometimes this space is referred to as an 'elevator shaft' in which disease processes can spread superior or inferior. As the space contains very few structures, most diseases within the parapharyngeal space arise from adjacent spaces.

Tumour pathology

As described above, most tumours within the parapharyngeal space tend to be malignant infiltration from adjacent deep spaces. The spread of infection is also commonly seen within the parapharyngeal spaces.

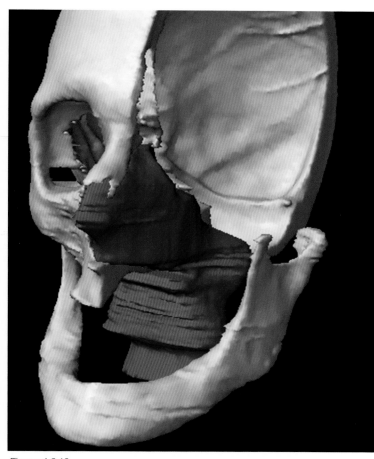

Figure 4.6.10

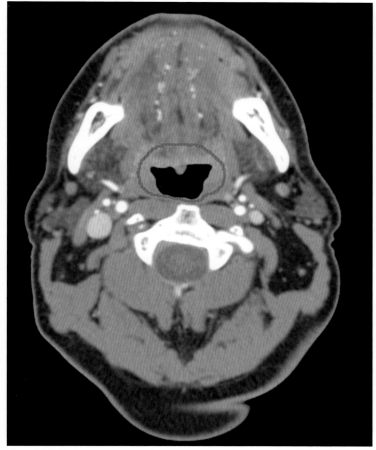

Figure 4.6.11

4.6.5 Pharyngeal Mucosal Space

The unpaired pharyngeal space is mostly suprahyoid and comprises the mucosa, sub-mucosa and immediate muscles of the nasal cavity, nasopharynx, oral cavity, oropharynx and hypopharynx. The space is a continuous mucosal sheet running vertically from the roof of the nasopharynx down to the epiglottis and hypopharynx. The pharyngeal space is not a true enclosed deep space, as there are no fasciae on its surface.

Clinical implications

The space is entirely superficial when compared to the other spaces, and tends to be bounded by fasciae, muscles and bones as opposed to cavities. Waldeyer's ring is included within the pharyngeal space. There may also be minor salivary glands located within the soft palate mucosa. Minor asymmetry within the pharyngeal space may be confused for tumours. High on the posterolateral borders of the pharynx, between the upper border of the superior constructor muscle and the base of the skull, there is a small indentation called the Sinus of Morgagni. The opening to the pharyngotympanic (auditory or Eustachian) tube is located adjacent to this sinus. These structures provide a route for the spread of disease from nasopharyngeal tumours into the skull base.

Tumour pathology

Lined with squamous epithelium, the space can be an origin for squamous cell carcinoma head and neck cancers. There may also be mucoepidermoid or adenoid cystic carcinomas arising from the mucosa. Other tumours are related to the lymphoid tissues, such as Non-Hodgkin's lymphoma. Although rare, there may also be minor salivary gland tumours.

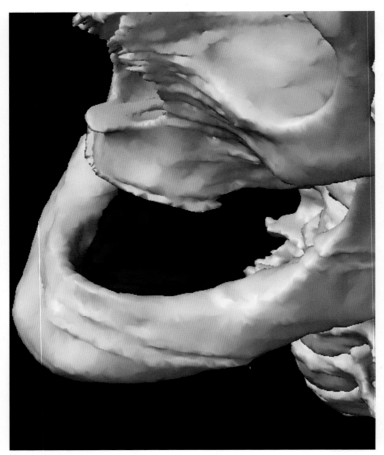

Figure 4.6.12

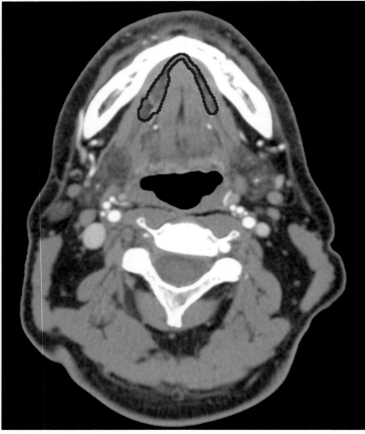

Figure 4.6.13

4.6.6 Sublingual Space

The sublingual spaces are paired, suprahyoid and located in the anterior floor of the mouth deep to the tongue. The two halves are separated by the roots of the genioglossus and geniohyoid muscles. Some texts also refer to this as the floor of the mouth space. The two spaces are linked anteriorly by a thin isthmus connecting the spaces anteriorly, posterior to the mandible. Viewed in a coronal section from the anterior, the sublingual spaces are described as having a teacup shape. Some texts also suggest one combined large space, rather than two left and right spaces separated in the midline by the genioglossus and geniohyoid muscle complex. The mylohyoid muscle forms the inferior boundary to the sublingual space. This muscle can be likened to a sling of muscles supporting the floor of the mouth. There are several important structures that pass through or lie within the sublingual space. These include the sublingual glands and ducts, sublingual lymph nodes, deep lobe of the submandibular gland, submandibular (Wharton's) duct, lingual artery and vein.

Clinical implications

There is no fascial tissue surrounding the sublingual spaces so infection or tumour spread can be relatively unchecked. Tumour spread from adjacent regions such as the submandibular space is not uncommon.

Squamous Cell Carcinoma (SCC) tumours crossing the lingual septum into the contralateral submandibular space are classed as un-resectable for cure. The deep tongue neuro-vascular bundles are all located in the sublingual space, so any tumours may affect the mobility and function of the tongue. Amalgam fillings in mandibular teeth may cause imaging artefacts on CT and MRI and may obscure tumour boundaries.

Tumour pathology

SCC of the tongue base and mucoepidermoid or adenocystic carcinoma of the sublingual glands can arise in this space.

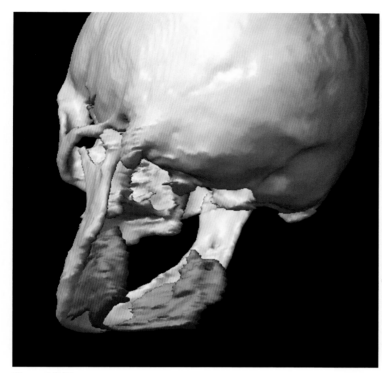

Figure 4.6.14

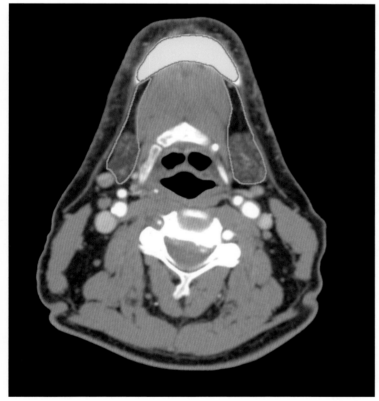

Figure 4.6.15

4.6.7 Submandibular Space

The horseshoe-shaped submandibular space is a singular, mostly suprahyoid region below the mandible. The inferoposterior aspect of the submandibular space extends into the anterior neck space below the hyoid bone. The structures that pass through or lie within the submandibular space include the superficial portion of submandibular gland, submandibular and submental lymph nodes (level IA and IB), anterior belly of digastric muscle, facial artery and vein and adipose tissue

Clinical implications

Obstructed and enlarged submandibular glands may give the appearance of a malignant lymph node associated with floor of mouth SCC. The superficial layer of the deep cervical fascia encapsulates the submandibular glands. A tongue like extension of glandular tissue (as seen in Figure 4.6.15) projects anteriorly into the sublingual space. The majority of lesions are associated with either lymph nodes or submandibular glands. Lesions within the inferior 'tail' of the parotid gland may be seen directly superior to the submandibular space and may cause confusion.

Tumour pathology

The most common malignant diseases within the submandibular space are lymph node metastases from SCC face, tongue or floor of mouth. Mucoepidermoid and adenocystic carcinoma of the submandibular glands or non-Hodgkin's lymphoma can also be found.

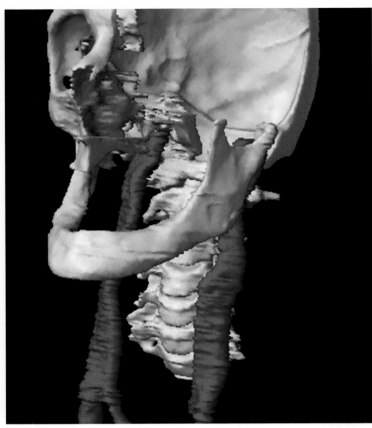

Figure 4.6.16

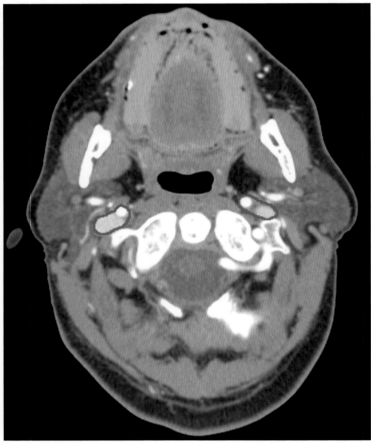

Figure 4.6.17

4.6.8 Carotid Space

The paired carotid spaces are long tubular structures running from the carotid canal and jugular foramen in the base of the skull to the aortic arch, lateral to the retropharyngeal space. The carotid space is sometimes referred to as either the carotid sheath or poststyloid pharyngeal space. As it is so long (as demonstrated in Figure 4.6.16) the carotid space is often divided into descriptive segments to help localise adjacent structures: nasopharyngeal, oropharyngeal, cervical and mediastinal. Other anatomical segments used for description are suprahyoid or infrahyoid. Within the suprahyoid carotid spaces are the internal carotid artery, internal jugular vein and cranial nerves IX-XII. The infrahyoid carotid contains the common carotid artery, internal jugular vein and cranial nerve X (vagus).

Clinical implications

Three layers of deep cervical fascia converge to form the dense carotid sheath. As the carotid sheath is so thick, it is rarely breached and disease tends to encase the sheath externally. Lesions within the carotid space consequently adopt a fusiform shape. Deep cervical nodes of the internal jugular chain lie adjacent to the internal jugular vein, but not actually inside the carotid space. A thrombosis in the internal jugular vein may mimic a necrotic lymph node.

Tumour pathology

The barrier of the carotid sheath ensures that most lesions within the space tend to originate from within.

Adjacent lymphadenopathy is the most common pathology, and may originate from SCC, thyroid, Hodgkin's and non-Hodgkin's lymphoma or nodal metastatic disease progression from lung and abdominal carcinoma. If the surrounding lymph nodes display peripheral calcification, this is indicative of previously treated lymphoma or silicosis. Enlarged cystic or hypervascular nodes tend to be associated with thyroid carcinoma.

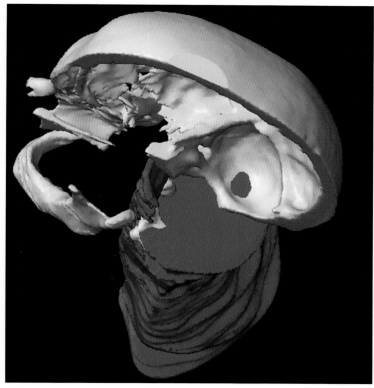

Figure 4.6.18

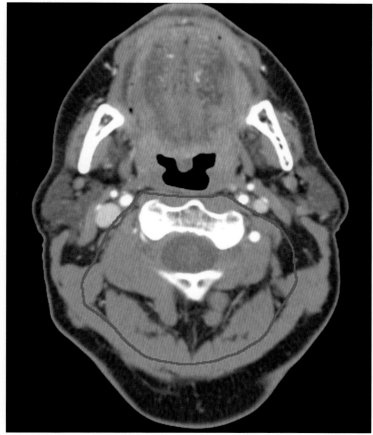

Figure 4.6.19

4.6.9 Perivertebral Space

The perivertebral space is one very large midline space, which extends from the base of the skull to just above T4 at the root of the neck. The space is surrounded by the deep layer of the deep cervical fascia, and encloses the cervical vertebral column, pre-vertebral and paraspinal muscles, anterior to and around the vertebral column, as seen outlined in Figure 4.6.19. The space is surrounded by a layer of adipose tissue within the posterior cervical space. Historically, the perivertebral space has been divided into two distinct components. The prevertebral space is anterior to and including the vertebral body and pedicles. It contains vertebral body and pedicles, intervertebral discs, spinal canal, brachial plexus roots and the vertebral artery and vein. The paravertebral space contains the posterior elements of the cervical vertebral column and the proximal brachial plexus.

Clinical implications

There is a very thin layer of areolar tissue trapped between the anterior aspect of the prevertebral space and posterior aspect of the retro-pharyngeal space. This is called the 'danger space' and is also considered part of the prevertebral space by some authors. The danger space runs along the length of the prevertebral space, and is not divided by any fascial planes supero-inferiorly. Disease can therefore progress within this space unchecked, and the spread of infection can be extremely rapid, leading to mediastinitis, emphysema and sepsis.

Tumour pathology

Most malignant prevertebral pathologies originate from the vertebral bodies and tend to be metastatic in origin, from lung, breast, prostate, thyroid and renal primary tumours. There may be rhabdomyosarcoma tumours in children.

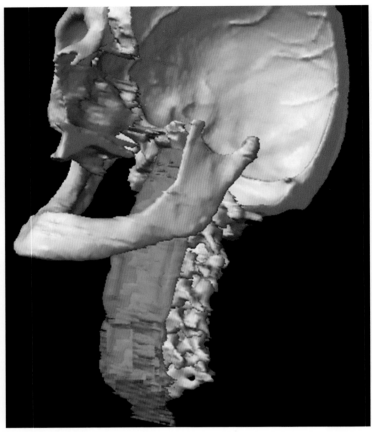

Figure 4.6.20

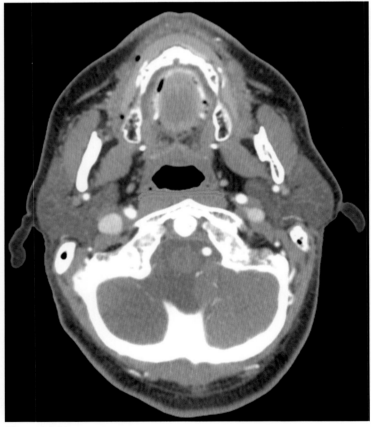

Figure 4.6.21

4.6.10 Retropharyngeal Space

The retropharyngeal space is a relatively thin potential midline space located directly posterior to the pharynx. It extends from the base of the skull to the upper mediastinum. The space is sandwiched between the pharyngeal mucosal space and 'danger space' prevertebral component of the perivertebral space. It is bordered laterally by both carotid spaces. The space is normally very thin in cross-section, as can be seen in Figure 4.6.21. The retropharyngeal space contains fat and lymph nodes within the suprahyoid region. These lymph nodes are grouped into 'lateral' and 'median'. Some of the nodes in the lateral group are also termed 'Nodes of Rouvière'. The eponymous node of Rouvière is found superiorly in the lateral group, close to the base of the skull. There are no lymph nodes in the retropharyngeal space in the infrahyoid region.

Clinical implications

SCC of the nasopharynx, posterior oropharynx and hypopharynx all drain into the suprahyoid retropharyngeal nodes. Radiation therapy of the head and neck region may cause oedema within the retropharyngeal space. A relatively high proportion of patients who undergo laryngeal radiation treatment suffer from an accumulation of fluid within the retropharyngeal space. This is normally seen approximately five weeks following therapy and can last up to six months. This will be demonstrated as a low attenuation area within the space with a mass effect pushing the fascial planes apart. It should appear symmetrical in cross-section, unless neighbouring lymphadenopathy distorts the anatomy.

Tumour pathology

Tumours within the retropharyngeal space tend to be direct extensions of SCC tumours from adjacent spaces. Nodal involvement is primarily spread from nasopharyngeal SCC. There can also be lymph node metastases from melanoma, thyroid carcinoma and lymphoma.

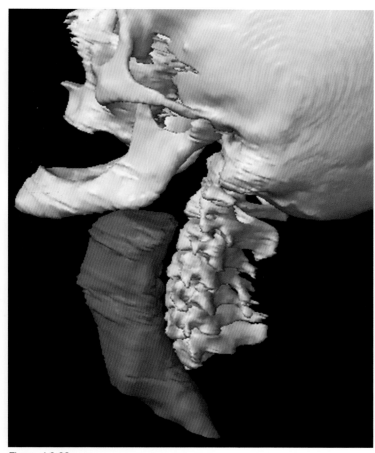

Figure 4.6.22

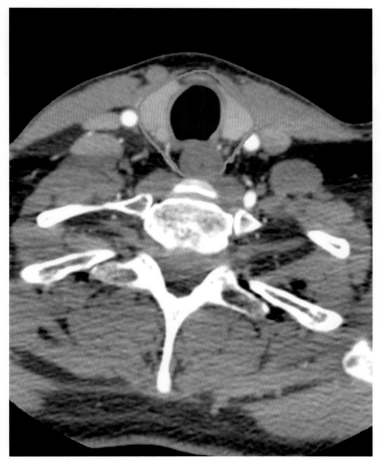

Figure 4.6.23

4.6.11 Visceral Space

The visceral space is a tubular infrahyoid space that extends from the hyoid bone to the upper mediastinum. Its boundaries are the carotid spaces posterolaterally and retropharyngeal space posteriorly. The visceral space can be further subdivided into four regions: laryngeal, thyroid, parathyroid and oesophageal. It is essentially the space that contains the infrahyoid viscera and contains the larynx, hypopharynx, cervical oesophagus, trachea and both thyroid and parathyroid glands.

Clinical implications

The level VI paratracheal lymph nodes are the first order drainage for thyroid malignancies which can then spread to nodes within the superior mediastinum. The prelaryngeal and pretracheal nodal groups are also located within the visceral space. The prelaryngeal nodes are located directly anterior to the larynx in the midline. Inferiorly, the pretracheal lymph nodes are seen in a similar location, directly anterior to the trachea. Lesions within the visceral space depend upon regional location thus laryngeal, thyroid, parathyroid and oesophageal lesions will present with different clinical symptoms.

Tumour pathology

Tumours within the visceral space will vary with their location. Typical tumours include SCC and chondrosarcoma of the larynx, thyroid carcinoma, adenoma of the parathyroid gland and oesophageal carcinoma. There may also be nodal metastases associated with SCC and lymphoma as described earlier.

4.7 Full Head and Neck CT Anatomy

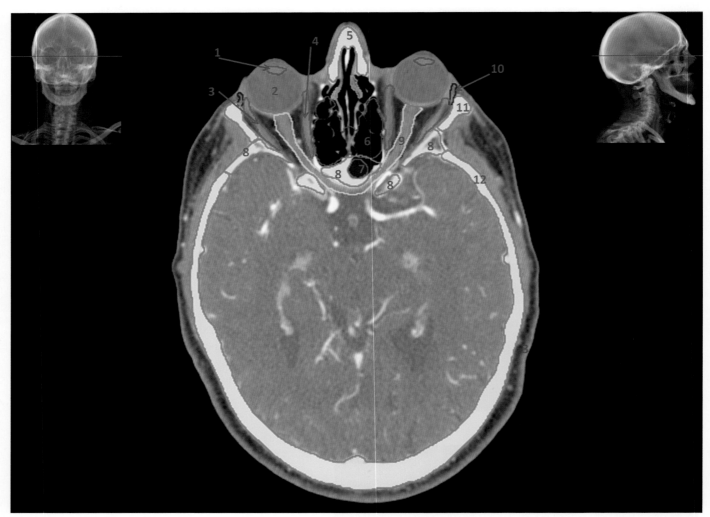

Figure 4.7.1

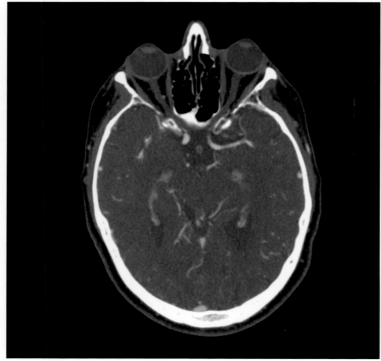

Figure 4.7.2

1. Lens
2. Eye
3. Lateral Rectus Muscle
4. Medial Rectus Muscle
5. Nasal Bone
6. Ethmoid Sinus
7. Sphenoid Sinus
8. Sphenoid Bone
9. Optic Nerve
10. Lacrimal Gland
11. Zygomatic Bone
12. Temporal Bone

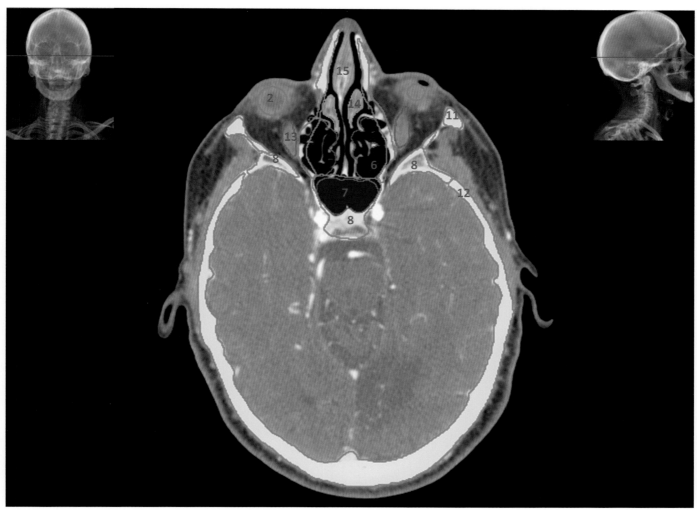

Figure 4.7.3

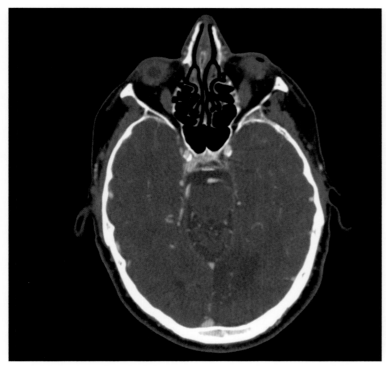

Figure 4.7.4

2. Eye
6. Ethmoid Sinus
7. Sphenoid Sinus
8. Sphenoid Bone
11. Zygomatic Bone
12. Temporal Bone
13. Inferior Rectus Muscle
14. Nasal Concha
15. Nasal Septum

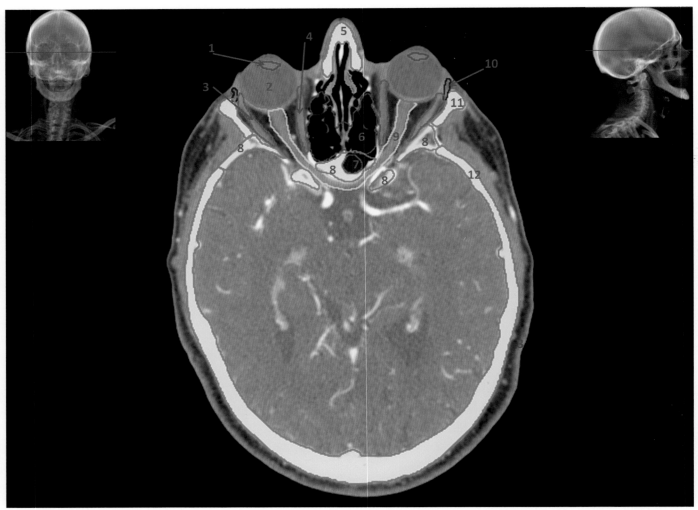

Figure 4.7.5

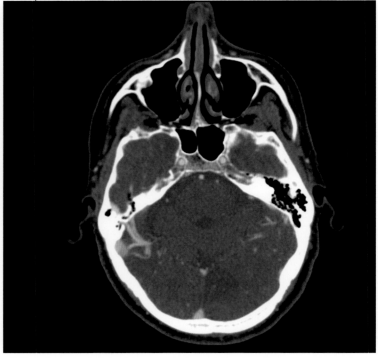

Figure 4.7.6

7. Sphenoid Sinus
8. Sphenoid Bone
12. Temporal Bone (Petrous Ridge)
14. Nasal Concha
15. Nasal Septum
16. Maxillary Sinus
17. Maxilla

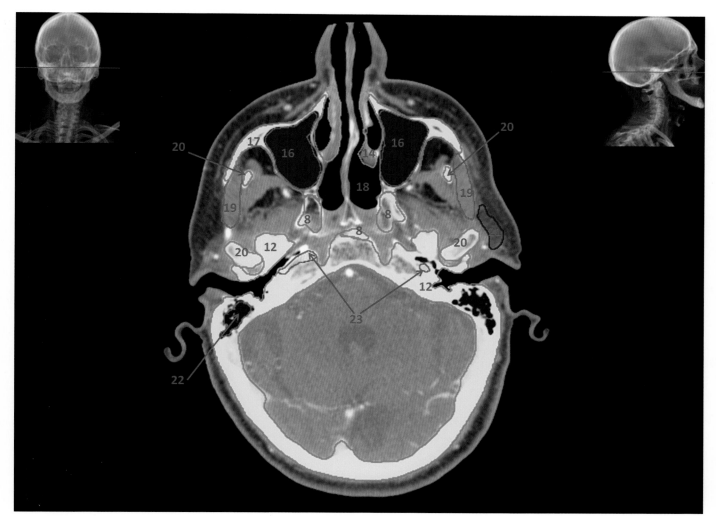

Figure 4.7.7

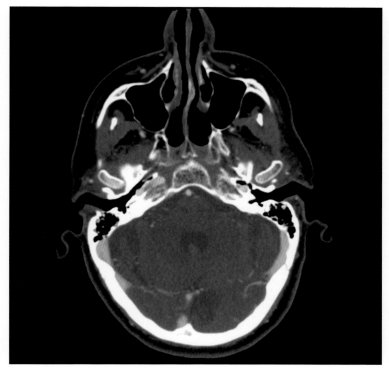

Figure 4.7.8

8. Sphenoid Bone
12. Temporal Bone
14. Nasal Concha
16. Maxillary Sinus
17. Maxilla
18. Nasal Cavity
19. Masseter Muscle
20. Temporomandibular Joint
21. Parotid Gland
22. Mastoid Air Cells
23. Internal Carotid Artery

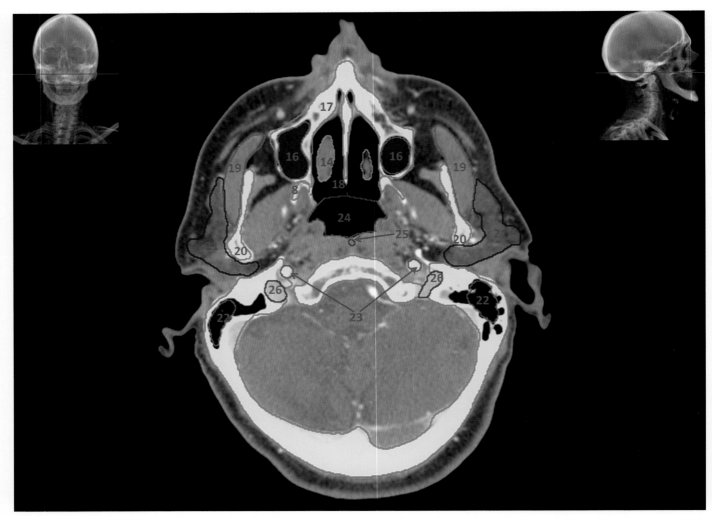

Figure 4.7.9

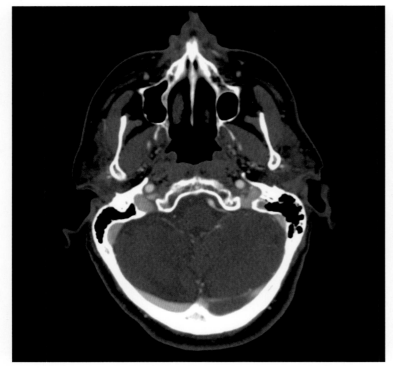

Figure 4.7.10

8. Sphenoid Bone
14. Nasal Concha
16. Maxillary Sinus
17. Maxilla
18. Nasal Cavity
19. Masseter Muscle
20. Mandible
21. Parotid Gland
22. Mastoid Air Cells
23. Internal Carotid Artery
24. Nasopharynx
25. Pharyngeal Tonsil
26. Jugular Vein

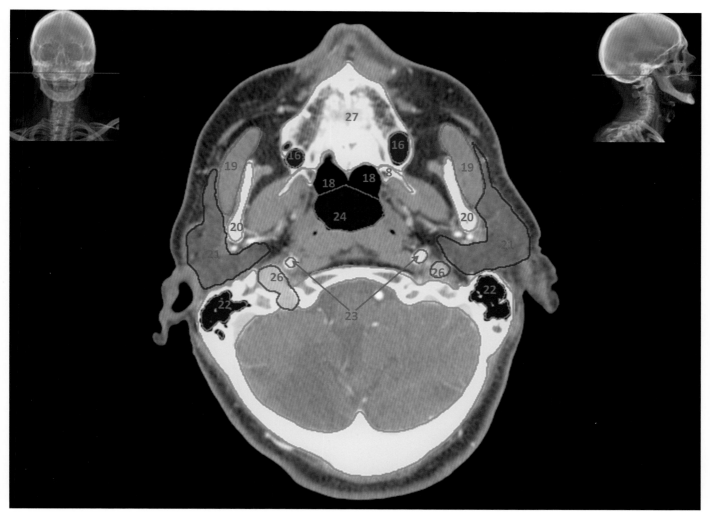

Figure 4.7.11

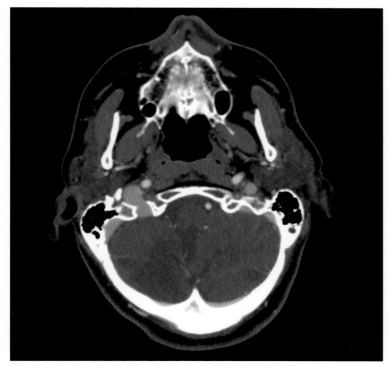

Figure 4.7.12

8.   Sphenoid Bone
16. Maxillary Sinus
18. Nasal Cavity
19. Masseter Muscle
20. Mandible
21. Parotid Gland
22. Mastoid Air Cells
23. Internal Carotid Artery
24. Nasopharynx
26. Jugular Vein
27. Hard Palate

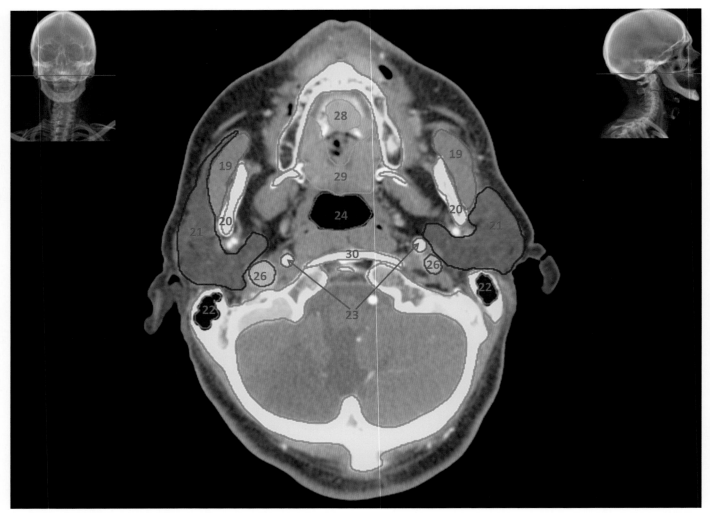

Figure 4.7.13

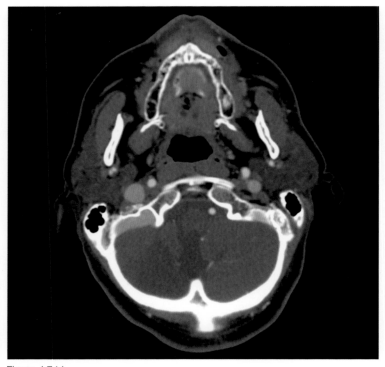

Figure 4.7.14

19. Masseter Muscle
20. Mandible
21. Parotid Gland
22. Mastoid Air Cells
23. Internal Carotid Artery
24. Nasopharynx
26. Jugular Vein
28. Tongue
29. Soft Palate

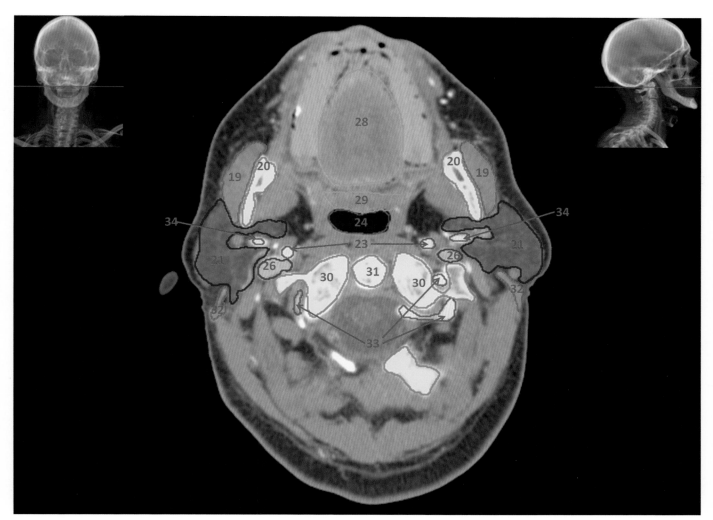

Figure 4.7.15

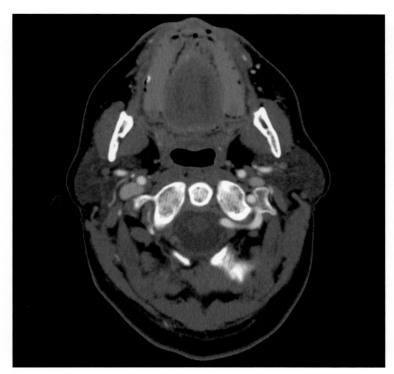

Figure 4.7.16

19. Masseter Muscle
20. Mandible
21. Parotid Gland
23. Internal Carotid Artery
24. Nasopharynx
26. Jugular Vein
28. Tongue
29. Soft Palate
30. C1 (Atlas)
31. C2 (Dens of Axis)
32. Sternocleidomastoid Muscle
33. Vertebral Artery
34. External Carotid Artery

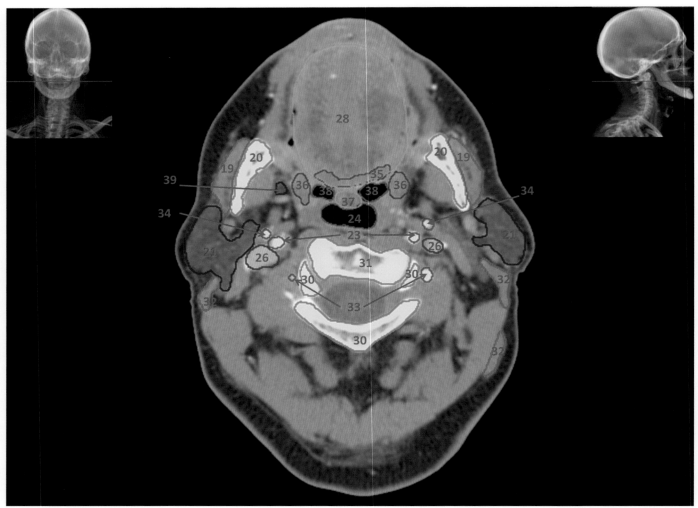

Figure 4.7.17

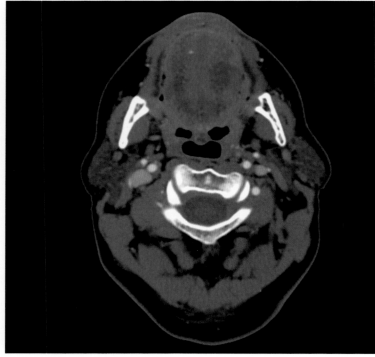

Figure 4.7.18

19. Masseter Muscle
20. Mandible
21. Parotid Gland
23. Internal Carotid Artery
24. Nasopharynx
26. Jugular Vein
28. Tongue
30. C1 (Atlas)
31. C2 (Axis)
32. Sternocleidomastoid Muscle
33. Vertebral Artery
34. External Carotid Artery
35. Lingual Tonsil
36. Palatine Tonsil
37. Uvula
38. Oropharynx
39. Submandibular Salivary Gland

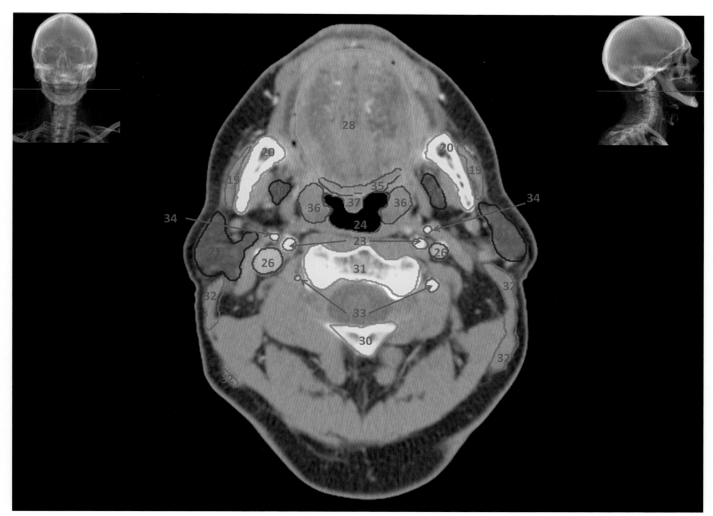

Figure 4.7.19

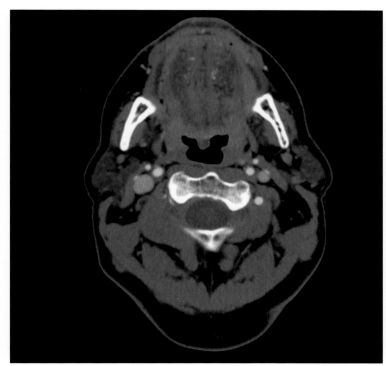

Figure 4.7.20

19. Masseter Muscle
20. Mandible
21. Parotid Gland
23. Internal Carotid Artery
24. Nasopharynx
26. Jugular Vein
28. Tongue
30. C1 (Atlas)
31. C2 (Axis)
32. Sternocleidomastoid Muscle
33. Vertebral Artery
34. External Carotid Artery
35. Lingual Tonsil
36. Palatine Tonsil
37. Uvula
39. Submandibular Salivary Gland

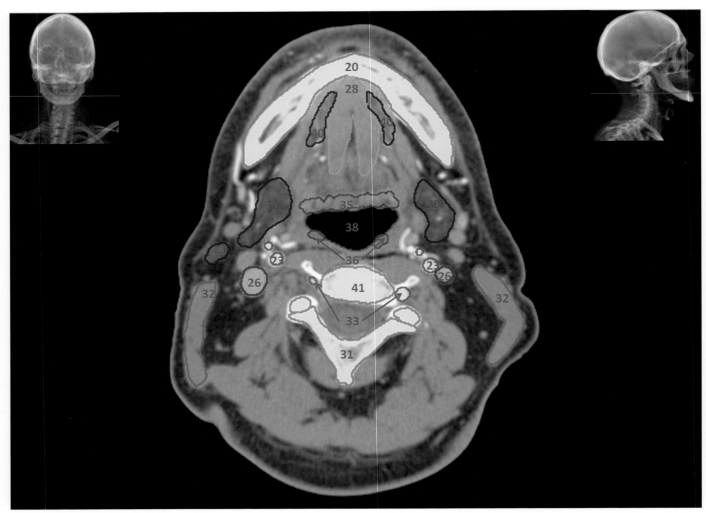

Figure 4.7.21

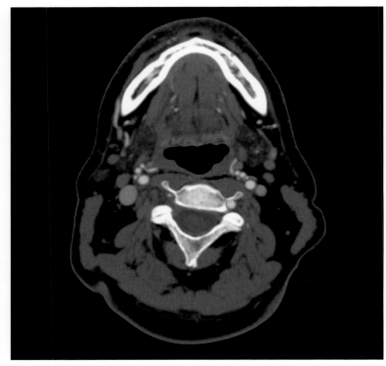

Figure 4.7.22

20. Mandible
21. Parotid Gland
23. Internal Carotid Artery
26. Jugular Vein
28. Tongue
31. C2 (Axis)
32. Sternocleidomastoid Muscle
33. Vertebral Artery
35. Lingual Tonsil
36. Palatine Tonsil
38. Oropharynx
39. Submandibular Salivary Gland
40. Sublingual Salivary Gland
41. C3

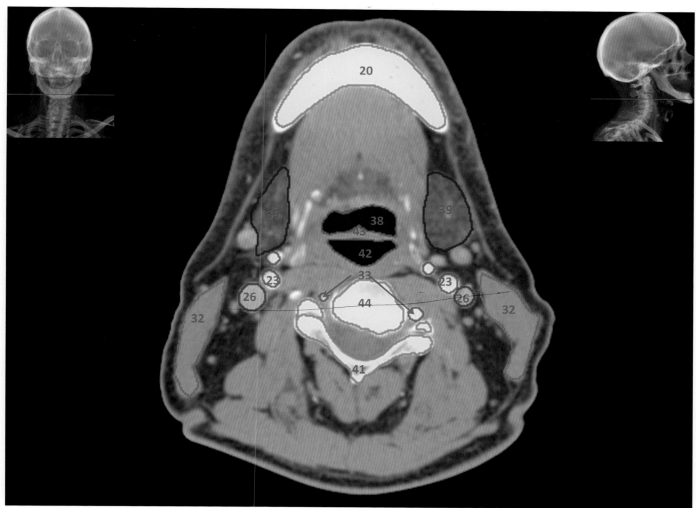

Figure 4.7.23

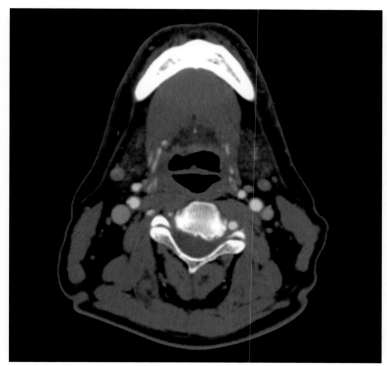

Figure 4.7.24

20. Mandible
23. Internal Carotid Artery
26. Jugular Vein
32. Sternocleidomastoid Muscle
33. Vertebral Artery
38. Oropharynx
39. Submandibular Salivary Gland
41. C3
42. Hypopharynx
43. Epiglottis
44. C4

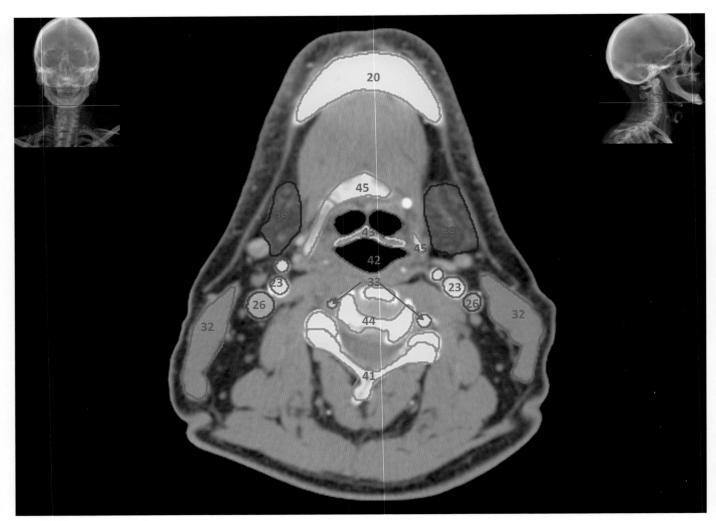

Figure 4.7.25

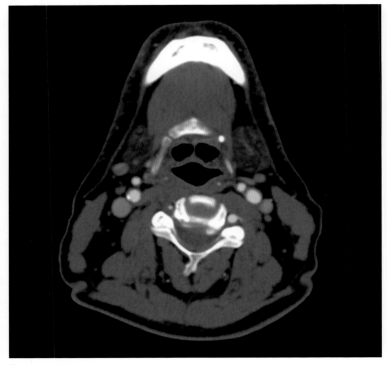

Figure 4.7.26

20. Mandible
23. Internal Carotid Artery
26. Jugular Vein
32. Sternocleidomastoid Muscle
33. Vertebral Artery
39. Submandibular Salivary Gland
41. C3
42. Hypopharynx
43. Epiglottis
44. C4
45. Hyoid Bone

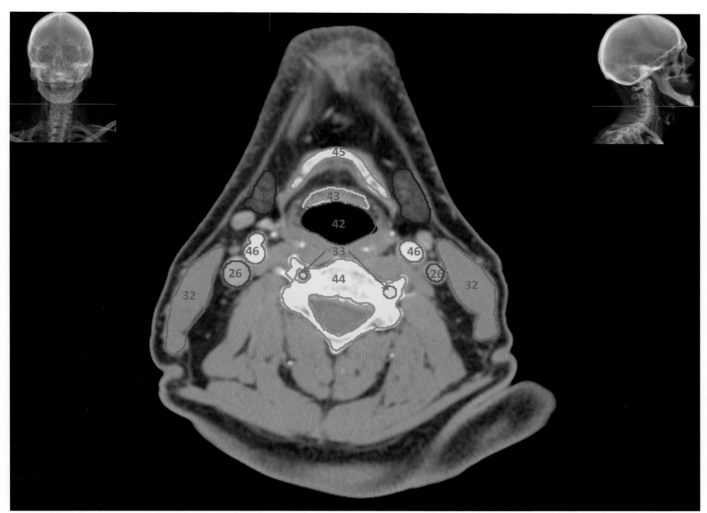

Figure 4.7.27

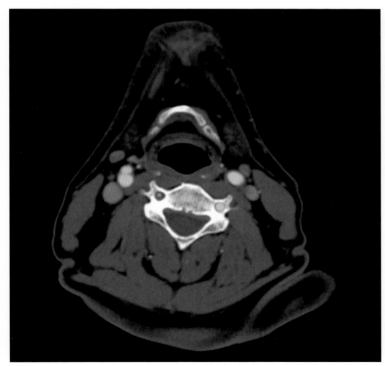

Figure 4.7.28

26. Jugular Vein
32. Sternocleidomastoid Muscle
33. Vertebral Artery
39. Submandibular Salivary Gland
42. Hypopharynx
43. Epiglottis
44. C4
45. Hyoid Bone
46. Common Carotid Artery

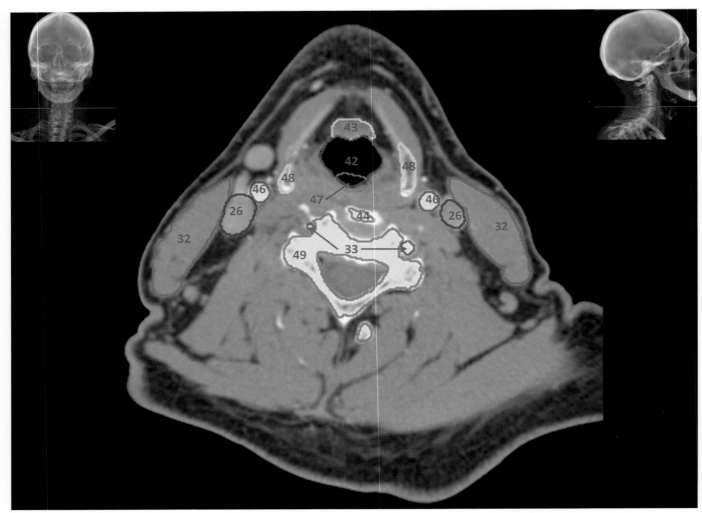

Figure 4.7.29

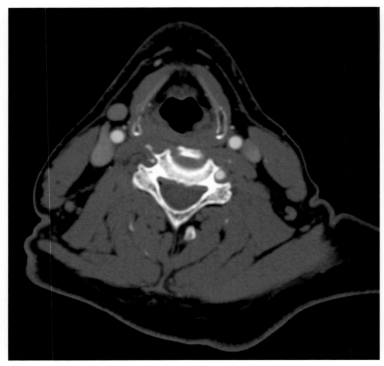

Figure 4.7.30

26. Jugular Vein
32. Sternocleidomastoid Muscle
33. Vertebral Artery
42. Hypopharynx
43. Epiglottis
44. C4
46. Common Carotid Artery
47. Oesophagus
48. Thyroid Cartilage of Larynx
49. C5

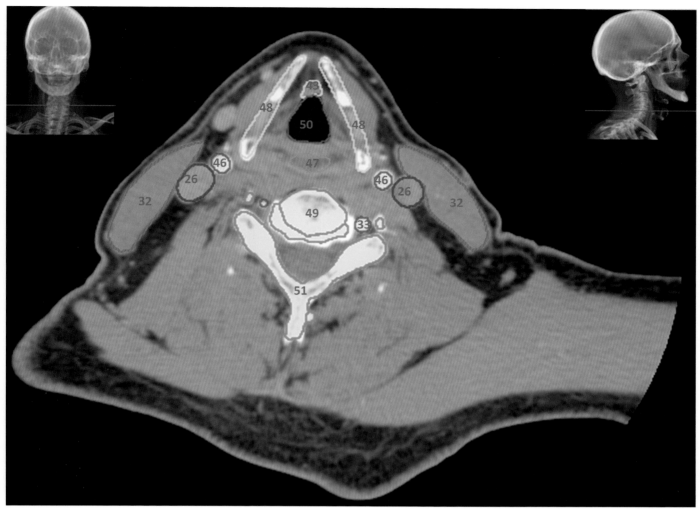

Figure 4.7.31

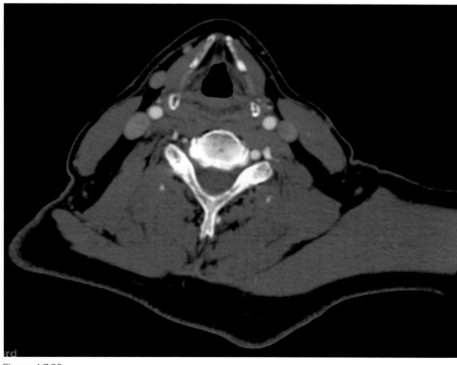

Figure 4.7.32

26. Jugular Vein
32. Sternocleidomastoid Muscle
33. Vertebral Artery
43. Epiglottis
46. Common Carotid Artery
47. Oesophagus
48. Thyroid Cartilage of Larynx
49. C5
50. Larynx
51. C6

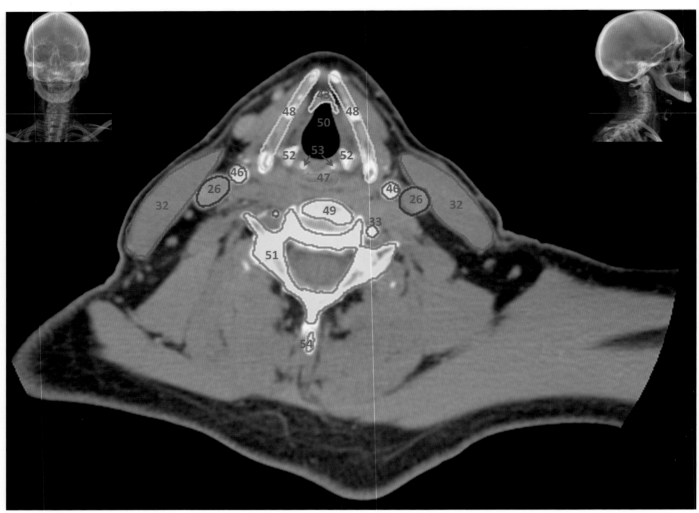

Figure 4.7.33

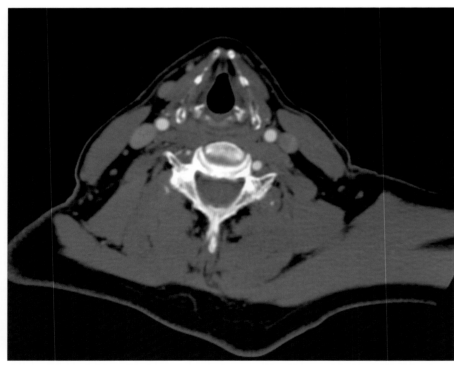

Figure 4.7.34

26. Jugular Vein
32. Sternocleidomastoid Muscle
33. Vertebral Artery
43. Epiglottis
46. Common Carotid Artery
47. Oesophagus
48. Thyroid Cartilage of Larynx
49. C5
50. Larynx
51. C6
52. Arytenoid Cartilages of Larynx
53. Corniculate Cartilages of Larynx
54. C7

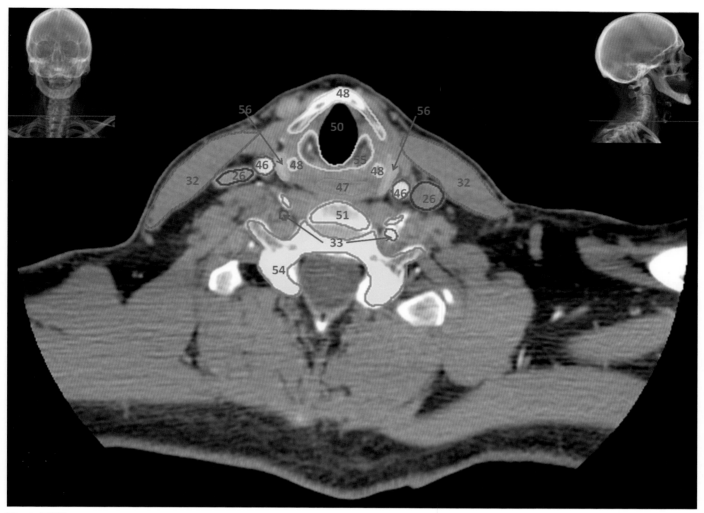

Figure 4.7.35

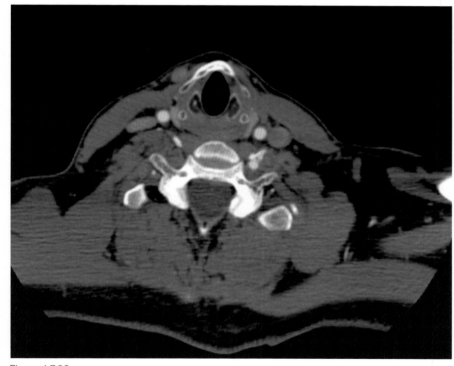

Figure 4.7.36

26. Jugular Vein
32. Sternocleidomastoid Muscle
33. Vertebral Artery
46. Common Carotid Artery
47. Oesophagus
48. Thyroid Cartilage of Larynx
50. Larynx
51. C6
54. C7
55. Cricoid Cartilage of Larynx
56. Thyroid Gland

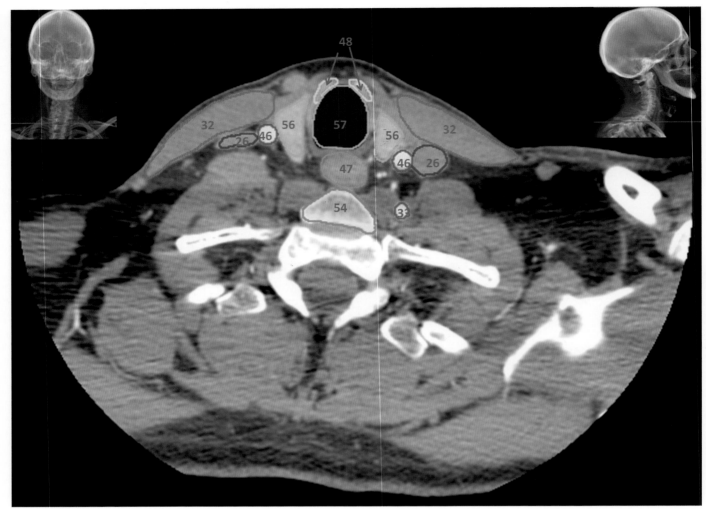

Figure 4.7.37

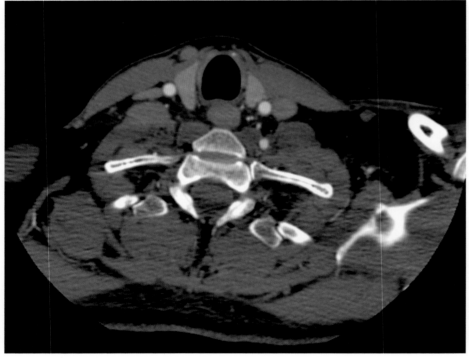

Figure 4.7.38

26. Jugular Vein
32. Sternocleidomastoid Muscle
33. Vertebral Artery
46. Common Carotid Artery
47. Oesophagus
48. Thyroid Cartilage of Larynx
54. C7
56. Thyroid Gland

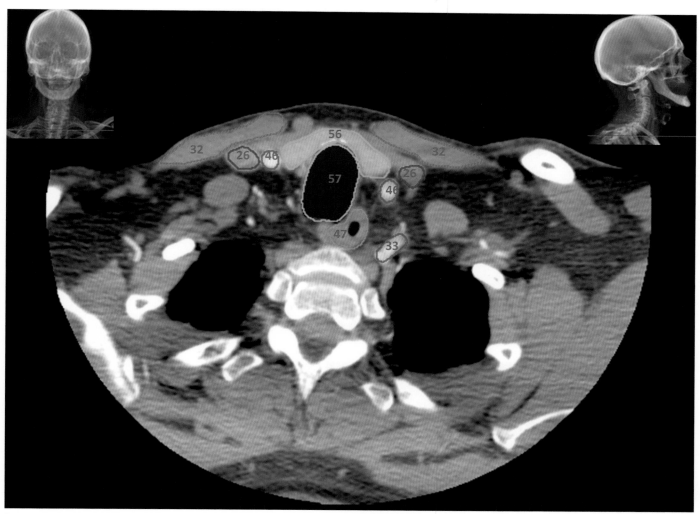

Figure 4.7.39

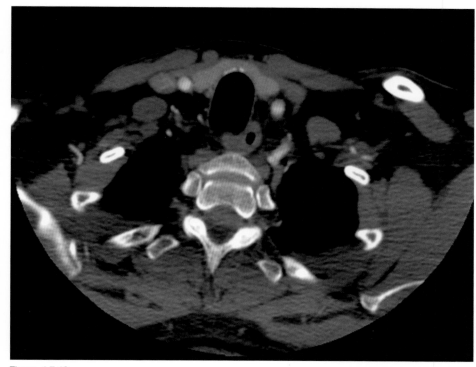

Figure 4.7.40

57. Trachea
26. Jugular Vein
32. Sternocleidomastoid Muscle
33. Vertebral Artery
46. Common Carotid Artery
47. Oesophagus
56. Thyroid Gland
57. Trachea

4.8 Common Head and Neck Tumour Pathology CT Appearance

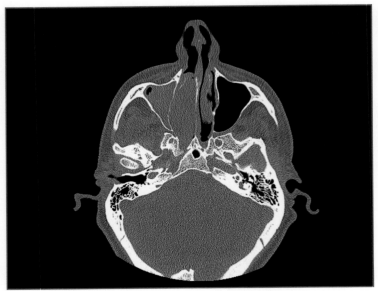

Figure 4.8.1

Sinus

Although the bony window settings in Figure 4.8.1 provide little soft tissue definition the tumour in the right maxillary sinus is clear to see. The tumour has almost completely occluded the right maxillary sinus and nasopharynx.

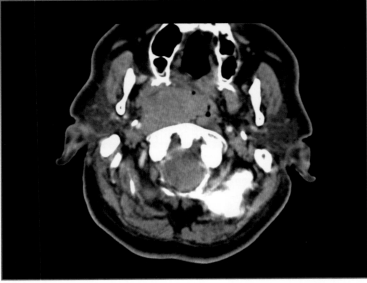

Figure 4.8.2

Nasopharynx

Like sinus tumours, nasopharynx tumours often present late due to the space available for them to grow in without impeding normal function. Figure 4.8.2 shows how the nasopharyngeal cavity has been completely occluded. The right-sided tumour is encroaching on the soft palate, right parapharyngeal and retropharyngeal spaces. Of these tumours, 75% present with lymphadenopathy and in this image the proximity of the jugular chain is evident.

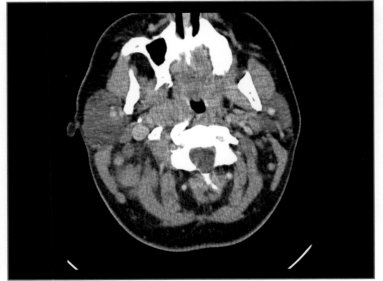

Figure 4.8.3

Parotid

The right parotid gland in Figure 4.8.3 is much enlarged compared to the left. In addition, there is evidence of multiple neck node involvement. The right jugular nodes in the carotid sheath are enlarged and there are enlarged nodes in the posterior cervical chain on both sides.

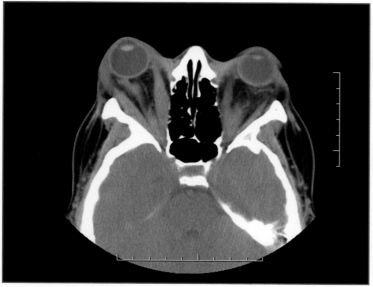

Figure 4.8.4

Thyroid eye disease

Thyroid orbitopathy is an autoimmune condition stimulating cross-sectional enlargement in the rectus muscles, resulting in the characteristic staring or bulging of the eyes (thyroid eye disease). Although all four muscles can be involved, the inferior rectus muscle tends to be more commonly affected. Figure 4.8.4 demonstrates the anterior displacement of both globes by the enlarged rectus muscles. There is also some stranding of the retro-orbital fat.

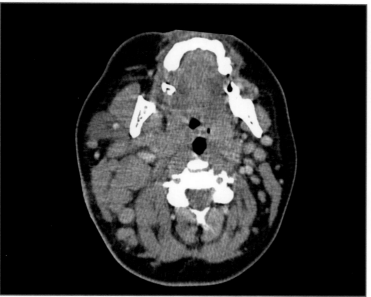

Figure 4.8.5

Cervical neck nodes

Figure 4.8.5 demonstrates extensive lymphadenopathy within all regions and levels of the cervical region. The nodes on the right are considerably larger than those on the left. The nodes are multiple, rounded, solid and of uniform density consistent with lymphoma. The head and neck region is by far the commonest site of presentation, with approximately 65–70% of cases demonstrating cervical lymphadenopathy.

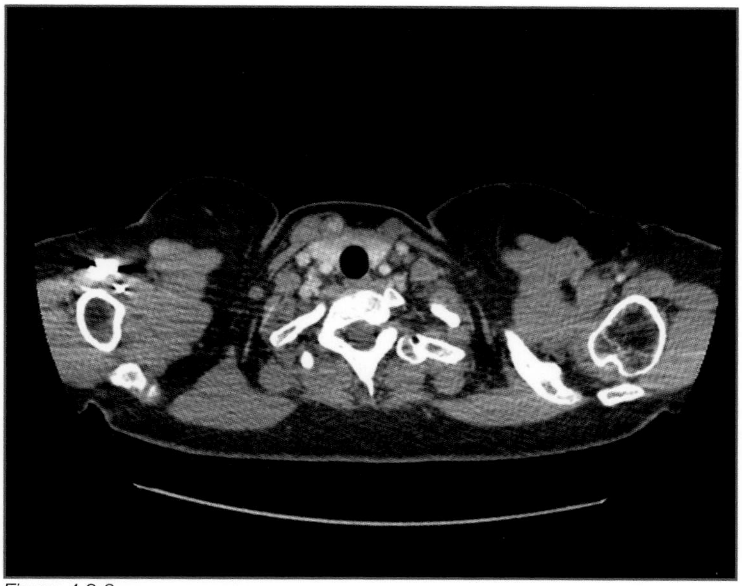

Supraclavicular nodes

The root of the neck can be a complex site to evaluate in axial section as there are multiple vessels, structures and deep spaces extending through the region. Unenhanced vessels will appear as rounded soft tissue in cross-section, similar to small nodes of uniform density; thus IV contrast is often used in this region. Figure 4.8.6 indicates the presence of several supraclavicular nodes within the root of the neck, displacing the sternocleidomastoid muscle.

Figure 4.8.6

4.9 Self-test Questions: Head and Neck

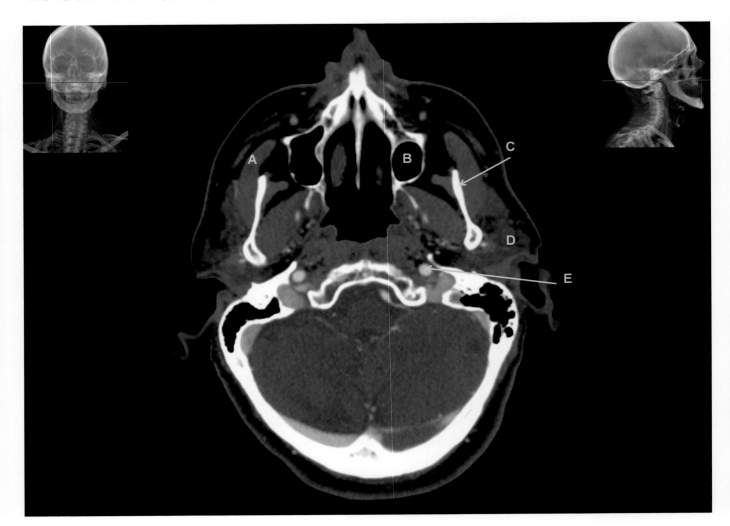

A

B

C

D

E

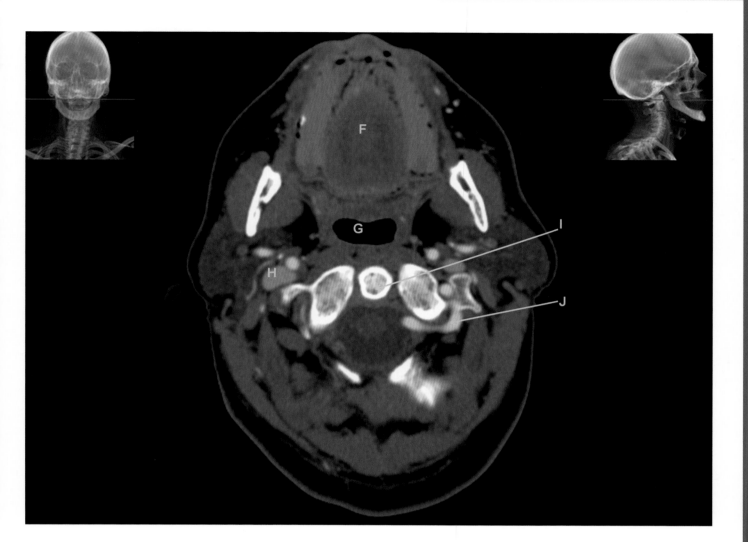

F

G

H

I

J

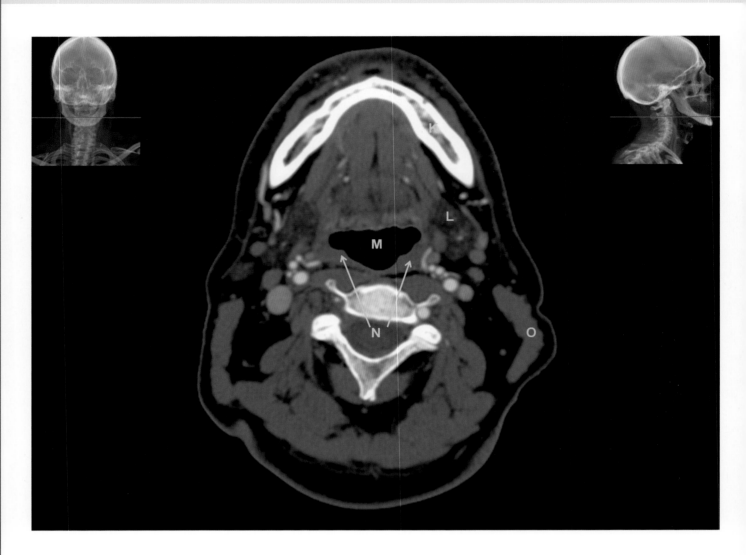

K

L

M

N

O

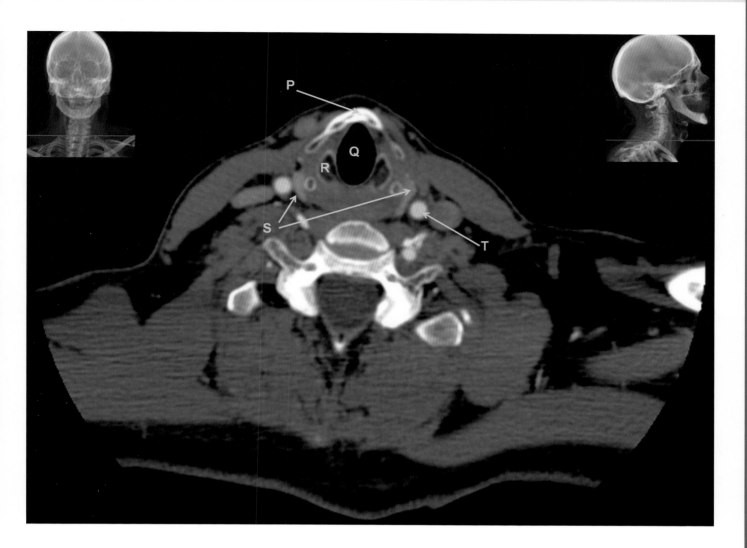

P

Q

R

S

T

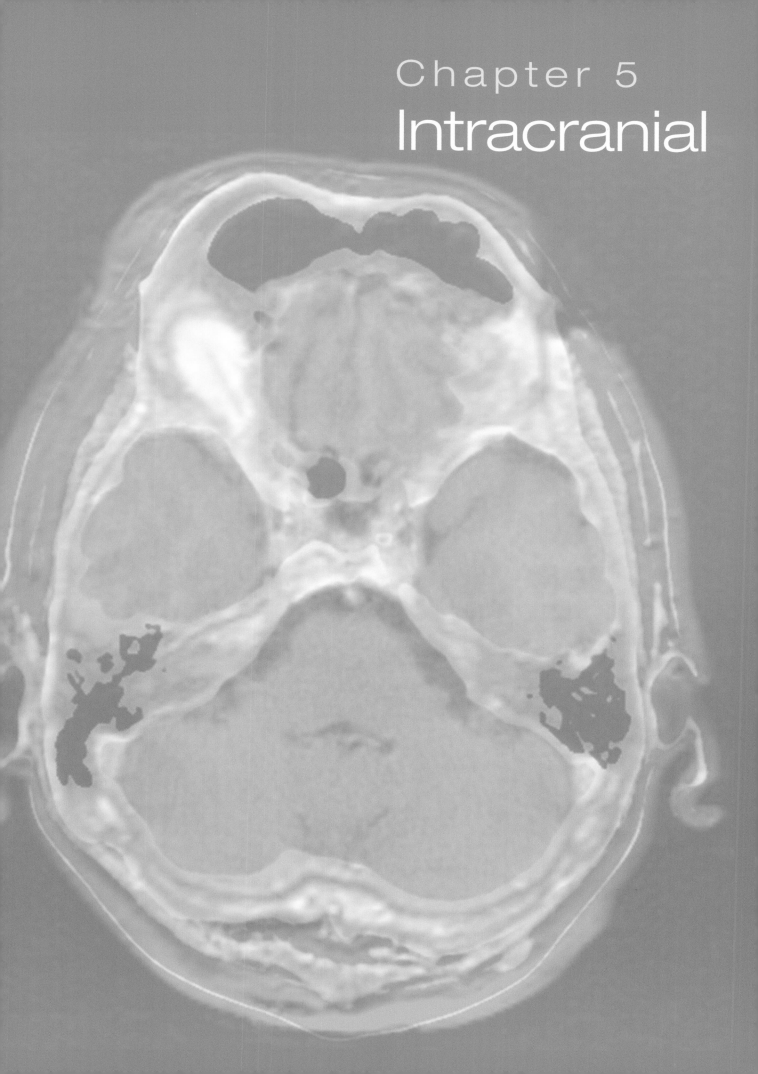

5.1 Cerebrospinal Fluid Spaces

The size, shape and distribution of cerebrospinal fluid (CSF) spaces are important indicators of space-occupying mass lesions. The intracranial CSF spaces will show distortion, compression and possible midline shift, depending on the severity and location of the mass. For example, dilatation of the ventricular system caused by obstructive hydrocephalus will not only manifest itself with expanded ventricles, but will also cause effacement of other subarachnoid spaces around the brain, such as cisterns and sulcal grooves. An appreciation of the intracranial CSF spaces is vital since the presence of CSF is evident on most, if not all, CT and/or MRI sectional images throughout the cranium.

CSF is predominantly produced via the choroid plexuses (*chorion* – Latin for delicate skin or outer layer, and *plectere* – Latin for plait or braid). CSF is essentially a watery, colourless fluid, of low density. When viewed on CT, it will have an appearance very similar to water, with approximately 0HU. This will give a natural inherent low density contrast when compared to adjacent brain tissue (about 36HU for grey matter, 28HU for white matter and over 200HU for the skull vault). As described earlier, it is vital to understand the location of the CSF, and there are two major CSF containing compartments: the ventricles and cisterns. Figure 5.1.1 illustrates the ventricular system, as seen from the left side.

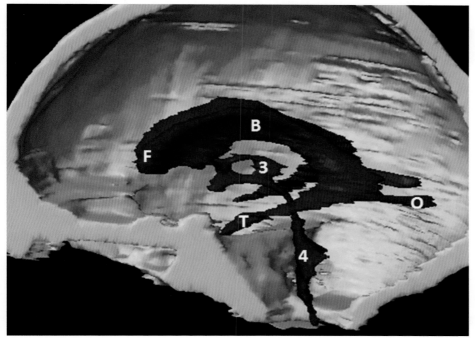

Figure 5.1.1

The largest ventricles are the two laterals. They each have a body (B) with three protrusions comprising the frontal (F), occipital (O) and temporal (T) horns. These penetrate the frontal lobe, occipital lobe and temporal lobe respectively. The two lateral ventricles are separated by a thin wall known as the septum pellucidum. Holes in this wall allow CSF to pass through. The lateral ventricles lead into the third ventricle (3) via the interventricular foramina of Munro. The third ventricle is a midline structure sitting inferiorly and medially to the lateral ventricle bodies. The cerebral aqueduct exits from the infero-posterior aspect of the third ventricle and descends before expanding into the fourth ventricle (4). After the fourth ventricle, the CSF is conducted into the spinal column via the central canal.

The cisterns are essentially openings in the subarachnoid space which are caused by separation of the arachnoid and dura mater forming the pools or collections of CSF surrounding the brain. This also gives rise to CSF sulcal spaces forming the readily recognisable patterns of cerebral and cerebellar sulcation between and surrounding the gyral convolutions on the external surface of the brain. The ventricular system and subarachnoid cistern spaces are fundamentally one space through which CSF circulates, and as such, the CT density appearances within each space should be the same.

The choroid plexuses form infoldings of the walls of parts of the ventricles through choroidal fissures, on the floors of the bodies and horns of the lateral ventricles, and the roofs of the third and fourth ventricles. Pressure within the ventricular system and various cisterns around the brain is relatively low at lumbar puncture, so has minimal mass effect on surrounding brain tissue. Therefore it is important to realise that a solid lesion or regions of high pressure due to haemorrhage, for example, will have a mass effect on the lower pressure ventricular system, cisterns and sulcal spaces. This will cause deformation or compression of the CSF filled spaces which will be apparent when comparing symmetry. As approximately 500ml of CSF is produced each day, any lesion that impedes CSF hydrodynamics will cause obstruction and subsequent dilatation of parts or all of the ventricular system, giving rise to hydrocephalus, which has recognisable traits in cross-sectional imaging.

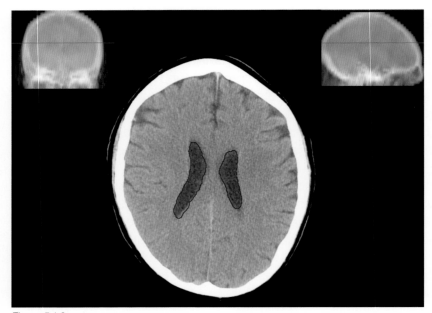

Figure 5.1.2

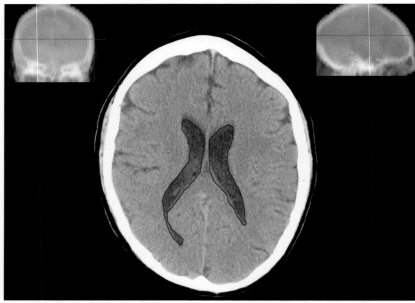

Figure 5.1.3

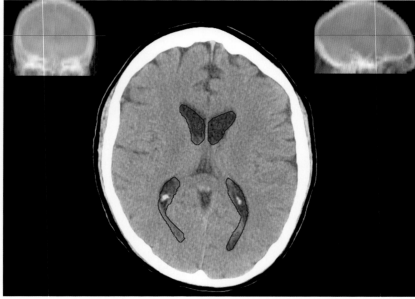

Figure 5.1.4

Figure 5.1.2 is the most superior of the images and shows the bodies of the lateral ventricles (5) either side of the falx cerebri. The left lateral ventricle displays minimal asymmetry when compared to the right; however this is within acceptable variances at this level. This could indicate slight discrepancies in positioning, but the rest of the anatomy is symmetrical, and this is more likely to represent mild normal ventricular asymmetry. The body of each ventricle displays a convexity away from midline with a curved appearance.

The CSF spaces on the external surface of the brain can be seen between each gyral projection. These are termed sulcus singularly, and each sulcus is a gap or mildly tortuous elongated depression along the cortex of the surface of the brain that greatly increases the cortical surface area.

Figure 5.1.3 depicts the lateral ventricle bodies forming the frontal and occipital horns. The right occipital horn (14) can be seen curving back into the occipital lobe, forming an 'S' shape. Within the central portions of the lateral ventricles (5) can be seen patchy feathered areas of slightly increased CT density. These are the choroid plexuses. The bodies of each lateral ventricle are separated in the midline by the septum pellucidum membranes. In 10% of the population, these two membranes are not fused, causing an elongated, CSF-filled projection between the lateral ventricles. This is the cavum septi pellucidi, and has in the past been referred to as the 'fifth ventricle'. This term however is more widely used to describe a small CSF cavity within the conus medullaris at the tail end of the spinal cord which is present in a small percentage of the population.

Figure 5.1.4 shows the frontal horns (13) of the lateral ventricles, separated in the midline by the anterior aspect of the septum pellucidum. The frontal horns are triangular in shape in cross-section, and are indented laterally. Figure 5.1.4

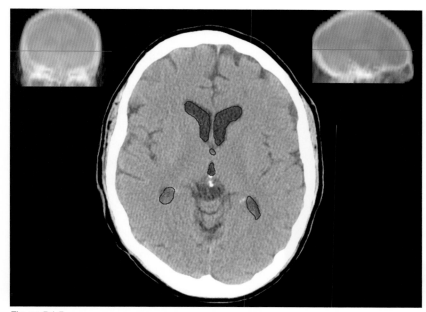

Figure 5.1.5

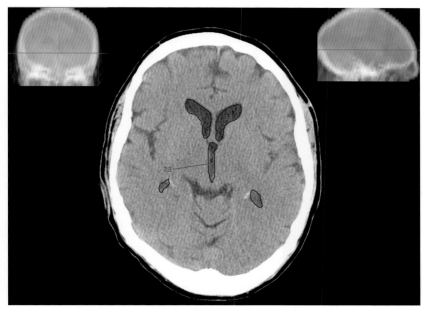

Figure 5.1.6

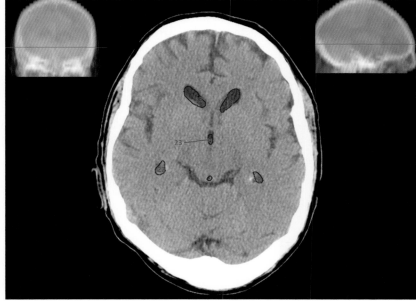

Figure 5.1.7

also demonstrates areas of increased CT density within each body of the lateral ventricle. These are calcifications within the choroid plexuses, and are an expected finding.

Extending from the posterior aspect of the body of each lateral ventricle, the narrower occipital horns (14) are tracking posteriorly deep into each occipital lobe curving around the corpus callosum medially towards the midline. Although relatively symmetrical in this example, it is not uncommon to show minor asymmetrical discrepancies in the size and shape of both the frontal and occipital horns. This should not be confused with disease.

Figures 5.1.5 to 5.1.7 show the temporal horns (22) of the lateral ventricles in short axis. They are quite small in cross-section. The temporal horns are narrow, ventricular projections curving laterally initially and then anteromedially deep into each temporal lobe. It is not unusual to lose sight of the temporal horns. They are sensitive to changes in intraventricular pressure and tend to display disproportionate levels of dilation compared to the rest of the ventricular system. This imaging sign is often used as an early prognostic indicator for obstructive hydrocephalus.

The third ventricle (23) is well demonstrated in Figure 5.1.6 as a centrally located CSF filled narrow structure. The third ventricle has several indentations or recesses caused by adjacent anatomy: optic and pituitary infundibular recess anteriorly and suprapineal and pineal recesses posteriorly.

Figure 5.1.8 shows the fourth ventricle (39). In three dimensions, this is quite a complex diamond shape with numerous indentations or recesses caused by adjacent neuroanatomy, similar to the third ventricle. In axial section, it displays a curved 'bean' shape, with a posterior concavity caused by the cerebellar vermis.

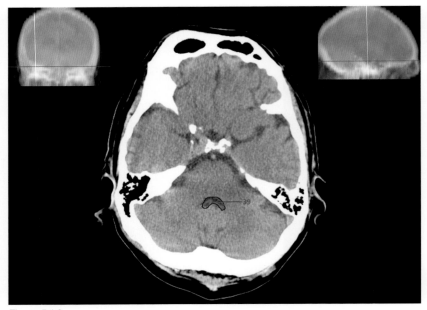

Figure 5.1.8

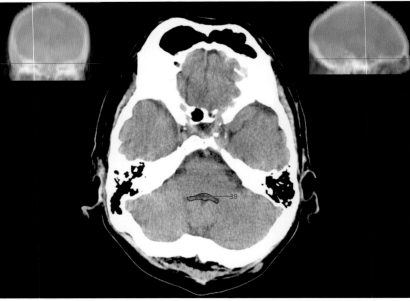

Figure 5.1.9

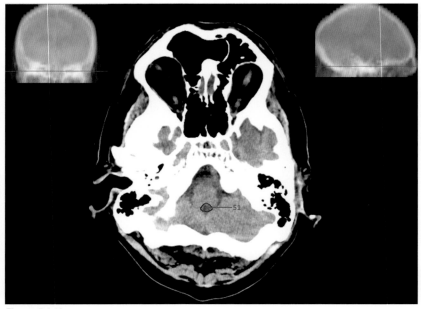

Figure 5.1.10

Slightly inferiorly as demonstrated in Figure 5.1.9, the posterior wall of the fourth ventricle has a blind ended pointed outpouching called the fastigium. Just inferior to this, visible in Figure 5.1.10, the three apertures or foraminae communicating with the subarachnoid spaces can be seen. The lateral foraminae (foraminae of Luschka) are seen laterally and the centrally located foramen of Magendie can be seen posteriorly from the fourth ventricle.

Figure 5.1.10 shows the CSF within the fourth ventricle communicating with the central canal (51) via the obex of the cord. From the three foraminae, the CSF circulates through the subarachnoid spaces and pools in various cisterns around the brain. The first cistern that CSF drains into is the cerebellopontine cistern, anterior and lateral to the cerebellum and pons as its name suggests. The pontine cistern is seen in Figure 5.1.10 surrounding the basilar artery. Another well recognised and described cistern is the quadrigeminal cistern seen in Figure 5.1.7 as a midline curved CSF space situated between the temporal horns.

Separating the temporal and frontal lobes, the lateral sulcus or 'insular cistern' can be seen in Figures 5.1.6 and 5.1.7. This cistern is more frequently known as the Sylvian fissure.

An easy feature to recognise when assessing CSF spaces for evidence of compression is a 'smily face', where on a midsection scan, the 'eyes' are formed by the frontal horns of the lateral ventricles, the 'nose' is formed by the third ventricle and 'smiling mouth' by the curved quadrigeminal cistern.

5.2 Circulatory System

Intracranial structures are supplied with blood by the internal carotid and vertebral arteries. The internal carotid arteries penetrate the skull through the carotid canals and then curve their way up along the lateral border of the clivus of the sphenoid bone before joining the Circle of Willis. The vertebral arteries curve over the first cervical vertebra and join in the midline to form the basilar artery. This then passes superiorly and anteriorly until it meets the Circle of Willis.

    The Circle of Willis is a ring-shaped anastomosis that connects these major arteries and thus ensures a constant supply of blood to the brain in the event of occlusion of one of these vessels. Figure 5.2.1 illustrates how the Circle is supplied by the internal carotid arteries (C) anteriorly and basilar artery (B) posteriorly. Note the formation of the basilar artery by the joining of the vertebral arteries (V). The right internal carotid is hidden by the skull in this diagram. Blood exits the Circle via the anterior (A), middle (M) and posterior (P) cerebral arteries. These in turn rapidly divide to supply the anterior, central and posterior parts of the brain respectively.

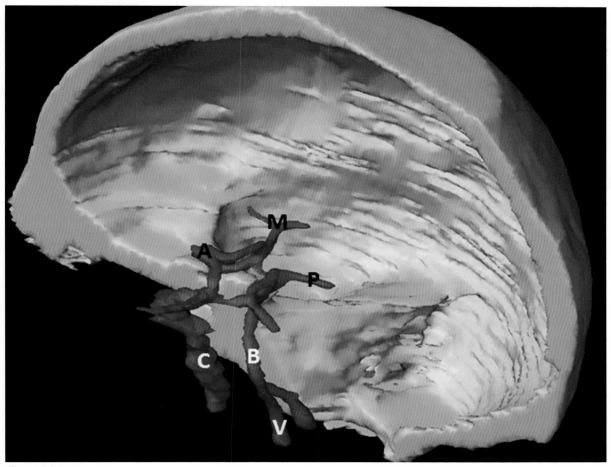

Figure 5.2.1

    Venous drainage in the brain is accomplished via interconnected veins that drain into large sinuses as illustrated in Figure 5.2.2. Blood from the peripheral superior region is drained into the superior sagittal sinus (SS). This runs along midline from the anterior of the skull over the superior aspect and down the occipital bone. More internal regions drain blood into the inferior sagittal sinus, while the centre of the brain drains via the great cerebral veins of Galen (G). The inferior sagittal sinus and veins of Galen meet to form the straight sinus (St). This runs posteriorly and inferiorly to join with the superior sagittal sinus at a widened region known as the confluence of sinuses (C). This is situated just beneath the occipital bone at the internal occipital protuberance. From the confluence of sinuses, blood runs laterally and anteriorly through the transverse sinuses (T) along the internal surface of the occipital bone. Once they reach the petrous ridge of the temporal bone the transverse sinuses form the sigmoid sinuses (Sig) and snake down to exit the brain via the jugular foramen to form the internal jugular veins.

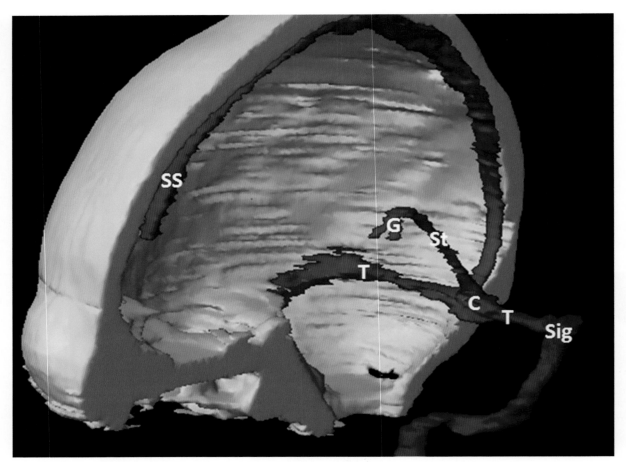

Figure 5.2.2

CT imaging the whole intracranial circulation on one series of images and subsequent reformatting is complex. This is usually achieved by a multiphased contrast-enhanced volume CT acquisition, resulting in two imaging runs, an early arterial phase, followed by a second venous phase or combined with the use of perfusion imaging. Current practices used for radiotherapy planning do not conventionally utilise these techniques. Other imaging modalities also tend to be used alongside or instead of CT, such as conventional angiography and MRI angiography (MRA). Therefore it is quite difficult to fully demonstrate intracranial circulation, both arterial supply and venous drainage, without utilising several imaging techniques. The following images demonstrate major intracranial cross-sectional morphology, ensuring standardisation of descriptive text and imaging. Creating a 3-dimensional model of the entire arterial circulation is challenging, as current outlining software struggles to demonstrate the tortuosity of more peripheral intracranial arteries.

To accompany Figure 5.2.1, the reader should also use Figure 5.2.13 to assist understanding of the whole arterial supply. This is a 3-dimensional CT volume rendered image acquired on a diagnostic platform, specifically designed for the detection of small vessel anomalies so the depicted arterial vascularity is highly detailed and complex.

The accompanying text also describes firstly the intracranial venous drainage (as this is most evident from the vertex inferiorly from Figure 5.2.3 and inferior to this level) and then the intracranial arterial supply, rather than mixing the two in the same body of text. Describing and understanding one vascular system at a time is less complex than learning both simultaneously.

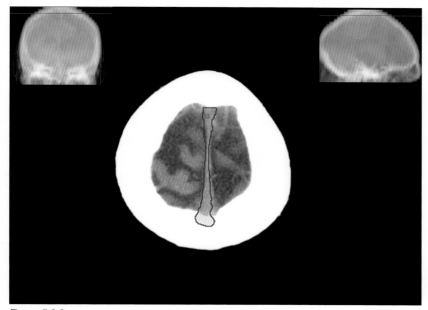

Figure 5.2.3

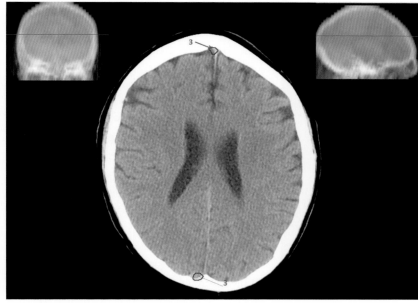

Figure 5.2.4

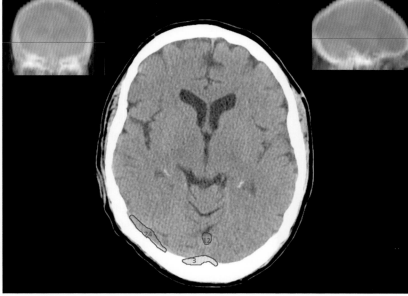

Figure 5.2.5

When assessing intracranial venous drainage there are essentially two main systems. The superior group comprises the sagittal (superior (3) and inferior sagittal sinus where visualised), transverse (24) and straight (12) dural sinuses (Figure 5.2.5). The basal group includes the cavernous and superior and inferior petrosal sinuses. Therefore, with a few exceptions, the vast majority of intracranial venous drainage ultimately flows into the internal jugular veins via the dural venous sinuses.

The superior venous sinuses are channels formed between layers of dura and internal periostial lining of the internal skull periosteum. CSF drains into the venous blood and back into the normal circulation. Unlike other venous channels within the body, these sinuses are just channels or cavities through which the blood flows. There are no valves or muscular walls present. This gives the sinuses their characteristic triangular shape in cross-section, as seen in Figure 5.2.4 in both anterior and posterior aspects of the superior sagittal sinus (3).

Figure 5.2.3 shows the superior sagittal sinus (3), formed by the two layers of falx cerebri folding inwards between the two cerebral hemispheres. The superior sagittal sinus (3) originates just distal to the crista galli on the cribriform plate and extends along the midline, enlarging in diameter as it tracks posteriorly. It may not be visible until level with the coronal suture. The superior sagittal sinus is normally a singular midline structure; however it may be slightly off centre and may even also bifurcate before its termination.

As the superior sagittal sinus (3) flows more posteriorly it descends towards the occipital bone where it joins the confluence of sinuses (26) seen in Figure 5.2.6 just superior to and anterior to the internal occipital protuberance.

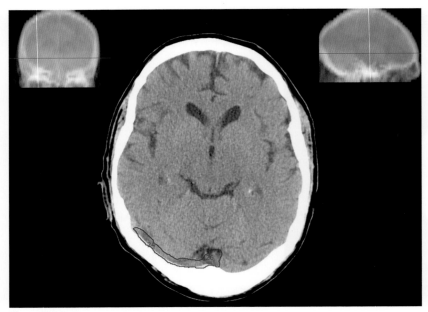

Figure 5.2.6

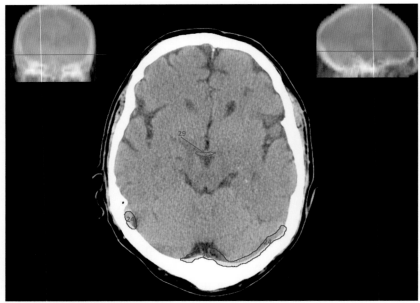

Figure 5.2.7

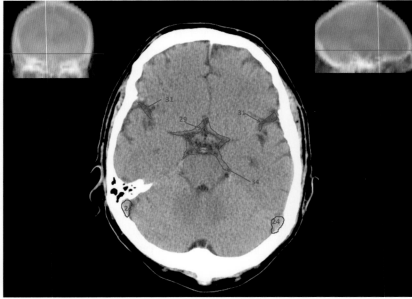

Figure 5.2.8

The straight sinus (12) is more central than the superior sagittal sinus and, rather than running along the inner calvarial vault, it is formed at the junction of the falx cerebri and the tentorium cerebelli (a sheet separating the cerebrum from the cerebellum). Thus it is normally a midline structure, although it can be offset towards the left, where it drains into the left transverse sinus (24), seen in Figure 5.2.7.

The smaller inferior sagittal sinus and internal cerebral veins also drain into the straight sinus along its course. As the straight sinus (12) descends inferiorly from the anterior edge of the tentorium cerebelli it follows a relatively steep descent and therefore is not normally seen in longitudinal cross-section. As demonstrated in Figure 5.2.5, it is frequently seen in a short axis cross-section.

At the confluence of sinuses (26) the sinuses split and drain laterally along the transverse sinuses (24). These are usually asymmetric and demonstrate a dominant side. As the transverse sinuses are relatively straight, instead of curvilinear, it is likely that a greater length will be visualised on axial slices such as Figures 5.2.6 and 5.2.7.

The transverse sinuses (24) change path at the base of the petrous temporal bone, and descend in a sigma shape as the sigmoid sinuses (45) as seen in Figures 5.2.7 to 5.2.10.

In Figures 5.2.11 and 5.2.12, the sigmoid sinuses can be seen draining into a dilated section called the jugular bulb, clearly seen in Figure 5.2.11 on the right, but not as clear on the left. From here, the sinuses drain into each internal jugular vein and exit the skull via the jugular foraminae.

Throughout many other parts of the body, both venous and arterial systems mirror each other so an artery will usually have a matching vein flowing in the opposite direction adjacent to it. The intracranial arterial supply is very different to its venous drainage, as seen in Figures 5.2.1 and 5.2.2.

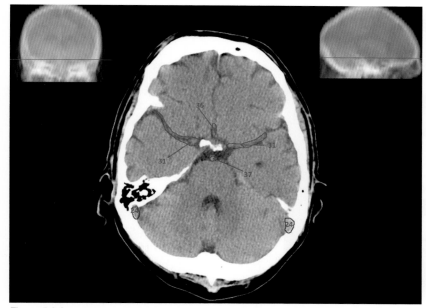

Figure 5.2.9

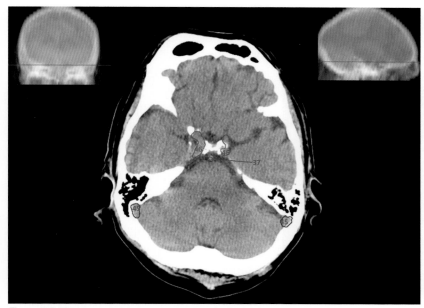

Figure 5.2.10

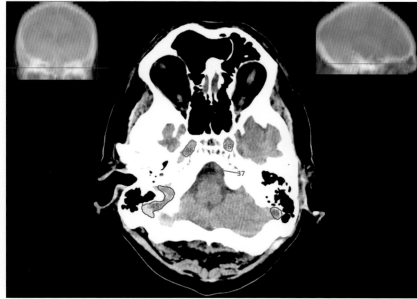

Figure 5.2.11

Figures 5.2.13 and 5.2.14 are more detailed 3-dimensional images of the intracranial arterial supply and the tortuosity of the vessels can be appreciated. Figure 5.2.13 shows the intracranial circulation from the posterior aspect and clearly demonstrates the various branches. Figure 5.2.14 demonstrates the same anatomy from the superior aspect, and the Circle of Willis can be seen central to the image, formed by anastomotic communicating vessels joining the six main cerebral vessels. These are the right and left anterior, middle and posterior cerebral arteries.

The anterior aspect of the Circle of Willis is supplied by both internal carotid arteries. One interesting point of note is the path of the internal carotid arteries. The internal carotid vessels undergo a seemingly unnecessarily tortuous path before supplying the anterior circulation of the Circle of Willis. The complex path of both internal carotid vessels (46) can be seen in Figures 5.2.13 and 5.2.14. Following their entry into the skull base via the carotid canal, they curve anteriorly and lie within the foramen lacerum either side of the sella turcica within the 'cavernous sinus'.

From here, the cavernous segments then bend sharply back on themselves in a U shape, known as the carotid siphon. They exit the cavernous sinus and the ophthalmic segments then project posteriorly before bending superiorly to join the Circle of Willis. This extremely tortuous path can be seen in axial section in Figures 5.2.9 to 5.2.12. The vessels are seen immediately lateral to the sella turcica in Figures 5.2.9 and 5.2.10. Various smaller vessels branch off the internal carotid artery before it joins the circle of Willis (29); however these are not usually seen on normal resolution CT scanning.

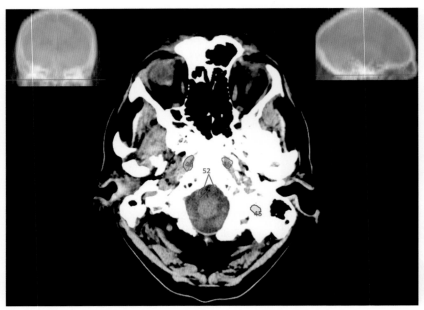

Figure 5.2.12

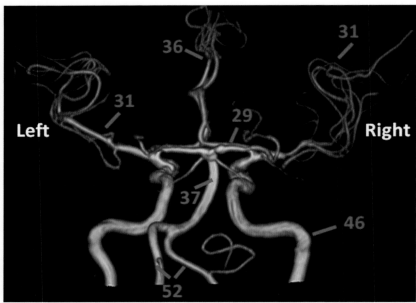

Figure 5.2.13

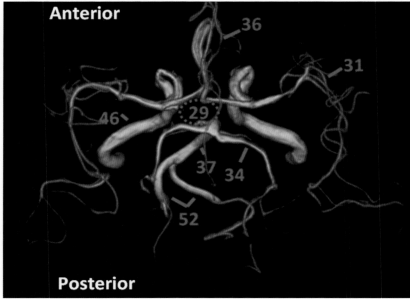

Figure 5.2.14

The posterior circulation is formed by the vertebrobasilar system. The two vertebral arteries (52) are well demonstrated in Figures 5.2.13 and 5.2.14 in three dimensions. Figure 5.2.12 demonstrates this in axial section, and the two vertebral vessels (52) are seen just anterior to the superior aspect of the spinal cord and immediately posterior to the anterior aspect of the foramen magnum.

Slightly superiorly, Figure 5.2.11 shows the presence of just one vessel, the basilar artery (37) following the fusion of the two vertebral vessels. From here the basilar artery ascends ventral to the pons in the midline, seen in Figures 5.2.8 to 5.2.10.

The basilar artery can be relatively eccentric and its path can extend off centre with varying configurations of smaller branches. The smaller branches are not well visualised on low resolution CT sections; however branches of the superior cerebellar and posterior inferior cerebellar arteries may be seen if contrast enhancement is sufficient.

Immediately superior to the superior cerebellar arteries, the basilar bifurcates into the right and left posterior cerebral arteries (34). The vessel curves posteriorly around the pons and travels through the ambient and quadrigeminal cisterns, as seen in Figure 5.2.8. Here the left posterior cerebral artery can be discerned in Figure 5.2.14. From here the vessels further subdivide and supply parts of the occipital and temporal cerebral lobes.

5.3 Central Nervous System

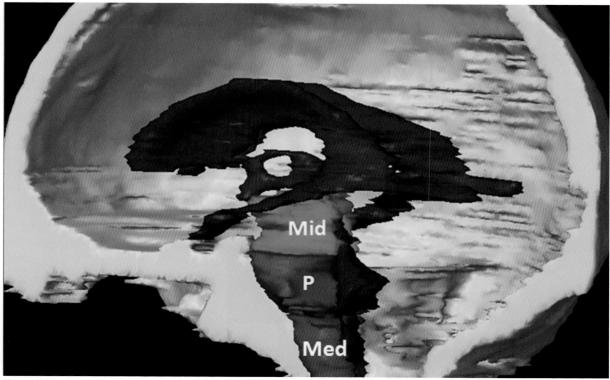

Figure 5.3.1

Although fabulously complex and intricate on a microscopic level, the macroscopic central nervous system (as seen on CT) is relatively straightforward. As the spinal cord penetrates the skull via the foramen magnum it bulges to form the medulla oblongata (Med), which is the most inferior part of the brainstem. Above the medulla lies the pons (P) with its characteristic double swellings on the anterior surface. Above the pons is the midbrain (Mid), which allows the brainstem to communicate with the rest of the brain. Figure 5.3.1 illustrates the relationship between these three components of the brainstem. The ventricular system is also illustrated, demonstrating the close relationship between the brainstem and fourth ventricle. The pons forms the connection between the cerebellum and the brainstem. The cerebellum lies posterior to the brainstem and comprises two hemispheres with a small central vermis. The pons and cerebellum enclose the fourth ventricle (4) with the cerebellum (C) forming the posterior wall, as seen in Figure 5.3.2.

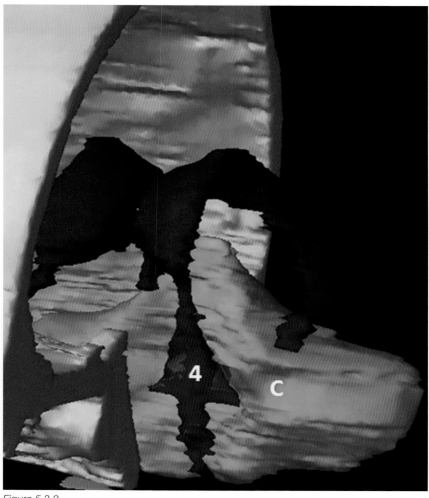

Figure 5.3.2

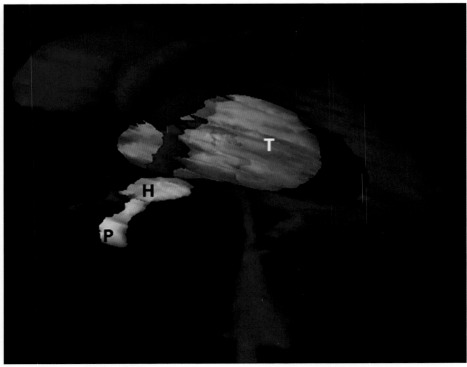

Figure 5.3.3

Superior to the midbrain can be found the paired lobes of the thalamus. The thalamus encloses the third ventricle, as seen in Figure 5.3.3. The thalamus (T) maintains several connections (anterior, middle and posterior fornix) that cross the ventricle and allow communication between the lobes. Although of limited interest to radiotherapy, the small pineal gland can always be seen on CT scans posteriorly to the thalamus. It is a useful and reliable landmark due to its calcification. In between the pineal gland and thalamus are the four rounded quadrigeminal bodies, associated with the visual system. Anteriorly and inferiorly to the thalamus lies the hypothalamus (H) region. This is a collection of small grey matter 'nuclei'. Extending inferiorly from the hypothalamus is the pituitary gland (P), connected by a thin stalk known as the infundibulum. The pituitary can be seen protruding from the hypothalamus in Figure 5.3.3. The pituitary sits in a depressed region of the sphenoid bone called the sella turcica (or Turkish Saddle). Due to its small size, it can sometimes be hard to visualise unless narrow slices are used.

There are other grey matter nuclei dotted around the brain and many of these are grouped together to form the basal ganglia. CT usually lacks the resolution to allow clear differentiation between the different nuclei and this book combines structures such as the putamen, globus pallidus and substantia nigra into the overarching term basal ganglia. Most of the basal ganglia nuclei are located laterally to the lateral ventricles. The caudate nucleus is perhaps the most easily visualised of the nuclei since it forms the inferior boundary of the frontal horn of the lateral ventricles. Each caudate nucleus curves over a thalamus lobe in a C-shape. The anterior section is enlarged and is known as the head. Figure 5.3.4 shows the caudate nucleus (C) curving along the lateral inferior surface of the lateral ventricle frontal horns. The rest of the basal ganglia (B) can be seen laterally to the thalamus (T).

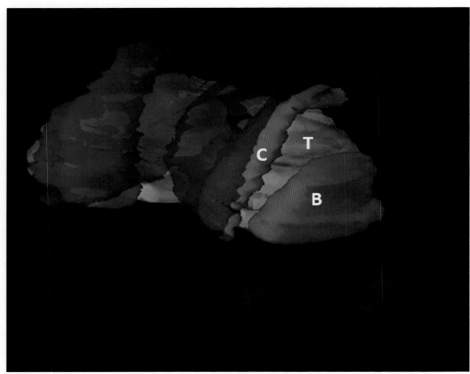

Figure 5.3.4

The largest part of the brain by far is the cerebrum. The cerebrum consists of two cerebral hemispheres that are almost completely separated by a fold of tissue called the falx cerebri. This is a fold of one of the meninges, which are the 'shrink-wrapping' of the brain. Trapped inside the fold just on the inside surface

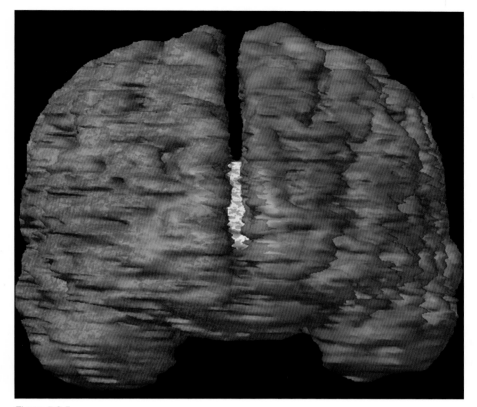

Figure 5.3.5

of the skull is the superior sagittal sinus, which has already been discussed. The falx cerebri bisects the cerebrum apart from the centre between the lateral ventricles. In this region the two cerebral hemispheres communicate via a wide band of white matter called the corpus callosum. The anterior part of this structure is the genu and the posterior is the splenium. The cerebrum itself forms lobes, named after the bones they underlie: the frontal, parietal, occipital and temporal lobes. Figure 5.3.5 shows the separation of the two hemispheres and the corpus callosum connecting them. Figure 5.3.6 illustrates the relationship between the cerebrum (pink), corpus callosum (white) and ventricles (dark blue) as seen from the posterior and superior aspect.

The most important consideration when viewing any axial or coronal cross-sectional intracranial anatomi-cal image is symmetry. All anatomy within the cranium is normally symmetrical, provided the patient has been positioned with their median sagittal plane perpendicular to the acquisition plane. Therefore, if an imaginary line is drawn centrally between the two intracranial hemispheres (the falx cerebri is a good anatomical marker for this) the anatomy of a normal patient will be the same on the left as it is on the right, notwithstanding any mild discrepancies. This relates to all intracranial anatomy, including the CSF containing spaces, although there are some minor recognised discrepancies, as already described in relevant sections. It must be stressed that relatively minor positioning errors can cause quite marked asymmetry, particularly within the ventricular system, and it is worthwhile spending a few additional seconds in taking care to align the patient carefully.

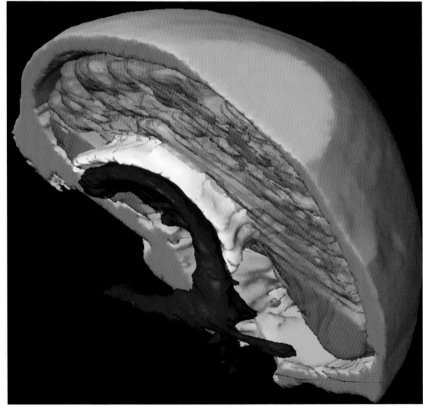

Figure 5.3.6

Following evaluation of any potential ventricular or subarachnoid space effacement, the next step is to assess evidence of soft tissue lesions that may be the cause of mass effects. On CT cross-section, it is important not only to evaluate global neuroanatomy, but also to recognise the differences between white and grey matter. To the inexperienced eye, this can be a relatively complicated task as most of the brain tissues have similar densities.

The grey matter forms an extensive 2–3mm layer that is evenly distributed around the cortex of the cerebral and cerebellar hemispheres. It follows the gyral projections and undulations on the outer surface of the brain. There are also pockets of grey matter deep within the brain.

The white matter is just deep to the cortical grey matter, and is predominantly composed of nerve fibres ('axons') extending between the cortex and the deep nuclei. These white matter tracts are covered with myelin which has high lipid content and therefore exhibit reduced CT density. Ironically, the white matter appears darker on CT than the adjacent grey matter which is composed of more densely packed unmyelinated nerve cell bodies. A narrow window width of 80HU with a window level of 35HU should be utilised for maximum differentiation between grey and white matter.

Potential changes to the white matter caused by the movement of fluid into the extracellular spaces can alter the CT density and appearance within the white matter. This peritumoural oedema is usually associated with the breakdown in the blood–brain barrier. Many tumours have structurally abnormal capillaries that allow plasma to leak from the endothelial cells within the capillary walls into surrounding white matter. This 'vasogenic' oedema usually only affects the white matter as fluid spreads along the white matter tracts relatively easily but is halted at the denser grey matter.

Differing tumour types and locations can affect the degree of peritumoural oedema and the differences can be quite marked. For example, a seemingly small metastatic lesion may cause a disproportionate amount of white matter oedema, compared to a similar sized primary lesion. Although in many instances the presence of vasogenic oedema will reduce white matter density (resulting in a much darker appearance on CT) and provide a visually darker background for some tumours, in many cases the actual tumour boundaries may not be immediately obvious. IV contrast agents are often used to aid demarcation of the shape, size, complexity and even multiplicity of lesions.

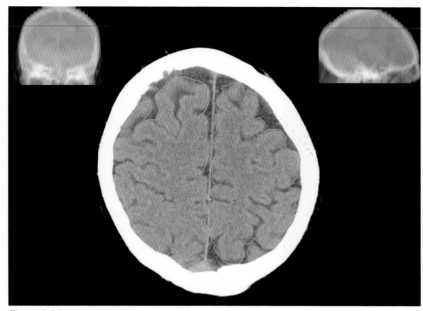

Figure 5.3.7

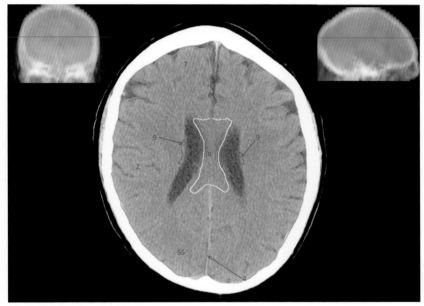

Figure 5.3.8

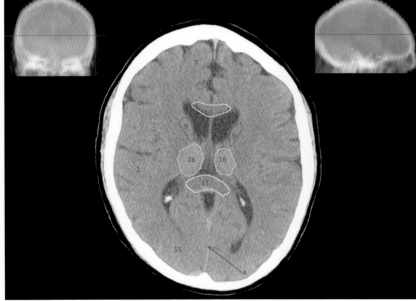

Figure 5.3.9

Figure 5.3.7 demonstrates a clear indication of symmetry. The thin, bright, hyperdense midline structure separating the cerebral hemispheres is the falx cerebri. The cortical grey matter is well demonstrated following the external surface of the gyral convolutions. The slightly less dense, homogeneous tissue deep to this in Figure 5.3.8 is the white matter within the frontal (7) and temporal lobes (2).

Also in Figure 5.3.8, the body of the corpus callosum (8) can be seen centrally. It is a dense body of axonal fibres linking both cerebral hemispheres, and is the largest white matter structure within the brain. The splenium (11) is the most posterior aspect of the corpus callosum. It is the widest part and two large bundles of nerve fibres can be seen extending into each occipital lobe, in Figures 5.3.8 and 5.3.9.

The falx cerebri (4) does not bisect any aspect of the corpus callosum, but curves over the superior aspect of it. The falx compartmentalises the brain within the cranium, and the location of the brain within these compartments can be compromised by a significant mass effect. Following sufficient mass effect within either hemisphere, a midline shift will occur.

Anterior to the genu (10) and posterior to the splenium (11) of the corpus callosum, the remaining aspects of the falx cerebri are seen as a thin, hyperdense midline structure separating the frontal lobes (7) anteriorly and occipital lobes (55) posteriorly. The frontal (7), parietal (2) and occipital (55) lobes are well demonstrated in Figures 5.3.8 and 5.3.9.

In Figure 5.3.9 the superior aspects of the right and left thalami (16) lie between the frontal and occipital horns of the lateral ventricles. Anterior to the thalami, the head of each caudate nucleus (9) indents the lateral walls of the ventricular frontal horns.

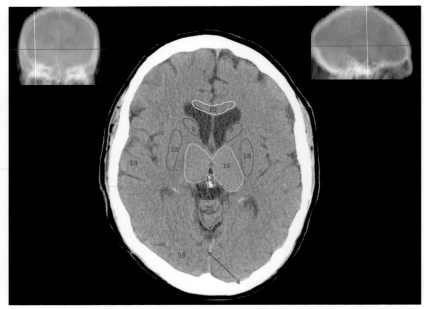

Figure 5.3.10

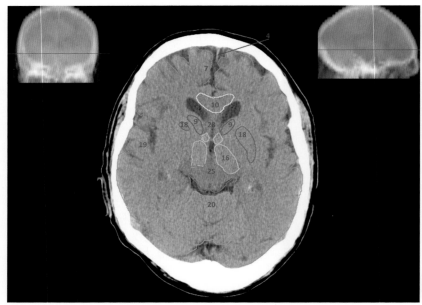

Figure 5.3.11

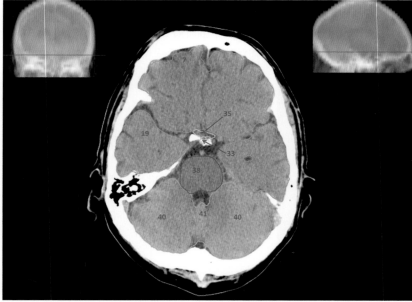

Figure 5.3.12

The paired thalami are ovoid in shape, and in Figures 5.3.9 and 5.3.10, their widest aspect can be seen in cross-section. The pineal gland (17) is well demonstrated in the midline, just anterior to CSF within the ambient and quadrigeminal cisterns. The pineal gland often displays some element of calcification.

Superior aspects of the temporal lobes (19) are visible in Figures 5.3.10 and 5.3.11. The temporal lobes extend from the inferior of the parietal lobes into the middle cranial fossae. The superior aspects of each temporal lobe are separated from the inferior of each frontal lobe (7) and anterior of each parietal lobe by the Sylvian fissure.

In axial section, the basal ganglia can be quite complicated to describe. These collections of paired grey matter structures are mainly sited lateral to both thalami and lateral ventricles. Figure 5.3.4 indicates the caudate nucleus (9) as a curved C-shaped nucleus, intimately related to the lateral aspect of the frontal horn. The putamen and globus pallidus form a relatively large lentil shaped mass of grey matter called the lentiform nucleus (18). This is well demonstrated in Figures 5.3.9 to 5.3.11.

Figure 5.3.11 indicates the location of the hypothalamus (28) anterior to the inferior aspect of each thalamus. Although not particularly well demonstrated in Figures 5.3.12 and 5.3.13, the pituitary infundibulum and gland are sited just inferior to the hypothalamus within the sella turcica.

Figure 5.3.11 shows the midbrain (25) below the inferior of each thalamus. Parts of the cerebral peduncles can be seen anteriorly extending posterior to each thalamic complex, and the quadrigeminal plate (tectum or colliculi) can be seen extending posteriorly into the quadrigeminal cistern.

The pons (38) is seen in Figure 5.3.12 as a large, central structure in the apex of the posterior fossa. The basilar artery can

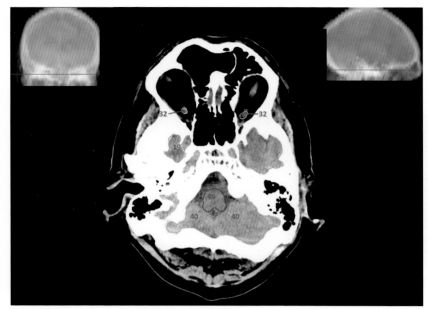

Figure 5.3.13

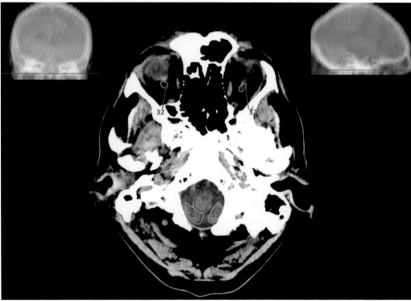

Figure 5.3.14

be seen tracking anteriorly to the pons within the pontine cistern. Fine detail within the pons and inferior aspects of the brainstem can often be obscured by the streak artefacts caused by the dense petrous bones.

The medulla oblongata (49) is seen in Figures 5.3.13 and 5.3.14, extending through the foramen magnum to the spinal cord. In axial section, the distinctive rounded projections on the ventral surface are the medullary pyramids, containing the corticospinal tracts from the cerebral cortex.

The location of the vermis of cerebellum (20) is shown in Figures 5.3.10 and 5.3.11, extending from the posterior fossa into the ambient and quadrigeminal cisterns. More inferiorly in Figures 5.3.12 to 5.3.13 the right and left cerebellar hemispheres (40) are seen within the posterior fossa. The cerebellar gyral convolutions and sulcal grooves are much smaller and more tightly arranged when compared to the cerebrum. The cerebellar tonsils (53) are seen in Figure 5.3.14, posterior to the junction of the medulla oblongata (49) and the spinal cord within the cisterna magna.

The optic chiasm and optic nerves are often overlooked, although they still represent an important clinical part of the central nervous system. The optic chiasm (35) can be seen in Figure 5.3.12 immediately anterior to the posterior clinoid process. This is of particular clinical relevance when considering pituitary adenomas. As the pituitary enlarges it expands laterally and superiorly, compressing the optic chiasm causing bitemporal hemianopsia. The optic nerves extend anteriorly through the optic canal and enter the orbital cavities. From here, each optic nerve (32) can be seen in Figures 5.3.13 and 5.3.14 extending from the apex of each optical cavity to the papilla within each eye at the central-posterior aspect of the globe. The window settings are a little too narrow to demonstrate detail within the optical cavities, and would need adjusting to wider settings (width 300 and level 30) to visualise the rectus muscles, retro-orbital fat and optical anatomy.

5.4 Full Intracranial CT and MR Anatomy

The following images comprise a labelled CT (top left), a blank CT (bottom left), a blend of CT and T1 MR (top right) and finally a pure T1 MR (bottom right). The reader is directed to Section 1.5 for a refresher on MR interpretation

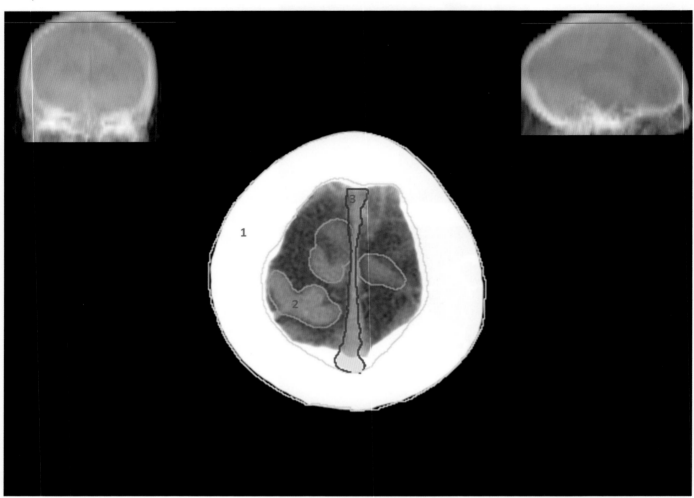

Figure 5.4.1

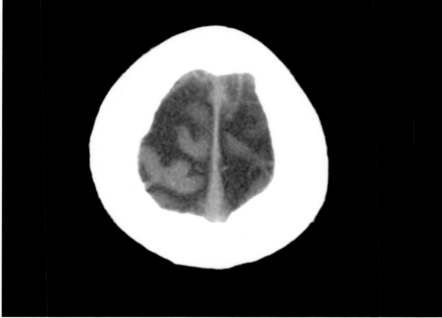

1. Parietal Bone
2. Parietal Lobe of Cerebrum
3. Superior Sagittal Sinus

Figure 5.4.2

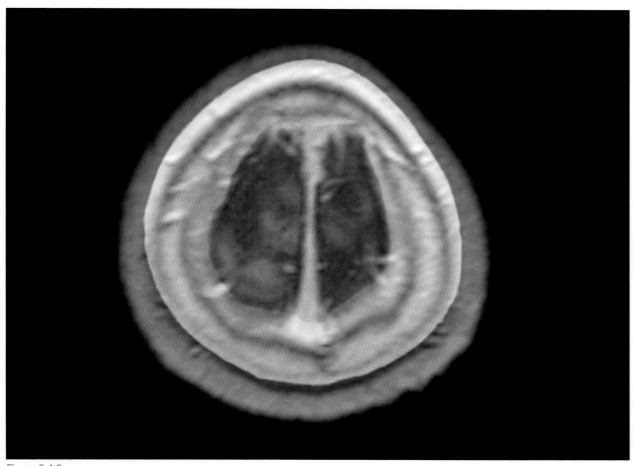

Figure 5.4.3

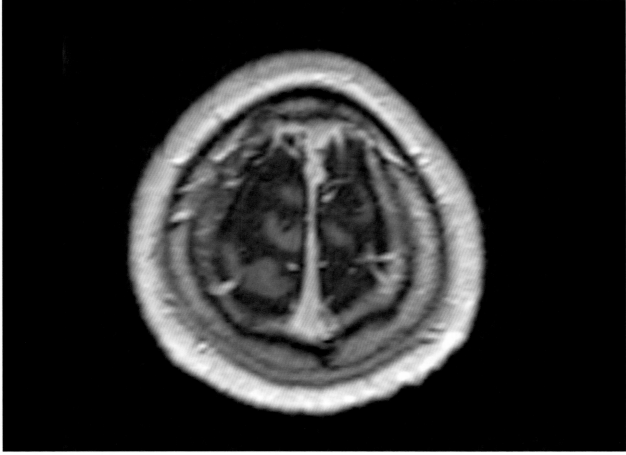

Figure 5.4.4

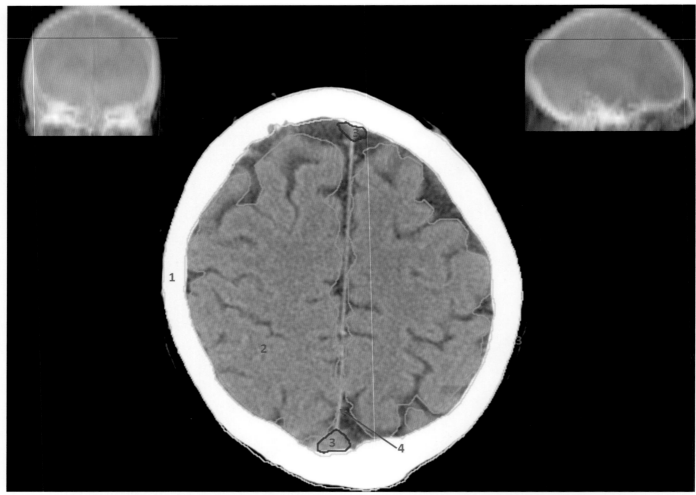

Figure 5.4.5

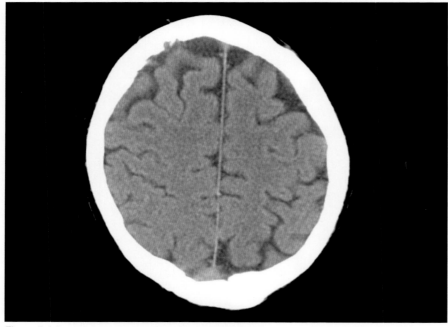

Figure 5.4.6

1. Parietal Bone
2. Parietal Lobe of Cerebrum
3. Superior Sagittal Sinus
4. Falx Cerebri

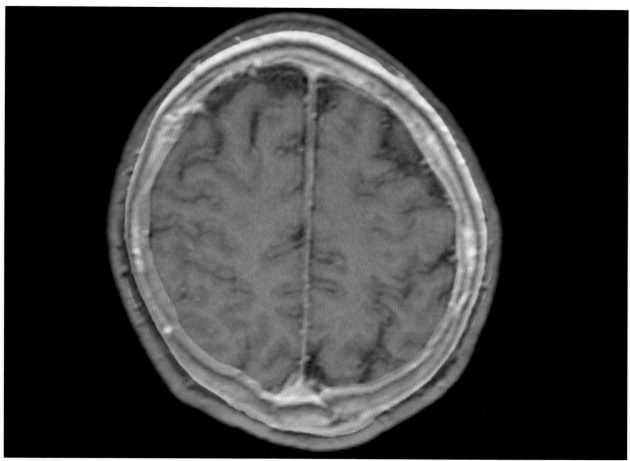

Figure 5.4.7

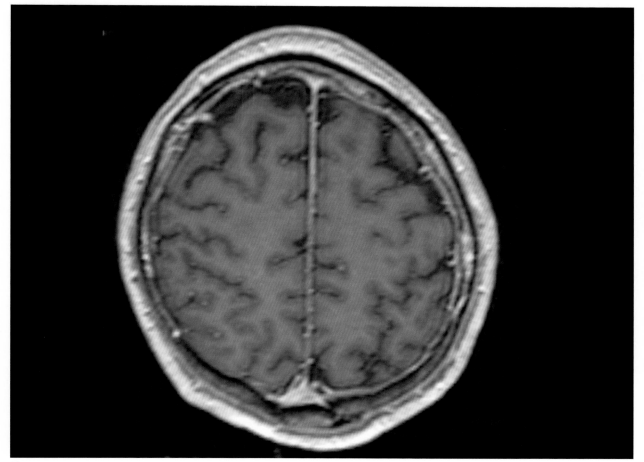

Figure 5.4.8

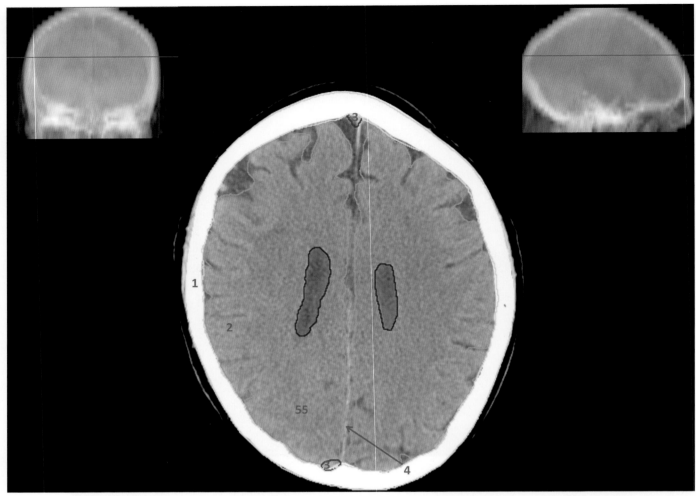

Figure 5.4.9

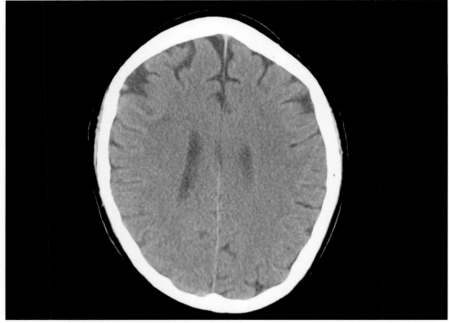

Figure 5.4.10

1. Parietal Bone
2. Parietal Lobe of Cerebrum
3. Superior Sagittal Sinus
4. Falx Cerebri
5. Body of Lateral Ventricle
55. Occipital Lobe of Cerebrum

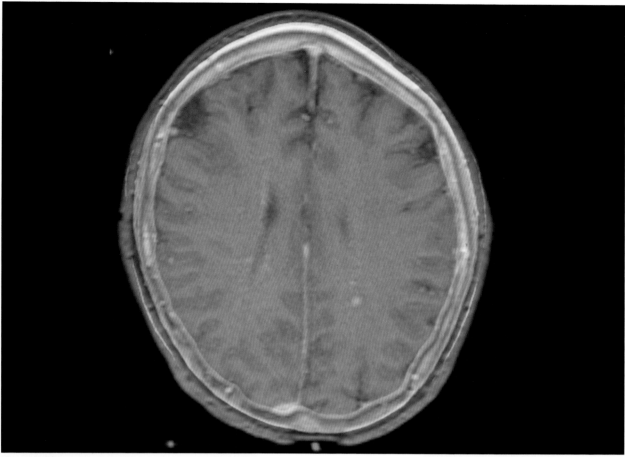

Figure 5.4.11

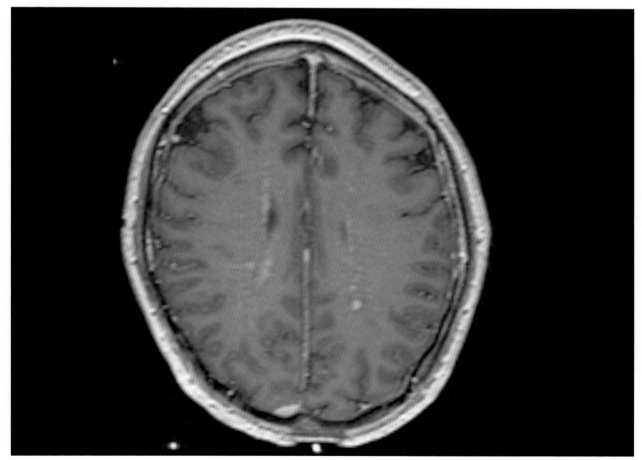

Figure 5.4.12

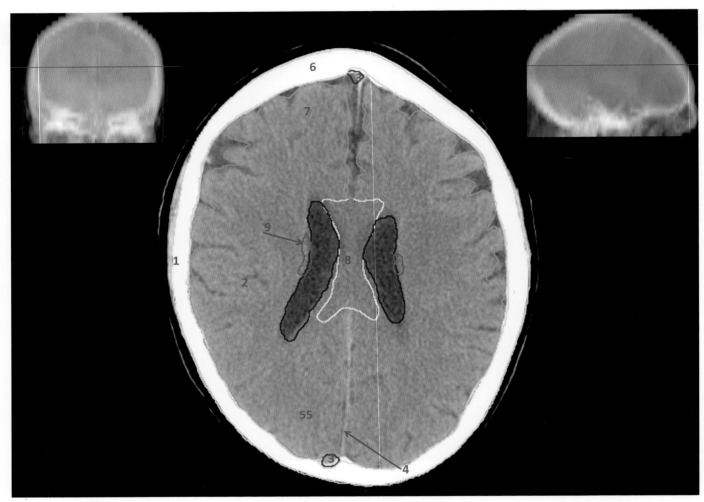

Figure 5.4.13

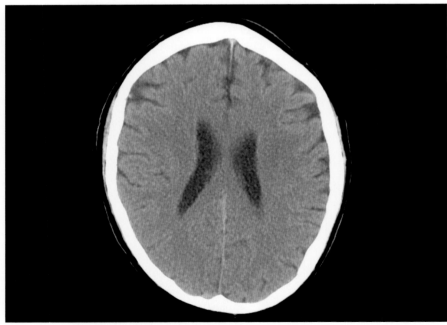

Figure 5.4.14

1. Parietal Bone
2. Parietal Lobe of Cerebrum
3. Superior Sagittal Sinus
4. Falx Cerebri
5. Body of Lateral Ventricle
6. Frontal Bone
7. Frontal Lobe of Cerebrum
8. Body of Corpus Callosum
9. Caudate Nucleus
55. Occipital Lobe of Cerebrum

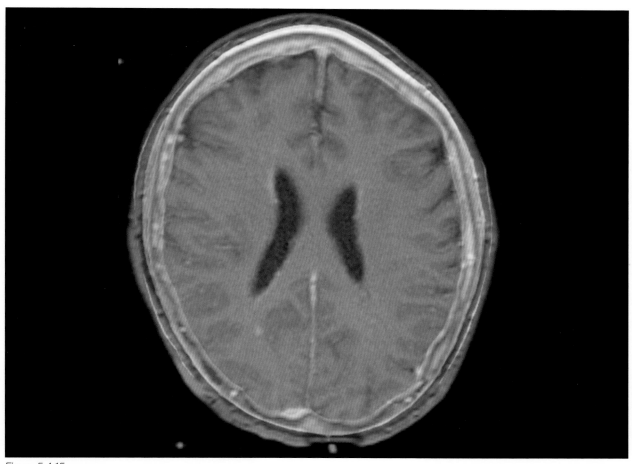

Figure 5.4.15

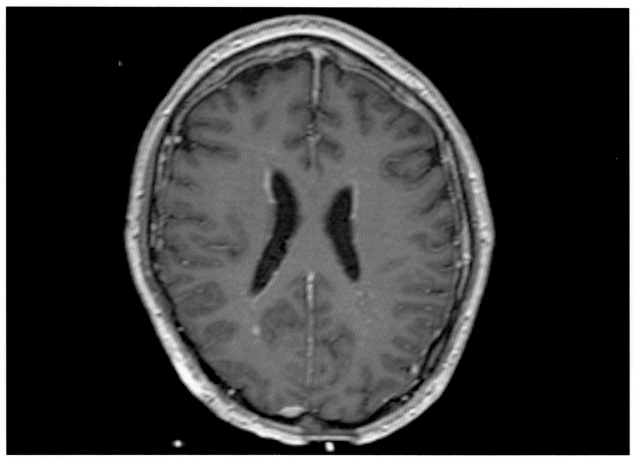

Figure 5.4.16

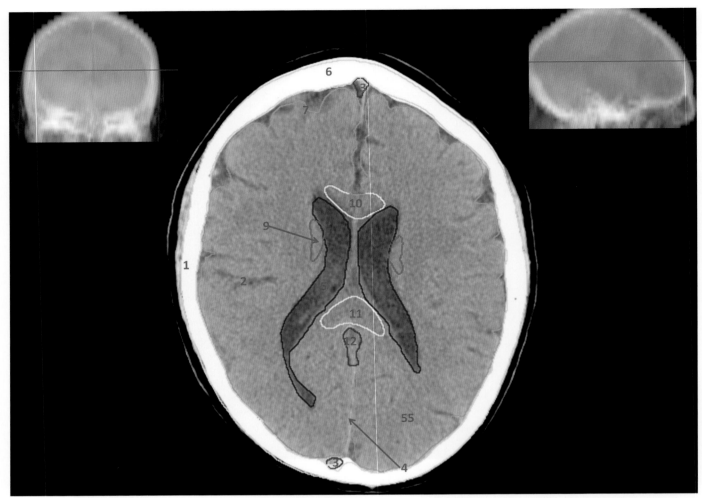

Figure 5.4.17

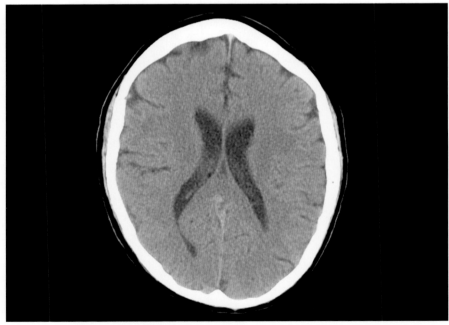

Figure 5.4.18

1. Parietal Bone
2. Parietal Lobe of Cerebrum
3. Superior Sagittal Sinus
4. Falx Cerebri
5. Body of Lateral Ventricle
6. Frontal Bone
7. Frontal Lobe of Cerebrum
9. Caudate Nucleus
10. Genu of Corpus Callosum
11. Splenium of Corpus Callosum
12. Straight Sinus
55. Occipital Lobe of Cerebrum

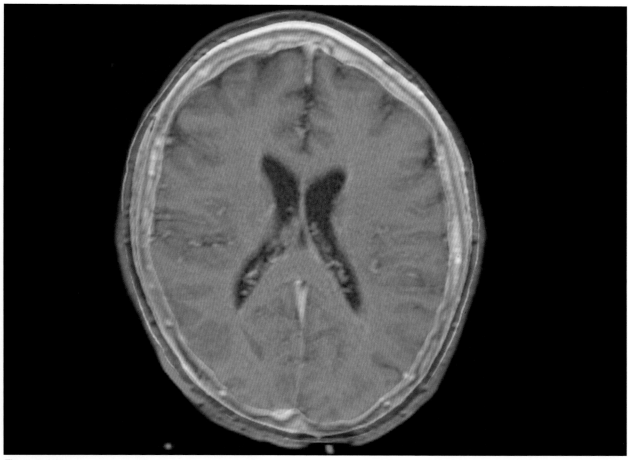

Figure 5.4.19

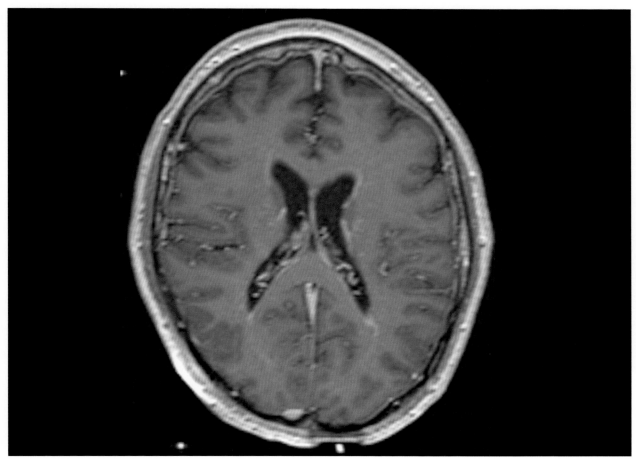

Figure 5.4.20

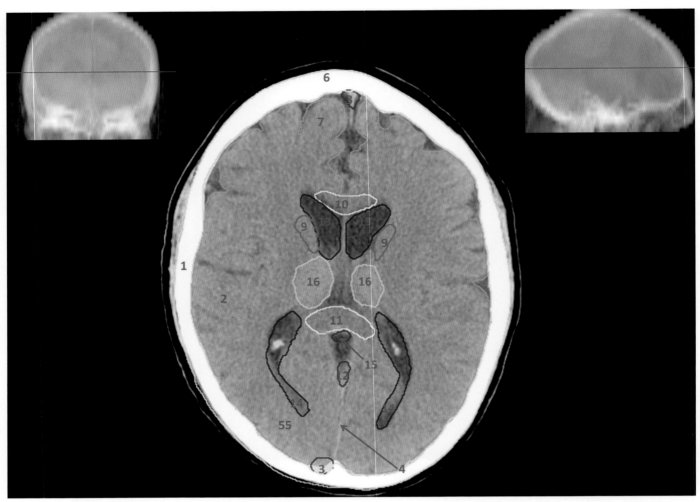

Figure 5.4.21

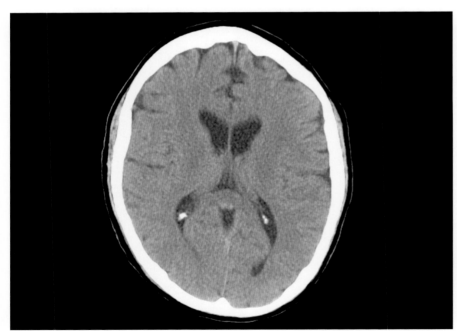

Figure 5.4.22

1. Parietal Bone
2. Parietal Lobe of Cerebrum
3. Superior Sagittal Sinus
4. Falx Cerebri
6. Frontal Bone
7. Frontal Lobe of Cerebrum
9. Head of Caudate Nucleus
10. Genu of Corpus Callosum
11. Splenium of Corpus Callosum
12. Straight Sinus
13. Lateral Ventricle Frontal Horn
14. Lateral Ventricle Occipital Horn
15. Great Vein of Galen
16. Thalamus
55. Occipital Lobe of Cerebrum

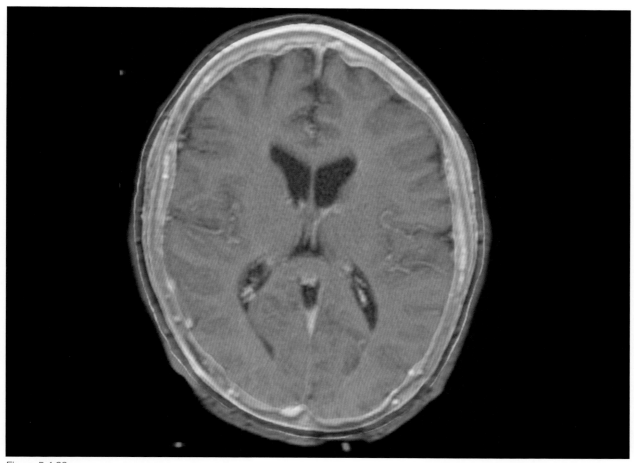

Figure 5.4.23

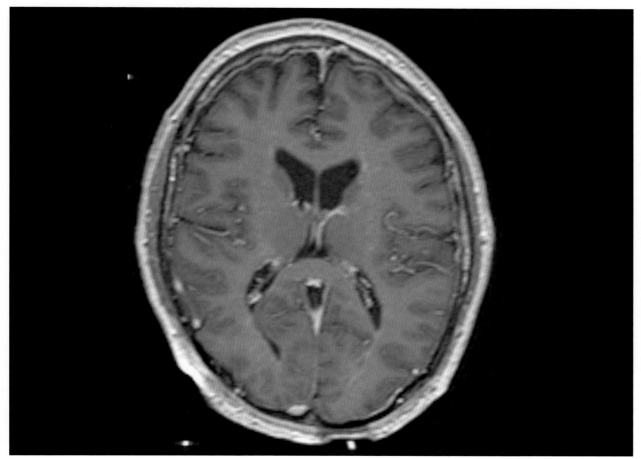

Figure 5.4.24

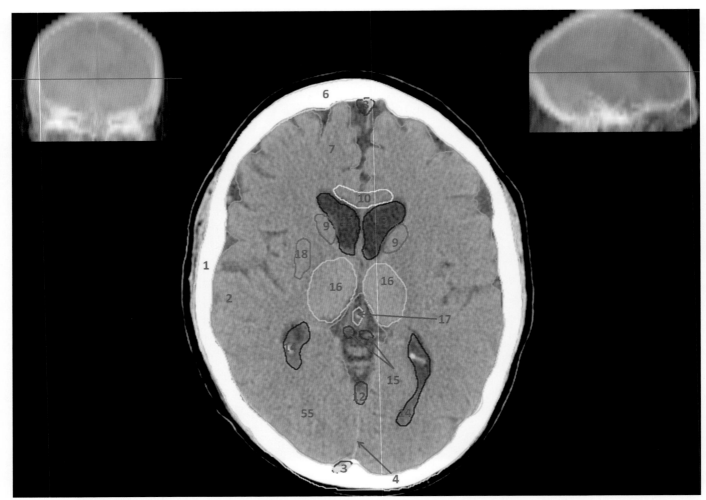

Figure 5.4.25

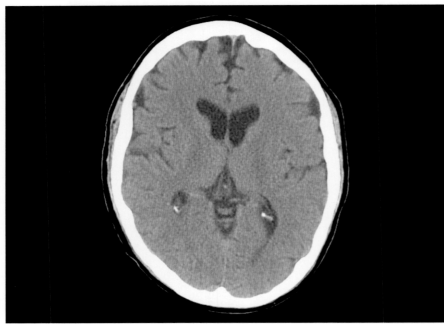

Figure 5.4.26

1. Parietal Bone
2. Parietal Lobe of Cerebrum
3. Superior Sagittal Sinus
4. Falx Cerebri
6. Frontal Bone
7. Frontal Lobe of Cerebrum
9. Head of Caudate Nucleus
10. Genu of Corpus Callosum
12. Straight Sinus
13. Lateral Ventricle Frontal Horn
14. Lateral Ventricle Occipital Horn
15. Great Vein of Galen
16. Thalamus
17. Pineal Gland
18. Lentiform Nucleus
55. Occipital Lobe of Cerebrum

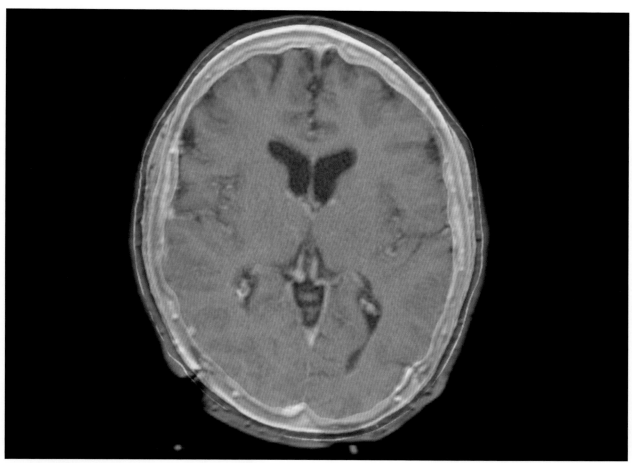

Figure 5.4.27

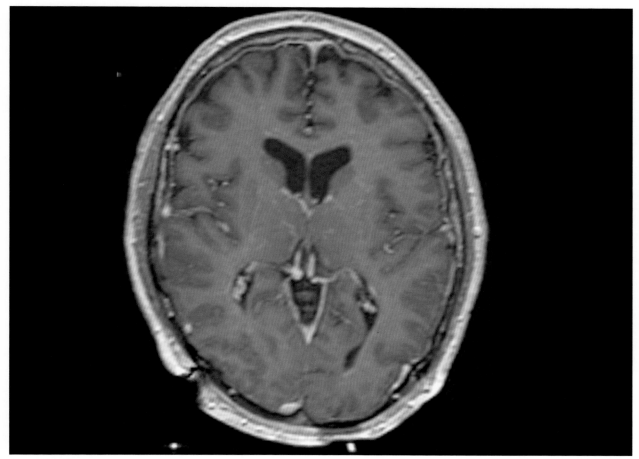

Figure 5.4.28

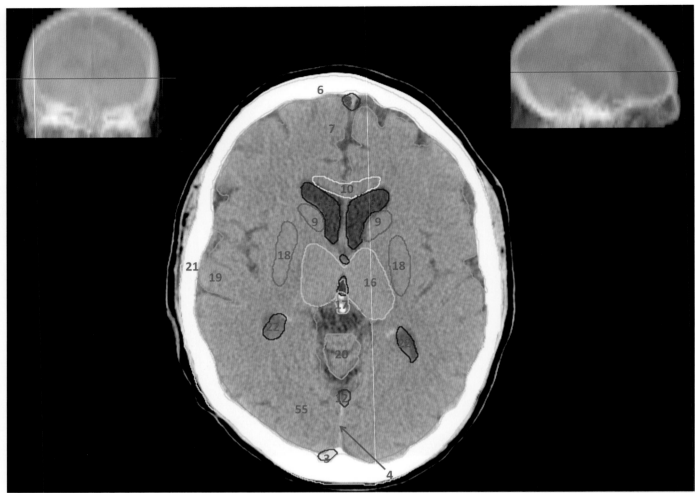

Figure 5.4.29

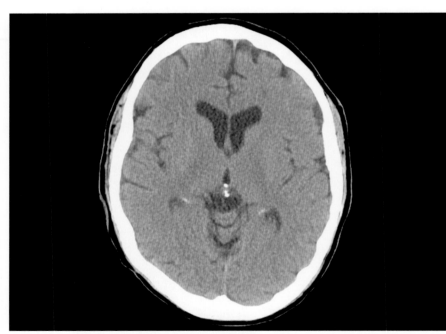

Figure 5.4.30

3. Superior Sagittal Sinus
4. Falx Cerebri
6. Frontal Bone
7. Frontal Lobe of Cerebrum
9. Head of Caudate Nucleus
10. Genu of Corpus Callosum
12. Straight Sinus
13. Lateral Ventricle Frontal Horn
16. Thalamus
17. Pineal Gland
18. Lentiform Nucleus
19. Temporal Lobe of Cerebrum
20. Cerebellum
21. Temporal Bone
22. Lateral Ventricle Temporal Horn
55. Occipital Lobe of Cerebrum

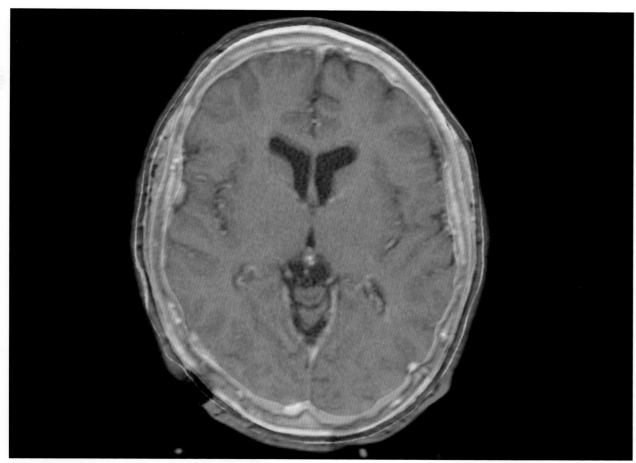

Figure 5.4.31

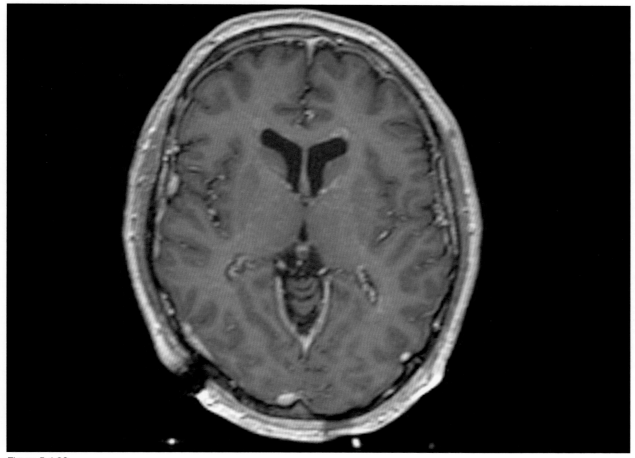

Figure 5.4.32

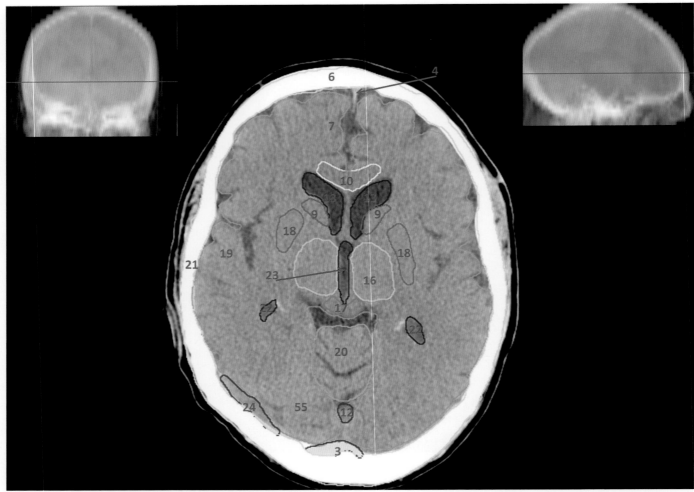

Figure 5.4.33

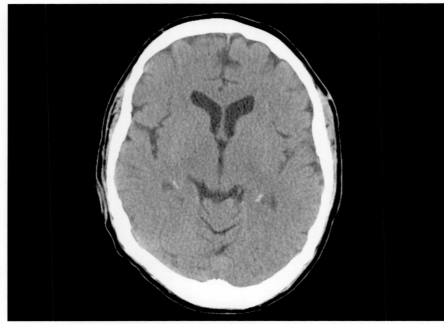

Figure 5.4.34

3. Superior Sagittal Sinus
4. Falx Cerebri
6. Frontal Bone
7. Frontal Lobe of Cerebrum
9. Head of Caudate Nucleus
10. Genu of Corpus Callosum
12. Straight Sinus
13. Lateral Ventricle Frontal Horn
16. Thalamus
17. Pineal Gland
18. Lentiform Nucleus
19. Temporal Lobe of Cerebrum
20. Cerebellum
21. Temporal Bone
22. Lateral Ventricle Temporal Horn
23. Third Ventricle
24. Transverse Sinus
55. Occipital Lobe of Cerebrum

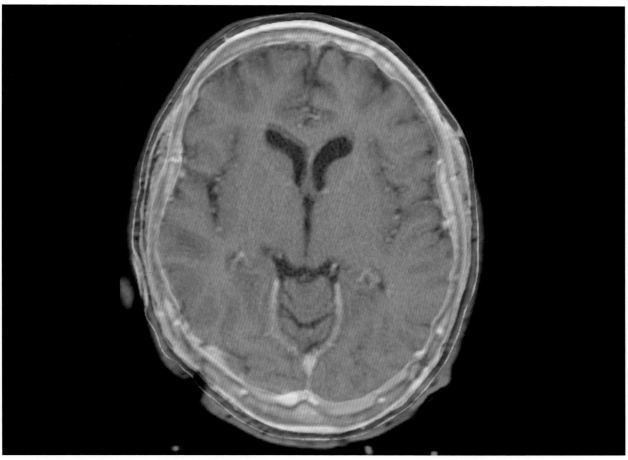

Figure 5.4.35

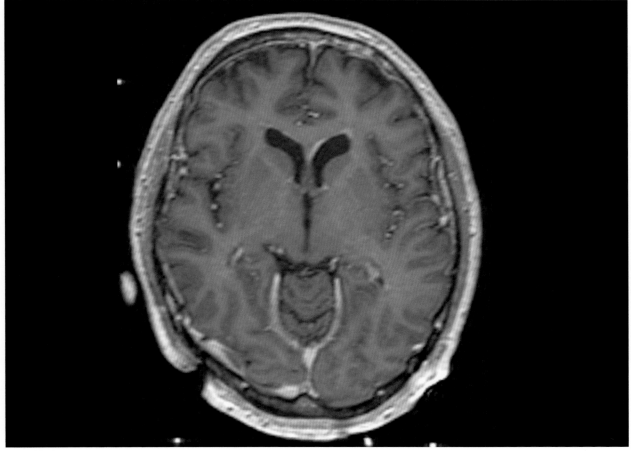

Figure 5.4.36

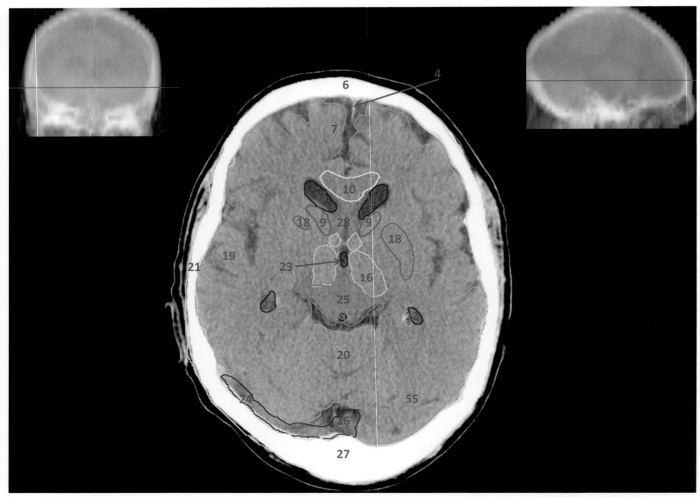

Figure 5.4.37

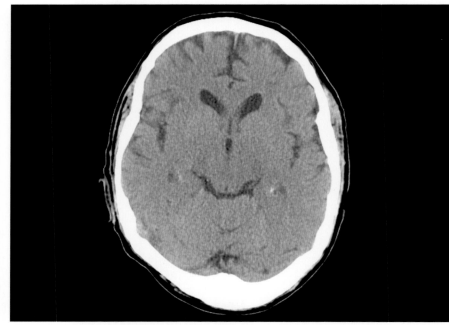

Figure 5.4.38

4. Falx Cerebri
6. Frontal Bone
7. Frontal Lobe of Cerebrum
9. Head of Caudate Nucleus
10. Genu of Corpus Callosum
13. Lateral Ventricle Frontal Horn
16. Thalamus
18. Lentiform Nucleus
19. Temporal Lobe of Cerebrum
20. Cerebellum
21. Temporal Bone
22. Lateral Ventricle Temporal Horn
23. Third Ventricle
24. Transverse Sinus
25. Midbrain
26. Confluence of Sinuses
27. Occipital Bone
28. Hypothalamus

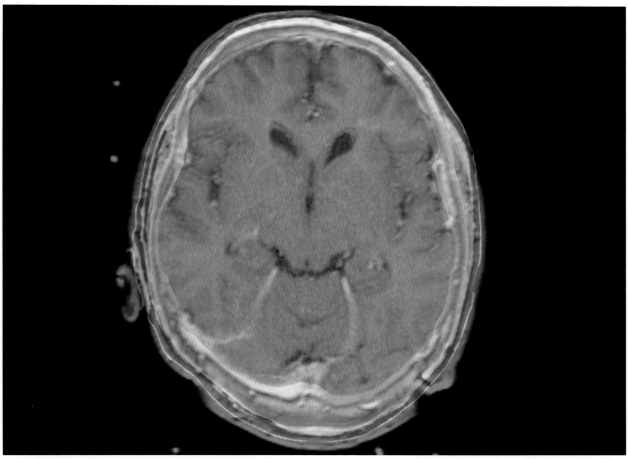

Figure 5.4.39

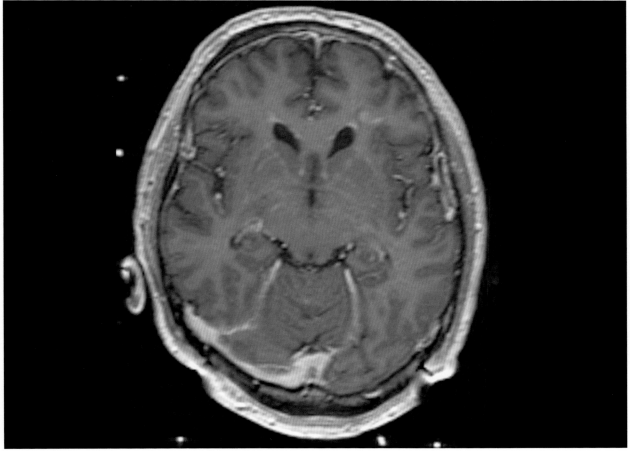

Figure 5.4.40

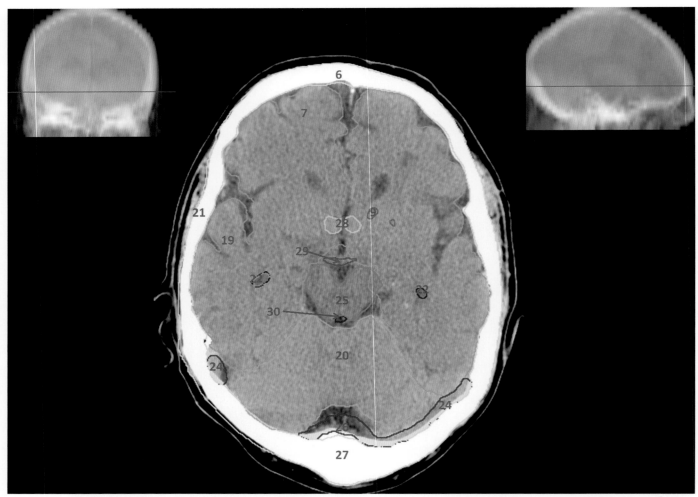

Figure 5.4.41

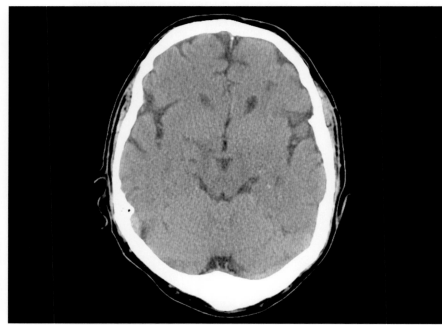

Figure 5.4.42

6. Frontal Bone
7. Frontal Lobe of Cerebrum
9. Head of Caudate Nucleus
19. Temporal Lobe of Cerebrum
20. Cerebellum
21. Temporal Bone
22. Lateral Ventricle Temporal Horn
24. Transverse Sinus
25. Midbrain
26. Confluence of Sinuses
27. Occipital Bone
28. Hypothalamus
29. Circle of Willis
30. Cerebral Aqueduct

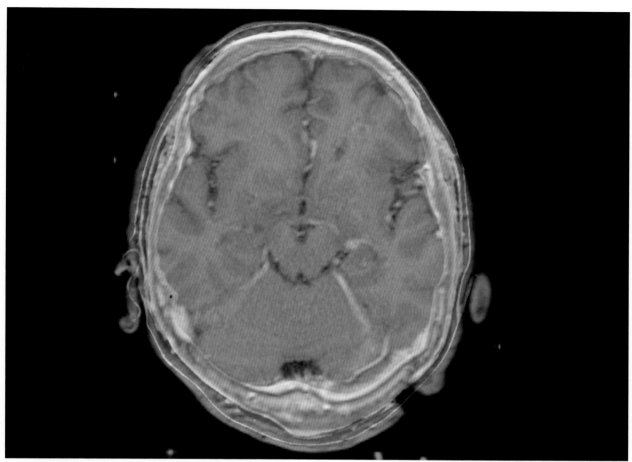

Figure 5.4.43

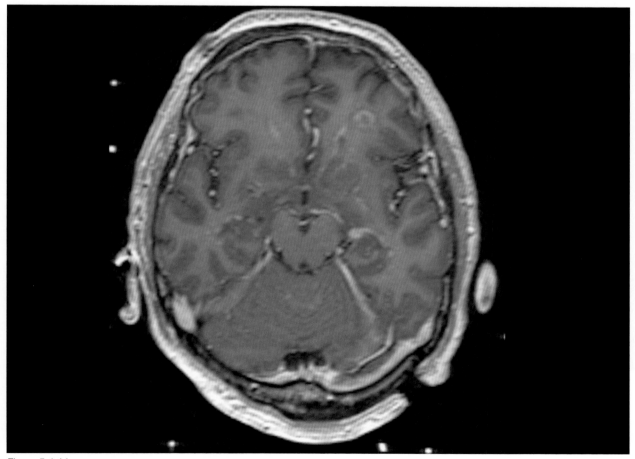

Figure 5.4.44

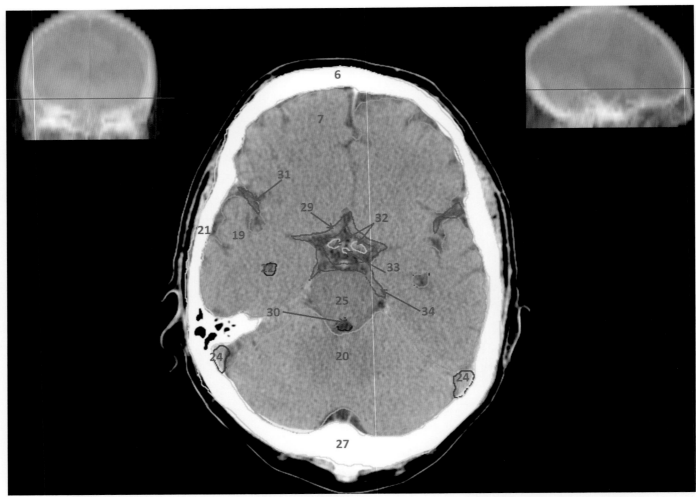

Figure 5.4.45

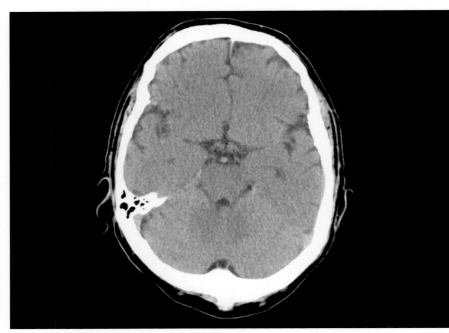

Figure 5.4.46

6. Frontal Bone
7. Frontal Lobe of Cerebrum
19. Temporal Lobe of Cerebrum
20. Cerebellum
21. Temporal Bone
22. Lateral Ventricle Temporal Horn
24. Transverse Sinus
25. Midbrain
27. Occipital Bone
29. Circle of Willis
30. Cerebral Aqueduct
31. Middle Cerebral Artery
32. Optic Nerves
33. Pituitary Infundibulum
34. Posterior Cerebral Artery

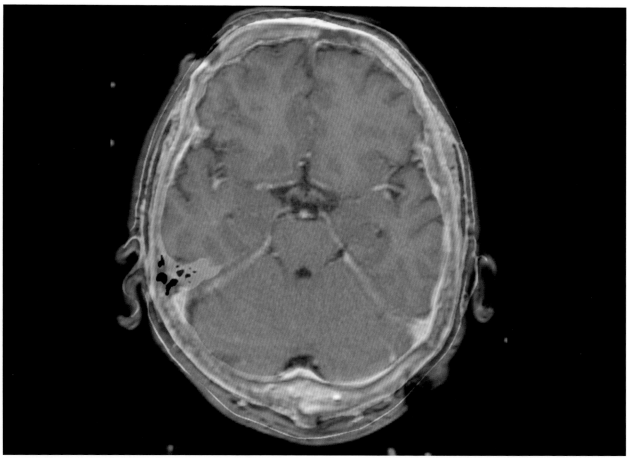

Figure 5.4.47

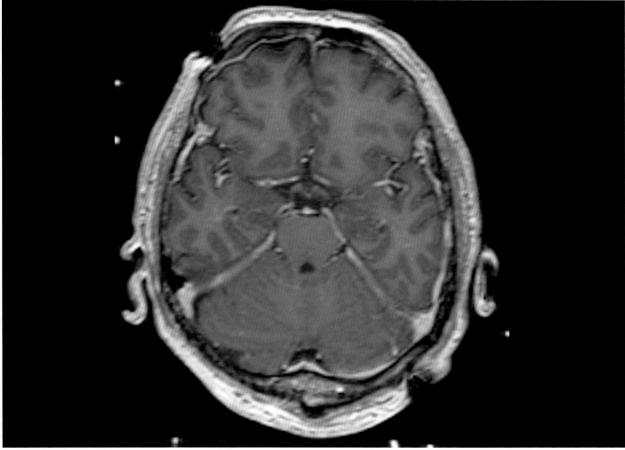

Figure 5.4.48

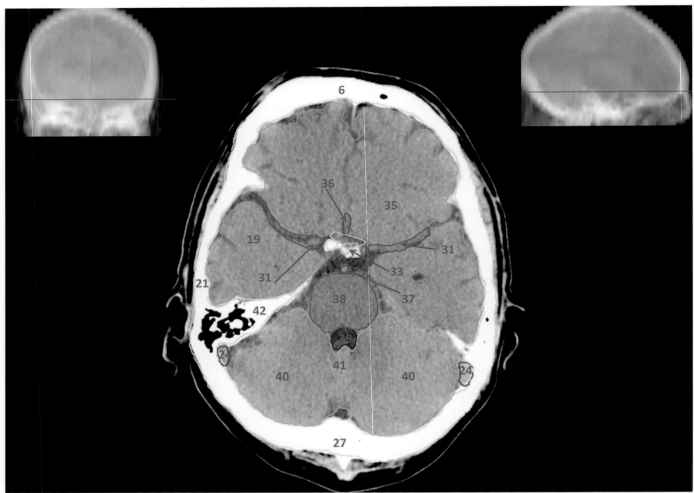

Figure 5.4.49

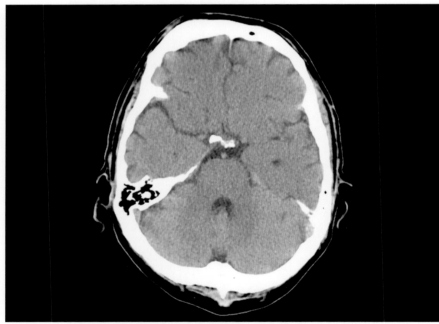

Figure 5.4.50

6. Frontal Bone
7. Frontal Lobe of Cerebrum
19. Temporal Lobe of Cerebrum
21. Temporal Bone
24. Transverse Sinus
27. Occipital Bone
31. Middle Cerebral Artery
33. Pituitary
35. Optic Chiasm
36. Anterior Cerebral Artery
37. Basilar Artery
38. Pons
39. Fourth Ventricle
40. Hemisphere of Cerebellum
41. Vermis of Cerebellum
42. Petrous Ridge of Temporal Bone

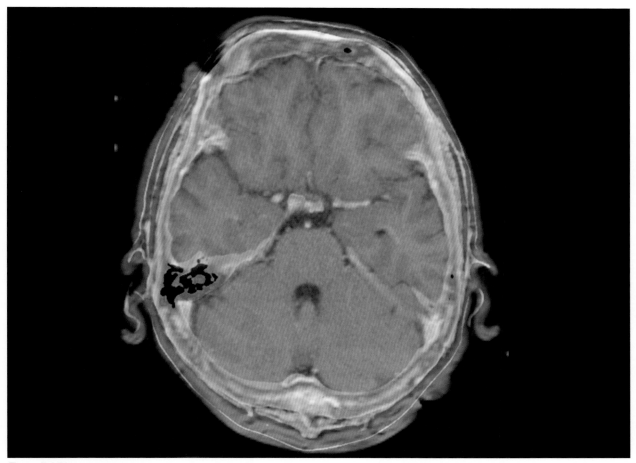

Figure 5.4.51

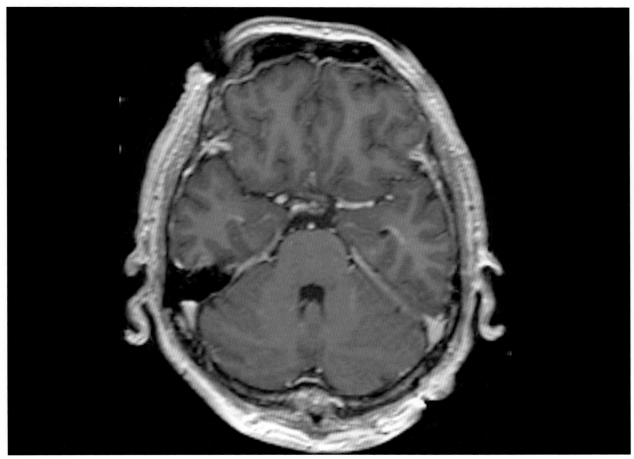

Figure 5.4.52

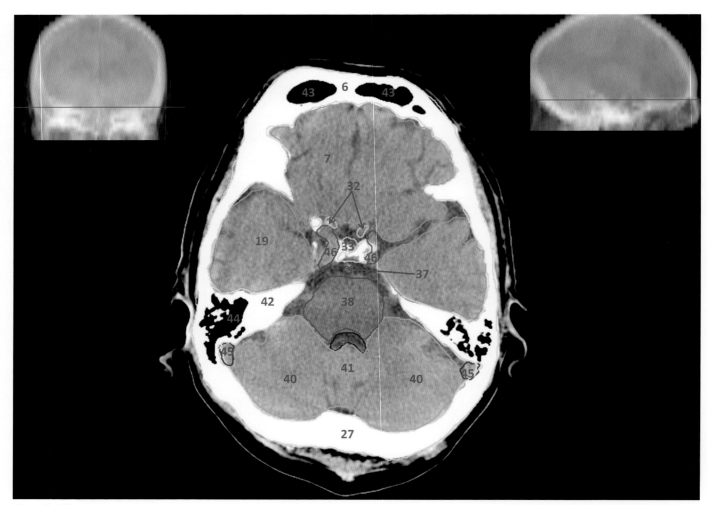

Figure 5.4.53

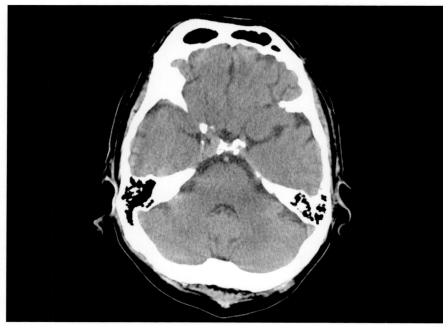

Figure 5.4.54

6. Frontal Bone
7. Frontal Lobe of Cerebrum
19. Temporal Lobe of Cerebrum
27. Occipital Bone
32. Optic Nerve
33. Pituitary
37. Basilar Artery
38. Pons
39. Fourth Ventricle
40. Hemisphere of Cerebellum
41. Vermis of Cerebellum
42. Petrous Ridge of Temporal Bone
43. Frontal Sinus
44. Inner Ear
45. Sigmoid Sinus
46. Internal Carotid Artery

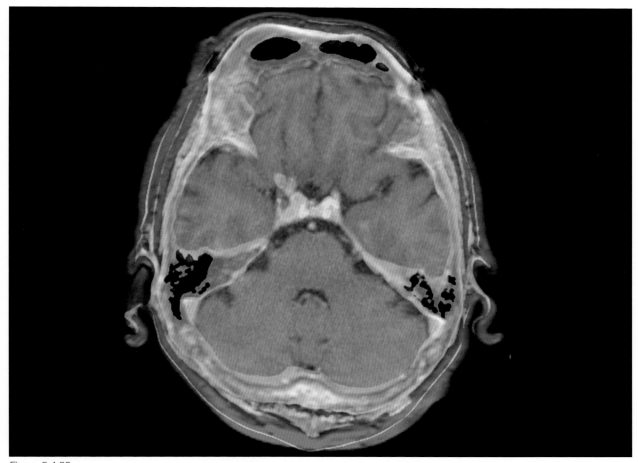

Figure 5.4.55

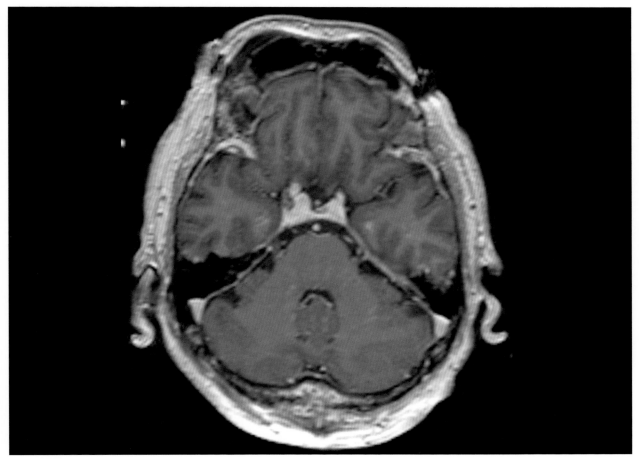

Figure 5.4.56

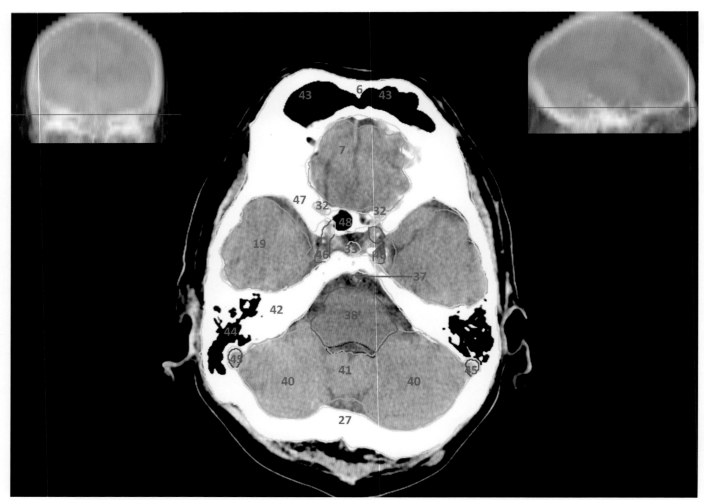

Figure 5.4.57

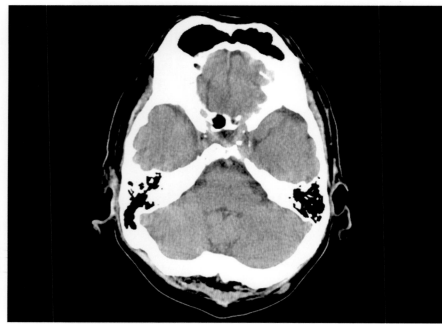

Figure 5.4.58

6. Frontal Bone
7. Frontal Lobe of Cerebrum
19. Temporal Lobe of Cerebrum
27. Occipital Bone
32. Optic Nerve
33. Pituitary
37. Basilar Artery
38. Pons
39. Fourth Ventricle
40. Hemisphere of Cerebellum
41. Vermis of Cerebellum
42. Petrous Ridge of Temporal Bone
43. Frontal Sinus
44. Inner Ear
45. Sigmoid Sinus
46. Internal Carotid Artery
47. Sphenoid Bone
48. Sphenoid Sinus

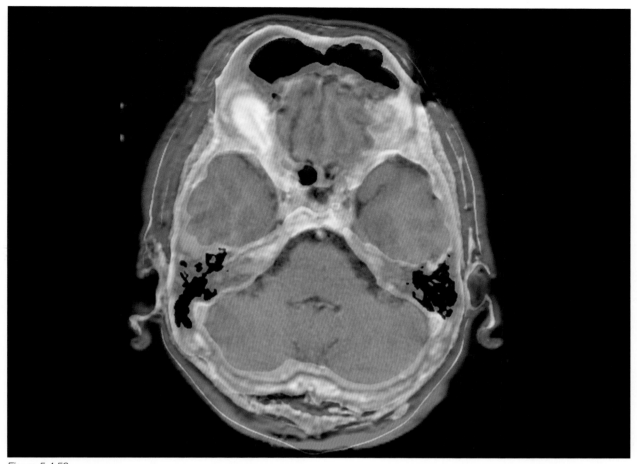

Figure 5.4.59

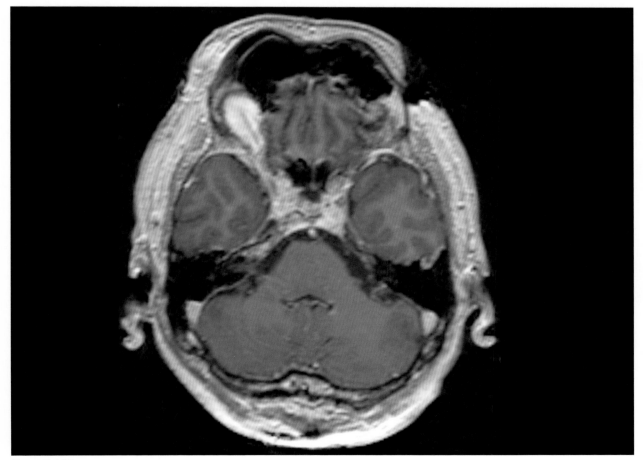

Figure 5.4.60

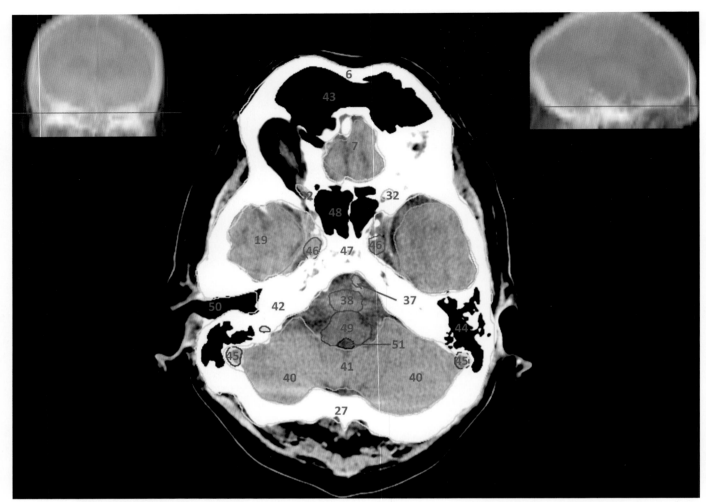

Figure 5.4.61

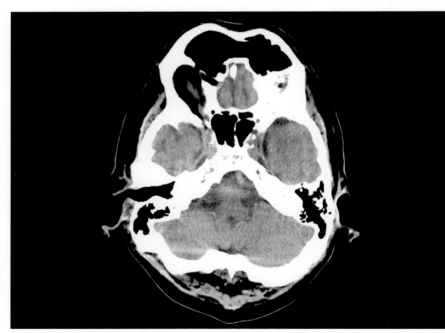

Figure 5.4.62

6. Frontal Bone
7. Frontal Lobe of Cerebrum
19. Temporal Lobe of Cerebrum
27. Occipital Bone
32. Optic Nerve
37. Basilar Artery
38. Pons
40. Hemisphere of Cerebellum
41. Vermis of Cerebellum
42. Petrous Ridge of Temporal Bone
43. Frontal Sinus
44. Inner Ear
45. Sigmoid Sinus
46. Internal Carotid Artery
47. Sphenoid Bone
48. Sphenoid Sinus
49. Medulla Oblongata
50. External Auditory Meatus
51. Spinal Central Canal

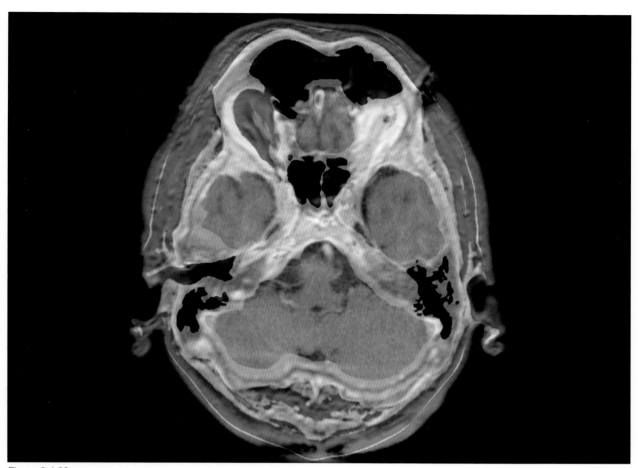

Figure 5.4.63

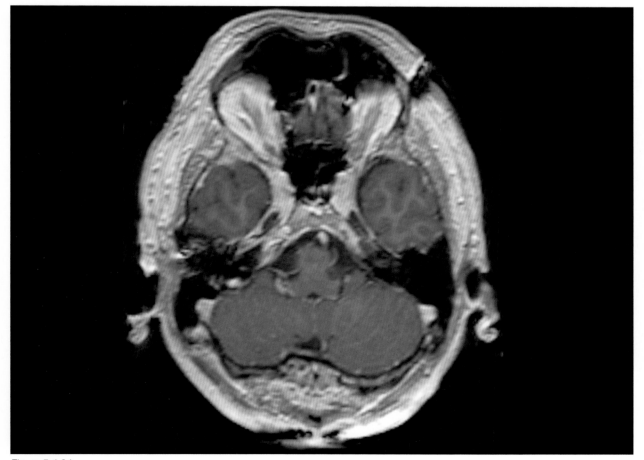

Figure 5.4.64

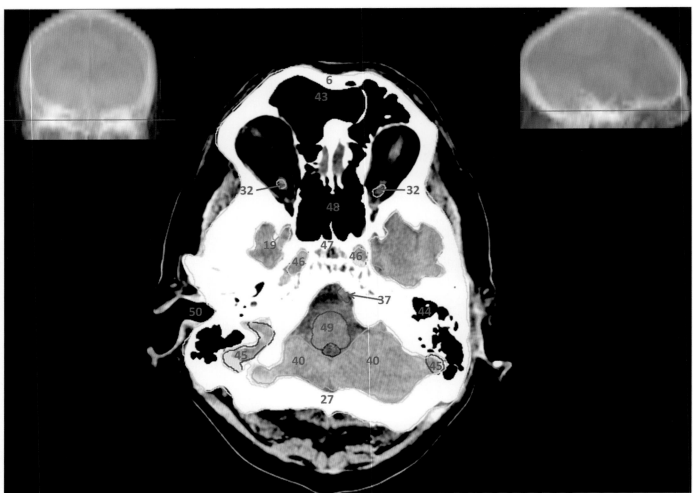

Figure 5.4.65

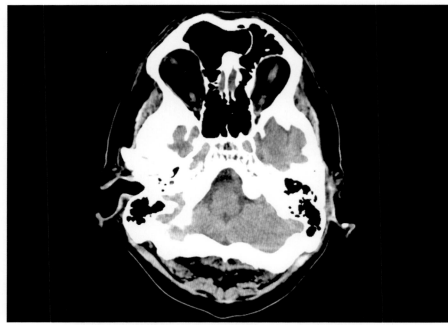

Figure 5.4.66

6. Frontal Bone
19. Temporal Lobe of Cerebrum
27. Occipital Bone
32. Optic Nerve
37. Basilar Artery
40. Hemisphere of Cerebellum
43. Frontal Sinus
44. Inner Ear
45. Sigmoid Sinus
46. Internal Carotid Artery
47. Sphenoid Bone
48. Sphenoid Sinus
49. Medulla Oblongata
50. External Auditory Meatus
51. Spinal Central Canal

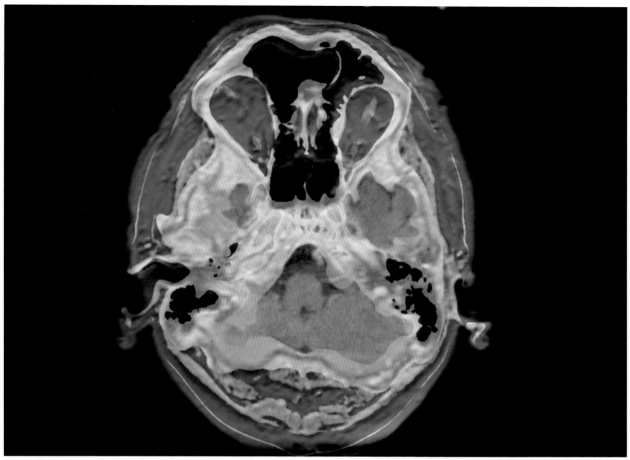

Figure 5.4.67

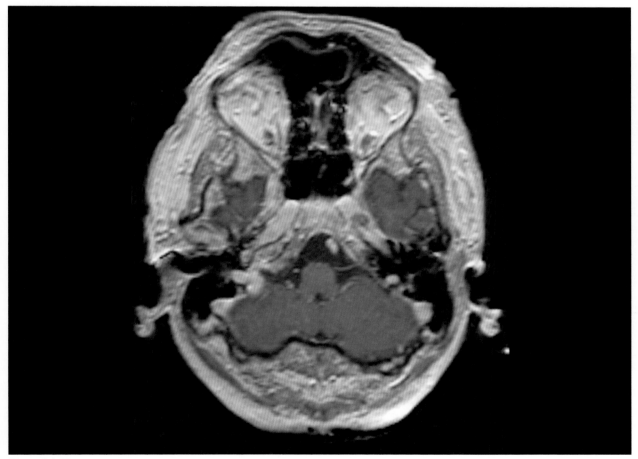

Figure 5.4.68

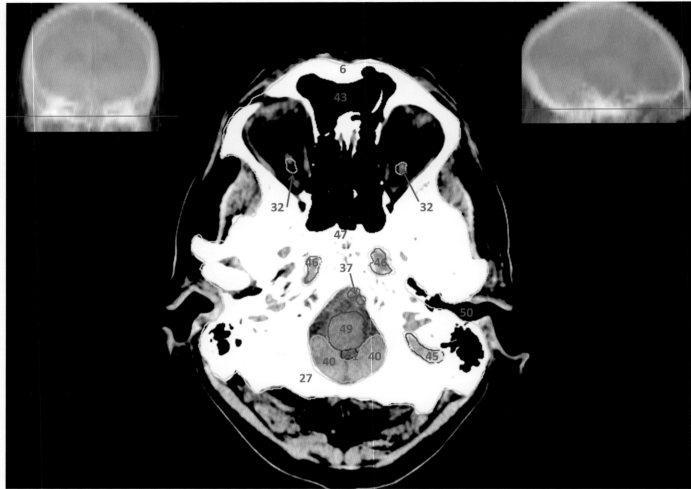

Figure 5.4.69

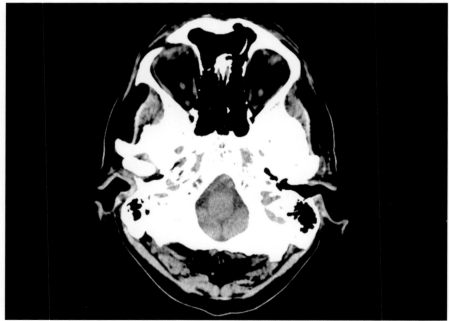

Figure 5.4.70

6. Frontal Bone
27. Occipital Bone
32. Optic Nerve
37. Basilar Artery
40. Hemisphere of Cerebellum
43. Frontal Sinus
45. Sigmoid Sinus
46. Internal Carotid Artery
47. Sphenoid Bone
49. Medulla Oblongata
50. External Auditory Meatus
51. Spinal Central Canal

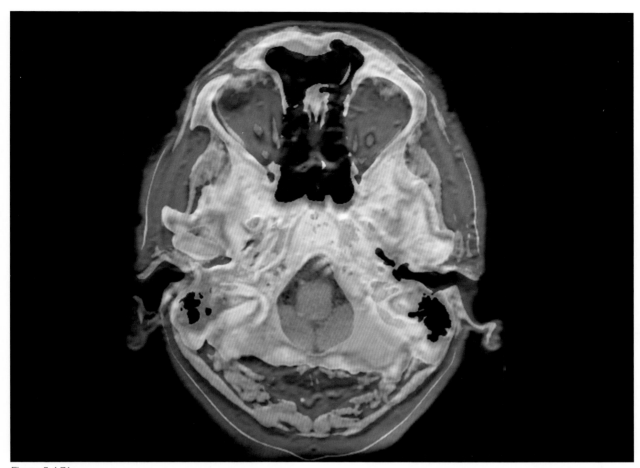

Figure 5.4.71

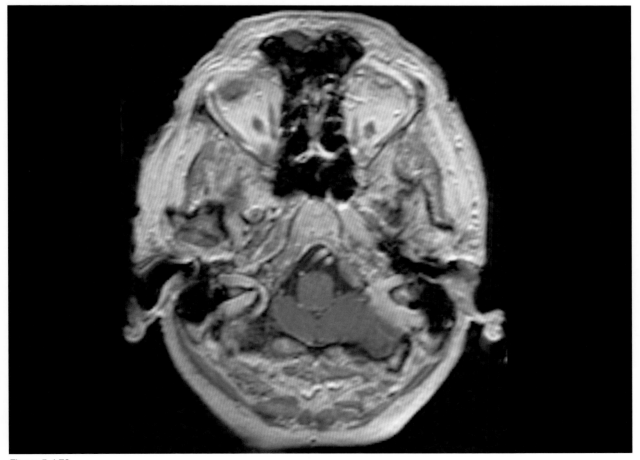

Figure 5.4.72

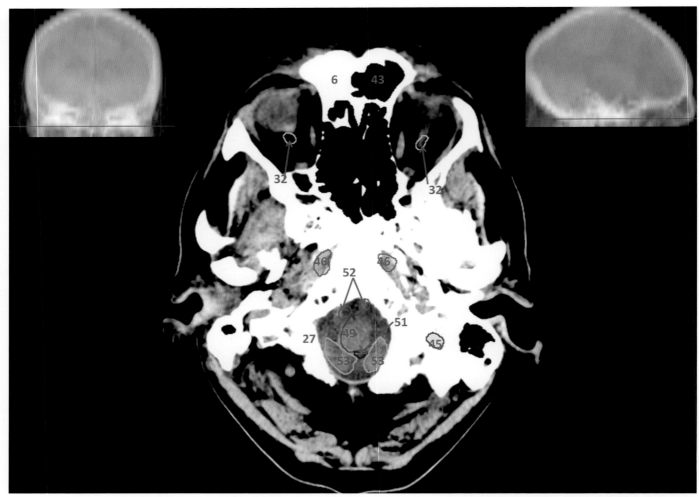

Figure 5.4.73

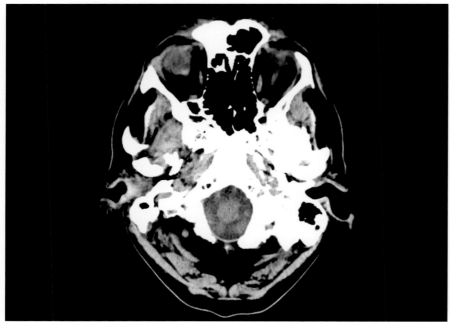

Figure 5.4.74

6. Frontal Bone
27. Occipital Bone
32. Optic Nerve
43. Frontal Sinus
45. Sigmoid Sinus
46. Internal Carotid Artery
49. Medulla Oblongata
51. Spinal Central Canal
52. Vertebral Artery
53. Cerebellar Tonsil

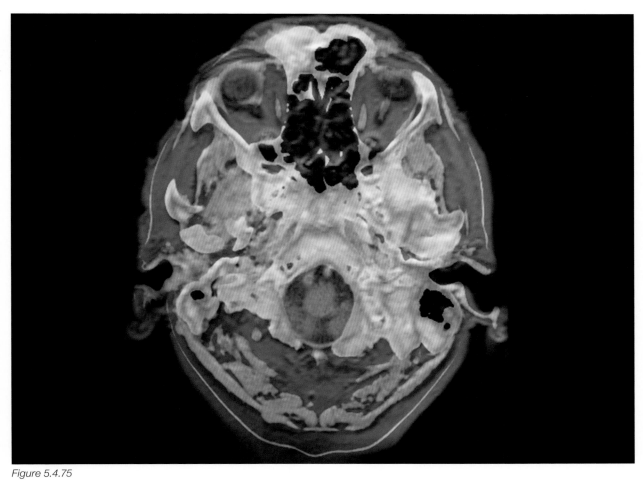

Figure 5.4.75

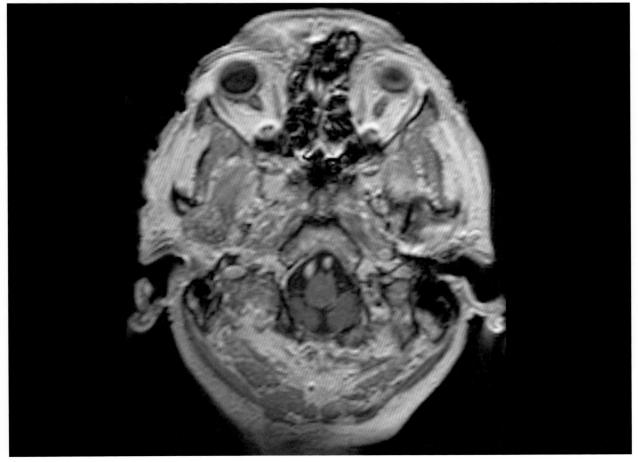

Figure 5.4.76

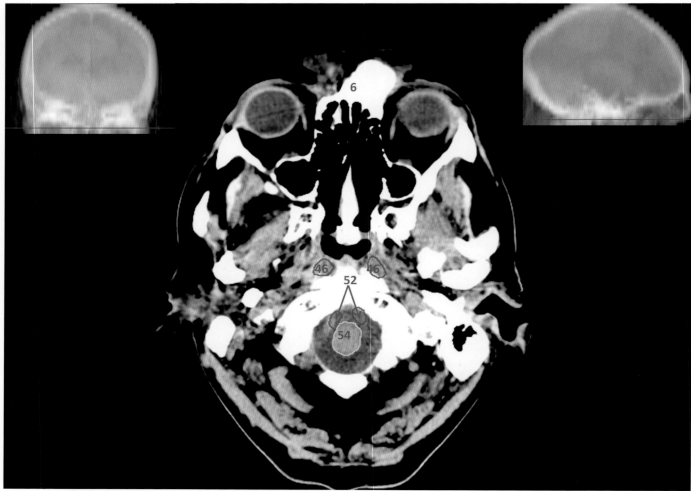

Figure 5.4.77

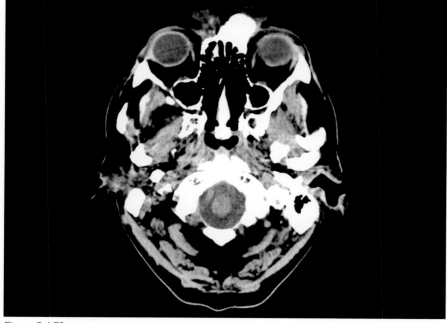

Figure 5.4.78

6. Frontal Bone
46. Internal Carotid Artery
52. Vertebral Artery
54. Spinal Cord

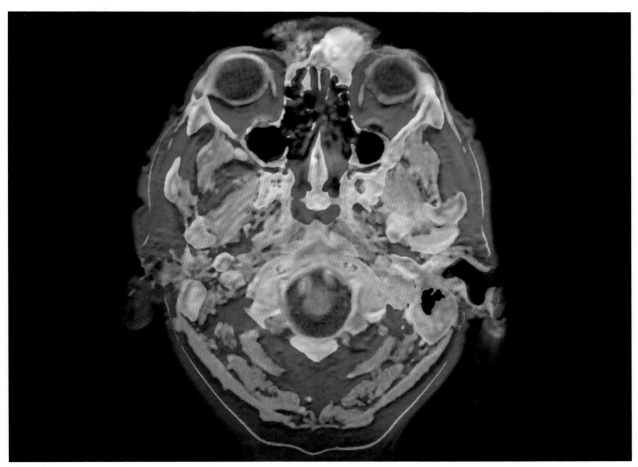

Figure 5.4.79

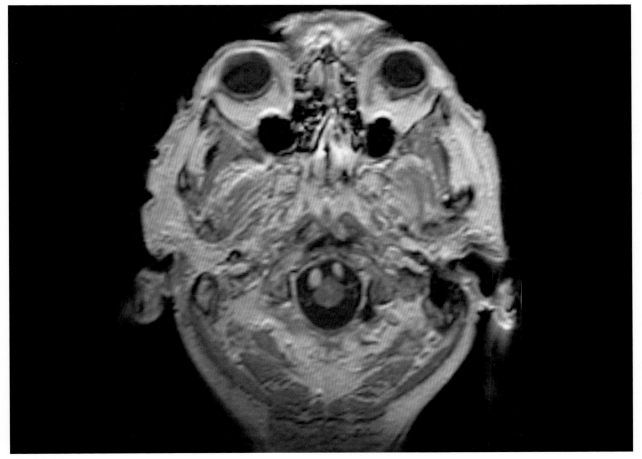

Figure 5.4.80

5.5 Common Intracranial Tumour Pathology CT Appearance

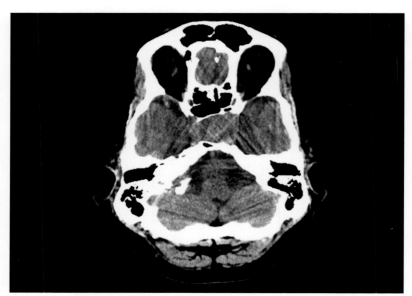

Figure 5.5.1

Pituitary macroadenoma

Figure 5.5.1 shows a relatively large, expansile lesion within the sella turcica. The anterior aspects of the pituitary fossa have been eroded. Without the use of IV contrast, it is difficult to demarcate the lateral extents and location of the cavernous sinuses. These are typical appearances of a pituitary macroadenoma (macro = >10mm). It is likely that this patient has some visual field disturbances as the optic chiasm is sited immediately superior to the pituitary gland and is likely to be compressed.

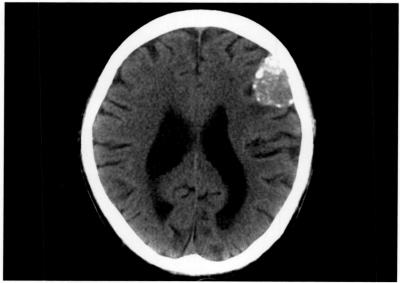

Figure 5.5.2

Meningioma

Figure 5.5.2 demonstrates a dome-shaped growth of mixed attenuation arising from the inner table of the left frontal bone. The lesion does not appear to have invaded the inner table of the skull (although bony window settings would be needed to confirm this). There are flecks of calcification present. The lesion is causing minimal buckling of the adjacent cortical gyral convolutions and little effect on other CSF spaces. This is a typical appearance of a long standing meningioma.

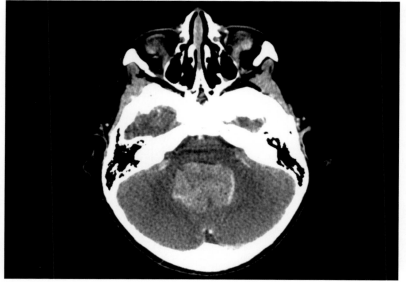

Figure 5.5.3

Medulloblastoma

Figure 5.5.3 shows a large, hyperdense mass within the posterior fossa. The lesion appears to be surrounded by the cerebellum posterolaterally and the compressed pons anteriorly. This is characteristic of medulloblastoma which usually arises from the fourth ventricle and subsequently causes obstructive hydrocephalus as the flow of CSF is limited. Axial scans above this level will typically demonstrate a dilated ventricular system and effacement of other CSF spaces.

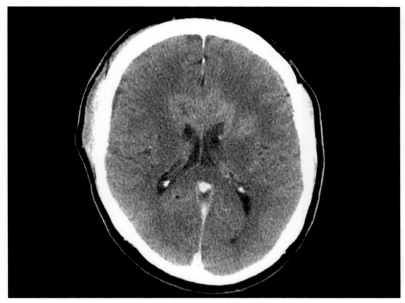

Figure 5.5.4

Intracerebral lymphoma

Figure 5.5.4 illustrates a relatively hyper-dense, slightly irregular mass lesion originating from within the genu of the corpus callosum. It extends anteriorly and crosses the midline laterally into adjacent white matter. The frontal horns of both lateral ventricles are minimally displaced; however the ventricles and surrounding CSF spaces are otherwise not affected. This is consistent with primary CNS lymphoma. Deep hemispheric peri-ventricular white matter such as corpus callosum is most commonly affected.

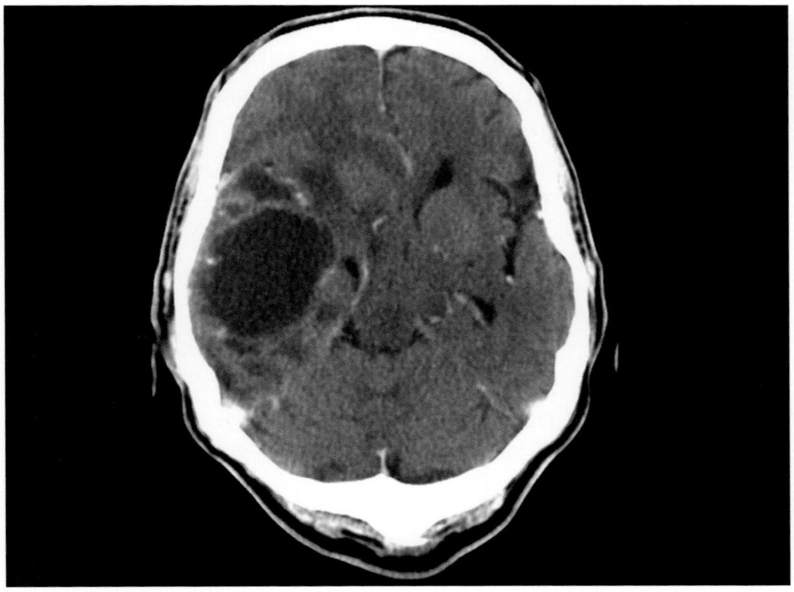

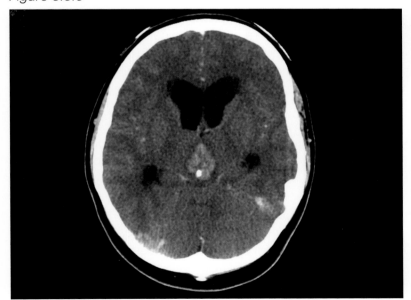

Figure 5.5.5

Glioblastoma Multiforme

Figure 5.5.5 shows a large, irregular rim-enhancing lesion of the right temporoparietal lobe within the deep white matter. The lesion is causing considerable midline shift, with effacement of the frontal horn of the right lateral ventricle, adjacent sulcal patterns and Sylvian fissure. The right basal ganglia are compressed and shifted to the left. This is a common appearance and location of a GBM, although frontal lobes are also affected. Haemorrhage, central necrosis and mass affect are all expected findings.

Figure 5.5.6

Pineal Germinoma

Figure 5.5.6 shows a small, lobulated, enhancing lesion central sited in the midline between both thalamic complexes. The lesion is either abutting the pineal gland (demonstrating similar patterns of enhancement), or arising from the gland itself. The ventricular system is enlarged, indicated by dilated frontal and temporal horns, suggesting that the lesion is compressing the cerebral aqueduct. All cortical sulcation patterns are obliterated and there is evidence of white matter CSF absorption within the frontal horns, further substantiating the presence of obstructive hydrocephalus.

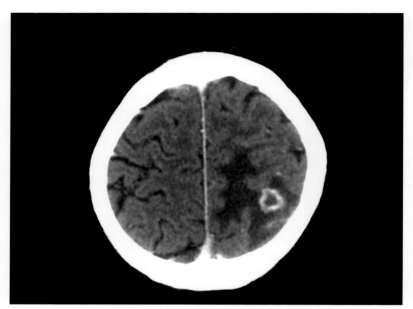

Figure 5.5.7

Solitary brain metastasis

Solitary brain metastases are sometimes treated discretely, especially if they are on the periphery of the brain. Contrast has enhanced the deposit in Figure 5.5.7, demonstrating a ring-like growth with a central low attenuation zone. In addition, this metastasis is surrounded by localised oedema. The CT appearance of solitary brain metastases can be difficult to distinguish from that of a primary brain tumour and biopsy is often needed to differentiate the two.

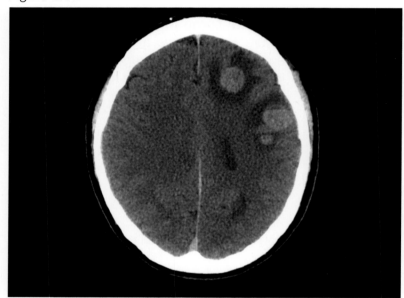

Figure 5.5.8

Multiple brain metastases

There can be little doubt of the diagnosis in Figure 5.5.8. These metastatic deposits are from a primary melanoma and demonstrate solid growths with surrounding oedema. The two hemispheres of the cerebrum have completely different appearances and the lack of symmetry is easy to identify.

Melanoma commonly metastasises to the brain, and approximately 40–60% of melanoma patients will present with brain metastases. Haemorrhage is also a distinctive appearance on CT.

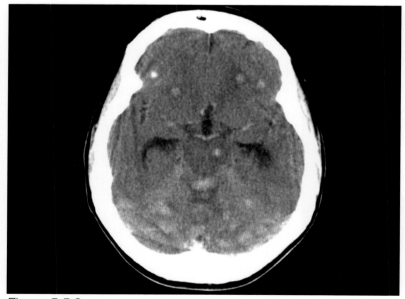

Figure 5.5.9

Multiple miliary brain metastases

Figure 5.5.9 indicates the presence of multiple, small, rounded uniformly enhancing lesions scattered throughout both cerebellar and cerebral hemispheres. Localised surrounding oedema is present around each of the lesions. There are a disproportionate number of lesions within the posterior fossa. This is causing mass effect and effacement of the fourth ventricle. There is subsequent obstructive hydrocephalus with marked dilatation of the temporal horns and third ventricle. These are typical appearances of miliary breast metastases.

5.6 Self-test Questions: Intracranial

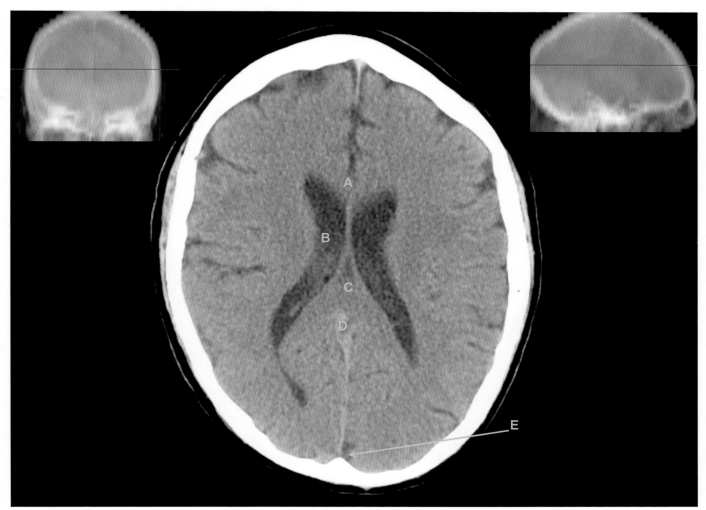

Figure 5.6.1

A

B

C

D

E

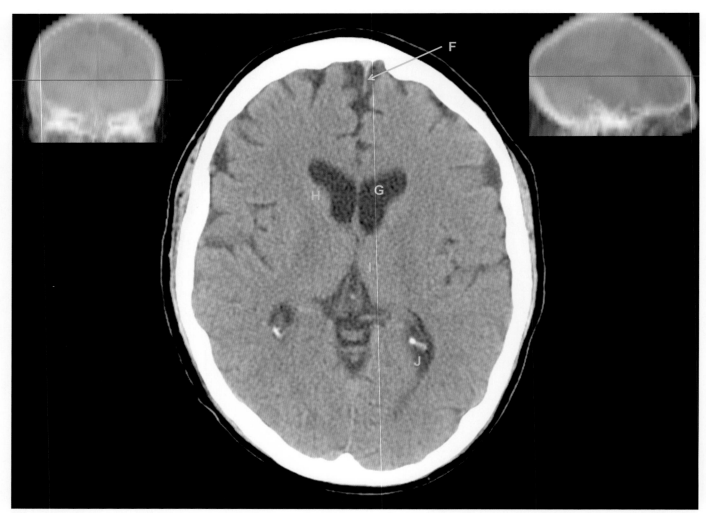

Figure 5.6.2

F

G

H

I

J

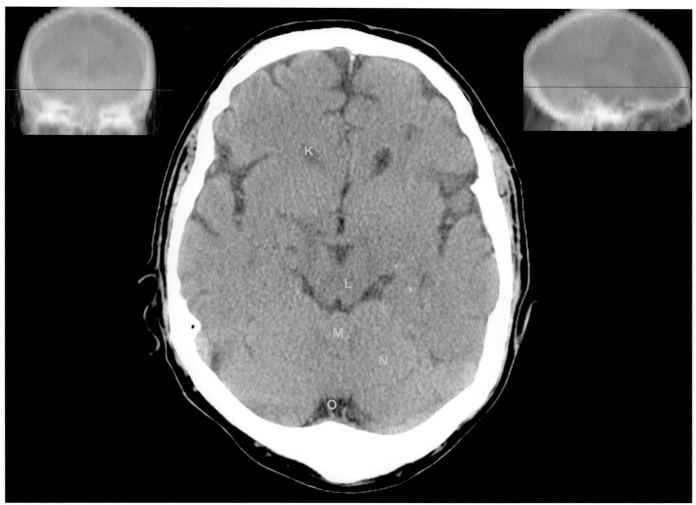

Figure 5.6.3

K

L

M

N

O

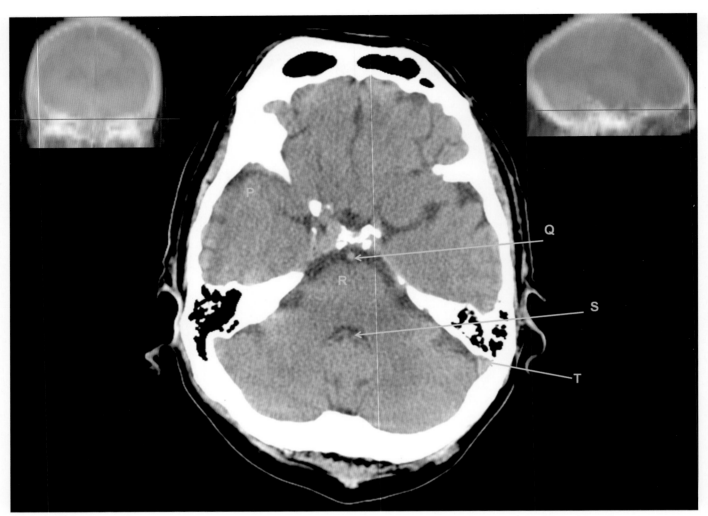

Figure 5.6.4

P

Q

R

S

T

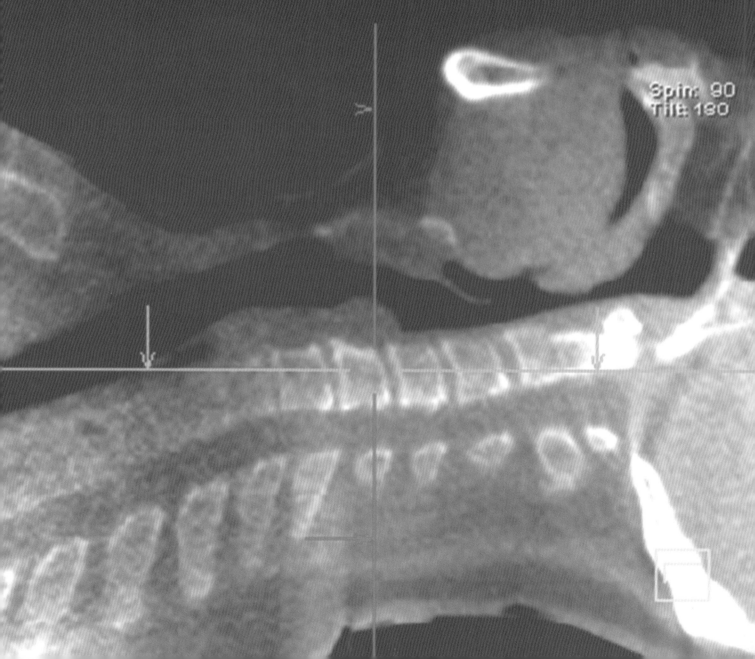

Chapter 6

CT in Radiotherapy

Since its inception in the 1970s, the CT scanner has steadily improved image quality, speed of acquisition and radiation safety. With the rapid development of technology, any description of current 'state of the art' equipment is doomed to obsolescence at time of printing and is beyond the scope of this text. The role of CT in radiotherapy in recent years, however, has expanded from its origins as the source of localisation data for treatment planning and is rapidly becoming a key verification tool. Separate CT scanners in the treatment room or integrated with the treatment equipment can produce diagnostic-quality images to assist with localisation and this process is known as Image-Guided Radiotherapy (IGRT). Modern treatment delivery systems are increasingly capable of producing CT images themselves on a daily basis to ensure radiation is delivered correctly without the need to move the patient. Given the increasingly more widespread use of IGRT technology, it may be of interest to the reader to examine some of these CT-based images and apply image interpretation skills to them.

6.1 Kilovoltage Cone Beam CT

Offering the nearest approximation to diagnostic quality CT images, the principle of cone beam imaging using kilovoltage generators and imagers is well-established. Cone beam refers to the use of a wide fan of x-rays used to obtain volumetric CT data in one rotation as opposed to single slice 'fan beam' acquisition. The kilovoltage tubes and image intensifier panels are usually fixed orthogonally to the treatment head and portal imager. Use of kilovoltage ensures that the photoelectric absorption process produces images with the best possible contrast. The only drawback to this technique (compared to a conventional CT scanner) is the length of time taken for image acquisition since gantry rotation is limited for safety reasons. The increased time can produce movement artefacts and blurring, although modern post-processing software can still provide excellent images.

Figure 6.1.1 illustrates a kilovoltage cone beam image of a male pelvis. It can be seen that the image lacks the sharp clarity of that produced by a diagnostic scanner. There is evidence of blurring and soft tissue definition is not as precise, for example muscle striation. Despite this, the reader should by now be able to identify bony structures, bladder, rectum, vas deferens, obturator internus muscle and external iliac artery and vein. Smaller structures such as ureters and internal iliac vessels are not so easily perceived, but overall the image is easily of sufficient quality for radiotherapy purposes.

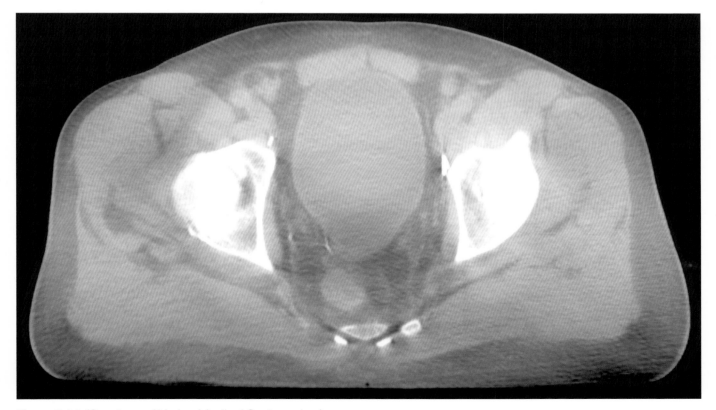

Figure 6.1.1 (Courtesy of Varian Medical Systems Inc.)

Figure 6.1.2 demonstrates the major drawback of linear accelerator-based cone beam CT. The image of a lung suffers from motion artefacts and associated blurring. The vastly increased imaging time compared to that enabled by enclosed circular gantry systems, such as traditional CT, encompasses several cycles of breathing. The effects of this can clearly be seen in the image.

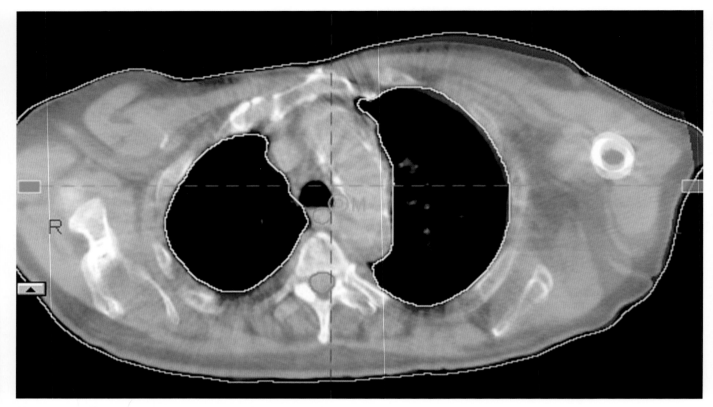

Figure 6.1.2 (Courtesy of Varian Medical Systems Inc.)

Many of the visualised structures have double images or blurred edges. The patient clearly has one arm above the head since the shaft of humerus can be seen on the left and only the scapula on the right. There is evidence of patient movement from the apparent blurring of the humerus. Note the reduced blurring at the posterior of the patient where motion is restricted by the couch top. Despite the motion effects, many of the structures can be identified, if not perfectly delineated. The trachea is demonstrating the classic 'horseshoe' shape and the lungs are obvious as ever. The position of the oesophagus should be clear behind the trachea. The sternum, thoracic vertebra, spinal cord, scapulae and humerus can also be seen easily. The arch of aorta is visible, but suffers badly from motion blurring. Between the ascending arch of aorta and right lung is the superior vena cava. The lungs themselves are clearly delineated from the surrounding soft tissue and the IGRT software has outlined them. There are visible soft tissue structures peppering the left lung and these are likely to be pulmonary vessels. Use of lung window width and level settings, as well as tracking on adjacent slices, would verify this.

6.2 Megavoltage Cone Beam CT

Megavoltage has few photons capable of interacting by photoelectric absorption and thus produces images with reduced contrast compared to kilovoltage radiation. It is possible, however, using sophisticated image processing algorithms, to generate useful clinical scans. The advantage of megavoltage cone beam is that it makes use of the treatment beam to generate images. There are currently two options for megavoltage CT equipment.

The first is a linear accelerator cone beam using a rotating megavoltage treatment beam and portal imager. This has the advantages of requiring little additional specialist equipment and reduced physical size of the apparatus. As with kilovoltage cone beam CT, the length of time to acquire the data can generate movement artefacts in all but the most cooperative patients and the limitations of gantry rotation speed can exacerbate this.

Another solution is to use tomotherapy. Tomotherapy equipment consists of a linear accelerator and megavoltage imager built into a ring gantry. This means that the speed of rotation can be drastically increased compared to cone beam CT and thus MV images can be produced with less movement artefact.

The key to both of these imaging systems is the image processing software which is able to enhance soft tissue contrast, despite the use of MV energies. Figure 6.2.1 shows some images from a linear accelerator-based megavoltage imaging system. This equipment has the advantage of maintaining the flexibility of a linear accelerator while providing a large field of view. When compared to Figures 6.1.1 and 6.1.2 from a kilovoltage cone beam imager, the reduction in image quality is evident. There is significantly reduced contrast, particularly between the soft tissue structures that are of such importance when determining accuracy of treatment position.

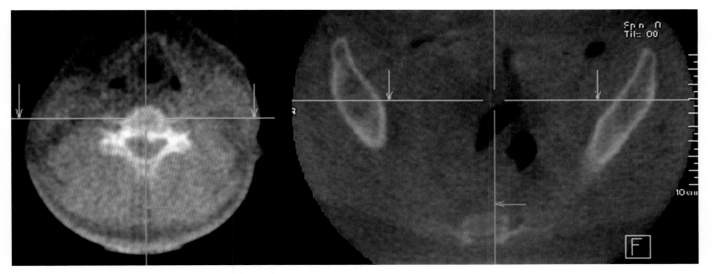

Figure 6.2.1 (Courtesy of Siemens Healthcare)

In the left hand head and neck image, the high contrast vertebra is easily seen. The air spaces of the larynx and pyriform fossae lie anterior to the vertebral body. The fatty spaces containing the carotid sheath are also visible but more detailed soft tissue structure analysis is difficult. The right hand image of the pelvis clearly shows the iliac bones laterally and the sacrum posteriorly. The air spaces visible illustrate the position of the large bowel, the sigmoid colon in this case. As with the head and neck image, the difference between muscle and fat can be traced but individual structures are hard to distinguish. The volumetric nature of the image collection, however, allows for very clear reconstruction in different planes. Figure 6.2.2 shows typical non-axial reconstructions for sagittal head and neck (left image) and coronal pelvis (right image). In both cases the bony anatomy is very clear and the head and neck air spaces are well defined. The artefact-free artificial hip implant in the right image highlights one of the benefits of megavoltage imaging.

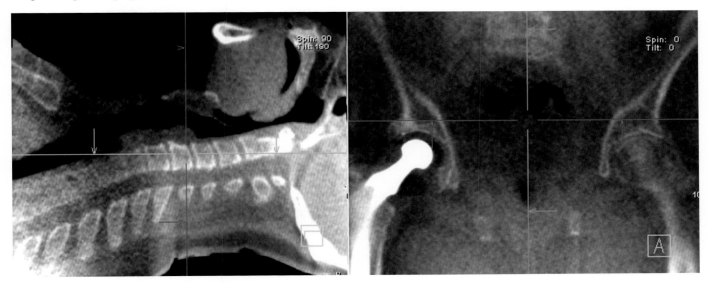

Figure 6.2.2 (Courtesy of Siemens Healthcare)

It must be remembered that the images need only be fit for purpose. If the aim of the image is radiotherapy planning, then a diagnostic quality scan, possibly enhanced by combination with another imaging modality will be required. If the aim is to judge reproducibility of treatment position and daily localisation, then image quality is of less importance. So long as target volume position can be determined, the important factors then become achieving this with minimum patient dose, time and cost.

Figure 6.2.3 is an image from tomotherapy equipment illustrating the benefit of speed of rotation and dedicated integrated hardware. The pelvic bones are clearly displayed and soft tissues such as the prostate, rectum, external iliac vessels and obturator internus muscle are easily distinguished. Image quality is of a high enough standard for use in planning, although the image still lacks the highly contrasting clarity of the diagnostic scan.

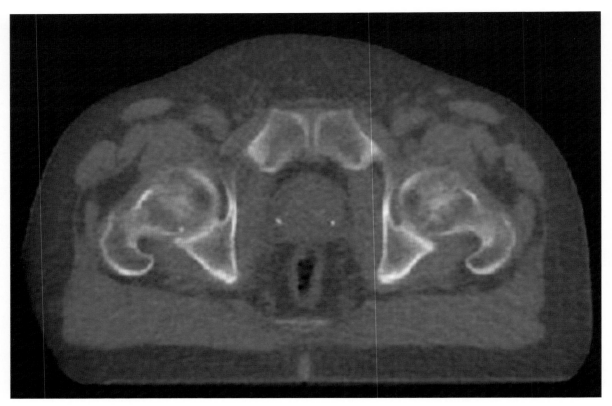

Figure 6.2.3 (Courtesy of TomoTherapy Inc®)

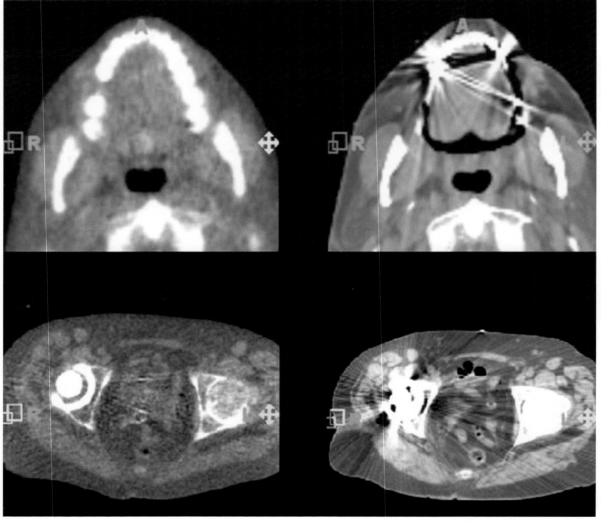

Figure 6.2.4

As has already been shown, one major advantage of using megavoltage beams for imaging is the reduced artefacts produced by high density materials such as dental fillings or artificial hips. Figure 6.2.4 illustrates megavoltage images on the left and corresponding kilovoltage images on the right. The top pair of images includes a dental filling. The kilovoltage image clearly suffers from white streaking artefacts across the picture and gaping black holes around the filling where there is insufficient data. The megavoltage image shows the fillings but without the artefacts. This is due to lack of photoelectric absorption and can provide invaluable data, particularly for tumour delineation close to high density materials. The bottom images highlight the problems caused by an artificial hip in the kilovoltage image on the right. The megavoltage image shows evidence of some streaking, but there are no gaps in the image and soft tissue structures near the high density material can be visualised with relative ease.

Answers to Self-Test Questions

	Male Abdomen / Pelvis	Female Abdomen / Pelvis	Thorax	Head and Neck	Intracranial
A	Stomach	Gall bladder	Sternum manubrium	Right masseter	Genu of corpus callosum
B	Liver	Inferior vena cava	Head of right clavicle	Left maxillary sinus	Right lateral ventricle
C	Descending abdominal aorta	Descending abdominal aorta	Brachiocephalic artery	Left mandible	Splenium of corpus callosum
D	Spleen	Left adrenal gland	Trachea	Left parotid	Straight sinus
E	Right kidney	Spleen	Right lung	Left internal carotid artery	Superior sagittal sinus
F	Left external iliac artery	Bladder	Ascending arch of aorta	Tongue	Falx cerebri
G	Left internal iliac artery	Round ligament	Superior vena cava	Nasopharynx	Frontal horn of left lateral ventricle
H	Sigmoid colon	Right ovary	Trachea	Right internal jugular vein	Head of right caudate nucleus
I	Right ilium	Uterus	Oesophagus	Odontoid process of axis (C2)	Thalamus
J	Sacrum	Rectum	Azygos vein	Left vertebral artery	Occipital horn of left lateral ventricle
K	Bladder	Right external iliac artery	Pulmonary trunk artery	Mandible	Frontal horn of right lateral ventricle
L	Acetabulum	Cervix	Left main bronchus	Submandibular salivary gland	Midbrain
M	Seminal vesicle	Vaginal vault	Left pulmonary artery	Oropharynx	Vermis of cerebellum
N	Left greater trochanter	Rectum	Descending thoracic aorta	Palatine tonsil	Left cerebellar hemisphere
O	Rectum	Sacrum	Spinal cord	Left sternocleidomastoid	Confluence of sinuses
P	Spermatic cord	Right pubis	Right ventricle	Thyroid cartilage	Right temporal lobe
Q	Right pubis	Urethra	Left ventricle	Larynx	Basilar artery
R	Prostate	Obturator internus	Right atrium	Cricoid cartilage	Pons
S	Right ischium	Vagina	Left atrium	Thyroid gland	Fourth ventricle
T	Levator ani	Anus	Oesophagus	Left common carotid artery	Sigmoid sinus

Structure Key: Chapter 2, Pelvis and Abdomen

1. Ilium
2. Psoas Muscle
3. Lumbar Vertebrae
4. Sacrum
5. Femur
6. Obturator Internus Muscle
7. Crura
8. Pubis
9. Ischium
10. Coccyx
11. Levator Ani
12. Kidney
13. Ureter
14. Bladder
15. Liver
16. Oesophagus
17. Stomach
18. Splenic Flexure
19. Gall Bladder
20. Duodenum
21. Pancreas
22. Small Bowel
23. Transverse Colon
24. Descending Colon
25. Ascending Colon
26. Appendix
27. Sigmoid Colon
28. Rectum
29. Anus
30. Vas Deferens
31. Seminal Vesicles
32. Prostate
33. Urethra
34. Penile Bulb
35. Penis
36. Uterus
37. Ligaments
38. Ovary
39. Cervix
40. Vagina
41. Descending Abdominal Aorta
42. Superior Mesenteric Vein
43. Inferior Vena Cava
44. Common Iliac Artery
45. Common Iliac Vein
46. Internal Iliac Artery
47. Internal Iliac Vein
48. External Iliac Artery
49. External Iliac Vein
50. Femoral Artery
51. Femoral Vein
52. Splenic Vein
53. Renal Artery
54. Renal Vein
55. Thoracic Vertebrae
56. Spleen
57. Coeliac Artery
58. Spinal Cord
59. Adrenal Gland
60. Superior Mesenteric Artery
61. Hepatic Flexure
62. Piriformis Muscle
63. Coccygeus Muscle
64. Hepatic Portal Vein
65. Greater Trochanter
66. Caecum
67. Spermatic Cord
68. Retrocrural Lymph Nodes
69. Superior Mesenteric Lymph Nodes
70. Para-aortic Lymph Nodes
71. Common Iliac Lymph Nodes
72. External Iliac Lymph Nodes
73. Sacral Lymph Nodes
74. Pararectal Lymph Nodes
75. Internal Iliac Lymph Nodes
76. Obturator Lymph Nodes

Structure Key: Chapter 3, Thorax

1. Clavicle
2. Scapula
3. Spine of Scapula
4. Head of Humerus
5. Thoracic Vertebrae
6. Rib
7. Pectoralis Major Muscle
8. Pectoralis Minor Muscle
9. Sternum
10. Xiphoid Process
11. Oesophagus
12. Trachea
13. Upper Lobe of Left Lung
14. Upper Lobe of Right Lung
15. Lower Lobe of Left Lung
16. Right Main Bronchus
17. Left Main Bronchus
18. Middle Lobe of Right Lung
19. Lower Lobe of Right Lung
20. Jugular Vein
21. Carotid Artery
22. Subclavian Artery
23. Subclavian Vein
24. Brachiocephalic Artery
25. Right Brachiocephalic Vein
26. Left Brachiocephalic Vein
27. Arch of Aorta
28. Ascending Thoracic Aorta
29. Descending Thoracic Aorta
30. Superior Vena Cava
31. Azygos Vein
32. Pulmonary Artery
33. Pulmonary Vein
34. Pulmonary Trunk
35. Left Atrium of Heart
36. Right Atrium of Heart
37. Left Ventricle of Heart
38. Right Ventricle of Heart
39. Inferior Vena Cava
40. Spinal Cord
41. Glandular Tissue of Breast
42. Supraclavicular Nodes
43. Infraclavicular Nodes
44. Jugular Nodes
45. Para-oesophageal Nodes
46. Paratracheal Nodes
47. Anterior Cervical Nodes
48. Deep Axillary Nodes
49. Interpectoral Nodes (Rotter's)
50. Paratracheal and Para-oesophageal Nodes
51. Anterior Mediastinal Nodes
52. Paravertebral Nodes
53. Superficial Axillary Nodes
54. Parasternal/Internal Mammary Nodes
55. Para-aortic Nodes
56. Subcarinal Nodes
57. Aorticopulmonary Window Nodes
58. Bronchopulmonary (Hilar) Nodes
59. Pericardial Nodes

Structure Key: Chapter 4, Head and Neck

1. Lens
2. Eye
3. Lateral Rectus Muscle
4. Medial Rectus Muscle
5. Nasal Bone
6. Ethmoid Labyrinth/Sinus
7. Sphenoid Sinus
8. Sphenoid Bone
9. Optic Nerve
10. Lacrimal Gland
11. Zygomatic Bone
12. Temporal Bone
13. Inferior Rectus Muscle
14. Nasal Concha
15. Nasal Septum
16. Maxillary Sinus
17. Maxilla
18. Nasal Cavity
19. Masseter Muscle
20. Mandible
21. Parotid Salivary Gland
22. Mastoid Air Cells
23. Internal Carotid Artery
24. Nasopharynx
25. Pharyngeal Tonsil
26. Jugular Vein
27. Hard Palate
28. Tongue
29. Soft Palate
30. First Cervical Vertebra (Atlas)
31. Second Cervical Vertebra (Axis)
32. Sternocleidomastoid Muscle
33. Vertebral Artery
34. External Carotid Artery
35. Lingual Tonsil
36. Palatine Tonsil
37. Uvula
38. Oropharynx
39. Submandibular Salivary Gland
40. Sublingual Salivary Gland
41. Third Cervical Vertebra
42. Hypopharynx
43. Epiglottis
44. Fourth Cervical Vertebra
45. Hyoid Bone
46. Common Carotid Artery
47. Oesophagus
48. Thyroid Cartilage of Larynx
49. Fifth Cervical Vertebra
50. Larynx
51. Sixth Cervical Vertebra
52. Arytenoid Cartilages of Larynx
53. Corniculate Cartilages of Larynx
54. Seventh Cervical Vertebra
55. Cricoid Cartilage of Larynx
56. Thyroid Gland
57. Trachea
58. Facial Nodes
59. Submental Nodes
60. Submandibular Nodes
61. Superficial Parotid Nodes
62. Auricular and Occipital Nodes
63. External Jugular Nodes
64. Visceral Nodes
65. Deep Parotid Nodes
66. Jugulodigastric Nodes
67. Spinal Accessory Chain
68. Superior Internal Jugular Chain
69. Middle Internal Jugular Chain
70. Inferior Internal Jugular Chain
71. Supra and Transverse Clavicular Nodes
72. Retropharyngeal Nodes
73. Node of Rouvière
74. Nuchal nodes

Structure Key

Structure Key: Chapter 5, Intracranial

1. Parietal Bone
2. Parietal Lobe of Cerebrum
3. Superior Sagittal Sinus
4. Falx Cerebri
5. Body of Lateral Ventricle
6. Frontal Bone
7. Frontal Lobe of Cerebrum
8. Body of Corpus Callosum
9. Head of Caudate Nucleus
10. Genu of Corpus Callosum
11. Splenium of Corpus Callosum
12. Straight Sinus
13. Lateral Ventricle Frontal Horn
14. Lateral Ventricle Occipital Horn
15. Great Vein of Galen
16. Thalamus
17. Pineal Gland
18. Lentiform Nucleus
19. Temporal Lobe of Cerebrum
20. Cerebellum
21. Temporal Bone
22. Lateral Ventricle Temporal Horn
23. Third Ventricle
24. Transverse Sinus
25. Midbrain
26. Confluence of Sinuses
27. Occipital Bone
28. Hypothalamus
29. Circle of Willis
30. Cerebral Aqueduct
31. Middle Cerebral Artery
32. Optic Nerve
33. Pituitary
34. Posterior Cerebral Artery
35. Optic Chiasm
36. Anterior Cerebral Artery
37. Basilar Artery
38. Pons
39. Fourth Ventricle
40. Hemisphere of Cerebellum
41. Vermis of Cerebellum
42. Petrous Ridge of Temporal Bone
43. Frontal Sinus
44. Inner Ear
45. Sigmoid Sinus
46. Internal Carotid Artery
47. Sphenoid Bone
48. Sphenoid Sinus
49. Medulla Oblongata
50. External Auditory Meatus
51. Spinal Central Canal
52. Vertebral Artery
53. Cerebellar Tonsils
54. Spinal Cord
55. Occipital Lobe of Cerebrum

References and Further Reading

American Thoracic Society (1983). Clinical staging of primary lung cancer. *American Review of Respiratory Disease* **127**: 1–6.

Butler, P., Mitchell, A.W.M. and Ellis, H. (2007). *Applied Radiological Anatomy*. Cambridge: Cambridge University Press.

Castellino, R.A. and Blank, N. (1972). Adenopathy of the cardiophrenic angle (diaphragmatic) lymph nodes. *American Journal of Roentgenology* **114**(3): 509–15.

Davis, W.L., Harnsberger, R., Smoker, W.R.K. and Watanabe, A.S. (1990). Retropharyngeal space: Evaluation of normal anatomy and diseases with CT and MR imaging. *Radiology* **174**: 59–64.

Ellis, H., Logan, B.M. and Dixon, A.K. (2007). *Human Sectional Anatomy,* 3rd edition. London: Hodder Arnold.

Fehrenbach, M.J. and Herring, S.W. (2006). *Illustrated Anatomy of the Head and Neck*, 3rd edition. London: Saunders Elsevier.

Harnsberger, H.R., Osborn, A.G., Ross, J.S. and Macdonald, A.J. (2006). *Diagnostic and Surgical Imaging Anatomy: Brain, Head and Neck, Spine*. Salt Lake City: AMIRSYS.

Hofer, M. (2007). *CT Teaching Manual: A Systematic Approach to CT Reading*, 2nd edition. Stuttgart: Thieme.

Kim, H., Han, M.H., Moon, M.H., Kim, J.H., Kim, I. and Chang, K. (2005). CT and MR imaging of the buccal space: Normal anatomy and abnormalities. *Korean Journal of Radiology* **6**(1): 22–30.

Kimura, Y. and Okano, T. (2003). The pharyngeal mucosal, parapharyngeal, and retropharyngeal spaces. *Oral Radiology* **19**(2): 4–16.

Martinez-Monge, R., Fernandes, P.S., Gupta, N. and Gahbauer, R. (1999). Cross-sectional nodal atlas: A tool for the definition of clinical target volumes in three-dimensional radiation therapy planning. *Radiology* **211**(3): 815–28.

McRobbie, D.W., Moore, E.A., Graves, M.J. and Prince, M.R. (2007). *MRI from Picture to Proton*. Cambridge: Cambridge University Press.

Moeller, T. and Reif, E. (2007). *Pocket Atlas of Sectional Anatomy CT and MRI*. Volume 1: Head and Neck, 3rd edition. Stuttgart: Thieme.

Moeller, T. and Reif, E. (2007). *Pocket Atlas of Sectional Anatomy CT and MRI*. Volume 2: Thorax, Abdomen and Pelvis, 3rd edition. Stuttgart: Thieme.

Moore, K.L., Dalley, A.F. and Agur, A.M.R. (2009). *Clinically Orientated Anatomy*, 6th edition. Philadelphia: Lippincott, Williams and Wilkins.

Mountain, C.F. and Dresler, C.M. (1997). Regional lymph node classification for lung cancer staging. *Chest* **111**: 1718–23.

Naidich, D.P., Webb, W.R., Muller, N.L., Vlahos, I. and Krinsky, G.A. (2006). *Computed Tomography and Magnetic Resonance of the Thorax,* 4th edition. Philadelphia: Lippincott, Williams and Wilkins.

Naruke, T. (1967). The spread of lung cancer and its relevance to surgery. *Japanese Journal of Surgery* **68**: 1607–21.

Osborn, A.G., Blaser, S., Salzman, K.L. *et al.* (2004). *Diagnostic Imaging: Brain.* Salt Lake City: AMIRSYS.

Prokop, M. and Galanski, M. (2003). *Spiral and Multislice Computed Tomography of the Body*. Stuttgart: Thieme.

Reiser, M.F., Takahashi, M., Modic, M. and Becker, C.R. (2004). *Multislice CT,* 2nd edition. London: Springer.

Rouvière, H. (1938). *Anatomy of the Human Lymphatic System*. Michigan: Edwards.

Seeram, E. (2008). *Computed Tomography: Physical Principles, Clinical Applications and Quality Control*, 3rd edition. London: Saunders.

Silver, A.J., Mawad, M.E., Hilal, S.K., Sane, P. and Ganti, S.R. (1984). Computed tomography of the carotid space and related cervical spaces. Part I: Anatomy. *Radiology* **150**: 723–8.

Tortora, G.J. and Grabowski, S.R. (2003). *Principles of Anatomy and Physiology*, 10th edition. Hoboken: Wiley.

Wei, Y., Xiao, J. and Zou, L. (2007). Masticator space: CT and MRI of secondary tumor spread. *American Journal of Roentgenology* **189**: 488–97.

Yousem, D.M., Zimmerman, R.D. and Grossman, R.I. (2010). *Neuroradiology: The Requisites*, 3rd edition. Philadelphia: Mosby.

Index